Riding the Bubble

The World of Housing is a Wild Ride

SCOTT BENJAMIN

 Scott Benjamin, 7777 N. Wickham Road, Suite 12-714, Melbourne, Florida, 32940. scott@ridingthebubble.com

ISBN: 0692405321
ISBN-13: 978-0-692-40532-1

DEDICATION

To the most understanding wife in the world, Jill, thanks for putting up with my absent mindedness, for my constant career changes, and for believing in me during all of my harebrained pursuits.

To my children, Noah & David, I am looking forward to seeing where life takes you both.

To my business partner Pete, what a wild ride we had – thanks for "making it happen".

To God, who provided for my family and watched over us each and every day.

CONTENTS

A NEW BEGINNING

Did you ever dream about what you would like to do for work if money wasn't an issue? I know, I know... if money wasn't an issue, then why would you work? But really, after getting bored with playing golf and traveling the world – what meaningful career would you truly enjoy doing? How would you contribute to society each and every day? For me, I always wanted to be a college professor. And I hear you: this is supposed to be a story about real estate, but be patient with me I'll get to that. My name is Scott Benjamin and I am a faculty member at a small business school in Melbourne, Florida – Florida Tech. I truly enjoy teaching college students about business. My day is incredibly rewarding as the "light bulb" clicks on for these future leaders and entrepreneurs. Yet, it's only recently that I have been able to pursue the dream of having this impact each and every day. You see, thirteen years ago I had a dilemma. If you know anything about college professors, you know we don't get paid a lot. How could I realize my dream while still providing for a family, saving for children's college educations, and setting aside retirement money? What tool could I use to create enough wealth in a short period of time in order to pursue my dream of becoming a professor? Enter "**real estate**".

I taught myself how to make money by investing in and developing real estate. I started small, with a single townhouse, and built up to subdividing land, purchasing office buildings, developing an apartment complex, and owning millions of dollars of residential properties. The book that you are about to read is a daily diary of my journey in real estate. What is truly unique about this book is that it is written in *real time* while as I learn the business. You will learn, right alongside of my own experience, how to find houses, flip houses, raise private equity, market valuation, and so many other lessons from the school of hard knocks. As a bonus, you get to feel the excitement of developing real estate during the biggest bull market in history, and live the misery I experienced losing millions of dollars during the crash of 2008. My goal in writing this book is to show people that learning something new and taking a chance in real estate is an available option for everyone. I don't possess any super powers and I didn't come from Trump style money – I am just a regular guy trying something new.

The book is written like a blog. There is no editor, no fancy publisher, and really no particular format. It is raw information, emotion, and experience being put down on paper. Periodically, I will sit down at the laptop and report on what is happening in a given week. I capture the process of finding and developing real estate; I capture the larger issues in the current real estate market; I capture the nuances of all aspects of the transaction; and finally, I capture the emotional roller coaster experienced during the process. By writing this in *real time*, you not only get the nuts and bolts of the "how to", but you also get insight into the other surrounding variables that affect a real estate flipper. I do want to issue a warning: after reading about my journey in real estate, you may find yourself wanting to buy your first investment property. So buckle up, because, you are about to *Ride The Bubble.*

April 2001

The date is April 1, 2001. It is really cold here in Maryland and I don't feel like heading outside today. Instead, I am wrestling with some decisions about career, life, future, and family. You know, the classic 'what do I want to be when I grow up' stuff. I have an idea of what I want the future to look like and I am developing a strategy on how to get there. I've always been fascinated by real estate, but never had the courage to throw my hat into the ring. Many of my friends have talked about investing in real estate, but it is all just talk. Nobody seems willing to pull the trigger. Today, I've decided that this is going to change. I am going to learn how to get rich through real estate. Instead of researching and reading, talking and analyzing, I am going to take action. I have no idea how just yet, but I am just crazy enough to take a shot. Before I get started, let me write down some thoughts about where I am mentally and financially, now, on April 1, 2001, and see how that changes over time.

Here is the vision, so bear with me. Today I want you to get to know me. I want to tell you about my priorities in life, my dreams, and my current financial state. Perhaps we share similar interests or are in a similar financial state. As the book rolls out, it should be chock full of real estate information and know-how, but right now, I don't have any: I promise it will some soon, though. So, meanwhile, try to get to know me in this first chapter.

Everyone has dreams, and I find that most of mine involve dreams of wealth. They could be material wealth, spiritual wealth, intellectual wealth, or the wealth of time. I am at a point in my life when things just seem to be confusing. I wrestle with the meaning of life, whether I'm a good father, why I spend most of my waking hours working, why there isn't more time for family and friends.... The more I think about these things, the more I realize that I need to create more "wealth" in areas which are more important to me. This book is not meant to be a feel-good book about my skewed vision of life. It is meant to be a daily diary of how to create financial wealth in real estate that will then open up many other areas of wealth. What makes this book so unique is that, right now, I have no wealth. This book is just a check box on my bucket list of creating $2,000,000 of wealth so that I can unleash some real areas of wealth.

At the tops of my list is the wealth of time. You may imagine what it might be like when the days are more fulfilling. You find yourself spending time doing things that you gather meaning from. It might be volunteering, exercising, learning to play an instrument, or traveling. What I do know is that I currently do not have – but sincerely crave – the wealth of time. Let me explain. Nothing gives me greater satisfaction than having a nicely manicured lawn. I know it sounds crazy, but I get some sick satisfaction from starting with the weed whacker, moving onto the edger, then to the criss-cross pattern with the mower, and finally blowing the clippings into easily disposable piles. When I finish the 3 hour activity of mowing...well, no, not just mowing, but sculpting my lawn... my wife thinks that I am crazy, as I stand in the street staring at my lawn with incredible satisfaction. Unfortunately, I can't remember the last time I gave my lawn the true and sincere attention that it needs. At best, these days it gets what I like to refer to as Olympic mowing. Sure, I can justify having found a way to combine the activity of mowing the lawn with my passions for exercise and running, but more than anything else, it reveals the lack of time in my life to do something that I enjoy. I literally run behind the mower at an 8 minute mile pace, just so that I can finish in order to move on to the next task on my to-do list. I'm now looking at family dinners as a wasted hour when I could stain the deck or continue finishing the basement that I have been working on for over six months. With two young children, I fear that this race, this lifestyle, will limit the time that I have to spend with them, and more than anything, I want to create memories. I am constantly jockeying with retirement planning, college tuition planning, current quality of life, and all with just a mere 24 hours in a day. I heard a statistic that a group of professionals came up with documenting the amount of time needed just to perform the typical duties of running your life on a day-to-day basis. Wouldn't you know, you need 36 hours in a day to effectively manage work and life? So, how do you handle the day-to-day concerns and also chase after that ideal wealth of time, and the freedom to spend it raising your children? If you are looking for an answer from me, stop reading, because at this point, I just don't know. However, if you hang around with me long enough, perhaps we can both figure it out.

Material wealth comes second. Put simply, I love money and I love nice things. Once in a while, my wife and I will go out to a nice steak house and dream what it would be like to dine like this more than just on a special occasion. The nicer things like vacations at beautiful beach resorts, luxury cars, and a bigger house capture my attention as I daydream about the future. Perhaps you are like me, and simply can't change the television station as you watch "Lifestyles of the Rich and Famous" or "Cribs". I live in Maryland, and I always pick up the real estate magazines and look at the homes on the water in Annapolis. There is something absolutely spellbinding about wealth. I grew up spending Sundays driving around neighborhoods and looking at houses that we couldn't afford. The catch to these two wants is that they are, or at least seem to be, mutually exclusive. Mutually exclusive is an interesting phrase, isn't it? It's almost like you have to choose one at the sacrifice of the other. The more I find myself chasing the dream of wealth, I catch myself missing my son's baseball games or not even connecting with my new baby. When I set aside time for them, my path to riches and retirement gets further and further away. So the challenge of chasing my dream is a way to accomplish both of these needs simultaneously. If you are looking for a reason for why I am writing this book, it is pretty simple. I want to have the time to enjoy every single day with my family, and the wealth so that their every need is satisfied. I am making a major assumption that I can use real estate as a tool to achieve this goal. If I am successful, this book may serve as a guideline for you to reach your goals.

You see, I have not made a nickel in real estate yet. Not today or yesterday for that matter, but I hope that over the next several years I will be able to create enough wealth so that I may enjoy my true passion…my family. I want you to see my current financial position and how it hopefully grows throughout the years. My goal is to obtain complete financial independence, getting ready for upcoming college tuitions, retirement planning, housing dreams, and expensive vacations, all the while keeping a family of four happy throughout these extremely important years of life. Keep in mind that I need to pull this off in a reasonable amount of time, without sacrificing the younger years of my family's development. The other day, I saw the CEO of a major corporation actually stepping down. Her goal was to spend more time with her family. I was impressed and touched that someone out in the big corporate world thinks like I do. Her youngest child was 13, and she realized that it was important to reconnect with her family. But wait... Hold the phone. Did she say that her youngest is 13? I am still impressed that she is giving up the corporate gig for family, but at 13, I imagine my kids are not going to want to have a whole lot to do with me, not by then. Right now, I am Superman to my 3 year old boy. I am his biggest playmate. These are the years that I want to spend with him.

When I read books by the great real estate investors, I have trouble assimilating with them. As a matter of fact, I am currently reading one by Dolf De Roos. His book is fantastic, and it excites me to read of his methods of investing. It gets the juices flowing to see how he made his fortune in real estate. However, I finish each chapter saying: 'it just can't be that easy'. It must have been a more difficult road than just simply buying low and selling high for big profits. I've read the entire Rich Dad, Poor Dad series, the Donald Trump biography... I've read them all. You see, the fundamental problem with these books is that they are written post hoc. That means, these guys have already experienced the successes and, unfortunately, have probably forgotten the failures.

They are recounting the events after they have been successful. They can remember fondly all of the wonderful deals they made and how they got rich, but I need the whole picture. I just cannot accept that their development into real estate gurus was all that easy. So, I have chosen a different path. I need you to see that it is not all that easy, but who ever said getting rich was easy? My goal of writing this book is for you to be able to walk my walk.

Don't think that this is a "how to" guide on getting rich in real estate. There are no tapes to purchase in three easy installments of $49.99. This book is a work in progress. I know that I will find success in real estate. That is why I plan to add chapters to this book every few months, documenting the processes I have implemented to create a successful enterprise. You can read the books of Donald Trump, Warren Buffet, or Jack Welch, describing what they remember about why they became successful, but something is missing…the **HOW**. The way I see it, I want to know how Donald Trump bought his first office building. What was his financial situation, how was his credit, how did he find the building to buy, how did he know when it was time to move to the next step, and what mistakes did he make on each deal that provided lessons learned for future his success? When I read his books, I see a fantastic view from 10,000 feet up. What I am lacking is HOW he got from being a young entrepreneur to a mega millionaire.

The structure of my book is completely different. I have nothing to look back upon and recount. Everything you read in this book is happening today!!! The events that I recount are happening in real time. I begin the book with a present day snapshot of my financial situation. Why? Because you need to see where I am in life. I make you one promise… I will not exaggerate a single detail in order to look like a pauper-to-prince story. I want you to finish this book and see that, if you have the passion to make money in real estate but are afraid to take the step, it is really not that hard.

I recently took a trip to Monticello down in Charlottesville,

Virginia. This is the famous real estate development project by Thomas Jefferson. There are many things that have fascinated me about Thomas Jefferson, but two particular things stick in my head even now. First...Throughout his professional career, he took copious notes about what he was doing at the time. He kept lists of his belongings, diaries of his sightseeing excursions, and general entries about what he was thinking. He took all of these notes knowing that what he was accomplishing was something fantastic. I look back on the exhibit with wonder at how he could be so arrogant as to list what he typically carried in his backpack during any given day, but he knew that he was becoming something important in American history, and that these artifacts would be something valuable for people to see. I don't expect that I will be quite as important as old TJ, but my goal in real estate will soon become a reality. I am so sure of it that I am taking copious notes about what I "carry in my backpack". (By the way, I have a pencil with a chewed-off eraser, a HP pocket financial calculator that my uncle gave me some 10 years ago, a legal pad, and a rice crispy treat in my brief case.) The second item I gleaned from the Monticello exhibit is the fascinating way that this national landmark was acquired by the Historical Preservation Society. After Jefferson died, his daughter took care of the property for quite some time. After she died, the property went into distress and dilapidation. Ultimately, the house was sold at a public foreclosure auction where General Lee bought it for $10. Talk about a prime opportunity to purchase discounted real estate. So, what is the house worth today…a whole lot more than $10. Perhaps these foreclosure auctions are worth looking into.

Here is the biggest question I face: When is it time to publish the book? When will people want to read a user's guide to developing wealth in real estate? How wealthy must I become? So, right now, on page 1 of the introduction written April 1, 2001, I will set that metric. This book will be published when my net worth is equal to $2 million. Why $2 million? Because in my head right now, I think that I can live comfortably on an annual return on assets of $200,000. This means that if I have $2 million in investments earning 10% per year, I can happily live on $200,000 per year. You see, I am actually a pretty simple guy. I love spending time with my kids (who are now 1 and 3). So, to me, $200,000 suits me just right. The risk to me, because all business decisions are based on risk, is that I never reach the goal and you never read the book. Therefore, I will have invested quite a bit of time writing when I could have been earning money. But, if I do make it and you do have this book to read, you can follow my process, adopt my knowledge, and hopefully accomplish my goal a whole lot faster than the time it takes me for me to do the same. I hope that this book serves as a user guide to success in the business, and as a wake-up call that – yes, it could happen to you.

LESSONS LEARNED

I am going to close each posting with a section called 'lessons learned'. This will be made up of a bulleted list of lessons gained through the school of hard knocks. At this point, I know nothing – so, therefore, I am simply going to pose some questions that have been percolating in my mind.

- There are different types of wealth – time, spiritual, money & family. How do you prioritize your wealth goals?

- Is real estate a viable model for achieving wealth?

FINANCIAL SNAPSHOT

I own a house. Crazy story, but long story short – I won $10,000 in a radio contest that allowed me to put a down payment on a 2,400 square foot house. My wife and I bought the house 5 years ago and have done very well with its appreciation.

Equity in House = $140,000

I am no rocket scientist, but as you can see, I have accumulated a ton of equity over a short period of time. You'll get some details on this radio contest story in chapters to come.

The stock and mutual fund markets have not been kind. I have two accounts:

Stocks = $19,000
Funds = $13,000

My wife drives a 1995 Jeep Grand Cherokee with 150,000 miles, and my car is a lease.

Equity in her Car = $3,000 on a good day

I do not believe in carrying credit card debt, so about $175,000 is pretty much my net worth picture at this point at this time. Just $1,825,000 to go to publication!

I have no IRA, no 401K, no secret piles of cash stored under my mattress. Subtract out the home equity and I am worth $35,000. I am 33 years old and do not have a retirement account set up. That depresses me every day that I think about it. At some point in life, I need to realize that I have grown up. I still think of myself as a college student living for the day. Carpe Diem...right? Children have changed this viewpoint. I have to get an IRA or retirement account. Let me say that again so that I can convince myself of its importance, **I must get an IRA account**. Don't get out the tissues for me just yet, though. I live quite comfortably. My wife does not have to work, we travel to see family, we go out to eat frequently, and I manage to spend a fair amount of time raising my two boys. The problem is…I am not saving anything for the future. I have managed to get some of the wealth of time, but as you can see above, I am missing financial wealth. The stocks and funds were purchased when my wife and I were DINKs (duel income, no kids). In the past three years, I have not put away a thing, and seem to be on the treadmill of life, living check to check. I have two college educations and a retirement to worry about, but still want to chase my real estate dream. Does that sound nuts to you? It certainly sounds nuts to my wife. How could I not take a nice salaried position with a big corporation, have security and retirement and benefits, and…..I can recite the argument in my head because Jill and I have it so often, but I certainly won't bore you with it. But you know…and I hate to say it…she is right. I am about to take on a venture with no income, no salary, no benefits, all with the hope of achieving financial security, and did I mention I have two kids to think about? Every entrepreneur must go through this iteration in his head. Why not stick with a secure job earning a steady income? Why go out and risk everything?

Read for yourself and see if my upbringing was anything like yours. My past will be quick since I think that you're looking forward to reading about the future. I grew up the son of an entrepreneur. My dad had many businesses, ranging from drug stores to ice cream stores. He owned several pack-and-ship businesses. I have a lot of respect for my father, as he worked extremely hard to make ends meet in the Benjamin household. We grew up in an average middle class neighborhood in Massachusetts. My mother stayed home with my brother and me for years, and finally went back to work as a teacher. We never vacationed, but never had unmet wants. Both my brother and I went to private high school and then to college. I graduated with a degree in entrepreneurship from the University of Miami with no student loans (thanks, mom and dad). So you can see, I did not start behind the eight ball. For those of you who can remember graduating college, you hit that moment that you wonder, now what? Think back to receiving that diploma, finding an apartment with two roommates to move into, and saying "here I am world."

At the time, I thought that I would like hospitality management. I took my diploma to the local fast food restaurant and got a job as an assistant manager for $25,000 per year. My parents were so pleased that they had just spent $50,000 on an education and I was flipping burgers. By the time my kids get to college, $50,000 won't cover textbooks.

Don't get down on me, though: I was young, and $25,000 was good money. I worked at this burger place for about a year, and moved over to manage a Domino's Pizza. Why Domino's? Well the program that they had in place was a profit-sharing plan. Each manager of a Domino's received a starting salary of $25,000, but also received 20% of the profits of the store. This was extremely appealing to a young budding entrepreneur. If I could build the sales, and manage the food and labor costs, I could make a handsome income. That proved true for over 4 years. I enjoyed the challenges of in-store marketing, lowering labor costs and improving profitability. I looked forward to month ending P&L statements and receiving that bonus check. I learned a lot at Domino's. Domino's serves one product, pizza. They do it incredibly well. They have mastered the system of taking the order and delivering the product within 30 minutes or less. I have several friends who have made substantial livings owning several pizzerias. Perhaps I should have continued down that Domino's path because the pizza business was fun and exciting. At any rate, I ended up in North Carolina working for a Domino's franchisee, with a salary and bonus of about $35,000 per year at age 24. Let me add, while in Florida and working for Domino's, I got my real estate salesperson's license. Even way back then, I had the lure of easy money twinkling in my eyes, and I knew that working for $25,000 a year was not going to get me there. My earnings from real estate in Florida, over a six month period from 1991 to 1992, was a $232 commission check when I helped a Domino's Pizza assistant manager buy a piece of land to start a tree farm. So, needless to say, I got out of the real estate business. Perhaps real estate was not the career that I thought it could be. I sniffed at it, but could not take the plunge into it as a career. In some ways, I wish that I had jumped into the career full tilt at such an early age, and without all of these adult responsibilities. My young professional life as a fast food manager did help develop me into a small business manager. I began to understand the concepts of marketing and advertising your product, systems for efficient operations, and how to deal with people and handle problems. I enjoyed the 5 years with the company and highly recommend it to entrepreneurs trying to learn on someone else's coin.

In 1995, we moved to my wife's home state of Maryland. I was again unemployed at age 26. My skill set was fairly limited. Although computers were just becoming an important part of the business world, I had extremely limited knowledge of how they worked. Computers have become such a pervasive part of our society that anyone with a little drive and a touch of experience has become rich beyond their wildest imagination over the past five years. At any rate, I had extremely limited computer experience, but I could type. I went to a local temporary agency and accepted data entry jobs for $10 an hour. My third temporary job was with a very small medical consulting company. The company was owned by an elderly couple and had two other employees. This would prove to be my first real introduction into small business. The office was about 2,500 square feet with a series of desks, computers, and file cabinets. Nothing elaborate, but enough to run a simple business operation. The initial job was data entry for a product that they sold to clients. The business concept was simple. They had about 50 clients who received a monthly product, sent out directly by a California manufacturer. This is called drop shipping the product. We never saw the product. Every month, we paid one large invoice to their manufacturer, and then we mailed out 50 invoices to their clients. It was a straight middleman set up. The situation was great. The product cost us about a dollar, and we marked it up to ten dollars depending on the quantity ordered. Furthermore, the state and federal regulations mandated that these clients use and renew the product every month, which created a continual cash flow without us having to do any further marketing or advertising. In addition to this service, the company did some consulting and offered continuing medical education seminars to physicians.

About six months before leaving the company, I began scouring the local newspapers for the next challenge. I came across a fast food restaurant for sale in one of the local shopping malls. Wow – I was going to own my own restaurant. Now this was something that I had always wanted to do. The asking price was $200,000, but by the time we had finished negotiating, the price was $99,000. The $200K was the sucker price, but I quickly learned that the $99K was still a sucker price. I can recall my wife thinking that I was a good negotiator when I managed to get the price almost cut in half, but what I learned is that he should have started at the $99K and had *that* cut in half. The seller didn't have very good financial records, and claimed that since he had many ventures and did not have the proper time to oversee this operation, he predicted that the manager was stealing a fortune. My thought was that I could swoop into this distressed business, clean it up quickly, stop the manager from stealing, and increase the sales, all as my ego told me I could. Not only that, but maybe I could resell it for $200,000 when I was done. So I went ahead and did it. I found a company out of California that would give me $67,000 as a loan against the equipment in the store, plus my personal guarantee and my wife's personal guarantee (big mistake), and the owner would hold the rest of the financing. Note the mistake here: Never get your wife to sign as a guarantor. Without her signature, they couldn't take the biggest asset we had, our house. But basically, I got into the business with $5,000 down. As I look back on this decision, I know what this guy was selling…potential. He had owned the store for three years and had never been able to achieve his goal. When he hard-sold me on the concept, he was telling me that if I was the owner-operator, then I could achieve these goals that he'd been unable to achieve as an absentee owner. Inexperience played a part in this decision because I took it hook, line, and sinker…and sink it did. Without reliving three of the toughest years of my life, I'll just tell you that we lost about $20,000 in year one (about ½ of my wife's salary), broke even in year two, and made about $25,000 in year three. I was certainly not skyrocketing the sales like I had predicted. If you think that $25,000 by year three was good, it equated to paying me about $3.25 per hour for my time.

Living expenses were difficult during these years. At the time, my wife was earning a steady income of about $40,000. This paid all of our bills and living expenses, but I did end up with some additional revenue during this time in my life. Almost simultaneously with my purchase of the restaurant, the elderly owner of the consulting company I'd been working for fell ill to cancer. Within months, he died from complications of a biopsy. I agreed to stay on, managing the company while his wife grieved and considered alternatives. For my help, guidance, and assistance during this time, I was allowed to create a company which would take over the servicing of the product accounts. This would prove to be a very good decision. The products division brought in about $15,000 per year in profit. I was able to carry the restaurant while it got on its feet. It is tough to remember this portion of my life because now it seems like quite a blur. At that time, I was logging in about 100 hours a week between both ventures, and not making much money.

Let me throw in my editorial on the concept of luck. I was in my late 20's, and owned a small medical products company and a restaurant. I was married to a lawyer and had recently purchased a 2,500 square foot house on a golf course. My peers would comment that somehow luck had something to do with my good fortune. Was it luck? I remember that as an undergraduate I took one of those 3 ½ hour classes that only met one night a week. The professor was an adjunct who had retired as the CEO of Montgomery Ward. In case you haven't heard of Ward, they were a large department store chain that somehow went bankrupt in 2000. The instructor brought to me and the class the concept of luckless success. His philosophy was that there were no outcomes for any event which have anything to do with luck. Sound confusing? Well, let me explain. We spent about an hour of class time throwing scenarios at him that were luck-related. He was lucky to become CEO of Ward's, we thought, but he simply responded that it was his late nights working and his aggressive desire to succeed that allowed him to become CEO. He was in control of his destiny to become CEO of Ward's. The football team had been lucky to pull off that 2 point conversion at the end of the game, but he replied that a weaker coach would not have tried the risky 2 point conversion, and perhaps not won the game. The coach made a decision which affected the outcome of the game. There is no luck involved in the victory. Finally, we brought up the winner of the Florida lottery who'd won $5 million, and had to be lucky. To which he asked if any of us students had bought tickets to the lottery last night. The winner put himself in a position to win by going to the local convenience store to buy the ticket. You can't win unless you buy the ticket.

So let us relate this to real estate. I am putting myself in the position to create my own luck: I need to buy my ticket, I need to try the two point conversion. Can I get any more cliché? I saw a nifty slogan the other day, that "Luck is where preparation meets opportunity." I believe that credit was given to Confucius for this saying. This book will give you some preparation, and now you just need to locate the opportunity, but first, I need to create my own luck.

Fast forward several years and you may get a better picture about where all of my entrepreneurial ventures have gone. At 30 years old, I have my first child. I have a pretty cushy work schedule. I have hired a very competent manager for the restaurant, and I typically work in the store from 10-2 each day. My income this year from the restaurant is $25,000, my income from offering medical seminars related to the products I sell is $24,000, and the income from the products' section is $15,000. All in all, at $64,000 a year, my wife can stay at home with the baby and I can spend time raising a family. It all sounds incredibly wonderful, but there is a catch. We spend all $64,000 a year. With the exception of some money we put away in savings while my wife was working, we are not saving anything. I am yet to really think about the words 'college education' or 'retirement'. I am happily trucking right along with a comfy lifestyle, and living in a nice suburban house with a white picket fence, located on a golf course in Maryland.

Why Real Estate?

My wife attended graduate school at the University of North Carolina when we were both 22 years old. For her twenty-second birthday, I bought her the cutest black Labrador puppy. This little black puppy quickly grew to exceed the 25 pound weight limit for pets in our apartment complex. I searched and searched for a place to live that would allow us to have this 80 pound beast. As I am sure that you can guess, I had no luck finding an apartment. My wheels started to turn and I thought that if I owned a place, I would have a home for our happy little family and I could always rent it out after she graduated, specifically to people with large dogs. Furthermore, with homeownership comes in-state residency. With in-state residency comes…you guessed it... in-state tuition. So, off I went to purchase my first house, a 2 bedroom townhouse on Canterbury Court, for $56,900. We got an FHA first time homebuyer loan that only required us to put down $2,500 of our own money. I had absolutely nothing to my name, but my wife had the down payment saved up in stocks that her grandparents had bought her years ago. Canterbury Court was a beautiful place, and with a field behind it for the pooch. We lived in this house for the next two years, and then I rented it out for the next 2 years to some other students attending UNC. After graduation, we moved up to Maryland, where I learned my first lesson in real estate: that long distance landlording is extremely difficult. I had several run-ins with my last tenant, and decided to sell the townhouse. Here is the interesting financial backstory about Canterbury Court; I ended up selling after 4 years for $74,000. At the closing table, I took home a tidy $12,000. Some quick analysis shows that we only put down about $2,500, and walked from the closing table with $2,500 in cold hard cash (actually, it was a check, but it's just fun to say cold hard cash). The return on that was about 500% in 4 years, but we also got a tax depreciation and interest deduction for 4 years, and we saved $5,000 per year in law school tuition. Don't analyze this deal too much: it is just in here to let you know that when I sold that house, I got bit by the bug for real estate. It is the simple concept of leverage that makes this work so fantastic. The $12,000 is only a 21% return on the original house price of $56,900, but I used $54,400 of the bank's money to buy the house. That's what makes the returns in real estate so fantastic that I can't imagine any other investment kicking back these types of returns.

Fast forward to our move to Maryland. We searched all of the listings in all of the areas for the perfect house. We had a choice to make – purchase a starter home for $150,000 or try to purchase as much as we could afford in order to maximize the leverage from the bank's money. We decided to build a house for $259,000. Wow, this was a daunting amount of money back then, but together we were earning over $100,000, with our combined income. We could afford the payment, but we just didn't have the 20% down payment to make. We went with an 80/10/10 mortgage. This product requires 10% as a down payment, then has two loans, one at 80% and the other at 10%. The reason for this type of product is twofold. One is that it only requires 10% down, and two, since the big loan is only 80%, it is a conventional loan which does not require the payment of that pesky mortgage insurance fee (basically, an insurance policy that you pay monthly to insure that you will make your mortgage payment). You need to ask a lot of questions to banks about products such as this, which can save a ton of money in the long term. At any rate, we needed to come up with $25,900 down. We had some money from that sale of the townhouse we'd owned in North Carolina, but were coming up $10,000 short. So with a little luck...or positioning myself for the opportunity for a lucky outcome, we came up with the money thanks to a local radio station.

You see, a local radio station was having their 7:11 A.M. wake-up game on a Thursday in March. I usually didn't listen to this station, but all of their television advertising prompted me to turn on my radio this faithful Thursday. Low and behold, if they announced my birthdate and if I could be the first caller to get through, I would win a prize. For some reason, this was going to be my day. The DJ indeed announced my birthday. The phone rang about 20 times before the DJ answered. Before I knew what was going on, he was telling me that I had just won $10,000. Maybe the result of a little luck, but by listening on that morning, I was suddenly positioned to purchase my dream house. We would spend that money as the down payment on the house. The house remained void of furniture for almost two years, but, hey, it was a big 4 bedroom model. Needless to say, we were proud of this accomplishment. Did I forget to mention that, since I had my real estate license in Florida, I simply took the test in Maryland to get my license? With this license, I saved $8,000 on the purchase on my house. I would do nothing else with my real estate license until 7 years later.

My next big decision was to return to school to get an MBA at the University of Maryland. At this point, I had achieved a reasonable success in obtaining wealth of time, but very limited success in financial wealth. I understood this, and could see that something drastic would have to happen in order to change the situation. You see, when your work days are thin, you find that there is a lot of free time for golf and leisure, and I'm just too young for that. For the next two years, my days were beyond full. Upon starting in the MBA program, I had become a full-time student, restaurant owner, medical products supplier, and father to a 1 year old. Now I was changing from my school clothes, to my shirt and tie, to my restaurant uniform, to my pajamas, where I would try to roll around on the floor with my baby boy. My vision was to graduate, sell the restaurant, and get a corporate job earning 6 figures. This vision altered somewhere along the way. During my last year of school, the restaurant was started to hemorrhage. Three managers later, and after a lot of lost sales, the store began to look like it had when I'd first purchased it, a disgusting mess. I finally felt the desperation the original seller had felt when I first inquired about the store. I sold the restaurant to another egomaniac like myself, who thought that he could white-knight this losing concept. I periodically go by the store to see if perhaps he is more successful, and it has not happened yet, but it's not my problem anymore. I wish him the best of luck. Incidentally, the original seller forgave some of my debt to him, and I subsequently exercised the same grace with the buyer who took it off of my hands. You see, being human in business plays into the abundance theory. Whatever you give will come back to you 10-fold.

In January of 2001, I enrolled in some real estate courses in my MBA program. I realized that I had to do something professionally in real estate, as I just kept finding my way back into this industry. There's just something about developing land and investing in income producing property that gets me excited. While in these courses, I met two other guys who seemed to have the same passion for real estate. We began discussing our plans for after graduation. I continued to interview for full time employment in corporate America, but had the fire in the belly for starting a real estate venture. As it worked out, both of these other guys had a similar fire. So Pete, Richard, and I started laying the foundation for a real estate company. Thus began Signature Properties, LLC.

LESSONS LEARNED

- Luck isn't something that simply happens. You need to create your own luck by being prepared for an opportunity. In order to make money in real estate, you need to be prepared for action and open to opportunity.
- Value in real estate is created through appreciation. Given the variable of time, the value of real estate tomorrow is worth more than the value of real estate today.
- Leverage is the concept of using other people's money. In real estate, the percentage return on your invested capital is far greater when you use as much of the bank's money to purchase the property as possible.

GETTING THE COMPANY GOING

The last semester of school, from January to June of 2001, was a period of investigation. I knew that a career in real estate was my objective, but where should I start? Early this last semester, Pete, Richard, and I did a case study on an industrial building located in Parole, Maryland. The study was to show how we could turn a distressed, vacant tire repair shop into a mini-auto repair mall. The building had 5 bays equipped with lifts.

We investigated the rehab costs of the building and the market rent for a quick oil lube/auto repair shop, paint shop, tire shop, etc.; we performed a complete MBA style analysis of the project. We looked at the market rent for light industrial space for that area. We looked at the various uses for the vacant lot behind the building. Our construction analysis included a new roof, new paving, subdividing the space, painting, and repairing the existing hydraulic lifts and everything else to create a top notch automobile mini-mall. We were super excited at what we thought would be the most convenient one-stop-shop for all of your automotive needs.

From a marketing prospective, it seemed great. The location was close to shopping options, and with a high density of residential dwellings. We thought that an individual could have auto repair, painting, tire replacement, and oil changes all in one location. The bottom line to the whole analysis was to come up with a final figure for what we could pay for the property and how rich we were going to get off of the cash flow associated with the project.

The result showed that we could pay up to $1.5 million for the building, and make a return of approximately 12% on our money invested after expenses. So far, so good....but we learned a few things from this case study. First, we learned the value of the saying "you need money to make money". Even though the three of us thought that we were players at the time, we learned from a local bank that a deal like this required 20% down. Where were we going to come up with 20% of $1.5 million, or $300,000? We also learned that, sometimes, the owners of real estate want far more money than what it's worth. The owner was asking $2.1 million – far more than our $1.5 million dollar valuation. Lastly, we learned that, in order to make money in real estate investment, you need a lot of real estate.

According to our analysis, this property would kick off a smooth $45,000 per year in net income. Divide that by 3, and Pete, Richard, and I we bringing home $15,000 each. Not exactly enough to support my future family. It was a great learning experience, and I thank Professor Baum, our teacher for this class, for teaching us some of the intricacies of analyzing a deal.

Recently, I did notice that the building was sold to a car dealership. This is actually a better fit for the property. There's a large lot in the rear of the property which lends well to the parking of cars. The bays in the existing building will work as the service center. The owner may have been able to get his $2.1 million because the buyer found a better use for the property than what our analysis had kicked out. We also learned a new concept – highest and best use.

We are learning every day, more and more about what is the best use for a piece of real estate. The big lesson learned from this case study was that, if we wanted to get into big projects for big bucks, we needed to establish a short term plan for cash flow. We know that the $1.5 million deals are where we want to be, but the more difficult question is: "how do we get there?". We've tried to think about what piece of real estate could be purchased for low capital requirements and where we could go for capital to get into the game. This quandary forced us to start from the bottom up.

Remember – and this is extremely important – when evaluating my start into the business, by the time I graduated school in May 2001, I had only the income from the courses and the products division. My wife was not working, we now had two kids, and we were surviving on about $40,000 per year. I will not go into the details of my partners' lives, but they had student debts and were not earning any income at all!

June 2001

June comes along. By now, we've figured out the short term cash plan. I renewed my real estate salesperson license, now in Maryland; Pete was working on getting his in Maryland, and Richard the same in Virginia. This part gets interesting. I knew that the three of us didn't have enough money to get into the real estate game. It was an expensive game to play. I knew that I needed to "Create my own luck". While looking through the local newspaper, I saw a tiny little ad for a real estate broker who was seeking licensed agents who wanted to flip houses. The game is called the elephant and the mouse.

At this point in time, I was the mouse and the broker was the elephant. I had no capital to invest, but a lot of time to work the street. The elephant had a line of credit that they were willing to expose if the mouse did all of the work. We'd split the profits after the property was purchased and rehabbed, 50/50. On the surface, this seemed like a good deal – he put up all the money and we would do all the work.

This local broker had established a great program. As his agent, I would scout out and buy distressed real estate. How I find these deals is another chapter all together, and I warn you that it is one you really want to remember. At any rate, when I find a shell or distressed property, I prepare the work-up sheet for the broker. The work-up sheet includes simple calculations, such as the buy-in price referred to as the acquisition cost, the repairs, the interest costs paid to the bank known as carry costs, the closing costs, and an estimated resale price. The formula is easy and fairly safe. The broker then provides access to his line of credit for the purchase of the house. The broker's line covers all of the repairs on the house as well. Upon completion, I list the property for sale as the listing agent, and hopefully sell the property for the estimated sales price. After the closing is complete, the broker cuts me a check for 50% of the profit. The importance of what you are reading now is that I found a way to get into the real estate development business with "no money down." I have always wanted to say that…no money down. Perhaps someday I will be on television at 2 AM telling you how to make money with "no money down".

But seriously, the elephant and the mouse is a great way to get into the business. Elephants are not hard to find, and if you look around at your local real estate investment club, you will likely find one. As of the writing of this chapter, I sincerely believe that this option was the best way for me to get started in the business. My goal is not to do small residential deals, but this appears to be the best method for gaining the experience with the smallest amount of exposure. My father would always tell me that it is better to learn on someone else's dime. This is exactly what he meant. If you are wondering whether it's difficult to find an elephant, it wasn't in my case. In the first three months, I came across three other brokers willing to make the same arrangement. (I was looking for a better profit split, but only found marginal differences.)

Before I complete this thought on the elephant and mouse game, something should be bothering you the way it bothers me today. If I am doing all of the scouting, locating, bidding, negotiating, construction, construction management, and then taking care of the resale of the properties, what exactly is the broker doing for 50% of the profits? If you are familiar with the venture capital model, you know they take an equity position in small companies with little to no assets or cash. The equity position is up to 50% or more of the company for the enormous risk they are taking by putting their money into a concept, technology, or prototype written on the back of a cocktail napkin.

With real estate, we are talking about a solid, resellable, collateralizable asset. The elephant is taking title to the property in his name, purchasing real estate for prices that are below assessed value, and making substantial profits for very little exposure. For this, they are rewarded with 50% of the profits of the deal. Don't get me wrong – I like the idea of getting into the business with no money down. My bigger question at this point is – can I become the elephant? Just a thought, for now.

Now that we had identified a source of capital, we needed to pick a market. We picked a market where we could find distressed residential properties which could have value added through rebuilding them into high quality rehabs. Our value proposition was that we could take an ugly property and turn it into a shining diamond. We needed a market that offered a lot of opportunities. We looked at many counties in Maryland, and settled on Baltimore. What made Baltimore so appealing was that the city was going through a transformation in and of itself. Many large businesses were moving to the city. Shopping and restaurants were on the rise in the city, and best of all, the employees of these companies were looking for the live/work environment. This meant that there were buyers looking for high-end city houses close to the workplace. The city housing in Baltimore is similar to any major city in the country. It is filled with rowhomes and brownstones which date back over 100 years. Many of these houses have not had any work done to them in about 100 years, and are presently uninhabitable. This became our model. We could purchase these "shells", which were nothing more than four brick walls and a roof for about $50,000, put in new plumbing, electric, HVAC, new drywall, kitchens, baths, hardwood floors, stainless appliances, and rooftop decks (altogether costing about $70,000), and resell them to the young affluent professionals in the city for $200,000. Our initial vision was to create a "Signature" look for each of properties. If we could build a brand in Baltimore, people would seek out our Signature product, and perhaps we could command a premium for our rehabbed products. The model looked promising, and Signature Properties was launched in June of 2001.

First, we set up a bank account and each put $1,500 into the account. I was fortunate enough to have this money in my personal account, but I know that my partners had to ask friends, family, and fools for the money. Next, we found an office downtown. We wanted to be close to where our core business was. We were so excited to locate a fantastic space. The office was a 10 by 15 room for $200 per month (six month lease), but we weren't even sure if we would still be in business six months from now. The space was located in a very old Baltimore building. The elevator ran super slow, the carpets smelled of cat urine, the walls were dirty…but it was our new home, and we were ecstatic. We then went to a "going out of business" office closure auction. This was our first auction, and the excitement of bidding on old, used office equipment was palpable. We purchased three desks, file cabinets, and a copy machine for about $200. With $30, we had business cards made up, set up a phone line, and voila, Signature Properties was born.

Pete and Richard in our first office on St. Paul Street in Baltimore

Alright, you can see that, so far, we have not accomplished any great feat, but I do think that we have put the wheels in motion to create something great. As an entrepreneur, I love the excitement, but also have some thoughts of my future. This is the point at which I am feeling fully pregnant. I am all in.

Pete stands proudly with our copier, purchased at auction for $25

Psychologically, I am wondering if I should have gone the MBA route and taken a corporate job earning 6 figures. I am hoping and dreaming that you will be reading this book and I will have reached my $2 million goal. If you are reading this, there should be nothing that I have described that anyone is not capable of doing.

I put up $1,500 of my money, and committed to taking a shot in real estate, but let's be realistic. I need to have a predetermined stop in my plan. What if I am not successful, and what if I spend all this time and risk all this money and fail? When is it time to "call it quits"? My thinking is that, in one year, if I have not seen the money or do not see any shot at the money, I will give up and find a job. This thought scares me because I hate failure. I have promised that I will be realistic in this venture. I have a 12 month self-imposed leash. If I do not see the money in a year, I am pulling the plug. It is a very exciting journey that I am embarking on – but also a very scary one.

September 2001

This morning, I bought a picture from this company called Successories. You may have seen their products: photographs with these motivational sayings under them. This one has a picture of a skier jumping off of a cliff, with the saying "Make it Happen". You see, we've been at this for several months now, and we are yet to make our first purchase. Each day, we search the internet, try networking with people, analyze different properties, but have yet to actually pull the trigger on our first purchase. We have been looking for properties for three months now, and for one reason or another, nothing seems to work out. Some of the properties are too expensive, some of them need too much work and most of them simply don't work when inputting them into our worksheet model. Today, I decided to hit the streets. I started driving around the city, street by street, to see what was available. As I pulled from the popular Federal Hill neighborhood into the up-and-coming Locust Point neighborhood, I found a house with a sign on it – For Sale by Owner – 1405 Andre Street. The house was in really tough shape. It was your typical Baltimore city middle row house. It had a brick front, broken windows, and little curb appeal. However, this house had a special feature – there were just three walls since the back wall was partially falling down, and oh yeah, there was no roof either. The interior had nothing salvageable. The house would need to be completely gutted, down to the bare walls.

This house was perfect. This would indeed fit our criteria, and seemed to be a great match for our business model. This was a perfect opportunity for redevelopment. I called the local telephone number on the sign and explained to the owner that I was an investor, and wanted to know how much he was asking for the house. He was asking $75,000. Hmmm, was that a good price or not? After a brief conversation, I went back to our $200 a month office space and began to analyze this deal. The house looked like it could be worth $200,000 if it was finished up with granite countertops, new cabinets, new baths, and yes, a roof and back wall as well. I met with Pete and Richard to discuss what we thought this house would require for construction and what it would cost. Our uneducated hypothesis was that $70,000 would do the trick. We literally used the back of the napkin at lunch today to figure out that a resale of $200,000, minus the $70,000 construction costs, less the $75,000 purchase price, could yield us a tidy $55,000 in profit. So, we set up a meeting with the broker and reviewed the financial worksheet. At his suggestion, we submitted a written offer for $65,000. I called the property owner, we met, and he countered with $67,000. I returned to Pete and Richard, excited like a school boy. We are pretty close to having our first deal in the hopper. The broker wanted us to get started, so he signed off on the $67,000 deal, and we are scheduled to purchase our very first house in 30 days. We are now under way. I am very excited, but at the same time, a little nervous.

We also started searching on the government sites. On the internet, you can access Housing and Urban Development (HUD) and Veterans Affairs (VA). These websites are great. You can go to any city in the United States, and find hundreds of properties being offered at a substantial discount with the click of the mouse. Furthermore, you can bid on these properties online, and with no risk. If you enter low bids and get the property, congratulations, you are now officially in the business! If your bids are not accepted, no big deal, but you put yourself into that position to be lucky. We quickly identified a property that we liked on the HUD website.

First and Second Floors of Andre Street

1405 Andre Street – Second Floor

This one was in a residential suburb of Baltimore on Belle Grove Road. So, again, we sat down to figure out what this would need in order to be shined up. This house was different than Andre Street. The ultimate buyer of this house would be a first time home buyer, looking to get into a property cheap. They would not need the granite and high end appliances. Our vision for this house was to give it a facelift. We could put new sheetrock over the paneling, new paint, newer inexpensive appliances, new carpet, and it needed a new roof and some curb appeal landscaping. We estimated the final selling price to be about $140,000. To get there, we would need to put in about $30,000 of work…plus about $10,000 in other costs. If we wanted to make $35,000 on the house, we could offer somewhere around $65,000. We first submitted an offer of $62,000 on the HUD website. Viola, we were the winning bidder at $62,000. The transaction was quite simple. Anyone can purchase a HUD or VA home with the assistance of a local real estate agent. On the internet, your agent will submit a bid to the government for the purchase of the house. All of the houses need some degree of work, and are discounted accordingly.

Bell Groves Road Exterior

Belle Grove Road Living Room

Within 24 hours, your agent is notified if your bid was accepted or rejected. Naturally, your bid should start low and slowly rise, until it is accepted by the government agency. So far, we have found one house by driving through the neighborhoods and one more on the HUD site – this has been a very productive month! Now if we can only turn these acquisitions into some income, my partners and I will all be happy. We haven't earned anything since we started this business and money is beginning to get tight.

So, now we had two properties under contract and were beginning to feel some mojo. Richard found himself out speaking with the contractors to do the work. He met with plumbers, electricians, roofers, and others subs that would be an integral part of helping us rebuild both Andre Street and Belle Grove Road. He was beginning to see that some of the estimates that we had made on the roof and the other work needed were, unfortunately, incredibly low. For instance, we had budgeted $5,000 for a new roof at Belle Grove Road, and the three quotes that he received were from $7,000 to $10,000. I guess this is part of the learning curve. The other thing that we have realized is that we need to make a more standardized template for analyzing the numbers. I am beginning to see that there is much which we don't know, and the thought of making mistakes is beginning to fester. So, this week, Pete and I have embarked on understanding all of the closing costs associated with both buying and selling the properties. We are trying to understand the fees associated with recording titles and purchasing title insurance. We want to know how property taxes work, along with fees and paperwork related to commissions, closing costs, and interest expense. While I have been preaching that it is not that difficult to get into this business, I do think that it is slightly complicated to get into a model that can be standardized for flipping more houses. So, while we are excited about the prospect of getting our first two properties under way, we are realizing that much work has to be done in order to make this process more efficient.

September 2nd Entry

This month, we were also turned onto foreclosure auctions. These happen on the court house steps each and every day. We began by checking the websites of all of the foreclosure auction houses. In Maryland, we looked at Alexcooper.com and ajbillig.com. These websites are fantastic. They list the street name and mortgage amount owed on each home. Now we could analyze 20-30 potential properties each and every week. We started to do a paper analysis to see if there's any potential equity in the respective deals. If there is, I take a road trip and look at 10-20 houses per week. Since these foreclosures are occupied, I can't get into the house to evaluate it. I am looking at the outside, peeking in the windows, and doing my best to evaluate some of the potential problems of the house. Unfortunately, this is making it difficult for Richard to price out the construction. Since I do not know if the plumbing works or if it needs a new water heater, how can we accurately estimate what the construction costs will be on these houses? While I like the fact that foreclosures offer a ton of opportunities, the thought of buying houses without ever seeing the inside of them is a little bit daunting. I haven't found any properties yet, but I have been attending the auctions at the courthouse steps and watching as other investors seem to be picking up properties each and every day. I do believe that this is a good method of acquisition, but will need a fair amount of further investigation before I am ready to risk the broker's money on it. Foreclosures seem to be exciting stuff – I look forward to learning more as quickly as possible so that we can get into this game.

Good news. We own three houses. We closed on Andre Street and on Belle Grove Road, and closed on another one a few weeks ago. The three of us have been working on Belle Grove Road. I have been learning a ton about construction. We have replaced cabinets, and installed toilets, sinks, doors, and knobs. We have had the carpet replaced and even hired one of our old MBA buddies to paint the house. The house is starting to take shape, and looks pretty good. Budget-wise, I think that we will end up coming in close to the $30,000 mark, but it is too early to tell. On Andre Street, we hired a general contractor to handle the entire process. This was a good deal – I think. We budgeted $70,000 for construction, and signed a contract with Clearspring Construction to do the entire project, soup-to-nuts, for $70,000. Once a week, I stop by and they are making some great progress. I hope to post some pictures of the process.

On the acquisition side, we purchased another property via the realtor database. This particular home was priced well below the market for the street. I am not really sure why other investors hadn't scooped this one up before us. After inspecting the property, it was obvious that the original floor plan with its funky kitchen reduced the value of the home significantly. We purchased the house with the intention of adding a full bathroom upstairs and reselling the house. We put this house under contract for $90,000. We envision selling it in the low to mid $200,000s. Another home was found for us by one of the construction workers from Andre Street. The owner had violations with the city due to the condition of the home, and had to sell immediately. We closed on this one relatively quickly – so we now own it, and out goes $46,000 more. As you can see, we spent the first 4-5 months really learning how to analyze, price, estimate market value, and learn the nuts and bolts of the industry. We are now becoming confident enough to fill our pipeline of properties.

December 2001

Quick post: I bought a house at foreclosure – Woodall Street. The house was vacant, so I managed to get inside and do a pretty good job of pricing out the construction. I found the house posted on alexcooper.com and the website showed a required deposit of $7,000. I needed to show up at the courthouse steps with $7,000 in certified funds. This meant that the property would most likely sell somewhere in the range of $70,000 in order to cover the defaulted mortgage with the bank. The area is growing, and we know that we could remodel this house and make a tidy profit. For this deal, we used the broker's money and it required no capital investment from us. Before we went to the courthouse steps, we did the following analysis to find out exactly how much we could spend.

Closing	$3,000	Expenses we would incur to purchase the property
Carry	$10,000	Interest money spent while construction takes place
Commission	$6,000	Money to pay the selling agent - we are the listing agent.
Repair Work	$60,000	Money to completely rehab the property
Resale	$180,000	Our best estimates as to what the property will be worth.
Closing	$3,000	Transfer taxes we will pay when we resell.
Profit	**$27,000**	**The broker looks for a 15% return on resale price.**
Buy In Price	$71,000	The most we could spend to purchase the property and realize a 15% return on resale for the broker.

This analysis is really quite simple. We start by estimating what the price will be when we go to resell the property. To accomplish this, we sought out comparable properties which have already been rehabbed and sold. Anyone can get this information from the internet. Property records are open to the public and available, at least in Maryland and most other states that I have checked, on their taxation and assessments website. Try Google searching for your 'county' and 'taxation and assessments' or 'appraisers' and I bet you will hit gold. I have heard of other publically available websites that are being developed to make this information public, as well. Next, we got a good estimate on rehabilitating the property. This can only be accomplished by talking with various tradesman and construction companies in the area. From there, we used percentages to estimate our expenses associated with carrying and closing the deal. The buy-in price is the final plug. After you have taken the fixed-up market value, subtracted out closing, commission, and carry and construction costs, and also subtracted out your required profit for the deal (we use a figure of 15% of the resale), you are left with the price at which you can safely acquire the project. According to this analysis, we could pay $71,000. Since the bank was looking for $70,000 at the foreclosure sale, we had a shot at this one if no one else showed up to the auction. Other people did indeed show up at the auction. The bidding opened at $70,000. I was a little bit nervous and raised my hand to indicate that I was willing to pay the $70,000. The auctioneer then bid on behalf of the bank with a bid of $71,000. I'd had seen this before. The bank will keep bidding until their debt is completely met. So I raised my hand again at $72,000. I realized that I was bidding higher than my max bid, but it was close enough. I mean, we were slated to make $27,000 in profit, so so what if it was only $26,000? We ended up being the only bidders on the property, and picked it up for $72,000. We signed the contract right there at the courthouse steps. The auctioneer informed us that these foreclosures take 60 days to close. How exciting – our first foreclosure purchase, and it looks like it could be a good one. We left the court house steps and I decided to run Pete and Richard by our newest foreclosure acquisition on Woodall Street.

This property happened to be vacant, and the neighbors informed us that it had been for quite some time. Perhaps this is the reason that the mortgage had been foreclosed on. At this point, I didn't own the property. I had a contract to settle on the property for the $72,000 price once the sale was approved by the court. While standing in front of the house, I had a thought. If it could be worth $180,000 when it was fixed up, maybe someone would pay me cash for the right to purchase it at $82,000. I'm thinking maybe flipping the contract for a quick $10,000. So, during this time, I hung a for-sale sign on the property with my telephone number. I didn't list a price or anything, just curious if I could "create some luck". I had about 6 calls on the house, and one good bite. These phone calls came from other investors looking for properties to rehab in the area. You see, the average investor is pretty lazy. They will drive around the neighborhoods to see if anything is for sale, but will not go the extra step of looking at the foreclosure sites. I priced the house in its present condition at $99,000.

I did find an investor ready to buy Woodall Street. We closed on the purchase of the property on a Monday. This means we showed up at closing with the broker's money, signed the documents, and got the keys to the house on Monday. On Wednesday, we sat down again at the settlement company, but this time with the buyer. The investor bought it from us for the full asking price or $99,000. Our gross margin was $27,000, but after all of the closing costs, insurance, commission, and carry, we netted about $14,000. From this, Signature Properties made $7,000 profit (remember, the 50/50 split with the elephant). While this does not sound like a lot of money, I certainly did not have to work very hard to make it. I put no money down, had no construction labor, and really invested no more work than the 15 minutes of paperwork on the courthouse steps. I could certainly get interested in the wholesale flipping of real estate to other investors.

I have now had the opportunity to flip 2 other properties which I bought at distressed prices, but I have opted instead to renovate them for a higher margin. If I focused on flipping properties, I could probably flip 15-20 properties a year with profits to the mouse of $5,000-$7,000 each. I always keep the option of a quick sale open. Right about now is when I began to realize that even though I'd made $7,000 on the flip, so had the elephant. Let's see: he put up $7,000 for the deposit, and put the entire closing on his line of credit. In return for his $7,000, he received a 100% return in 60 days. Wow... do this all year long, and he makes a 600% return on his money (one every two months). I continue to keep my eye on the prize of becoming the financial capital behind the deals instead of the working labor on the deals. For now, I am beginning to see some of the money coming in from these first couple of transactions, and so far so good.

LESSONS LEARNED

- Goal setting is extremely important. Start by setting financial goals and then mapping out a course of action to get there.

- Capital is a very important component of real estate. The person with the money makes the rules. Quickly become self-funded.

- Finding deals is difficult. You always need to be scanning multiple sources in order to locate deals and keep your business flowing forward.

THE JOURNEY CONTINUES

January 2002

Let me now fill you in with a snapshot of the deals that I am presently involved. We currently have 3 houses under construction and 5 houses under contract. I'm excited to see how we do on all of these projects. We did sell the house that we bought on Belle Grove Road. At the end of the day, it sold for $137,000 – which was pretty close to the original $140,000 that we anticipated. The profit on the deal was $13,800. This ended up being substantially less than we had anticipated. We underestimated the construction budget substantially, as well as underestimated some of the closing costs associated with the deal. I guess these are typical rookie mistakes we're making.

Over the months, we have accumulated properties from a variety of sources. We are becoming pretty adept at identifying opportunities all around us.

If 8 houses sounds like a lot of real estate to purchase within 6-months, it's really not. I can find about 2 houses per month which have enough equity to yield a profit. Every day of the week is an auction, whether they are foreclosure, estate, private sale, or by guardian. These houses are fantastic opportunities to buy from motivated sellers. Next, you can check with your local real estate agent. They have access to bank owned properties, fixer upper properties, and other motivated sellers. Finally, if you let people know that you buy distressed properties for cash, opportunities tend to come to you. A contractor brought us the #1 Wolfe deal and a disgruntled investor brought us the #2 Pratt.

In looking at our recent successes, you can see some really good deals, but I want to point out something else. Take a look at Belle Grove Road. This was our first project. Pete, Richard, and I put a lot of sweat into making this deal happen. At the end of the day, Signature Properties made $6,900. This was great. Combine this with the $7,000 we made flipping Woodall Street, and the company had a pretty good couple of months. We made almost $14,000!!!! Remember, the elephant also made $14,000. So, a couple of months ago, we all started to noodle a little bit on the idea of how to cut the elephant out and keep all the profit.

Here's what has happened. It does not take a genius to realize that the mouse does all of the work and then shares the peanuts with the elephant. So, when you analyze what the elephant brings to the table, it is simply his line of credit and some closing cash. Some of these deals required about $10,000 in closing cash, and good credit for a construction loan. Well, both my partner and I have great credit, but we lack the cash. I had two options. So, a couple of months ago, I went to BB&T (the bank that holds the mortgage on my primary residence) to discuss how I could tap the available equity in my house to come up with the $10,000 in cash. A quick visit to the bank and a friendly branch manager revealed that I could qualify for a $50,000 personal line of credit. I was unfamiliar with how a personal line of credit worked, so the manager went on to explain. Since I had impeccable credit, the bank was willing to extend me $50,000 just for signing my name. The manager did inform me that she has been in this business for 20+ years, and the opportunity to get unsecured money like this is really uncommon. She strongly suggested that I put in for the $50,000 line of credit right away! Since I wanted to keep my wife out of the loop and really not let her know that I was going into personal debt to finance this venture, I opted for the personal line. Sorry, Jill, but some secrets will just help you sleep better at night. When I told my partner Pete about this, who has been a full time student for the past two years without any income, he was also able to qualify for the same $50,000 line of credit. So, now we were in business. Here is a deal update. Some of the deals that I talked about were purchased without the elephant's money. This is huge – because if we make $15,000 to $20,000 on these deals, we keep it all. For the past six months, I have continued to extend my line of credit to support this venture and for living expenses.

So, here is the problem with establishing a line of credit – you use it. While we have been making some money flipping houses, the money is simply not enough to support all three of us. Richard has since departed from the company, so just Pete and I are left. I have been using the line of credit as living expenses. This was supposed to be reserved for acquisitions. Yikes. On this date, January 20, 2002, I owe my bank $27,000. My partner is in debt over $50,000. Some days go by when this fact really bothers me. Not only am I in debt for all this money, but the opportunity cost is on my mind as well – that of not working a corporate job for the past 6 months, where I could have earned $50,000 since June – and this is also becoming a stark reality. I'll be honest, some of my MBA buddies are right now purchasing big beautiful houses and driving some nice cars. I am heading in the wrong direction by living off of fumes and life support and my line of credit. Yikes…it feels worse writing it down. I marvel at the support of my wife. She has supported me each and every month, and really helps me stay in the game. She has given me the emotional support to keep plugging away, but also the financial support to continue. You see, we now have two kids and no other income. This means that we have gone into frugal living mode. We cut as many corners as possible in order to reduce our burn rate as much as possible during these periods of poor cash flow. I have trained her in the ways of a frugal pauper quite well. I remember coming home from my in-laws house one night. Both kids were quietly sleeping in the back of the Jeep. My wife asked if we could stop by the grocery store so that she could pick up a pie crust for a pie she planned to bake. As we got closer to the store, she asked if I could turn around and go home to pick something up. It ended up that she was willing to risk the kids waking up in the back seat, and add another 10 minutes to our travels, so that she could pick up a coupon she had at home for the pie crust.

There was a short period in our dual income life when she was purchasing nothing but high-end organic groceries from the store. Over the past several years, she has really adapted back to how it was when she originally married me, the then pizza delivery guy. I continue to feel the pain of extending myself further and further along with this line of credit. Some days go by when I question whether the model will work. How long can I afford to continue to run up credit in order to live? I am presently at $27,000 but what happens when I hit the $50,000? Do I start a home equity line, and at what point do I just throw in the towel? When we originally set up the company, we predicted profitability within the first six months. These issues weigh incredibly heavy on my mind at this point in my extremely young real estate career. The problem is that I had no idea how long we would have to wait in order to really cash in on some deals. We had great luck with the first couple of deals yielding an incredibly quick $7,000 each, but nothing has materialized since then. We wait patiently for the construction to be complete, but nothing. Time seems to drag by. As partners, we didn't even take any money from that $14,000 in deals since we have debts to pay like rent, parking, phone tolls, realtor fees, copies, supplies, and everything else that adds up so incredibly quickly. If you are not getting the picture from this chapter already, know that life is pretty tough these days for Signature Properties. There is the excitement about what could be, but that excitement is squashed almost immediately by the reality of little cash flow, small deals, and huge lines of credit debt.

It really depends what hat I put on when I get dressed in the morning, and that dictates how I feel about this business venture and about real estate in general. Some days, I am constantly daydreaming about the next 3 or 4 deals closing, and how I am going to spend the $100,000 I will make, and other days I look at the debt or the deal that just closed for peanuts, and think that I have made a grave mistake. It may be time to revisit the original business plan. It wasn't supposed to start out this way. What keeps me sane and focused on the long term game is the chart of properties above. I can taste and smell the money. I am getting so close to completing this first cycle of investment properties that I can't wait to close what we have and find more deals. I tell Pete every day that I love dreaming about the money. I can look at the chart above and spend the money a thousand times in my head. When Wolfe closes, I will buy this, and when Pratt closes, I will buy that. For now, however, I can only think about paying off this line of credit. I am not one that lives off of credit. I pay my credit card bills in full each month, and have never missed a payment in my entire life.

January 21, 2002

A few weeks have passed since my past entry, and things are not as doom and gloom this week. Let me introduce you to one of the interesting properties on the chart above, #1 Pratt Street. #1 Pratt Street has an interesting story. It showed up on the foreclosure list for a Friday auction. The deposit for the property was $8,400. From the street, it looked like every other Baltimore City rowhouse. It was big, it seemed to be well maintained from the street, it was occupied, and the blinds were closed so that I couldn't really get a good look inside. At any rate, the property could be worth up to $250,000 if it was fixed up nicely. It was a large 3,000 square foot house, and would cost every bit of $100,000 to fix up. So, I did the analysis and thought that we could pay up to $90,000 for the property and still make a tidy $40,000 profit after all of the expenses. I took the write-up to the elephant (broker) and asked him for a check for $8,400 to bring to the auction the next day so that I could buy this deal. If the bidding began at $84,000, I would buy that, put in about $100,000, and hopefully resell the property for $230,000 to $250,000. I think that the broker was in a bad mood that day because he scolded me about giving him more advanced notice on getting a check for the auction, and he refused to give me the check. I still don't know what his deal was on that particular day, because he usually got me checks right on the spot. At any rate, I showed the deal to Pete. He agreed that the paper analysis looked good, so I hit my personal line of credit for $8,400 so that we would be armed and ready for the auction the next morning. We went to the auction at the courthouse steps in Baltimore City that day, and wouldn't you know it, we were the only bidders there. It is really strange the way things happen. My wife will tell you it's a God thing, but we needed a big victory, and buying this property for under $90,000 may be just the start that we needed. The bidding opened at $83,500 and we took it for $84,000. We were pretty excited about the purchase, but we were nowhere near prepared for the excitement that we were about to experience.

With buying houses at the courthouse steps, we've learned a process known as 'cash for keys'. Right after leaving the steps with the contract in hand, we head over to the property and knock on the door. When the defaulting homeowner opens the door, we explain that the bank has foreclosed on the property and that we are representatives for the investment company that bought the house. Usually, people are aware of the foreclosure and are not as aggressive as one might anticipate. Our hope is to make a friendly introduction with the homeowner, and convince them that they should pack up their goods and move out. We have, of course, found that they have no money to move out, and need something as a deposit to move into an apartment. So, I have found that if I offer them $500 in cash if they move out in 30 days, the whole process goes much smoother. We call it 'cash for keys'. So on this beautiful sunny day, we went to the house that day to knock on the door to let the homeowner know that we had purchased his house at auction, and we wanted to make arrangements for him to move out. After knocking about a dozen times, the door slowly opened. It opened slowly because there was a pile of unopened mail below the mail slot, about 2 feet high, and the door had to push the pile aside. The owner was a young adult in his mid-twenties, somewhat disheveled looking. Apparently, this guy was going through a tough time in his life, had become a hermit, and had just stopped opening up his mail. We spoke with him briefly about the fact that we'd bought his house at the courthouse steps, and that he would need to make arrangements to move out of the house in the next 30 days. He didn't invite us into the house, but what we saw when Pete and I looked into the house was nothing short of awesome. When he closed the door and we sauntered back to the street, we were slightly speechless. We looked at each other, slowly cracked smiles, and asked the other if he had gotten a good look inside the house. We had budgeted $100,000 to fix up the house. Since, when purchasing property at a foreclosure auction, you cannot see the inside of the house and you are bidding solely on the exterior appearance, we typically assume that the entire house needs work done. The $100,000 represents potential updates to the electric, plumbing, HVAC, sheetrock, paint, and just about everything else. To our delight and utter amazement, the house had been completely remodeled about 5 years back. All of the electric, plumbing, HVAC, sheetrock, floors... all was all relatively new. The shock and excitement at budgeting $100,000 and not needing nearly that much was beginning to sink in. This now was going to be an unbelievable deal! Even more unbelievable, we'd bought this with our money in the name of Signature Properties – our first acquisition without the broker.

I've decided to retroactively insert what happened on this house in June 2002. I know I am violating my rule of a chronological timeline – but it ends up being so incredible that I wanted the story to come to a logical end right now: We did get into the house in March. The house had been updated closer to 10 years prior, and would indeed need some work. We did end up dropping about $45,000 in repairs. We ended up dropping a new kitchen into the house, redoing the upstairs au pair apartment, and putting in nicer lighting fixtures. And remember, this one was not financed by the elephant, so we hit the lines of credit again to close on the property, carry the mortgage, and fix up the property. This was going to be the first deal that we self-financed, so we needed to find a bank that would give us a loan. We went to this local mortgage broker who could get us 90% financing on the shell and 100% of the construction money. That seemed pretty good to us. This guy was a local mortgage broker with a retail office right there on Pratt Street. He did construction financing, so we thought he was just as good as anyone else. His financing package was a great deal, and he got everything square for settlement. He did not do it for free…he took 2.5 points on the deal, which cost us about $4,500, but he got the deal done, and for that I am extremely thankful. He did the financing through a local Annapolis bank. So we bought the shell for $84,000, had about $10,000 in closing costs (including his $4,500 mortgage broker fee), put in $45,000 in rehabilitation costs, and spent maybe another $6,000 in carry costs, so all in, we had about $145,000 in the deal. When the work was completed, the house looked really nice. It was large, had an open floor plan, had decent fixtures and finishes, and should be able to command something at the higher-end of the market.

We put the house on the market last week for $245,000, and within one week, we had an offer on the property for $236,500. At this level, we would net about $90,000 on the deal. We countered their offer at the full $245,000. Trust me – it was not easy saying no to this kind of cash, but I'm optimistic that they will come up to my level. My plan is to take my portion of the money, clear out my $36,000 in debt, though actually my line is probably more than that when you add my portion of the carry on this deal, and I will then leave $5,000, or whatever is left, in the account for the next purchase. I am incredibly excited about the possibility of just clearing out my debt. Looking at the chart above, this year should be really good. If all things were to work out, I could make $100,000-$200,000 this year. I hope that when I reread this chapter in several years, that this does not sound like a lot of money, but right now…..WOW. I'll let you know how the Pratt Street deal ends up once it closes. Once again, there is excitement in the real estate game.

Before I depart writing for the month, I would like to bring you to a deal that I think will be one of our most profitable this year. Pete and I love this deal. The address is on Lombard Street in the city. I would call it a house, but it really is only one wall (the front wall). The investor who owned it was digging out the basement of this home during his rehab. They hadn't structurally supported the walls sufficiently, and the end result was that the entire house collapsed... with the exception of the front wall. He has been fined numerous times by the city housing authority for unsafe conditions. Recently, the city condemned the property, and threatened to demolish what is left at his expense. I hope that you can see that this is a real opportunity, because I like to think that the uglier the house, the more the opportunity for making big money. So far, I have talked to the assistant State's Attorney about what needs to be done to this house to bring it out of condemnation and back to life. I have also spoken with the city housing inspector to see what structural damage needs to be completed for this property and the surrounding properties, which were also damaged. Tomorrow, I will meet the structural engineer to see if reconstruction is structurally possible. The engineer will run $200. I put together an offer of $5,000 for the property, whose assessed value for the land is $35,000. To a lazy investor, this house is a black hole. This house is a nightmare that could take on many fines and expensive legal fees. I have thick skin, though, and I am willing to take this bull by the horns to make the deal work.

Here is my vision for this property, and it will be interesting to see if my numbers are remotely correct. The buy-in of the property should run us about $7,000 with closing costs. Right now, I do not have my half of the $7,000, but I love this deal so much that I will throw another $3,500 onto my line of credit. I have already had a contractor take a quick look at the project, and he believes that to rebuild a new house on that property should run about $165,000. Therefore, we are in at $7,000, spend $165,000 to rebuild the house, and will have commissions, carry, and costs of about $20,000. I am predicting this house to hit the market in 9 months (September 2002) for $300,000. Let's do the math, 300-20-165-7 = $108,000. I have trouble typing when I see these kinds of numbers. Right now, this deal is pretty exciting to me. Did I neglect to mention that the bank should give me a loan of 70% of the appraised value? That equates to $210,000, and I only need $165,000 to do the renovation. So, I am in this opportunity to make $108,000 on this one deal, and for $7,000 down. Does this sound doable to you? Just for clarification, Pete and I are 50/50 partners and purchase everything together. We invest the same amount each and own exactly half of all of our purchases.

Lombard Street Lower Level

Shot from Inside of Lombard Street

Thus, this chapter will come to a close. I am at a point in my real estate career when things are just about to happen. I love what I do; I look forward to going to work each day; I feel the deals getting bigger; I have a flexible schedule, and I enjoy the time I spend with my family, but I am far from financially wealthy…but I can taste the money. My goal will be to continue the next chapters in about a month. I want to give some of these deals a little time to develop.

LESSONS LEARNED

- When credit is available – cautiously take it. It may not always be available.

- Plan your deal conservatively. Use today's comparable numbers for your analysis. Never gamble on appreciation. If it happens, you may hit a homerun.

- Risk definitely equals rewards. You will hit more homeruns if you are willing to take on deals that other investors fear. Just be careful!

MAKING (SOME) MONEY

February 2002

I just sat down with my spreadsheet program to calculate the net revenues that Pete and I should make with the existing 10 properties under construction. You see, something exciting is about to happen. On Tuesday of next week, we are going to close Pratt Street. If you recall, this was the property that we picked up at a foreclosure auction for $84,000, put in about $45,000, and now the offer that we have is for $236,500. Not bad for a couple of rookies. We have learned several lessons with this property. The biggest one, which almost cost us the deal, was to be more vigilant when reading the contract. We received the offer for $236,500 (we were looking for $245,000). The house came out fantastic. It had hard wood floors throughout, stainless appliances in the kitchen, a spiral staircase, and a swanky entertainment room. As of today, the deal is scheduled to go through at $236,500 in two days. I am hoping for a big win and a nice dinner to celebrate this week.

So, back to my spreadsheet, where I listed the properties out with estimates of profits in various columns. Now keep in mind that, with half of our properties, we only have a fifty percent interest and the elephant owns the other fifty. If we do not pick up another project for the rest of the year, Pete and I should split $358,000. This weekend, I went to my local book store and bought a real estate investing book written by one of the well-known investor/authors. His angle is on buying property right, letting it appreciate, renting it out, never selling it, and cashing in big time on refinancing the projects. I got so excited when reading this book that I called Pete early in the morning to tell him that I thought that we needed a meeting to discuss strategy this week. Perhaps we should be picking up rental properties in our portfolio in addition to flipping houses.

Let me explain some of the concepts that really hit home. The main concept was the one of leverage. You see, Pete and I are already using leverage to our advantage, but we have never really calculated the true meaning of the leverage we're using. Allow me to explain. I earlier referenced the condemned property that we closed on last week. The final cash down on this deal was $6,400. When it comes time for the construction loan, we should be able to finance 100% of the construction costs because we really bought right. When this thing is all said and done, we should make about $75,000-$100,000 by the end of the year, all using just $6,400. Pete is the accountant, but to me, that looks like over 1000% return on cash. That is unbelievable if you ask me. So, the next line of thought is that I have set up a line of credit of $50,000 with my local bank. Now, if I could find a project similar to the condemned wall, but which required $50,000…and I could receive the same 1000% return, now we are talking…. Where is Pete when I need him? …That looks like $500,000 within one year on one project. I am not going to have to do too many of these deals before you will be reading this book. You see, the book I'm reading says the deal of the decade comes about once a week. Maybe once a week is a bit much, but I believe that it comes probably 4-5 times a year. So, this week I need to start focusing on bigger projects, and I am beginning to realize that while residential was a great way for us to cut our teeth, the only way to quickly accomplish my financial goals is going to be launching into the commercial arena. So, here we go.

April 2002

As I sit down to write the next bit of notes, I find humor in reading my thoughts during the previous several months. As a quick recap to February's thoughts, we did indeed have a swank dinner after closing on the Pratt Street property. I went to the closing and handled the paperwork for our side of the deal. That meant signing the deed and some other ancillary paperwork. I met the young couple that had fallen in love with the property, and they seemed excited and pleased with the house. This brought a certain sense of accomplishment. I know that I am doing this for the wealth side, but seeing someone genuinely pleased with something that I designed, renovated, and built gave me sort of a peace in accomplishment. It is hard to explain, but knowing that we created something was very satisfying. Well, back to the money. Not many people know the feeling, but when you are sitting at the closing table and the settlement attorney hands you a check for $99,000, your hands start to quiver. What a homerun deal! That is a lot of numbers on one check. I took that check back to the office and made several photocopies of it. The first one I have taped to my desk to remind me that this is why I am in the business. This is the excitement that gets me up in the morning with the fire in my belly. Then, I made a copy to bring home to my wife. I guess I just wanted to show her that I indeed was going to succeed in real estate. When I got home, I showed the check to my father in law; Pete faxed his copy of the check to his in-laws. Isn't that interesting, that we both sent the checks to our in-laws? I wonder if this is some subconscious reaction to showing them that we can and will take good care of their daughters. Needless to say, Pete and I took the wives out on the town and dropped almost 4 bills on a dinner at Morton's Steakhouse. We ordered just about everything possible on the menu. We had drinks, appetizers, soups, steaks, desserts (why not?); we were living large. Now, this is the kind of living that I could get used to. This moment was an extremely important point in my career. This deal is what made me and a lot of other people believers in what we were doing. Not that people didn't think that we were capable, but it's not until the check is in your hands that it truly hits home that "we made it happen". It took almost one full year before we hit our first homerun. Something more significant is also happening to us with this closing. Pete and I have decided that we really don't need to rely on the elephant as much anymore. We are now completely debt-free, and have some cash in the bank for living expenses and down payments. We have each set up lines of credit, and have begun to establish a nice working relationship with the bank. This is indeed a very significant point in the growth of Signature Properties. While there were many times that I thought of throwing in the towel... I am glad that I decided to hang in there now.

Since February, we closed 2 more deals. One we bought at an estate sale for $62,000 at an auction. We dropped $12,000 into cosmetic changes, including carpet, paint, roof, and a new kitchen. We sold it almost immediately for $117,000. Again, I sat at the closing table and was handed a check for $40,000. This deal was 3 months, from start to finish. The other deal was a foreclosure property that was bought on the courthouse steps for $126,000. It took close to 3 months for the debtor to move out after the auction, but she left the house in pristine condition. We did very little work, put it onto the market immediately, and I had three offers on the house within a week. We took the offer for $169,000, another nice return for us.

As for my present deals: I bought two houses last month. Both are shells in Baltimore City. They need to be completely gutted and rehabbed. The neighborhoods are strong and the numbers work as rehabs. One could net about $20K and the other about $40K. We decided to try something different with these two houses. Remember when I flirted with flipping the contracts on Woodall? This was the deal we bought and settled, but never really took possession of the house, and then turned around and resold it for a quick profit. Now that I was far more experienced, I decided to take another shot at flipping the contracts. We put contracts on both of them with the typical 30 day closing period. As soon as we were the "contract owners" of the properties, we put ads in the *Washington Post* and *Baltimore Sun*, in the investment properties sections, for the sale of two shells in desirable locations. The ad reads "rehab and win big". You see, our angle here is looking for the amateur investor who doesn't know the market or what they should be paying for shells in the city. The real estate market is on fire right now, and people are throwing around stupid money to get into the game. Again, I didn't seem to get anyone to bite on my contract flipping scheme, but I did get some interest in both of the properties. I did end up having to close on the first property last week at $65K; however, I already have a contract on it for a Washington, DC investor to pay $99K. The second one I close on next Monday for $68K, and I already have a contract on it for $90K. Let's look at the math for this month's work on these two properties:

	Project 1	**Project 2**
Buy in price	$65,000	$68,000
Closing Expense	($3,000)	($3,000)
Carry (one month)	($1,000)	($1,000)
Transfer out	($2,000)	($2,000)
Total Cash In Deal	$71,000	$74,000
Resale	$99,000	$90,000
Net for this month	$28,000	$16,000

TOTAL PROFIT FOR THE MONTH: $44,000

Pete and I will make $22K each this month, just from these two deals. People in the industry call this flipping property. This is when you really are not injecting any real value into the project – you are simply buying a property at an undervalued price, and then exposing the property to a larger market and generating a higher sales price. Of all of the work that we have done so far, this is by far the easiest money to be made in real estate. We are only owning these properties for about a week, and netting out crazy money. I should have another $10K coming in from commissions and other sales. The money seems to just be falling into place. Someday, I want to look back and say that $22,000 per month is not that much money. Boy, would that be great. So, what comes next?

The money is just too easy to make. I wonder if it's because we are in a strong market, or is real estate investing just this easy? Will I look back at the year 2002 and say, "Wow – this was just one of the best real estate times in history." There is an incredible value brought to the process by purchasing discounted property. My goal is to put 2 homes per month under contract. If I can reproduce this success 24 times per year – it'll be a homerun year. One of the limitations is my time. I am trying to figure out all of the methods for buying these discounted properties, but I think that I am going to need help going through all of the available information, available properties, and submitting contracts. I decided to enlist the help of students at the local colleges. I remembered being a student and receiving some great mentoring as an intern. So, I contacted the University of Maryland and Towson State University career development centers for help. We hired a part-time entrepreneurial sophomore from Maryland, and have had three other interviews in search of a full-time employee. I am seeking an aggressive undergraduate who wants to become insanely rich at a young age. This 19 year old part-timer does not realize how much he can make if he finds me 2 deals per month. To me, that represents about $50K a month in income to the company. So, that's my primary focus this month, hiring and training two new employees to pump deals into our system. Time will tell if that pans out for us in the future. For now, we have a part-time intern from the University of Maryland and we will see if he turns out to be an asset to our little growing company. This week, the part-timer already turned us onto a single family house in the county that has wonderful potential for subdivision. The lot is large enough for two houses. The seller has not priced the property appropriately for the premium of building a second house on the lot. Our thoughts are to purchase the small single family existing house, subdivide the lot into a second buildable lot, build a 2,000 square foot colonial on the back of the lot, and sell off both houses to make a quick $90K. Our offer was for $10K over the asking price, with the sale contingent upon the satisfaction of a 30 day study period. This means that for the next 30 days, we can look at the zoning and permitting on the building of this lot. If for any reason we decide that we do not like anything about the deal, we can bag the whole deal and get our deposit returned. I'll let you know.

The next big adventure that Pete and I are embarking on is the introduction of commercial property into our portfolio. There are two reasons that we are looking to jump into the commercial arena. The first reason is for cash flow and tax sheltering. With all of these transformational deals going on, we estimate that we will have to pay over $100K in taxes to the government. While we shouldn't mind paying this money because it means that we will earn near $400K this year, the thought of paying this really burns me up. For this reason, we are leaning towards buying a building, holding it for the cash flow that the rental brings, and possibly refinancing the building years down the road if we want to cash out and not pay any taxes on these earnings, since we are not selling them. The second reason for us to jump into commercial is the size of the deal. Even after just one short year in business, we both realize that the bigger the deal, the bigger the profit. So, here we go again.

Several weeks ago, Pete found an underperforming office building in Baltimore. The building is currently 25% occupied, and has been for almost a year and a half. The market for "C" class space in the city is currently a 90% occupancy rate. This building is truly operating at well below the market occupancy rate. We're wondering why this building is sucking wind. We looked at the building, and by our amateur estimation, the building appears to be desirable and rentable. The appraisal on the building, as provided by the selling agent (for what it is worth), is $1,400,000. They are asking $900,000. We submitted an offer for $700,000, with the seller to finance $140,000 and provide $50,000 in closing help. For those of you who can analyze a deal, our offer is really weak. If you're wondering why we presented such a weak offer, we did the analysis of the project and, as of today, the owner is losing $12,000 per month. So basically, we are offering a lot of money for the opportunity to lose $12K per month. Right about now, you must be wondering what our angle is. The current rent on comparable space is about $13.50 per square foot. We want to deep discount the market to about $11 or $12 per square foot. Fill up the space, and make marginal profits for the first year or two. But after the place is 100% occupied, slowly escalate the rate, and eventually get that appraisal in at $1,400,000. Keep in mind that we want to pay a net of $650,000. That would be a tidy four or five years' work.

So, after a few pages, I will depart. From this chapter, take a few things away about what is happening... We are starting to make some coin. So much coin that Pete will by buying a Mercedes by month's end, and I am soon to follow. Next week, I am buying either a 28 foot Cobalt Speed Boat or a 27 foot Sea Ray. For the boating enthusiasts, that is a $65,000 boat, and I can't wait to cruise the Chesapeake in it. Things are good and we hope that they continue to grow that way.

LESSONS LEARNED

- Interns are a great method of leveraging human capital.
- Commercial property is just as easy as residential properties – but the numbers are much larger.
- Perseverance pays off.

INTERNS CAN BE GREAT

May 2002

Things did not exactly fall into place after last month. Some of my predictions did come true, but others varied for better or for worse. Pete did indeed purchase a brand new Mercedes. He's now found that his job of negotiating with contractors has become more difficult, as he pulls up to the job site in his shiny new car. And I did indeed buy a speed boat; I went with a 27 foot Sea Ray. I pick up the boat next week and am looking forward to it like a young schoolboy. We are approaching just one year in the business, and so far things have met and slightly exceeded my expectations.

The office deal fell through, however. We submitted our no money down deal and the seller countered with a cash rich proposal which simply did not fit our model. We plan on continuing to negotiate on this deal. The intern has proved to be a fantastic investment. We pay this college student $10 per hour and he works about 25 hours per week. In his first week, he found a condominium that was going to foreclosure auction at around $100,000. The market in this area is red hot, with condos in this particular development selling with only 10 days on the market. The average sales price is about $160,000…so, there is plenty of profit in this deal. We were greeted by all of the regular players at the auction at the courthouse steps. The deposit was $10,000 which we had in hand. My upper limit was $125,000, and we picked it up for $126,500. We were pretty stoked after the auction, but not nearly as stoked as the next day. We knew that the property was fairly stable since it was located within a brick condominium building. Therefore, the electric, plumbing, HVAC should all have been in fairly good condition. The next day, Pete and I went to the building to see if we could knock on the door and let the homeowners know that we'd purchased their house at foreclosure, and that they have about 45 days to move out. Much to our surprise, the house was vacant. The next door neighbor told us that they'd simply gotten up and moved one day when they got notice from the bank that they were in default on their loan. Furthermore, the neighbor was on the board of the homeowners association and gave us immediate access to the place. This proved to be a great surprise.

The condo was in fantastic condition. With a little paint and carpet, this house was ready for the market. The board member allowed us to change the locks on the house since we technically were the new contract owners. In the last three weeks, we have painted and carpeted, and the house hits the market tomorrow. Now, it could be somewhat risky because we did all this before we actually owned the deal. This is particularly risky, and I will explain why. Without a deed in hand, some element of the deal may fall through. We have a contract that we signed on the courthouse steps for the purchase of the condo at $126,500. This contract is subject to ratification by the court and the receipt of the clean title. If something happens with the title or the court doesn't ratify this sale, we are out all of the construction money and all of the time invested in this project. So, although we are aware of the risks of this type of transaction, I am slightly concerned with the outcome of the transaction. Secondly, we technically do not own this property. Pete and I have discussed at length our legal interest in project.

We have $7,000 in deposit tied up, and we have a contract interest in the property, but we are really unsure if we should be entering or disrupting this house without the consent of the present homeowner or the bank. This is all new territory to us. If we can clean it up before the 90 days it takes for the court to approve the foreclosure sale, we could potentially assign the contract. This would save us thousands of dollars by not having to close on it and then reclose on it with the final buyer. These items weigh somewhat heavily on our minds, but we continue to push onward and upward with the completion of this transaction.

The intern is really turning out to be a wiz-kid. He has an incredible knack for searching out opportunities. This kid is going to make me a ton of money…and himself a pile of cash in the process. The intern found the deal above in his first week of employment. During his second week, he found a vacant foreclosure opportunity in another hot market. We bought this one on a Monday for $60,000 (we put up a $6,000 deposit). Following the auction, I stuck one of my realtor signs in the window of this vacant property. Someone driving by called me and I made arrangement for the gentleman to see the property. Since we only owned the contract on the property, I technically couldn't write up a contract for sale. So, what I did was write up a 2 page assignment contract. This allowed the gentleman to take my position in the foreclosure sale and close on the deal as if he were me, upon court ratification. If it sounds confusing, it really isn't. Upon signing the contract, this gentleman gave me a check for $18,000. This money represented my $6,000 deposit and a $12,000 assignment fee just for going to the courthouse steps. By the way, this happened on Friday. So, between Monday and Friday, I made $12,000. My goal is similar on the condo listed above. We bought it for $126,500, we are putting in about $5,000 in carpet and updates, and we hope to assign this contract for $170,000. The beauty of assigning contracts is that we don't have to pay any of the closing costs associated with taking possession of the house. On the $12,000 deal, if we were to close on this transaction at $60,000, we would have to pay $1,800 in transfer costs (the buyer pays all transfers in a foreclosure sale), $1,800 in carry costs (the buyer pays the carry between auction date and court ratification), and $2,000 to close the transaction on the buy side, and another $1,200 to close the transaction on the sale side.

All added up, a double closing takes an additional $6,800 in transactional fees out of the profit. So, now you can begin to see the power of flipping.

I continue to look into all types of available methods for acquiring properties. Now, let me clue you in on another angle that I am in the process of learning – the annual tax sale. Keep in mind that at this point I am completely unfamiliar with the process, but I'm sure that there's a gold mine awaiting in this process each and every year in each and every county. About 2 weeks ago, I went to the Baltimore City municipal building and bought a catalogue of tax liens on over 16,000 properties in the city. For three days this week, an auction company will go through each property and auction off the right to purchase these liens. Most of the tax debts are around $1,000, which represents the unpaid liability the homeowner has to the city. In an effort to collect these debts, the city auctions off these liabilities to investors who then attempt to collect the debts from the individuals. The upside is that the investor has the right to tack on 18% interest to these debts. The auction is dominated by several extremely savvy investors; I think that they might be attorneys. These guys buy $3-$4 million dollars worth of tax liability. Now, I am not sure of their angle, but I think that they attempt to collect the 18% plus legal fees and interest, making the return on the money about 20% per year. This year, Pete and I bought four tax liens. Our angle is slightly different. We do not want the homeowner to redeem the tax debt and pay us the little 18% return. We want the six month redemption period to expire, and allow us to begin the foreclosure process. During the redemption period, the homeowners have the right to give us our money back plus the interest, but that is not our strategy. You see our strategy is to take possession of the property at a discounted rate and resell it at market value. The four properties that we bought were at rates about $25,000 below market. So, if our theory is true, we plan on owning four already vacant properties with a margin of about $100,000. The lure to the bigger dollars will cause us to further evaluate the investor model.

My guess on the institutional guys bidding is that they're putting about $4,000,000 toward purchasing around 800 tax certificates. If all 800 redeem within the six month period, they should receive 18% interest on about $800,000 (the $4 million includes the buyer's premium, which is not interest bearing). So, now they are sitting on about $144,000 in interest per year. The big bucks come from the legal fees. I think that these folks are lawyers and they tack on $500 per certificate in redemption fees. If this is the case, they just took in another $400,000 in legal fees on 800 certificates. Add them up and, in the six month process, they made $544,000. Let us suppose that they promised the financial backer 10% per year or 5% per six months on the $4,000,000. They give the backer $400,000 in return and have to suffer earning $144,000 for an easy six months' work. I'm sure the process must have some bullet that I'm not considering, but if this is as simple as it appears, Pete and I need to find someone with $4,000,000 and a few more hours in the day to crunch some numbers.

Speaking of more time in the day, we are growing. I gave you the skinny on the intern that we hired. In his first month, he has generated about $45,000 for the company. The company has also started looking for a full-time candidate. We recruit through the entrepreneurship program located at the University of Maryland. After getting the word out at the school, we got several interested parties. The most impressive candidate was a young man with some entrepreneurial skills. Upon receiving his resume, we realized that this guy is the valedictorian of this year's graduating class at Maryland and a Rhode scholar semi-finalist. I'm not one to be impressed by academics, as I graduated with a straight 3.0 GPA, but this guy has a lot going for him. We interviewed him and he appears to have all of the right moves to succeed in this business. We put together an aggressive offer and, wouldn't you know it, he accepted. Our goal with this guy is to have him take over the residential division. We'll hire another several interns for him to manage, and hope that he can match the residential success that Pete and I have had this past year. If this is the case, he should make six figures in his first year out of school. So, now we enter the newest challenge in the extremely young life of Signature Properties. We are looking for alternative sources of income. At this point, we feel that we have a good grip on the residential model, and are hoping to move into the commercial arena and land development. I'll keep you posted.

July 2002

Well, not a lot has happened over the past several months. We continue to plug along as a residential development company. Currently, we have about 9 properties on the books. We are pretty excited about a foreclosure property that we recently acquired. I think that I've mentioned the intern that we hired in April from the University of Maryland. This young man is a true winner. He is perceptive, does fantastic analysis, and I'm sure he will do extremely well in real estate. Right now, he is just a sophomore in school, and already he's bought and sold his first residential property, netting over $100,000 in the process. We hired him to exclusively cull through the 100s of foreclosure listings each week, and he's even finding deals that we would have missed. He's paid a base $10 per hour, before extra property income, and has found 5 properties in three months. With just these 5, he's made the company $75,000. There really is something about his intern that is very impressive. He has great instincts that will make him a lot of money in the business. I just hope that he hangs around me long enough to make me a lot of money.

I mentioned in my last journal entry that I was picking up my new 27 foot Sea Ray. Well, on the day that I went for sea trials, the intern saw a foreclosure for a $300,000 property in a town north of Baltimore. This was an expensive property, and the deposit alone was $20,000. We got him the check, thinking that the auction would certainly be cancelled since the property was worth about $400,000. Needless to say, I got a call while on the boat that this young kid had just spent $330,000 of my money on a house that neither I nor my partner had ever seen. The slight catch to this was that I had told him to bid up to $315,000, and he bought it for $330,000. I try to picture the auction setting in my mind, the auctioneer getting bids from homeowner and investors up to $325,000, and then a 20 year old kid dressed in shorts and a tee shirt ups the bid and drops the gavel at $330,000. First, my partner and I were pretty upset and concerned that he'd upped our maximum bid amount, but after investigating that market, I actually think we should be pretty safe. We spoke with the homeowner, and he voluntarily left the property before the closing. I closed on it last week, and after painting for $4,500, landscaping for $2,000, and cleaning the carpets up for $500, the property is on the market this week at $425,000. Hopefully, this should yield a tidy $45-50K.

Our first full-timer started two weeks ago. This is the valedictorian that I previously wrote about. The guy is extremely intelligent, but even after two weeks, I can see some potential mismatches between his style and ours. I can see that things have come pretty easily to this guy for most of his life. Real estate, and particularly what we do, requires a lot of perseverance. You really need to look at 100 properties before you will buy one good one. I'm not sure this guy is going to be cut out for this business. The real estate business is not as easy as everyone thinks. You know those infomercial folks that show tons of people making tons of money with little or no money down in their spare time? Yeah, it is just not that easy, and this guy is learning that firsthand. I sure do hope he gets the hang of it, though, because I would like to see him succeed. Time will tell if he survives the residential market. I will state that the intern and the full-timer have prompted us to start looking at the bigger picture. Now that these guys will be taking the residential division on, it has freed up my time to pursue some commercial deals. At present, the four of us are crammed into 225 square feet. The word cozy barely covers it. We are in our original space. That was great when it was just the three of us, but as we grow, our space needs are growing as well.

I want to close with one last property this month. Remember

1405 Andre Street? This was the very first property that we ever bought. We purchased it with the elephant's money for $67,000. Well – on August 28, 2002 – we finally sold it. Boy, did we underestimate what would be involved in this property. We thought that it would sell for $200,000. We were estimating appreciation into our formula, and didn't try to make the numbers work based on current day comparable properties. It sold for $189,900. We estimated $70,000 in construction costs. Our final expense ran us $82,000. When we bought this property, our analysis was extremely weak. We forgot to include substantial expenses like closing costs, commissions, carry costs, taxes, and a bundle of other expenses. These ran us an additional $30,000. At the end of the day, the property netted $10,900. Divide this by 50% for the elephant, and Richard, Pete, and I split $5,450. Well, we needed to get into the first deal, and this property started it all.

First floor of a completed Andre Street

Second floor of a completed Andre Street

LESSONS LEARNED

- Flipping contracts is a mid-level solution to rehabbing houses. It is less work, and incurs less risk, but results in less profit.

- Real estate is a game of numbers. You need to look at a lot of properties to find the diamond in the rough.

- Remember to enjoy the spoils along the way.

THE NEXT LEVEL

January 15, 2003

It's been a few months since my last journal entry, and a lot has happened. I hope to accomplish two items with this journal entry. The first item will be to update some of the information that has progressed of late, including some follow-up data to past deals. Next, I want to take this opportunity to update my balance sheet. You see, it has been one full year since I started writing this book. I am truly curious how I am doing in route to my $2 million goal.

I wrote about the 27 foot Sea Ray. It is a blast. We took it out several times a month all summer long, and if anything could give me the taste of real estate wealth, these little material things will surely do it. I can remember sitting on a park bench down at the city docks of Annapolis, eating ice cream with my wife. We watched as the boats would come in and out of this little alley of water right in the heart of Annapolis. How could you not be envious of the life of the people floating down the alley, drinking a beer, and watching everyone on the dock? Now that I'm a boater, I've learned that the little alley of water that people parade their boats down is called Ego Alley. How appropriate, as people sport their vessels in front of everyone else to see. Doesn't that seem crazy, that people's egos about their material things are so great that they have to show them off to others? Yikes, and I do it now!!! I know that this is an incredibly shallow thing to do, but I have worked hard this past year, and taking the boat out is just one small reward for all of the work over the past year.

The Deal Update

One thing to realize about rehabbing houses is that it always costs more money than you think. If you remember, I was pretty excited about the condo that we bought for $126,500. My initial thoughts were to put in $5,000 and assign the contract for $170,000. Well, we did assign the contract, but not before sinking $15,000 into the unit. It needed carpet, paint, appliances, vinyl flooring, and other cosmetic fixes. On this particular deal, we underestimated our market. The typical condo owner in this neighborhood wants a pristine unit ready to be moved into, and most potential buyers are retired empty-nesters looking for a low maintenance way of living. As such, we ended up sending three different cleaning crews through this place to clean it out. We thought that we could get by with the appliances that were already in the unit, but after feedback from the agents who showed the property, we quickly came to realize that the prospective buyers really wanted new and shiny appliances. The water heater ended up going while we were working on the house. People in the industry have always told me to assume the worst when pricing out a job, and this is a perfect example of why you would do just that. We started our pricing at $170,000 and ended up at $156,000. After paying out the commission and other concessions, we netted $9,000 on the deal. I shouldn't complain, because we really did not do that much to the property, but it simply didn't go as expected. On this particular deal, the money was not earned by renovating or rehabilitating the property: the value was created through my ability to assign a foreclosure contract. You see, at $156,000, we would not have sufficient margin to close the transaction, then fix it up, then sell, and then close the transaction again. So we basically manufactured the $9,000 by finding an agent who could work with their buyer so that they felt comfortable assigning a foreclosure contract. If you remember, when you get stuck closing on the property and then having to close again to resell, you incur about 5% (or $7,590) of the foreclosure contract when you go to close the first time. This would have just about wiped out the profit on this deal. When you are dealt lemons, you learn to make lemonade.

Now, you may remember the big $400,000 house that we bought, which the intern bid on at $330,000 ($15,000 more than approved). This proved to be a difficult deal. In our analysis, we thought that the market in this area was extremely strong, and in that analysis, we estimated our carry period being about 1 month. So, think about us planning on closing and reclosing very quickly (almost like an assignment). The one month carry on $300,000 should have run us about $2,100. This proved to be a bit aggressive. You see, the 1 month period is great on a home which has been updated throughout the years, but this house was a 5,000 square foot house built in 1970, and had not had any updates done to the property over the previous 30 years. Buyers are quick to pick up on this, and while traffic through the property was pretty strong, we did not have any offers for 90 days. Now, do the analysis: we carried the mortgage and taxes on this property for 3 months to the tune of $2,100 per month. That was all calculated profit in our analysis stage. During the 3 months, it seemed that everyone that went through the property had an issue with it. Every issue had a solution and every solution cost us more and more money. This was money that we had not budgeted into the deal. Now, I am not going to say that this deal kept me up at night, but carrying the deal and not having any end in sight was beginning to wear on my typically uninhibited sleeping patterns. We finally got an offer for $375,000. The problem was, after all of our expenses, including commissions, construction, and carry, we were into this property for $385,000. We haggled back and forth, and ended up somewhere around $390,000. After the home inspection yielded a faulty roof and many other problems, the actual offer was valued at $385,500. So, when we finally bailed – and I do mean bailed – on this deal, we pocketed a tidy $500 in profit, and for risking $385,000. While we didn't actually lose hard money on this deal, this will always be known as a losing deal to me. I put a ton of hours into this deal.

Let me take a quick moment to discuss how I was feeling throughout this negotiation. The buyer had an extremely astute agent. He found out how much money we'd paid for the property and knew approximately how much we were paying in carry costs while this thing sat empty. I consider myself a pretty good negotiator, and usually I'm able to capture most of the pie when I deal with typical agents and buyers. In this scenario, the other agent was an equal match. He negotiated on the sales price, the seller contributions, the home inspection returns, the well inspection kick back…basically, I was exhausted by the time he was through with me, but I didn't want to risk this buyer leaving. We had waited a long time to get a fish on the line and I was leery of recasting. We were carrying the property to the tune of $2,100 per month. When the buyer submits an offer, they have several contingencies. Two of the contingencies on this deal were the well and the home inspection. You typically give the buyer 10-14 days to conduct these inspections. Two weeks on this deal means I am out another $1,000 in carry. These buyers had an aggressive closing date (which was one of the reasons that I liked the offer). So, when they asked for an additional few thousand dollars here or there, I was thinking that giving in a little bit was certainly better than having to remarket the property, wait for another offer, and then go through the same contingency inspection process as this one. If you equate this to dollars and cents, which my partner, Pete the accountant, always does, rejecting this offer based on the nibbling negotiation translates into what could be 3 more months of carry or $6,300. So, when the buyer asked me for an additional $5,000, I was hard-pressed not to negotiate with him.

From this property, we gleaned a few quick lessons. On the higher-end properties where the carry expense is more than the little deals, we certainly need to build in more carry expense and higher margins to compensate us for the additional risks. Second, when we come up with an analysis and a final bid number, it is important that we stick to this analysis and not deviate. I guess we were correct in questioning the intern's gumption in bidding

$15,000 more than he should have. This proved to be an expensive lesson to learn. As I am sure that we will suffer losses on future deals, let it be known that this is officially the first loser for us. Even though we pocketed chump change on the deal, we didn't take a commission on the sale and we essentially worked for free. In my book, this is a loser.

Now, if you are wondering if we fired the intern for this debacle, allow me to redeem him quickly. I think that I have sung this guy's praises enough for you to realize that we think he is extremely talented. He has gotten us into many fantastic deals, and we have realized plenty of cash through his acquisitions. Frankly, I have made the mistake of becoming too emotionally attached to deals at foreclosure, and I have set the precedent for bidding higher than my limit. The next deal that I am about to describe is just another description of why this kid is so talented in what he does. The auction process requires a deposit in a certified check at the courthouse steps in order to bid on a foreclosed property. Typically – and here is the key – the deposit required for bidding is approximately 10% of the estimated defaulted loan amount of the property. For example, if the deposit is $10,000, we automatically assume that the bank is owed $100,000. This is typically where the bidding begins. Now, this rule of thumb of the auctioneers setting the deposit at roughly 10% of the mortgage debt is a wonderful method of deciding whether or not further analysis is required for the property. In any given week, there are over 200 properties being offered in the eastern Maryland Counties that we analyze. The deposits are printed on the auction websites. This allows the interns to look at the market value for the property and compare that with the debt amount owed on the subject properties. Of the 200, there are only about 20-30 a week that warrant a visit to the courthouse steps for the auction. The rest of the properties have a debt that is so high that you simply cannot make any money if you have to close, repair, and resell. We call this being under water. So anyway, the intern requested a check for $14,500 for an auction in Pasadena, Maryland. Pasadena is a great real estate market where things typically don't stay on the market for very long. The property was worth about $135,000, so don't ask me why the intern was wasting my time with a check. If you do the analysis, the payoff on the property should have been $145,000 for a house that is only worth $135,000. I would estimate that about 90% of the foreclosure deals that we analyze on a weekly basis have little to no equity in them. Basically, the bank has made aggressive loans on the property, only to have the home owner default. After the legal fees and foreclosing fees are added up, the total buy out sometimes exceeds the market value of the property. So, this clearly seemed to be the deal on this property. Either the bank had made a loan that was aggressive, at some high loan to value ratio, or it's a relatively new loan that, after you add on the legal and auction fees, has everything add up to more than the property's market value.

Back to the intern who needed the check for $14,500; he had gone one step further in his analysis. The public record, which is the state document showing the assessed value of the property in addition to transfer dates and amounts, showed this property had transferred in 1988 for $88,000. If the property had not been refinanced and a second mortgage had not been drawn on the equity, this mortgage redemption should be around $70,000-$80,000. So, why was the deposit $14,500? We had no idea – thus we decided to send the intern with the $14,500 check. Well, his hunch proved correct. The 20 year old kid went to the auction and the bidding began at $89,000. Going once, twice....he offered $89,500. "Sold to the young kid for $89,500" were the auctioneer's final words. So immediately, you get the idea that he just bought a property worth $135,000 for just $89,500. I like the phrase "buying dollar bills for 66 cents". The other investors standing there at the courthouse steps, awaiting the auction for the other properties that had equity in them, didn't even know what had just happened. You see the same group of investors show up each day to bid on the good properties. They're doing the same sort of analysis that I have been doing for months, comparing the market values with the deposit amounts. Therefore, they hadn't analyzed this deal, and didn't have ready checks since they thought that there was no equity in the deal.

To make a long story short, I went to the purchased house ready to explain to the defaulting homeowners that my company had bought their property at the courthouse steps, and that they had to make arrangements to pack up and move. After doing this several times, I have learned a valuable lesson. These people are going through hard times. By being human in dealing with them – and what I mean by that is understanding that they are going through hard times and have just lost their home – I find that they will typically work with you. I knocked on the door and a very polite couple answered the door together. They were clearly a working class family, judging by the meager interior decorations to the house. They could not have been friendlier as they invited me in to have a cup of coffee with them. They were fully aware that they were losing the property. Apparently, they had a tax lien on the property that they would have had to settle if they'd sold their house on the open market. After doing the analysis, they learned that they simply could not afford to sell the house. So, here they were: they couldn't afford to keep the house and they couldn't afford to sell the house. My first goal was to see if they would willingly agree to move within 30 days, so that I could hopefully flip the contract once they got everything out of the house. They did indeed agree to move, and then they even went one step further. They allowed me to hold an open house on that Saturday, to show the house in an attempt to assign the contract. They said that they were going out of town that weekend, so they would leave the key under the doormat for me to have an open house. Does this really happen in this day in our society? Well, it did. I think that this is just the power that you get from being nice to people. So, I put the property into the multiple list service so that all agents could see the property for sale, and know that the open house would be held Saturday from 2 until 5. Wouldn't you know it, but I had three offers by the end of the day on Saturday, and went with the one for $132,500 (which I might add was $7,500 over my list price).

The real estate market is on an unbelievable hot streak. I don't know how long this is going to last, but I am putting properties on the market for one day and getting multiple offers – and technically, I don't even own the houses yet. I am then calling the agents back to have them increase their offers, and they are escalating their offers. Quite frankly, this house in Pasadena was in tough shape. From the incredibly amount of yard trash to the mold growing on the seventies-style basement, this house would need at least $30,000 just to bring it to what I think would be acceptable condition. The market is so tight right now with inventory that people surprise me each time I put something out there. Not only that, but I'm not even selling the property. I'm selling a position in a contract that I bought at the courthouse steps. The entire process seems crazy to me, but for some incredible reason, it seems to be working for us. So, this deal went through, and after some commissions and other expenses, I netted $35,000 on the deal. This is really getting fun. I know you hear about these stories on the late night infomercials, but they really do happen. The value was created by looking at the right information, talking politely with the homeowners, and ultimately finding a buyer who was willing to assign a foreclosure contract. We are not even taking possession of these properties.

Some of our ongoing construction projects are shaping up great. Next Friday, I should have a nice downtown 3 bedroom rowhouse renovation on the market. We bought this one for $50K, invested another $60K, and it should hit the market around $180,000. Our pride and joy is ready to hit the market in March. This is the mammoth 3,000 square foot renovation that we took from being a condemned wall to a newly constructed custom-built palace. We call this one Lombard, as it sits on one of the more famous streets in Baltimore City. The entryway will be a two story open air foyer, the kitchen was professionally designed with awesome amenities, and the house is really going to be a masterpiece. The numbers, which I am always optimistic about, show that we bought it for $5K, invested $165K in renovations, and I have hopes of getting upwards of $400,000 on the sale. I think that we originally thought that the house would sell for $300,000, but as the market continues to heat up, so follow our dreams for this property. My goal is to pocket $150,000 on this deal. We will see how it turns out in future chapters.

Now, let me introduce you to one of my better purchases. The big palace I just described, located on Lombard, sits right across the street from a non-profit organization specializing in housing and jobs. After visiting the palace, I stopped in to ask if the non-profit organization had any real estate that they were looking to divest…regardless of location or condition. I got a return call from the director of the organization, elaborating on a 12 unit apartment building located in the ghetto of Baltimore. The units were split into two connected buildings, one with 6 units in need of complete renovation and the other with 4 rented units providing $1,850 in monthly revenue. The properties were in disrepair and were basically a thorn in the organization's side. The organization was specializing in senior living, and a previous director had bought these units years ago for the wrong reason and then just never divested the group from them. The mortgage on them was $180,000; I almost immediately offered them $150,000 and we settled on $170,000. My motivation for purchasing these units was slightly different from what you might expect and what I'd experienced before. I just had a feeling.

Real estate is truly a two-part business. The first is analysis. You have comparable data, rent rates, sales information, construction costs, and commissions and the like. Pete tells me that everything can be reduced to a spreadsheet analysis, and for the most part, he's right. The part that he is missing is the GUT. Sometimes, we get into a project because I just have the gut feeling that the project will make money. So, for these rundown ghetto properties, I just had the gut. As of this date, March 2003, the stock market has been tanking for well over a year. Many people had lost a fortune in the stock market over the last 3 years, and today, people were looking for safer more diversified places to put their money. Real estate has become the newest investment trend to hit the streets. Everyone wants to be a landlord, and everyone wants to flip real estate. Hopefully, another chapter will be titled "The real estate seminar" because I am surely looking for a way to capture this market of rookie investors. This 12 unit apartment deal will have appeal to someone. I don't know who or why – I'm just trying to capture some of the exuberance in the market. I have no interest in owning these properties – just scalping a few dollars and getting out. This would be the first commercial purchase for us.

So, here is the deal for 2 run down 6 unit buildings that I just purchased for $170,000. First, let me go into the (1) why, and then the (2) how, and ultimately, (3) the spoils. Now, I told you that the current rent, if you could collect it without having to pack a 9 millimeter gun, totaled $1,850 per month. The mortgage payment and tax payment on $150,000 is approximately $1,200 per month. So, with the current rent roll, I should have been able to carry the debt for both buildings, barring any major renovations required on the property. I convinced Pete and the bank that, if my flipping strategy did not work, we could always have a positive cash flow investment with some potential appreciation, if the neighborhood would be gentrified like the rest of Baltimore City. This was not my goal on the property, but it's always good to have a plan B. Allow me to describe the two buildings for you, as they stood at purchase. The first building was in dire need of a complete renovation. It's full of garbage, old furniture, hanging drywall, and flaking paint. I had no intention of doing anything to this property. The better building had 4 rented units and 2 vacant units. The two vacant units needed kitchen updates, new baths, paint, windows, and flooring.

So, first, understand why I bought these units. I've been to many auctions for multi-family housing. There is just a sense of auction fever that pervades these venues. Buildings that should sell for $300,000 are going for as high as $400,000 at auction. All of my market analysis showed that a completely occupied 6 unit building should be worth $225,000. This does not take into consideration the 6 unit building that needs complete repair. That would be my bonus. If I could paint and rent the two remaining good units, I would have a solid building worth around $200,000. Then, if I could get $50-$60,000 for the shell, I would net a tidy $75,000 on the project. Here is the way it actually went down...

I bought the property for $170,000. With a pretty good track record with the bank, our loan officer went to bat for me on this one. You see, the loan committee hated the deal. It was a terrible building with terrible tenants in a terrible location. At any rate, she got us a loan, but it required us to put $50,000 into the deal. We raised some debt financing for $30,000, and put $20,000 on a credit line, and we were in business. We took possession on November 1, 2002. In the next four weeks, we spent $15,000 on paint, some windows, and a lot of cosmetics to make the vacant two units get into fair condition. I had them rented by December 1st for $600 per unit. Now, we had an asset kicking out $3,050 per month, and the opportunity to fix up the other building and have a sweet $6,000 per month in revenues. So, off I went to the auctioneer and signed a listing for him to auction it off on December 12, 2002. I was extremely bullish on the deal, and excited to get to the 12th. When the 12th came, the sun was out, and it was a perfect day for auction fever…or so I thought. Most auctions get a crowd of about 30 people. Ours got a crowd of 8. When you sell a package of two buildings, the auctioneers use a different formula. They offer each building for sale separately. They auction building one first, and then they auction building two second. After this is completed, they auction both buildings together as a package. Whichever scenario brings in the highest total is the auction that stands.

Separately, the good building sold for $150,000. Not exactly what I had in mind. The shell brought in $57,000. So at the total of $207,000, we were losing $8,000. What had I done wrong?

Here, I thought that my analysis was solid, my rent rolls had been increased, and the market was rising... so why didn't these 8 potential buyers see what I saw? After him auctioning them separately, my stomach dropped to the street; I could actually feel my Adams apple inflate like a balloon, and I quickly and swiftly apologized to Pete before I broke out into public tears. Perhaps I could have been wrong in the whole analysis. The next step was the auctioneer selling the buildings together as a package. If this price exceeded the individual price – then we still had a shot at walking away with a few bucks. Then the auction opened up the package at $207,000. The minute between when the second individual auction ended and the package bidding started felt like an hour. I went through the numbers in my head again and again, and thought: "we are going to actually lose money on this thing." We waited... $207,000 once, twice…and then someone bid $208,000. Then $209,000, $210,000…this went on until these two bidders ran the price up to $265,000. The hammer dropped, and sold at $265,000. Now I did the math, and realized we'd netted $50,000 on the deal. I got to thinking about it, and $50,000 in 42 days is really not that bad. This was our first entry into the commercial real estate business. We are big time, now! Since the auction, we have been property managers of this building, and will be, until the closing date which should happen on February 10th. I am looking forward to another steak dinner.

As I review my last entry, I can quickly update that the closing did indeed happen, and we took the entire office out for a righteous lunch. Entire office, you say...? Well, yes, phase two has included some major changes to Signature Properties.

The Company – Office and Personnel

Pete and I are finally getting some traction in the business. We have a steady cash flow from carrying 10-12 projects at any one time. If I were doing this business out of my house, I would probably be earning a few hundred thousand dollars per year, but I have a goal to create a bigger company. My vision is one which has a constant and incredibly large cash flow from year to year, at the same time as enabling investing for an early retirement and a comfortable way of living for me and my family. So, now we are focusing on creating a real estate company, and not just a salaries. Our personnel situation has gone through some changes. The valedictorian, our first full-timer who we ended up being unsure about, as to whether or not he could weather the storm of real estate…well, the gamble failed. I have to reinforce that the real estate game is really one of determination and perseverance. Money in real estate does not come easily. You need to cull through countless opportunities, be able to multitask and manage the entire process, and have thick skin, or you won't be able to sleep at night. This young man had little to any of these qualities. He simply did not understand that a real estate investor needs to look at hundreds of deals to find the cherries. He was looking for the magic tree outside that would constantly fill our pipeline with deals. Another element which was lacking was financial analysis. I guess Pete and I take for granted that a true real estate investor can institute basic real estate analysis on the fly. The simple elements like carry costs, construction costs, rental revenues, and resale expenses need to be understood, both inside and out. The numbers are not that difficult, but you really need to be able to do those elementary school arithmetic calculations on the fly. I am talking about subtraction from the sales price, multiplication used for transfers taxes as a percentage, and then have the ability to store these numbers in your head to ultimately come up with a buy-in price on the fly. Don't get me wrong: we use a spreadsheet and computer to analyze deals before we buy them, but on a daily basis, we probably go through 5 deals in our heads to rule them out or go forward. So, needless to say, we had to cut this fellow loose before it cost us too much money. I felt bad having to let the guy go, but he didn't have the arithmetic skills, nor the drive, for this particular industry. He was a brilliant guy and will do well in whatever field he chooses (as long as it's not real estate). Upon a little follow-up,

I've found that he's currently planning to attend the best law school in the country, and hopefully someday will look at our decision to let him go as one of the best things to happen to him.

We recently received a call from the University of Maryland Real Estate Development Club. The club was requesting that Signature Properties put on a two hour lecture on exactly what we do. You see, the university does not offer many opportunities for business or architecture majors interested in getting involved with real estate development. So, two students created this club to help students network and learn about the industry. One of our professors from graduate school passed on our contact information to the students, and they requested that we do a presentation to the club members. The presentation itself was quite enjoyable, but the true value came in the after-hours discussion following the presentation. Many of the students stayed later to ask questions and receive input on their career tracks. By the end of the night, Pete and I had 4 interns willing to help us investigate and analyze deals. Over the past several months, these interns, who get paid the same base $10 per hour we planned out for our first intern, have found four or five good deals which we have bought and subsequently profited from. We are culling through hundreds of opportunities per week, looking at dozens of houses, attending 15-20 auctions per week, closing on 2-3 houses per month, keeping 5-8 houses under construction at any one time, and hopefully remaining sane throughout the whole process. By bringing on some cheap but pretty well-skilled labor, we could stop working "in" the business of acquisitions, and focus "on" the business of growing a real estate company.

Here is a little story that illustrates how we knew that we were too busy, and it was past time to bring on some additional labor. At times, I felt like we just had the Midas touch. Everything that we touch was turning to gold. I'm smart enough to know that some of this comes from being in an industry that is taking off like a rocketship, but other days, I do tend to get a big ego about our success. Case in point – to save time, we stopped driving by the foreclosure auction properties, and buying them just based off of a paper analysis. On a day-to-day basis, we would purchases homes for anywhere between $50,000 to $150,000 without ever looking at the product until we were under contract to buy it. Think about this for a second, because this is a phenomenon that is becoming popular with sites like eBay. If you are like me and you buy things on eBay, you are very tentative about purchasing a used item that you cannot see and touch. I usually look for sellers with good eBay ratings. That way, at least I have a better chance of getting a good used product. I would never buy something like a car on eBay. That's just too risky, buying something that large without ever seeing or touching it. I mean, a car could be $10,000 or more! So wait a second and think about it. Why would I ever consider buying a $150,000 house which has a pretty good chance of being trashed (I mean, it is someone who is losing their house to foreclosure), without ever seeing the property? It's a good question….in hindsight.

One day, I bought a house that looked fantastic on paper. When I say on paper, I mean just the financial spreadsheet, no pictures and no visual aids. It was located in Pasadena, the city where we already had such great luck flipping properties. On paper, the house was a 2,000 square foot single family home worth anywhere from $240,000-$260,000. The house had been built in 1985, so it should have been in pretty good condition. I mean, how much damage could be done to a 20 year old property? The bidding on the property started at $190,000, which seemed to leave a sizeable margin for the flip. I was the one and only bidder, and I would soon find out why. So, I bought the house for just over $190,000. I was pretty excited at this point, hoping to make a quick $20,000 in this hot area. After contracting to purchase the property, I decided to see the gem that I now owned, or was at least contracted to own. Words cannot describe my disappointment when I got to see the house. As I rounded the corner of the street and drove closer to the number of that house, I could see what looked to be the biggest eyesore in the entire neighborhood. As I got closer, it looked vacant, had a huge dismantled dumpster in the front yard, and had more broken windows than not. The house was vacant, and had been for about a year. In my analysis, I have budgeted it taking $20,000 to fix up the property (we use a $1,000 per year old rule of thumb). Well, since the property was in such disrepair, it would take about $60,000 to fix up the property. If you've been following and absorbing my analysis process thus far, that does not leave anything for carry, commission, or closing costs. Basically, if we chose to close on the deal, fix it up, and resell it, we would suffer a loss of about $25,000, at minimum.

That is one of the few projects that did keep me up at night. I guess, in hindsight, I could have wallowed in the pity of making such a horrible decision, but instead I decided to tackle this one head-on. We hired a temp crew to meet Pete at the property to clean it out. It took 4 dumpsters just to get the mammoth amount of trash and debris out so that we could get it into a shape where it did not look so overwhelming. I then flipped the contract to an unsophisticated investor looking for a handyman special for $200,000. After paying a commission to the other agent, and the clean-out fees, this one would still turn out to be a wash. But trust me, I have no complaints about that. The lesson that came out of this one was not to spend $190,000 on something that you have not even looked at. Allow this lesson to sink in for just a minute. In our daily lives, we haggle over pennies, and here our arrogance had taken us to spend that kind of money without doing any due diligence. Well, I said that you would learn through my wins and my failures, so chock this one up as a significant failure with a very lucky ending.

So, with more going on in the office than Pete and I have hours in the day to cover, we've decided to hire a full-time administrative assistant/office manager and a full-time field assistant. We just finished interviewing our first candidate yesterday, and will proceed to interview several more before making our final decision.

Imagine this, if you will: we have a 200 square foot office with sometimes 4 or 5 people trying to work. The demand quickly arose for a larger office space. As a result, last week, we moved to a 900 square foot office space for $766 per month. This place feels palatial compared to the old digs. I have my own office with a door and two windows. We set up a wireless computer network, and have 5 phone lines and a DSL on order. We certainly have not "made it" yet, but this office sure does feel pretty good. So, we are indeed hiring a full time administrator to organize our lives. The goal is to have this person handle all of the closing activities on the buy-and-sale side of each transaction, organize the foreclosure process in order to make sure that all opportunities are evaluated, and basically run the day–to-day operations of the office. In addition to the office manager, we are looking to hire a full time field assistant, as I mentioned. I spend a fair amount of my time running to fix items at properties, looking at different opportunities, and heading to auctions to bid on projects. These are all items that can be handled by a field assistant, thus freeing up my time to find the next big deal. At least this is the theory. So, these two hires are on our plate for the next couple of weeks. The challenge with hiring on two new people is the commitment of payroll. As of today, we really have not had a high overhead expense. Once we bring on two full-time employees, we had better make sure that we can establish some more cash flow to carry these expenses.

March 7, 2003

We are settled into our new office. We have maps on the wall, a 'new' used copier, 6 computer workstations, a network that Pete worked 10 hours to hook up and which for the most part works to share files, a DSL hookup that works 75% of the time, a board room with used furniture donated by my father-in-law's law firm, and two new employees. We bit the bullet and hired both a field assistant and an office manager. Thus far, both have been great. The field assistant now takes a digital camera and looks at every auction property we consider. The interns prepare the paper analysis packets with photos for the properties. I review the packets and view the pictures for each deal, and then our office manager cuts a check for the field assistant to go to auction whenever we deem that that's the next step. The process has worked very well so far, and we've been able to purchase 4 decent foreclosure properties over the last several weeks. The office manager is slowly taking on more and more of my responsibilities. While not there yet, the addition of these two employees should free up sufficient time for me to start networking my way into the next big deal.

LESSONS LEARNED

- We are currently in a unique real estate market. Realize that this simply can't last forever.
- When buying at auction, set a limit and stick to it.
- Time is a valuable resource. Growth requires leveraging human capital.
- Be very careful. Always **look** at each house and analyze each deal.

NEW SOURCES OF MONEY

The Fund

We have realized a problem with our initial business model. Over the past 18 months, we have completed the cycle of about 15 properties. This includes both houses that have been flipped and houses that were repaired and sold. This has all been great, and Pete and I have realized some of our hoped-for financial successes with this performance. The problem lies in the scalability of the model. Assuming that we can find many real estate opportunities, enough qualified contractors to handle our business, and sufficient staff to coordinate the components of the deals, we still have one huge problem….capital. I believe that I've already commented on the fantastic relationship that we have with our bank when it comes to loaning money on these deals. Typically, we can get 90% loans on each project, which only requires us to carry the 10% down payments and the closing costs of each deal. We use credit lines to cover these expenses, and with $175,000 available through credit lines, we can be into around $1.5 million dollars worth of deals at any one time. Therein lies the problem. In order to grow faster, we need to be into more of these smaller residential deals, or else bigger deals in general. Thus far, we have raised some money by taking on debt from friends and family. We have accomplished this by simply issuing a personal promissory note for loaned money giving the lender 12% interest. And through this vehicle, my brother gave us $20,000, and we found another investor for an additional $50,000. Somewhere, in our current vision, we see the need for much larger numbers, and subsequently we are going to need to shift our focus onto fund-raising capital. I remember when $175,000 of cash on those lines of credit seemed like something that we could never imagine using up. Not only that, but we now have another $70,000 in debt financing to use or squander. The next phase of our business requires even more capital. I am quickly learning that one of the largest keys to success in real estate is capitalization. You simply must have large amounts of cash and solid banking relationships to succeed in this business.

Raising money through debt is really quite tough. When people see you making all that return on the different deals, they want a piece of the action. I look at 12% as a pretty good return on your money, but all of our contemporaries are looking for higher potential returns. Perhaps we are missing the boat by not seeking people who are simply looking for stable returns, as opposed to major profit, but it seems like everyone we talk to wants to be involved in the excitement of real estate. Our friends don't mind the element of risk, and they want the upside of the market. In these current days, real estate is a topic of discussion at every neighborhood picnic and every cocktail party. People like to talk about how much equity they've made in their primary residencies. Everyone knows how much so and so's house sold for up the street, and they then tend to extrapolate how much their own house should be worth. The more savvy people talk about how they've been investing in stocks of the major builders in the country, and the real estate investment trusts. Our ears have been open to this, but we've not had a need yet for such large amounts of capital. Now, we are beginning to have this need.

So one day, while taking the Sea Ray out with our interns and another MBA buddy, I got an education in capitalization. This MBA buddy suggested an equity play. When people give us money, they will own 25% of the project, and we will pay them a 6% preferred interest rate, plus 25% of the profits of the deals. Enter *SIGNATURE PROPERTIES FUND 1.*

We did some research on the various financial tools that were out there that could help businesses raise money. We found that the best match for us was going to be a SEC filing called a Regulation 504(d) (named after the IRS tax code). We made a visit to our local attorney who explained to us the way that this fund raising vehicle worked. We will start the process of assembling this vehicle by developing our business plan. In hindsight, Pete and I should have developed our business plan before we started the company, oh well. This business plan will include our resumes, the company's financial history, and a report of our entire portfolio of past house flips. In addition to the business plan, we will lay out how we will use the investors' money to purchase new deals and how the investors would make money. Our marketing packet will include a spreadsheet summary page about the projects that we have completed over the past year. These will have buy-in prices, closing costs, construction dollars spent, and ultimately the profit. The nice thing about having been through some successful projects is that we now have some data to make some projections. We actually have a track record. This document will serve as a prospectus for potential investors. We will then show how much an investor would have made in each of these projects had we had the fund set up for these specific projects. Also in the packet will be our business plan.

We plan on sending it out to any interested party. Our goal is to raise $600,000 with this fund, in order to invest in real estate projects. Using the bank's 90% rule, that puts us into somewhere around $6 million in real estate deals. With the attorney's guidance, we should be able to set up the Signature Properties Fund with 100 shares priced at $6,000 per share. If we can sell all 100 shares, we will reach the maximum subscription of $600,000 in cash raised.

Here is how the investors' return on capital is going to work. If we are as good as I think we are, and we raise $600,000, we can begin using this money (combined with the banks financing) to purchase some properties. The first 6%, or $36,000, in profits goes straight to the investors. This is called the preferred interest rate. Pete and I don't make a cent until we've paid them the 6%. After the 6% has been paid, we then will split any profits leftover at the rate of 25% them and 75% us. On the surface is looks like a pretty good deal for both the investors and for Signature. For Pete and me... well, yes, we are giving up a percentage of the pie (which I truly hate doing), but I see a greater vision now, and this truly appears to be the best method to achieving that vision. If you look back on our successes and put the 6% interest / 25% ownership plan in place, it appears that the investors will have made about 30% on their money over the past year and a half.

We hired a pretty large law firm, with pretty large prices, to handle the document preparation and filings. The total legal bill will be $6,000, but the nice part about it is that we don't have to pay the bill until we raise some money. For this investment, the law firm will do filings with the SEC in each state that we are pursuing investors. He is going to file in about 10 states to start, where Pete and I think that we have potential investors lined up.

So, if you are looking for an investment in real estate, perhaps our timing is pretty good on this thing. For those of you in real estate or new business creation, we are targeting the 3-F's. These would be friends, family, and fools. It's just a saying for people that would invest in a startup business without a lot of track record. Pete and I are so confident in our real estate business model that you would have to be a *fool* not to invest in our company. Everyone knows that we have been in the business for a while, and a lot of these connections would jump at the opportunity to give us some money to play with, and perhaps make some tidy returns. To date, we have not received any checks to start up the fund, but our initial rumblings have been quite positive. I am estimating that we should have about $300,000 raised in about 6 weeks. The next challenge that we will face is in how we spend that kind of money. Hopefully, the next chapter will have great projects to discuss.

The Rental King

Let me start this section by describing one of my wife's pet peeves. I've been an entrepreneur for the last 8 years. Sometimes – well, maybe many times – she's gotten the feeling that we are living from check to check. In a way, she's right. I have never drawn a steady salary from any of the businesses that I have started. None of the ventures has been large enough to actually have an entry as salary for me on the income statement. This actually violates one of those rules I learned in the Entrepreneurship program at the University of Miami. The entrepreneur is always supposed to put a value on their time. This is called their opportunity cost, which represents what you could make if you were doing something else. That cost shows up as an owner's salary on the income statement. I really struggle with inserting an opportunity cost into my analysis. I believe that it will sometimes kill the deal – but that is exactly why I should put it into the entry. If I can make more money working for a large corporation than I can flipping a house – then perhaps I should work for a large corporation. In all of my businesses, I have yet to be convicted enough that I should have that entry, and this real estate business is no different. As I look back on my success in this business, I have had a pretty good run flipping houses, but I do not have a steady income that I can rely upon for a *salary*. When a deal closes, we get a sizeable check, but when it's dry for months, we end up having to put money back into the company to carry the salaries of our employees and the expenses of running an office. They call this the burn rate, and it really does burn me up. When a property sells, I take a small draw, and then reinvest the rest into another great deal. The nature of this business is that you must continually invest capital for new deals. It is not like typical businesses where you have a large start-up cost and then the company is underway. In this business, you have a large start-up cost to buy some projects, and then you have large capital calls throughout the year as you buy more projects. It seems like you are always reinvesting your money back into the company. It is beginning to be somewhat frustrating to feel like I am making a ton of money but not taking a ton of money home to the family.

Bear with me over this next paragraph because I am going to write about the unique nature of real estate as a capital intensive business. Read the whole paragraph before getting down on the real estate industry. At Signature, Pete and I will take small draws from the business, which helps pay our personal mortgages and the bills, but the lion's share of the money goes back into the company to cover the overhead and to buy more and more properties. I have realized one reason why the business has taken a few years off of the end of my life. Even though I can write about the excitement of making $20,000 on this deal and $40,000 on that deal, I actually am not seeing that money. We end up perhaps taking $5,000 out of the $20,000, and perhaps $10,000 out of the $40,000. The other money goes into the carry costs of all of our projects and the acquisitions of future deals. So, in your head, you are seeing a deal kick off a $30,000 profit, but in actuality, after Pete and I reserve 50% for new project investment and then split 50% of that, my personal bank account is only seeing $7,500 . This has been playing psychological warfare on me. As a consequence, over the years, my wife has become quite accustomed to the check to check lifestyle of an entrepreneur. The part that she's not getting accustomed to is the lack of savings. Without a formal 401K or company contribution, I never seem to get on board with saving for my retirement or children's education. I still have not invested in my stock market accounts or set up any formal retirement account. This is getting to be a problem, as my oldest son is almost 5, and I now sit at 34 years of age. In my head, I see that I have accumulated a lot of "paper" net worth in future deals, but my bank account would report differently. So, I have been developing a forced method of creating a retirement vehicle.

I've read numerous books about real estate investing, and am smart enough to understand all of the merits of rental properties, but I still refuse to put all of this knowledge into practice. Think about it: you purchase a rental house for $150,000; it takes about $20,000 of your money to invest, or you just put that on your line of credit. You rent it for, say, $1,600 per month, or enough to cover your mortgage, taxes, insurance, repairs, etc., and attempt to have a few hundred dollars of positive cash flow per month. Reinvest the extra cash flow into your principal, and viola, you own an asset worth $150,000 in about 20 years. Over the 20 years, however, this asset has appreciated at a rate of 3% per year (which is not unheard of). Now your asset is worth $300,000. In addition, your rents have doubled over that 20 year period, and now you are receiving $3,200 per month in rent. So, hypothetically, at age 54, I could sell this asset and take the $300K to live off of, or keep it invested in the real estate market and have gross revenues of about $40,000 per year to live off of. Now, while these numbers may not seem very exciting, if I could own 3 of these rental properties, I would have $900,000, or $120,000 per year. Maybe I could purchase 10 of these and have $3,000,000 or $400,000 per year. Now we are talking. Thus begins the excitement of the Signature Properties rental business. Even though I am longing for the cash you receive at the end of a project, we seem to continue to reinvest into other projects. With rental properties, I can create paper net worth, which someday will hopefully pay for my kid's college educations and support my retirement.

The challenging thing about rentals is finding them. You see, you simply cannot pay market value for properties, and then keep them as rentals. The way the financial model is set up, current rental rates just barely cover your mortgage, interest, and other expenses. The perfect rental property is one that's distressed, and requires value to be injected into the process through renovations or negotiation. Does this sound vaguely similar to what we do when we flip and construct property? Well, it is. If a property analysis works for a flip, which means that we would have a 20% margin built into the deal, then it probably works equally as well as a rental property. So, sometime over the last four months, I realized that I needed to make a decision. Although originally slated for resale as cash-out projects, we had about 7 properties on the books which could work well as rentals once they were built or renovated. We could sell each of the properties and capture the $90,000 - $120,000 equity in the projects, or we could keep them as rental properties. The decision can be broken down into a cash-now or cash-later decision. I like to call this decision my growth versus income. When you buy stocks, you buy some of them with the goal of providing dividends for you to live off of, or income (these are my construction projects that have nice $20,000 paydays), and you buy other stocks for the long term growth opportunities (these will by my rentals), and I hope to eventually have a balanced portfolio of growth and income properties. I have had this discussion with Pete, and I think that we are both on the same page. We both like the cash flow now, but we also both see the need for a long-term retirement strategy. Well, we decided to take these 7 and have them be a cash-later retirement annuity. The rents on the 7 properties are $725, $825, $850, $1075, $1100, $1300, and $1300. So the monthly cash flow on these properties which we decided to keep as rental totals up to $7,425 per month. The current valuation of the 7 properties is $725,000. In 20 years, I hope that all of these properties are paid off in full, and both the rents and valuation have doubled. Therefore, Pete and I will share equity of $1.45 million and have $15,000 per month in gross revenues. Again, this is not a ton of money, but if I can keep 7 properties a year as rental units over the next 10 years, each year after 20, I will have another $1.5 million in equity. Run these numbers in your head. I will be 64 in 30 years. So, in 30 years, when I own (in full) all 70 properties, my portion of this portfolio will be about $5 million dollars. I will happily retire on that at age 64.

Managing rentals requires some property management skills. I am still a rookie at property management, but I truly think that people are overly concerned about what it takes to be a landlord. Once we have completed the paint, carpeting, and updates to the given house, I will run an ad in the newspaper for rent. We just ran an ad for a 4 bedroom townhouse that we painted and carpeted on Cedar Barn Way. The dynamics of the deal are as follows: We purchased the house at a foreclosure sale in December of 2002 for $90,000. The property is worth about $125,000. I stopped by the house to let the homeowners know that we had recently bought their home at foreclosure. The owner knew that the foreclosure was coming, and informed me that he would be cleared out within 30 days, and would leave the front door unlocked for me. We settled on the transaction at the beginning of February, with a total of $14,000 invested in the deal. By March 1st, we had the crew clean, carpet, and paint the unit. We put in about $6,000 in construction, and had a total of $100,000 in the deal with all closing costs included. Our payment is now $800 per month, including taxes. Throw in the $20 per month HOA dues, $30 per month insurance, and $50 reserved for repairs and maintenance, and we are at about $900 per month. We ran the ad for rent on the 1st and 2nd of March. The phone rang off the hook with people looking to pay $1100 per month. With 15 applications in hand, we had a lease signed the following day. So, here is your scenario, yielding $200 per month positive cash flow. Keep in mind that I have done this 7 times in the last 4 months.

LESSONS LEARNED

- Real estate is a finance driven business. Spend plenty of time focusing on raising capital.
- Always be talking about your business. You never know when someone will enlighten you.
- Rentals, rentals, rentals - true net worth is accumulated via real estate ownership.

THE "BIG KAHUNA"

Previously, I touched upon some flips that my super summer intern found for me. One of the flips was a townhouse that needed some work, over in a blue collar neighborhood called Dundalk. Before closing on the foreclosure, I flipped the contract to a savvy investor. This guy was about 60 years old, and over the past 10 years, had accumulated 156 rental properties in Dundalk. While I made $5,000 quickly by flipping the property to him, I got far more from the education this veteran gave me. This investor is a great guy, and kindly mentored me as a landlord. Not only that, but he, his son, and his daughter-in-law are all University of Miami Hurricanes…like me. He had me over to his house one afternoon for a beer and introduced me to his wife, and we talked shop for a few hours. I told him that I was interested in college rentals, and wondered whether he knew of any in the Towson area near the state university. I really wanted to get into college rentals. The numbers just seemed too good to turn up, or turn down, for that matter. His portfolio was full of these blue collar rentals. He liked the $200-$300 per month in cash flow, and I imagine that with 156 of these, he was doing quite well at it. He'd started buying them with his son (who was about 24 year old at the time) and by now his son was well on his way to owning a large fortune in real estate.

Personally, he didn't have any college rentals, but one of his golfing buddies did. He gave me the phone number of this guy and I started the dialogue. I met this guy for lunch up in Towson at a seedy little diner. This guy was a local, and liked this local hang-out where all of the waitresses knew his name. I guess being on his turf made him feel important and like he'd have the upper hand. I treated him to lunch this time, and about 5 more times, as I found that he had an interest in mentoring me about building and managing real estate. As luck would have it, this guy was a retired builder who was looking to retire to Florida. He had built just about everything over the course of his career, and was still holding 5 college rental townhouses in a community of 20 that he had built back in the 1980's. He didn't know what they were worth, nor did he care. He didn't need the extra money, and my timing was right because he didn't want the headache of managing the units. So I opened up the dialogue as to his selling me these units. I've learned that there's a question that most people simply cannot ask. This question is how fortunes are made.

Ask, "so, how much do you want for these properties?" And don't say anything after that. Don't say I think that they are worth "x" dollars. Don't say, "would you take 'x' dollars for them?". Simply say nothing. The next person who speaks will typically lose. He told me that he wanted $65,000 each, bottom line, and did not care how I wrote up the offer or the contract. He said "just send me on my way with $325,000". Now, I could have tried to negotiate with the guy. I could have said my usual…"wow, that's kinda high", but instead, I said 'no problem'. Truth be told, I simply don't understand why it is so difficult to let other people get what they want. He stood to get his price (which made him happy), and I stood to get into the college rental business and buy a group of assets at well under market value (which made me happy). This is the quintessential win-win solution. So, here was my strategy:

First, I evaluated the worth of these five units. Individually, they should appraise somewhere around $90,000 each. My goal was to get into these houses for no money down…or even for cash back. My ready offer was to purchase the property for $85,000 each. If my bank were to get an appraisal of anything higher than

$85,000, I should qualify for 90% financing. This meant that I would have to come up with $8,500 each, plus closing costs, to get into the deal. That translated into about $42,000 of cash up front in order to settle. Now, here is where a little creativity comes in. Remember that the seller only wanted to bottom line $65,000 from each deal. As a licensed real estate agent, I had him agree to list them with me with a 10% commission coming back to me on the final settlement statement. I wrote up the contract for $85,000 each, or at a total of $425,000. The bank did indeed finance 90%, or $77,000 per unit, I got my commission of $42,500 and I paid all of the transfer taxes. After all of the ink had dried and the numbers worked out, we came out owning the package with not only no money down, but a check for our commission totaling $42,000. This is probably the best deal that I have ever negotiated. The seller left with his $65,000 per unit, and happy to not have to manage these college kids, the bank had a well collateralized loan, and we were now in the rental business. The five townhouses he had rented for $850 per month, but I have quickly raised the rates for next year's leases to $1,000 per month. I intend on creeping the rents even higher over the next several years. So, think about this as a ROI deal. I have literally nothing invested in the deal, my mortgage for all five is $2,800 per month, and I am receiving $5,000 per month in gross revenues. The cash flows are slowly but surely beginning to add up. We have a total of 12 properties in our rental portfolio, with positive monthly cash flow after all expenses of about $3,500 per month.

About 6 months ago, Pete and I put down some short-term goals for the company on the used dry erase board hanging in our 200 square foot office. There was our 12 month strategy:

- Networking – attend 2 events per quarter
- Fund raising – raise $100,000
- Rentals – find 5 residential rental properties
- Flips – find 10 flips

- Commercial – buy one commercial investment

The goals will expire on March 31st, so here is where we stand. We joined both the Baltimore City and Baltimore County chambers of commerce. We have gone to breakfasts and happy hours and have met many useful contacts. This is an area that we will continue to focus on as we see the merits of networking in the community. We successfully set up Signature Properties Fund 1 as a formal SEC filed offering. To date, we have raised $200,000 for the Fund and have put the fundraising efforts on hold until we cycle this initial money through. You see, we are paying 6% interest on the money, and only receiving 2.25 % in the money market account. To date, the money has come to us, and we really have not had to focus on the fundraising. The previous section shows that we have doubled our goal of residential rental properties, and this really excites me. We are coming up short on the flips. The flips are now exclusively run through the Fund. We bought one in January, one in February, and 3 so far in March. We would have to find 5 quick ones in the next 3 weeks to reach the goal we set for ourselves. Finally, we come to the commercial rental.

Pete and I have been searching for an office building for a long time. Before signing our lease, we put in several offers on buildings we wanted into in order to relocate our office. On each deal, we came up short in our offer price and have not yet had an accepted offer. Therefore, we signed a lease, and more or less gave in to the idea that commercial just takes time. One month after we signed our lease, we went to a foreclosure auction for a 15,000 square foot office building. You don't typically see commercial properties falling into foreclosure – so, yes, this one really caught our attention. We jumped in the car to go check out the property. It was a 1970's style medical arts sort of building. It looked like it was in decent shape from the outside and the inside needed some tender loving care. New carpets, repairs in the bathrooms, new paint and new ceiling tiles will go long way in sprucing this thing up. Financially, we had limited information on the property. We walked up and down each of the 3 floors in the building, and judging by the names on the suite doors, the building appeared to be about 60% occupied. Since we could not see the leases on the units, I had no idea on what the rental rates were in the building. I called up similar buildings in the area and found that their rates were between $12-$14 per square foot. I thought that residential foreclosures are difficult because sometimes you can't see the inside of the house, but without any real data, commercial transactions are completely nuts. We really did not have enough information about the building to make a truly sophisticated analysis. You see, when you buy foreclosure property, you cannot look at the income statements. You do not have balance sheets with a study period to crunch the numbers and make a logical offer. You only have a view of the exterior of the building, and nothing more. This type of investing is risky, but also exciting. As we stand in the parking lot of this building, Pete and I can only guess and imagine what the revenues and expenses are for this investment. We have a deposit check in hand, and we are poised and ready to throw out a bid without any financial information. Are we nuts? We could only estimate that with 9,000 square feet, or the total 15,000 square feet renting for $10 per square, the gross revenues on the building should be about $90,000 per year. This number is, of course, an estimate based off of 60% of the total square footage. We certainly do not know if that 15,000 square feet includes elevator shafts, bathrooms, or common area maintenance.

Having absolutely no experience with office space, what exactly is gross rent, and how is it calculated? We are armed with nothing but our inexperience at the auction. Without prior financial statements, we did not have a line on the expenses. What are the fees in owning a building, and what is the electric bill, maintenance, trash removal, or any other expense associated with the building? We were not afforded the luxury of having a building inspection performed on the building to tell us if the roof needed to be replaced, if the heating and electrical systems were in working order, or even if the elevator was remotely in compliance with code. So, this left us in a precarious position. How should we evaluate what to bid on this building? I looked at the project extremely quickly. The first time the building was sold, about 9 years ago, it sold for $750,000. Since then, the building has sold 2 times, respectively for $295,000 and $305,000. Basically, I went into this assuming that, based on revenues of $90,000 and estimating that it would take $50,000 to run the building, this left us $40,000 per month, or $3,200 per month to service the debt. At this point, assuming that the building had a current revenue of $90,000, which would mean that it was indeed 60% occupied and that these tenants were paying rent (and that there rent was indeed about $10 per square foot), we would break even. Basically, we are not losing money, but we also wouldn't be compensated for our time leasing the building, renovating the building, or for any of the risk that we have now exposed ourselves to by purchasing the building. I came up with the magic number of $300,000. Don't ask me why I chose this number: it just seemed to fit (back to that GUT feeling). I mean, $3,200 per month can service a debt of around $300K, and the last two times it went up for sale, it sold for the low 300's.

We are so completely out of our league on this deal, but we both know that already. Not only that, but we have been flirting with commercial for so long that we know we are going to have to jump in with both feet in order to learn. I recall when we looked for months for our first residential deal, and ultimately just plunged in feet first to learn the process. The foreclosure auction happened right there on the steps of the building. About 4 prospective bidders showed up for the auction. The bidding opened at $200,000. I was pretty excited to at least see, at this price, that we were in the game. From there, we let the other three bidders run up the numbers. You see, we have developed a bidding style. We let the other investors get the adrenaline rush early. They peak right before we get in. Basically, they're mentally exhausted by the time it appears that we are just jumping into the game. So, in this instance, the other 3 bidders ran the price up to about $255,000. The auction says going once, twice, three times, last and final call, and then Pete steps in with a bold and confident $256,000. Now, one of the other investors is a guy I haven't recognized from any other auction. He was there with his wife, and we certainly didn't know his reasons for purchasing the building. Maybe he was looking to relocate his company, in which case we were certain to be outbid. Well, this gentleman stepped back in at 257. Pete goes straight to 260. Gentleman in blue hat to 261, Pete authoritatively straight to 265. At this point, Pete was trying to intimidate the other bidder into thinking, "I should probably bail out since this guy seems pretty serious about picking up this investment." Well, sometimes things do not go quite as planned. Pete and the other guy bickered back and forth until they had gotten the bidding up to $325,000. Now, keep in mind, this was $25,000 more than I wanted to pay. Pete kept nodding to me with that look in his eye that said not to worry, that this was going to be his pet project and he would make it happen. To make a long auction short, because it really was short, we ended up paying $350,000 for a piece of property, without having any inspection, leases, or financials. Some would consider this foolish…and so would I. Pete and I discussed and re-discussed the purchase. Was it good, was it bad, or was it just downright irresponsible. Oh yeah, another small problem or two: Did we have the money to close this deal? How much would it cost? I guess that, truth be told, completely irresponsible was the right phrase. All of that didn't matter because, at that moment, we were finally the rightful owners of a piece of commercial real estate.

Now put yourselves in my shoes. We just bought a building at foreclosure. The courts would take 60-90 days to ratify the sale. During that period, the old landlord had very little incentive to upkeep the building or spend anymore time on the project. I, on the other hand, did not own the building, but had every intention of keeping the tenants happy so that they didn't move. The next 2 months were a see-saw balancing act of how much money we should spend on a building that we didn't own and how much work we should do to keep the tenants happy and reassured that, if the court ratified the sale, and if we could procure financing, then after 3 miserable months, we were planning on investing big bucks into making this the best address in town. So, during the 2 months, we fixed the heat, got a dumpster company to empty the trash, made sure the electric company did not turn off the power, plowed the driveway several times during snow storms, replaced exterior light bulbs for safety, and so on and so on. We contacted our bank in order to arrange financing. They said that as long as the appraisal came back clean, they would probably finance 80% of the transaction. That left Pete and me to come up with 20% of $350,000, or $70,000 plus closing costs. All in all, we needed about $98,500 to close the deal. Here is the breakdown:

Down payment	$70,000	
3% transfers	$10,500	Remember, with foreclosure, we pay it all.
3% interest carry	$10,500	Again, buying foreclosures is expensive.
Closing fees	$2,000	
Bank charges	$4,000	
Appraisal	$1,500	
Total to close	$98,500	

So, the next question I needed to answer was where in the heck we could come up with $98,000 to close the transaction. We had already put up $50,000 as our deposit. This came straight off of a line of credit which was now maxed to the limit. We needed to find $50,000 within 60-90 days, or risk losing our deposit. As far as I'm concerned, this is one of those examples that makes me confident we'll succeed in real estate. We hop into deals that we are confident make perfect sense, and worry about the minor details like financing after we have already committed to a contract! So, now we had a contract on a mediocre deal at $350,000, it was time to work some magic and get another $50,000 in order to buy this thing. When you buy these things, you put up a deposit of $50,000, in this case. If you cannot come up with the additional money to close or if your bank just will not give you financing to close the deal….well, you are just out of luck. You have just given up your $50,000 since these foreclosure transactions are not blessed with a financing contingency (which most normal transactions have). At any rate, now it was time for Pete and I to shift gears and focus on raising some capital, or else we risked losing our deposit. Around this time, Pete had been exchanging emails and keeping up with an old entrepreneurship instructor from our MBA program. He was asking how our venture was going. We told him about all of the exciting opportunities that we had going here at Signature Properties. You see, when you graduate from an entrepreneurship program at a university and actually create a venture, which not too many entrepreneurship majors actually do, the instructors like to know how you are doing in your business. It's almost a direct correlation to how successful they are as teachers in relation to the success of your business. We explained to him our business model, shared our successes, and even hinted that my brother and other investors were enjoying a 12% return on their money. If nothing else, we are good at talking smack about our business and making it seem to be the best deal around. Then, ever so subtly, we drop hints that we are letting outside investors capture some big returns by being involved with our company. Wouldn't you know it, but he was liquidating another investment and had $50,000 that he was looking to plunk down on a venture. The pen went to paper pretty fast that day, then with a meeting for lunch, and a check in the bank by 2 o'clock. We signed a promissory note for $50,000, promising him 12% interest on his money. Sometimes, I think that we impress ourselves.

Well, we had solved the financing problem about getting enough down payment money, and now onto the challenge of getting the bank to approve our financing. Appraisers are an interesting group. They are independent contractors hired by the bank to give an objective opinion on what they think a particular piece of real estate is worth. When it comes to analyzing residential properties, their job is relatively easy. They look at all of the houses that have sold in a particular neighborhood. From there, they compare the square footage, lot sizes, house styles, bedrooms, baths, and ideally, they like to find the most similar house to the subject property in order to really be sure of their appraisal. Then they make minor adjustments for garages, decks, finished basements, pools, and other items that may make a property slightly better or even slightly worse. With this data, they come up with a price for the property that it should sell for in the current market conditions. The problem with the setup is that banks are in the business of lending money. Loan officers, who are the people that originate the loans for the banks, are in charge of choosing which appraisal company does the work. These loan officers only make money if the bank actually makes the loan. And the bank only makes the loan if the property appraises properly. Do you see where I am going with this? The appraiser needs to come up with a number that makes the bank feel comfortable. If the number is too high, the appraisers open themselves up to liability when the bank loans the money and the borrower defaults. If the number is too low, this will squash a loan, which in turn means that the loan officer does not get their commission, meaning that the next time the bank needs an appraisal done, they may not call that appraisal company again. At any rate, I feel that one of the most important aspects of getting a good appraisal is meeting the appraiser out at the property and subtly leading the appraiser to come up with a number that you are looking to pay. We know what we see in the deal, and then we call our loan officer and try to sell her on what we see in the deal. That means explaining to her the current market rents for an office building in that area, and discussing how the bank is well-protected in giving us money on a particular deal. Finally, I need to convince the appraiser to see what we see in the deal.

It really seems like I spend a lot of time convincing people to see what I see in any given deal. For instance, on this building, we had absolutely no idea what the appraisal would be. If you looked at it from a straight net operating income approach, using the $90K in revenues minus the $50K in expenses, your net operating income (NOI) for the project was $40,000. Now, appraisers use a number called a cap rate, which represents the return on the project if one was to invest all cash in the deal. This number incorporates risk and cost of capital, and can range anywhere from 6% to as high as 13%. The higher the cap rate, the more risky the investment. I am not a financial guru, so you will have to take me at my word when I tell you that the number is somewhat arbitrary. In my head, I made up a number of 10% that I thought the appraiser might use. So, a 10% cap rate would mean that this project should appraise at $400,000. This is found by dividing $40,000 in NOI by the 10%. In my mind, this project had more than average risk associated with it. The neighborhood is older and run down; and the commercial district is deteriorating, not increasing, so if I were a commercial appraiser, I would assign this thing a cap rate of 12% (which indicates more risk). Using the same formula, a 12% cap rate would equate to a valuation of $333,333. This is about what I thought the building was worth. Pete, on the other hand, has been selling me on the future valuation of the building. Pete's argument is that once we invest $75,000 into landscaping, lighting, roofing, signage, driveway resurfacing, carpeting, and updates, the building will be more appealing. Now, with a more appealing building, we can lease up the remaining 40% and raise the rent to current market conditions, or $12 per square foot. So, at 100% occupancy at the $12 on 15,000 square feet, we would have gross revenues of $180,000 per year. Our expenses would increase slightly with 100% occupancy, putting them around $60,000. Therefore, the future estimates of our NOI would be $120,000. At the same cap rate of 12%, this investment now should have a valuation of $1,000,000. Interesting how Pete and I can be so far apart on our valuations for the building. It will be even more interesting to see what happens.

At any rate, I need to convince the appraiser toward our vision for this building. So, I meet the appraiser at the building on a cold Monday morning in March. I show him the enthusiasm and excitement that I have about the prospects of this building, channeling my partner's positivity in terms of this particular building. I explain numerous examples of how good we have become at residential rehabilitation. I emphasize the numbers, the same raw profit numbers that make my mouth water: you have seen the stuff that I have been writing about for over two years now, and you have been reading about these same mouth-watering numbers for some time, so I know you have an idea what I'm talking about. Next, I am selling him on what I see for this building. I see new carpet and paint, updated bathrooms, a new sign out front with a newly paved parking lot. This will be one of the nicest community buildings around. The tenants will include doctors, lawyers, and accountants. The rents will be around $12 per square, with 100% occupancy. I am beginning to believe the vision myself, and I call Pete to tell him how excited I am about the building, and that $350,000 was not a bad price to pay. By the end of the meeting, the appraiser is ready to write down whatever number I want him to write down. I make sure that he understands the purchase of the building as a price of $350,000, and that we are looking to get about $100,000 in fixer-upper financing from the bank. From there, we shake hands, talk about playing a round of golf in Annapolis, and part ways.

Pete and I wait out the week to see how the appraisal comes back. Finally, we get the call from the bank. After construction and repairs, as we have stipulated in our loan package (spending $75,000 in cosmetic updates), this appraiser feels that the building will be worth... Are you ready for this one? $850,000. If that hasn't made an impression on you, you probably should put the book down and forget about real estate, because what just happened is incredible. Think about this: we bought a building for $350,000. We promised to put $75,000 into the building, and the appraiser tells the bank that it will then be worth $850,000. If we needed cash for future deals, we can now refinance the building for $740,000 (80% of the $850,000), pay off the existing mortgage of

$280,000, give back the entrepreneurship professor his $50,000, pay off that line of credit for $50,000, and have a tidy $360,000 in cash…in my pocket. Now, I own a building for "no money down" and I have $360,000 in extra money to invest elsewhere. Keep in mind that there are two quick roadblocks to taking this kind of cash out of the building. First, the building really needs to be fully occupied at strong rents in order to service the debt on $740,000, and second, if I go to sell the building, I hope that the market agrees with the appraiser and I can sell the building for more than $740,000. But if both of these items are satisfied, I get my piece and have just created, out of all but nothing, $180,000 in net worth. All of this is just fantasy. Probably my favorite part of real estate is dreaming, and deals like this are certainly the core of these types of dreams. There is a lot of work which needs to be done to fix this building up. Pete has never really had to do rehabilitation of a commercial property, and these new mechanical systems could certainly present a major stumbling block for him. Second, I have no clue on how to lease commercial space. This could prove to be a stumbling block as well. I try not to allow these minor problems to worry me or keep me from being extremely excited about the prospects of owning commercial property.

May 2003

It is now 60 days later, and we have closed on the building. Over the past month, we have secured leases from all of the existing tenants. The building did indeed end up being about 50% occupied. We have a trickle of cash flow coming in to service all of the bills, and we are beginning to get the picture of what all of the expenses should come out to be on an annual basis. Pete has contractors working on the HVAC system, roof, bathrooms, signage, and the like. Once the building has some appeal, I will then take it and run with the leasing side of the building. Our goal will be to fill it up, raise the rents, and enjoy about $30,000 in annual cash flow for the next 20 years. Then we can either sell it and capture the cash or continue to rent it for $70,000 a year in cash flow. Either way, this is our first attempt at commercial space, and we are really excited about the outcome so far. Oh yeah... it is not all peaches and cream, of course. All of our analysis was based off of the 15,000 square feet published in the city tax assessment. Sure, the building is 15,000 square feet of gross space, but by the time you take out the room with the HVAC unit, the hallways, the elevator, the lobby and similar non-renting spaces, we are actually only renting 9,000 square feet. So, our gross rents just dipped some $7,200 per year due to this rookie oversight. Oops.

Our first commercial purchase at 6314 Windsor Mill Road, Baltimore

LESSONS LEARNED

- Cash flow is king. Rentals provide a combination of appreciation and cash flow. If nothing else – buy some rentals now.

- Find the good deals and raising capital is easy. Believe in your vision and be able to sell it to investors. Windsor Mill is a perfect example.

- A capitalization rate is an important component of commercial transactions. Lower cap rates equate to lower risk.

WEEKEND AT THE BEACH

I need to digress for a chapter so you can try to see the things that I see going on around me. I am writing this chapter on a return flight from South Beach, Miami. As I sit here crammed into a coach seat with just enough room to set up my laptop, I am jealous of the folks relaxing and lounging up in first class. Some of these subtleties and the glitz and glamour of South Beach in Miami have rejuvenated me to tackle the growth of my real estate empire. As a parent of young children (mine being almost 5 and almost 2 now), you really get run down with the day-to-day routine of working hard and being a father. Every once in a while, you just need to get a weekend with the fellas. My wife is a fantastic mother to my children, and extremely giving when I need time to get away to recoup and regroup. At any rate, I am a dedicated father, and only take one weekend a year away from my family. Working in real estate limits my travel also, so once in a while, the weekend away fills a need.

This particular weekend was a guy's weekend in Miami. Over the past 10 years, Miami has become a Mecca for the rich and famous. Models speckle the beach and money exudes from every pore of the city. I have a childhood friend, Arthur, who is quickly becoming my most successful protégé. Arthur has always known his dream for success and wealth, and has chased it with reckless abandon. Since graduating college, he took a job in Manhattan with an investment banking firm, then got an MBA degree at Wharton, and went on to one of the most prestigious positions in investment banking in the city. After working several years for this firm and earning a salary that most people can only dream about, Arthur quit his job to start his own firm. In the last five years, Arthur has built a company with the title of the second largest average account in the investment banking industry. Needless to say, along with this comes plenty of cash. This weekend, we were meeting at Arthur's place on the beach. The other player for the weekend was Howard. Howard was my college roommate at Miami. As a biomedical engineer, Howard took several decent positions with large engineering firms in Texas and California. About 5 years ago, like Arthur, Howard quit his job and started his own firm, originally operating out of his garage. Since then, his little company was bought by a larger holding company, and today he is the CEO of this same small firm, with growing revenues. Both players are in their early thirties and both players are well on their way to success and wealth. You just get that feeling when you listen to them talk over lunch or dinner.

The venue for our weekend was Arthur's seasonal rental in South Beach, Miami. It's funny what happens when you get together with other business-driven individuals. The conversation is always centered on financial wealth and success. We never discuss salaries, savings, income, or investments. It is a dance that we do, over and over again, asking questions about how business is going. Nobody is blunt enough to ask how much we have or how much we make, but every conversation circles around and dances around these details. I know Arthur's assets under management at his firm. That was published in an article in *Forbes Magazine* that I read. The dude was quoted in *Forbes*. Art, if you are reading this (which means my book was actually published) and I forgot to tell you, I am proud of your accomplishments in Forbes. Anyhow, what it comes down to is that, from there, I can extrapolate his success even without having been told about those details I mentioned above. I am figuring that his company has a management fee of 1% and he has a half of a billion dollars under management. So, his company has a pretty healthy operating income. Arthur has been thinking about buying a winter place in

Miami, so this year he thought that he would bite the bullet and try a seasonal rental first. Miami Beach has many nice places to live, up and down the beach at all price ranges. Arthur chose Il Villagio for his seasonal dreams. If the name Il Villagio conjures up Las Vegas style amenities, the rental lives up to your vision. The building is a 17 story structure located right on the beach. It is by far the nicest looking building on South Beach, and from what Arthur tells me, it's the highest priced property, as well. The unit that Arthur is renting costs $1.5 million to buy and $8,000 per month to rent. If you run those numbers in your head, Arthur is paying $24,000 for his three month seasonal rental. I don't know about you, but that is more than I pay for my mortgage…in a year.

The view from the 11th floor is an uninterrupted view of the Atlantic Ocean. The term million-dollar-view gets its name from units like this. The amenities at Il Villagio are second to none. From the valet who takes your car, to the elevator doorman who programs your private elevator, to the towel girl who sets up your chair at the beach, this is truly living the lifestyle of the rich and famous. At this point in my life, I am just not accustomed to those kinds of amenities…but I certainly could get used to them. The weekend included a $150 round of golf at a local beach country club, a $400 chartered fishing boat for evening Tarpon fishing, drink tabs that ran over $200 per person, and clubs that you have to wait in line for in order to give them $20 per drink. As I read this section, I still feel out of my element. I am a family man, totally not into this style of living, upset at myself for even dreaming of having the desire to live this style of living, but I can't help myself for wanting it. The cars in the garage at the Villagio were Porches, Mercedes, Hummers, and Rolls. The question constantly runs through my head, what are these people doing for all of this money? I think of myself as smart and able, but how do I accomplish this style of living? Without dragging on with all of the weekend's activities, the purpose of this chapter of the book is, simply, "the conversation".

"The conversation" started as soon as I arrived and continued intermittently throughout the entire weekend. When you have three young budding entrepreneurs put into an extravagant location for a weekend…the purpose of the discussion is clear: how can we do the Miami lifestyle full-time? How do we acquire this amount of money for retirement, and I mean to live this kind of lifestyle for retirement, and more importantly, *what is the number?* The 'What is the number' question is one that's been hanging around in the back of my mind for several years, but I have never had a system for calculating that number. The other two players have gone one step further. When the question came up, that 'what is the number' question, they had the answer armed and ready. Their answers had been calculated down to the exact penny. As I vaguely talk about "the number", it seems clear that it means different things to different people. The number, very simply, is how much money it will take to retire in the lifestyle of your dreams. Everyone's dreams are different. Each number is different because each player has different goals and aspirations, but the question of what the number is really put a bug in my head. The question comes down to how much money one needs to stop working and retire with a lifestyle that will satisfy them for the rest of their life.

The three players we're talking about here are 33, 34, and 34 years of age, respectively. Retirement is now becoming the most pressing question for each of us. We all have goals of early retirement. How much money is it going to take to accomplish this goal, and how many years is it going to take to get there? You know my financial situation, so you are going to be involved with my decision in calculating my number. I am going to focus the next month toward calculating every penny I will need for a happy retirement. Hanging out with these guys isn't good for me. I know that I put down the number $2,000,000 in net worth for a condition needed in order to publish this book, but after this weekend, I can quickly see that the return on the $2,000,000 will not be enough to sustain my lifestyle, nor sustain a lifestyle that I am jealously seeking. At any rate, I am going to hold firm to my initial goals of $2,000,000. This weekend proved to be an eye opening weekend on the cost of retirement. When you put a few smart guys (actually two smart guys and me) together with some critical thinking, you see that my $2 million number is flawed. Let me look at the players and tell you a little bit about their numbers.

Howard was the first one to ask me the number question. Howard's situation is quite unique. He started his company several years ago, and was given an option to sell his option of stock worth several million dollars. In other words, if Howard were to quit working today, he could exercise his option and receive several (after tax) million dollars. Ka-chunk, here is a lump sum of money. If Howard were writing this book, it would already be going to press. Howard has already done the math. The current risk free rates on investing this money and living off of the interest it produces is about 2.5%. He is confident that he could invest and receive 5% return on his money in a fairly safe investment. Therefore, Howard could stop working now, at age 34, and live off of over a hundred thousand dollars per year. Don't ask me twice: I would be done. The problem with Howard is that, as the CEO of the company, he has been earning a more-than-healthy salary. He has ratcheted up his lifestyle to the point that his burn rate is far higher than mine. Howard has larger dreams. He would like to have a $1 million sail boat to sail around the world in. He would like to have a house on the beach. And in order to accomplish these goals, he needs to have a larger number. We went through the calculations for what it would take for Howard to live the life without having to rely on working. The big decision for Howard is to continue to work for the salary and save up his money, or to take the cash and invest it, or start another venture. There is a law of return called the law of 72. For quick calculations on return, you can divide any interest percentage into the number 72 and calculate how many years it will take your money to double. For example, let's say I had the $2 million and I could put it into an investment yielding 6%. By dividing 6 into 72, I see that my $2 million would become $4 million in 12 years. Then, in another 12 years, it would be $8 million. Using this formula, Howard is well on his way to achieving his goal.

Now, let us take a look at Arthur's situation. I don't have any hard-core numbers on Arthur since he is fairly tight-lipped about his situation, but I have a feeling that he has an even larger burn rate than Howard. Arthur, however, is really living the life, and is driven towards his goals. Arthur is in the business of managing money for some of the wealthiest people in the world. Arthur's clients take him fishing in Panama, skiing in Aspen, flying on their private jets, and just about every other lavish expense that can be thrown into the mix. Arthur is truly used to being waited on hand and foot at hotels, restaurants, and clubs. He is the consummate salesman. Even this weekend, when we wanted to get into one of the hippest clubs on the beach without a reservation, Arthur was negotiating with the doorman, quickly slipping him a $50 bill, and in we went. He schmoozes everyone he talks with and closes with the best of them. The one key element about Arthur is his drive. He knows what he wants, sees it in front of him, and drives towards it like the goal line in a super bowl game. He always has his game face on, and he just loves the smell of money.

Alright then, so this gets me to reevaluate my number. I know that my number was $2 million when I started the book. I look back and see that the number was based on a 10% return on my money, and living off of $200,000 per year. I still think that I can live off of $200,000 per year, but after talking with these guys, my number probably should be $4 million. Their point was that, in order to have a somewhat risk-free investment, you should calculate around a 5% return. The other challenging question for me will be what material items I need to have paid for (in full) before I accomplish that $4 million after-tax number. When I retire, I would like to have certain things that will make my life more enjoyable. I would like to have a condominium in Florida. It does not have to be a $1,000,000 view, but a waterfront condo which allows me to enjoy my morning cup of coffee looking at the sunrise each morning before my round of golf is certainly in the cards. I am guessing that this property will cost me about

$500,000. I want to maintain a house in Maryland. Perhaps my present address will suffice, but the payoff for this house is currently $200,000. I would like a bigger boat to retire with. My present boat is a fun runabout deck boat. The boat that I need will be one that I can take weekends away on, in the Bahamas, Bermuda, and the Caribbean. Large enough to take trips up to Cape Cod, but not so expensive that it exhausts my $200,000 in annual income to maintain. I am guessing that the boat will run me about $200,000. These items will take about $900,000 to buy, which will run my total retirement number up to $4.7 million. I need to back in to that number and figure out a plan that lets me arrive at it. I realize, as I am flying home, that I need to spend some time focusing on my financial goals and developing a real strategy focused on obtaining them. So, what better way to tackle this goal setting than to investigate my current situation again? I haven't really done this since I started this entire journey

March 2003 – Update on current situation

Let me see how close I am to the $2 million by figuring out how my net worth has grown over the past year. At the beginning of the book, I calculated my net worth as $175,000. Let me perform the same analysis about two years later.

I am paying off the house we live in. We bought the house 6 years ago and have done very well with its appreciation.

Equity in House = $180,000 – appreciation has been good to us over the past year.

The stocks and funds markets have not been kind. The recession continues to hit, and my portfolio continues to dwindle. I have two accounts:

Stocks = $15,000
Funds = $12,000

In response to my guys' weekend away, I finally have set up a simple IRA.

Simple IRA = $17,400

I have set up two 529 educational IRA accounts for my children.

Total invested in education = $4,000

My wife still drives a 1995 Jeep Grand Cherokee, but now it has 165,000 miles, and my car is a lease.

Equity in her Car = down to $2,000 on a good day
Equity in SeaRay Boat = $5,000 (I took a large debt on the purchase)

I do not believe in carrying credit card debt, so $235,400 is pretty much my personal net worth picture at this point in time. Yes, this number has grown from $175,000 last year. If I had not started in the real estate business, it is quite possible that this $235,400 tells the entire story. You see, I have managed to save about $55,000 over the past year, between savings and real estate appreciation. I love appreciation; I'll say it again: I love real estate appreciation. But, you see, you are not getting the whole picture of my net worth from this simple analysis. You see, with every deal that Signature does, Pete and I continually invest in more and more deals. We are building up a pretty substantial paper net worth in real estate. This is where it gets really fun!

Let me roll through the number that Signature Properties owns, and run a quick net worth picture if we were to sell each property right now.

Residential Rentals	Appraised Value	Mortgage	Total Net Worth
Arncliffe	$75,000	$51,000	$24,000
Scotia	$95,000	$68,000	$27,000
Cedar Barn	$128,000	$90,000	$38,000
5 College rentals	$485,000	$287,500	$197,500
Terrace	$120,000	$90,000	$30,000
Streeper	$157,000	$120,000	$37,000
Fleet	$157,000	$120,000	$37,000
Yarnall	$85,000	$30,000	$55,000
Windsor Building	$850,000	$380,000	$470,000
Total Rental Equity			$905,000
My portion of the equity			$402,500

Now add this $402,500 to the $235,400 I have in savings and personal assets, and we are now up to $637,500 in net worth. So far, so good, right? Well, I am not done yet. You see, in addition to all of the rental properties, we currently have 14 properties under construction. Much of the equity built up in these properties is questionable. I say questionable for two reasons. First, we have not realized the profits from these investments because they are currently under construction. Therefore, the net worth created by these investments is merely my estimates of what I hope to sell them for when we are complete. Since it is difficult to give a current under construction valuation, I will use the final value, since we should be wrapping them up within the year. Second, we have quite a bit of credit line debt, which has allowed us to purchase this portfolio of spec houses. So, without trying to sugar coat the number and without confusing you with the debt associated with each house, I will give you a snippet of just the big deals. The house on Lombard Street... you remember the one that was just a wall when we started? Well, this house should and will sell for a minimum of $400,000. As I stated before, I recently put this house into the market for $450,000. I have already had several calls for the property, and one extremely serious prospect. I am not quite complete with the construction, but I have listed it now in an attempt to give the buyer a chance to customize the house with carpeting, colors, paint, and other cosmetic fixes. In addition, I am trying to time the closing date with the completion date so as not to waste any additional money in interest carry. But, I digress: my point is that, when the house sells for $400,000, we stand to receive $200,000 in cash from that deal. So, let me run down the list of properties that we own and the total expected cash in each deal.

Lombard	$200,000	Bay View	$10,000
Pratt	$38,000	Charlcote	$50,000
Washington	$45,000	Greenbank	$130,000
Wolfe	$10,000	Bellhaven	$4,000
Sunset	$3,000	Cross	$10,000

Total Equity $502,000

So I am anticipating about $251,000 in cash over the next 6-8 months. Now, let's tally up the total net worth picture:

Savings, etc.	$240,400
Rental Equity	$402,500
Spec Equity	$251,000

Total Net $894,000

Wow... almost half way there in just about two years. Not exactly. I should not include the speculative equity of the $251,000 because that is what I live off of as my salary. This is not really net worth money. Using that is like saying that you get a salary of $100,000 per year at your job, and you use that number to calculate your net worth. So that number could be somewhere around $800,000, but still a pretty good year!

June 2003

I had a conversation with Pete today about the direction and strategy for Signature Properties. You see, I love rentals. If I could find a way to locate and purchase 100 rentals tomorrow, I would. The reason that I love rentals so much is that in 30 years, at age 64, I want to own as many pieces of passive income properties as possible. Right now, we make about $50K per year in positive cash flow, just with the existing 14 rentals in our portfolio. If I had 10 times this number, I would have $500K per year in positive cash. In this scenario, I would just be a property manager, manage 140 rental properties, and live off of the cash flow generated. Now, in 30 years, when all of the mortgages are paid off, the cash flow goes up significantly. My goal is to have all of them paid off by the time I'm 65 years old. So, just say that I do not acquire another rental property for the next 30 years, and just pay off the 14 that we have right now. These 14 currently pay about $25,000 per month in rent. That works out to be around $300,000 per year in revenues. Without any mortgages to service, one could net about $200,000 per year after maintenance, insurance, and taxes. So, that alone is exciting. If you take this analysis to the next level and put 140 rentals into your portfolio, now you are living off of $2,000,000 per year. So, obviously, my goal is to get to 140 rental properties as quickly as possible.

Pete has a different mantra for the company. He is looking to cash out today on the profits of some of our flips and rehabs. This cash, which could be reinvested into rental properties, is going straight to us, toward running the company and living off of the excess. Now certainly, we need the cash for day-to-day operations, but I would love to try to buy more rentals, and it is a daily chore to push Pete in that direction. Now, in fairness to Pete, he is an accountant by training. He pays all of the bills and has a much better understanding of our cash burn rate and how much money he needs to see in our bank account to meet those cash needs. I may be too aggressive in trying to build a rental portfolio without truly understanding the cash needs of our little company. Our company is currently expensive to run. We have three full-time employees and soon to be four, with a total payroll of $130,000. We have overhead and office expenses of about another $50,000. Therefore, the first $180,000 of our year goes to running the company. This is a difficult nut for a small company, but a required piece if we are planning growth. The tools are in position, the model has been developed, the employees are in place, and now we just need to maximize our operations at full tilt.

Competition is another problem that we are running into. Now, I am sure that everyone has seen the late night infomercials about how to get rich in real estate. The great artists of the day are Carlton Sheets, Don Lapre, and Russ Whitney. These guys get on television with numerous student testimonies about how wonderful their get-rich-quick real estate program is. What they detail in their books is how to locate, finance, fix, and sell real estate. Their programs are 100% absolutely true and accurate. The information is exactly what Signature Properties does, and how we have built a company over the past several years. The commercials are so exciting that even my brother invested $1,500 to attend a three-day boot camp for Russ Whitney. The only thing that these guys don't do is actually take you to an auction and help you buy real estate. What they have managed to do is allow anyone with $10,000 in their pocket, or a line of credit, to get into the real estate game. Even over the past 2 years, I have seen the crowds of investors grow for each auction at the foreclosures. The increased competition has driven up the prices of the houses, almost to market value. At one point in time, there were just a few hardcore investors who would show up at each auction, and there was plenty of inventory to go around. Now, when we show up at an auction, we are bidding against every Tom, Dick, and Harry with a $5,000 deposit check. As rookies to the business (not to say that we are the wily veterans), these guys have not really analyzed all of the numbers. Combine this with the fact that they are willing to take on the project at lower margins, just to be in real estate, and you now have a formula for the market outbidding us each and every time.

For example, I went to an auction this week where the house in question will be worth about $190,000 when it is fixed up. I drove past the house, and it had a car on blocks in the front yard, grass up to my ass, and needed a roof, windows, and who knows what else on the inside of the house. At any rate, my numbers could substantiate about $130,000 at the courthouse steps. After the commission, carry, transfers, construction, and other fees, we then stood to make about $15,000. I was flabbergasted to see the house sell for $167,000. Could you imaging paying almost market value for a house that you haven't even seen the inside of? Once you throw in the additional carry costs for buying a foreclosure, and the double transfers, you will be in the house for $177,000 on day one. This is further proof that Signature Properties needs to look for some sort of change in order to grow. The deals that we have managed to get into over the past several months have been houses that need a lot of work to complete (the rookie investors being afraid of these deals) and houses that need substantial deposits. Just to refresh your memory, here's a reminder we set up the Fund which has about $300,000 in cash in it, so we can afford to get into somewhat larger deals than the average investor. Judging by the 3 or 4 players that buy and sell foreclosures in the Baltimore area, we probably own the most real estate at this point in time. We are the big fish in a little pond of foreclosure people. We really want to find a way to jump over to the bigger pond and be the little fish there for a while.

As we continue to run around just to keep up with our current pace of growth and our number of investments, we are beginning to think that it would be a nice thing if we could have larger projects (and fewer of them). Recently, Pete has gone through the public records and sorted out all large tracts of land zoned for multi-family buildings, and sent letters to all of these land owners to see if they are interested in selling their property. At the same time, I have gone through every office building owner with a property that shows less than 50% occupancy, and sent them letters to see if they have any interest in selling their buildings. Over the past 2 years, I have learned that the low hanging fruit is not always the sweetest tasting fruit. What I mean by this is that the foreclosure auctions are what I consider the low hanging fruit. At the courthouse steps, that property is guaranteed to sell. This forces a fierce amount of competition among investors, often driving the price up to market values. The difficult apples on the tree to reach require some cold calling, direct marketing, and alternative measures of acquisition. This was proven by Lombard Street, which was acquired by networking and Park Avenue, the apartment building that the non-profit sold us. If you take one nugget of information from this entire book, this is it. So, pay attention: In order to get rich in real estate, you need to step outside of your comfort zone for acquisition. It is as simple as that. We now know that we can putter along with spot-build deals, flipping properties throughout the city, and make a fine salary of six figures each year. Furthermore, we can acquire rentals here and there to supplement our cash flow and retirement. The key to consistent growth is going on to the next level. That level requires us to step outside of our comfort zone and start acquiring bigger deals. You see, distressed properties are at all levels. Buildings can certainly be distressed due to functional failures and market changes, as well. The key to Signature Properties' growth, in this stage, is economies of scale. Several years ago, we took the plunge in residential houses with our first purchase on Andre Street. Then we jumped into commercial when we bought the building at Windsor and the 12 unit apartment building on Park. It is time again for us to climb onto the trampoline of real estate and jump into the next area. We need a subdivision where we can build 10 to 20 houses or townhouses. Pete's mailing campaign yielded three leads. I'm tempted to call them hot leads, but that potential is for future chapters. At any rate, one of the landowners called Pete to discuss selling his property. This piece of property would allow us to build 12 townhouses in a fantastic residential development. Now, remember that we have absolutely no idea how to subdivide land, put in storm water management, cut curbs, run streets, or address engineering and architectural concerns, or anything else that we haven't had to do before for that matter. We are proceeding cautiously, but certainly not letting our naiveté keep us from getting into the deal. The first call was to an engineering firm. We simply picked one out of the phone book and off we went. We had the first meeting with the firm last week. Upon initial review of the plans, the engineer certainly thought that the lot was buildable. His statement to us was more along the lines of how much we wanted to spend on the building.

We are learning that, as long as the zoning matches our intended use, the next step is just a function of money. This is exactly where we want to be as we proceed to the step of making an offer on the land. Next week, we hope to set a meeting up with the county zoning and planning department to see exactly what they think we can do with this piece of land. From there, we will estimate a budget from the engineer on how much he thinks the subdivision process will take. And from there, we can put together a letter of intent for the seller, and hopefully, this letter matches what he wants.

Fells Point Insanity

Before I cut out for this month, I want to describe a project that we just bought yesterday. This was an auction in Fells Point, Baltimore. If you are unfamiliar with the area, Fells Point is a post-college hang-out residential area. It is located on the Baltimore Harbor, and has cute little shops, restaurants, and, of course, bars. The residential scene in Fells Point is pretty hopping. The houses are the same rowhouse style that we have been building for the past two years. The closer that you get to the harbor, the hotter the resale price. I noticed an auction of 4 connected buildings about 3 blocks from the harbor. The buildings looked run-down and needed a complete and thorough rehabilitation to turn them into any kind of useful real estate. I gave the project to Dan, an MBA guy in our office who's trying to get rich in real estate, for him to analyze and come up with a course of action. His analysis returned 4 luxury townhouses with garage parking underneath. If you have ever lived in the major city, you know that a realtor having the ability to provide garage parking is key. Each of these 4 townhouses should yield about $350,000. The estimated total revenue for the project was $1,400,000. Here is what the analysis looks like, as Dan handed it to me about 2 hours prior to the auction.

Revenues	$1,400,000
Construction	$540,000
Closing	$40,000
Commission	$92,000
Carry	$75,000
Total Expenses	$747,000
Gross Profit	$653,000

Purchase of the land at auction $400,000

Net off of the deal $253,000 (18% of revenues)

So, off to the auction we went. We being myself, Dan, and a college intern who was dying to see the excitement of an auction. We all loaded into my Mercedes E430; did I mention that I bought that a few months ago? This should motivate you even more, because just about 2 years ago, I was not even imagining that I would be driving such a sweet automobile! I bought my wife a Toyota Sequoia, by the way, one of those ultra huge SUVs capable of carrying 8 people, and then I bought myself a Benz. Little by little, I am slowly cracking a smile at for the fact that this book may indeed get to print. I have set a goal, and at some point over the next few years, I may attain my financial goals. At any rate, I digress; we got to the auction about 20 minutes prior to the start, with our check for $32,000 in deposit money. This was not your typical auction. It was four vacant houses that had been combined into one large meeting area. Given that it wasn't a foreclosure, we could actually tour the property. The places looked worse than I'd thought on the inside. It had apparently been used as a bar not too long ago, and suffered complete damage due to a fire. The lot was a whopping .11 acres. That is not 11 acres, but one tenth of one acre. The location was outstanding, though. If we could get this thing for under $400,000, and be able to build our vision, this could be a big project for us.

We took our place amongst 50 or so attendees. At an auction of this size, most of the attendees are lookers-on, and few have the money to close on this size transaction. The bidding opened at $150,000. It went on in $5,000 increments for about 2 minutes, up to $300,000, and then it slowed down. I stumbled a little bit on a bid of $335,000 and this guy across the room shot back $340,000 without missing a step. In fact, he's bidding so confidently, I thought he might go up to $400,000. So, I took one more stab, at $345,000, and within seconds, the guy just nodded at the auctioneer, telling him that $350,000 was no problem. Meanwhile, I'm done, exhausted, beaten, and frankly confused. If my limit is $350,000 and I go to $355,000, and this guy doesn't bid again, I buy it, but really over what my limit was. So I quit. Going once, twice, third and final call, are we all done bidding…? And then Dan raises his hand at $355,000. Going, going, gone. So, there you have it, we bought it for $355,000, and plus you have to tack on a 5% auctioneer fee, bringing our total to $367,500. Backing into Dan's analysis, this deal should be able to kick back $285,500. But still, I ask Dan, "What are you thinking?" – and he tells me, "I've got a gut feeling on this one".

So, now we own this piece of land in historic Fells Point. What do we do next with it? As soon as I returned from the auction, I sent an email to our loan officer over at Severn Savings Bank. Now comes some of the salesmanship. My email says how excited we are to have just acquired this fantastic and unbelievable opportunity in Fells Point. I quickly give her the financials of the deal, and ask her what kind of pitch packet she would like to have to present this deal to her committee. Then I add an update on the two properties that we currently have under contract. I tell her that the one on Charlcote should close July 24th for $422,500, and we have a loan on it for $315,000. Now she knows that she is getting her money back, and that I am making about $80,000 on this deal. Then I tell her about Cross Street, which will close at $203,000, whereas our loan is $132,000. Again, she is getting some money back and I am making about $50,000. This update serves two purposes in my mind. One, I want to let her know that the bank is getting back $447,000 of their money, and two, that we should make about $180,000 in profit off of these two deals. It is sort of like tooting your own horn, but I am always conscious of creating a positive mind share in my loan officer's mind. This helps her sell my loan requests to her committee more successfully, and in turn gets us into more deals. How successful we are at what we do? Well, this is how we do it. Remember, the bank is also making a ton of fees and income off of me.

Let me get back to the reason that I have set down this month to write in my journal. I just told you about the experience at the auction for the purchase of 4 residential lots in historic Fells Point, Baltimore. Right now, on the site stands 4 completely burned-out shells. They are literally burned out because I believe that there was a fire which gutted them all some years ago. This purchase is exactly what Signature Properties needs at this point in our growth. I've alluded to the difficulties that we're having with spot building and spot investing in various properties throughout the different counties. These projects are difficult to visit, purchase, build, remodel, and sell. They take substantial amounts of my time to manage, and certainly begin to put a limitation on the number of deals that we can coordinate at any one period of time. If you look at the big dry erase board in my office, you see 13 different addresses listed on the board. Two years ago, I would not have believed that we would have 13 different projects going at once. What I am realizing at this point in my career, though, is that we are beginning to see our capacity limitations. We are at a point when we have to make a decision on the future growth of our enterprise. We can be the king of the small $20,000 deals and hire more people to increase our portfolio, or we can begin to focus on larger deals.

There was a time when I was so excited about a $20,000 deal. We could find a shell, spend a year developing and building this house, and when we got to the table some 12-14 months later and received that check for $20,000, I was in bliss. It seemed like it was taking candy from a baby. Now, when the interns in the office (4 in number) bring me these deals where I can make $15,000-$20,000, I find myself scoffing at the numbers and telling them that I have no interest in tying up $15,000 in capital for 6 months just to make 10 or 15 thousand in cash. Is there something wrong with me, where I don't want to double my money in 6 months? Actually, it is the work and headaches that I have to endure in order to make that $10,000, leading to my becoming lazier and more unwilling to accept the potential deals. So Pete and I decided that I have to start focusing on larger deals where $50,000-$100,000 in profits becomes the normal margin on these deals. This is why I have begun to focus on commercial projects, including office buildings and shopping centers, while Pete focuses on subdivision of residential tracks of land. At any rate, the numbers on this Fells Point deal are exactly where we need to be. The first step in developing this project is to get an architectural diagram of exactly what we want to do to the buildings. Once we have this plan approved by both the city and the historical district board, we will bid out the project to several larger construction companies. This is hugely important. Over the past year, Pete has really struggled with our current contractor. The contractor has delayed our projects and has caused a significant amount of stress in the office. We suffer these setbacks in order to save money, but we've quickly come to understand that it would be better to pay top dollar for a quality contractor, and not have to constantly worry about meeting deadlines and having the expense of carrying these loans for longer periods of time. So, here we are now, poised to offer a larger contractor a job worth $500,000 to $600,000 in construction revenues. Our goal will be to have several bids come in, and select the contractor that has the best quality and is able to manage the project with the most efficiency. It will be interesting to see how this project turns out, as it really does symbolize the next step in the company's growth and future.

Before I cut out for the month, I want to jot down a few thoughts on my present state of mind regarding both my happiness in real estate and in my personal life. I cannot help but feel that the decision I made several years ago was one of the best decisions of my life. When you get into your thirties and are raising a family, you start to look at life through a different lens. I am starting to think about life and what is most important in my life. I have two young kids that love me to pieces, and I love them more than words can describe. I enjoy spending as much time as possible with them at these early ages. You see, when kids are young, you are their hero. When I arrive from work, they can't wait to jump into my arms, give me a hug, and have some quality time with their favorite playmate. I try to savor these moments because I know that they are fleeting. There will come a time when they just do not have any time or patience to spend with their father, and their friends will take my place as their favorite playmate. I know that this time will come, and I have certain self-inflicted rules that just do not get broken. It is incredibly important for me to be home with my family every night for dinner. Many of my friends leave for work before their kids awake, and then return home after their kids are asleep. It would break my heart to go a full day without seeing my kids. I intentionally put less emphasis on my work schedule than on scheduling time to spend with my children. Another rule which I am slowly adopting is the protection of my weekends. You see, real estate is typically sold on weekends. People go shopping for houses on weekends, and agents need to get in touch with me on weekends. I seldom go into the office or show a house on a weekend day, though, and recently I have moved to not even answering my cell phone as it rings all weekend long. I sometimes wonder how business was conducted without the constant accessibility of the cell phone. By choosing real estate as my career, I have managed to reduce the time away from my children and I have managed to really get a grip on my daily schedule. This aspect of my personal life has meshed well with my professional aspirations. The recurring problem with my plan is time.

As I approach 35 years of age, I realize the limitation time has on my goals. With two kids soon to attend private school, college tuitions to start saving for more earnestly, and finally retirement, all these concerns are lingering as a constant question of how much time I can really afford to give my kids now, without risking their or my financial futures. This is where I think real estate has been one of the best decisions of my life. Through the constant flipping and developing of projects, I can earn enough day-to-day income to support my family and save for college. Saving for retirement is truly one of the most difficult portions of the equation. Assuming that I was not involved with real estate and had still hoped to save the magic $2 million, I would have to have saved $100,000 for about 20 years running in order to have that kind of money in my retirement account. Sure, that does not take into consideration the time value of money, but even if I had Pete go through the exact numbers, they would still be more that I could afford to put aside in any given year. Rental properties all but force me to set aside money now for retirement – it just makes too much sense not to, since that's why we have them in many ways. Furthermore, if I continue to own the properties for 30 years, and have them all paid off, this becomes my retirement nest egg. As far as I am concerned, real estate provides me with the completeness of spending time with my family, having a substantial enough annual income to enjoy all of the joys of an affluent family, and allows me to save and earn tons of equity towards retirement. Whether or not real estate works out and this book ever makes it to publication, Signature Properties has really given me all that a career could give someone.

LESSONS LEARNED

- The Law of 72 states that your money will double as a function of interest rate and time. Divide your interest rate into 72 to see how long you have until your money doubles.

- Flipping is great for income, but owning is great for growth. Buy and hold some real estate.

- *Who Moved My Cheese?* – When the profits from one area start to dry up due to competition, keep moving to other areas in order to maintain high profits.

FELLS POINT

August 2003

These last 2 months have really been a roller coaster of ups and downs for both me and Pete, as well as the company. My last chapter talked about the excitement that we experienced with the purchase of the Fells Point property. We'll go to closing this week on that property, and let me explain to you a few of the details of the deal that has transpired. Here is where we stood 60 days ago, when we had just purchased the property at auction: We were excited about the prospects of what we were going to do with this bar. We had discussions about what we think will be the best use for the piece of land. The existing structure had elements that were originally constructed in the late 1700's, so we knew that we would run into some conflict with the historical preservation society in Baltimore City. The gentleman that was selling the property is a local physician. He bought the property with a vision for 4 small apartments on the upper level and a Spanish style café on the lower level. This idea would be perfect for this part of town. You see, people like to come to this area to window shop and walk the streets. There is also a segment of yuppies that like to call Fells Point their home. After many hours of discussions and hypotheticals, we decided to build four luxury garage townhouses. Over the past 8 or 9 years, sections of this area have gone through significant renovations. Townhouses are now selling for up to $500,000. So, here we were deciding on what to build on this tavern lot in Fells Point, and we came to the conclusion that we are going to build the nicest, most elegant, spacious houses that we could have ever thought of putting there. To top it off, we will have off-street parking and a location that should be able to command great market values.

Now that we have come to the decision of what we are going to put there, how do we do it? Our first meeting came just 10 days after the auction. This was a meeting with the Baltimore City Zoning and Planning Department. We went to this meeting prepared with designs and plans and packets and folders. We weren't sure what they were going to ask us, and quite frankly, we were scared that they might not let us build the vision that we had. So Pete, Dan, Jeff (a new full-time employee) and I all went to the meeting down at the city offices. Much to our surprise, the gentleman handling our request was easy to talk to, helpful, and basically put us at ease, saying that putting four residences there, with off-street parking, is probably the easiest plan to get past the community and historical committee. For over 10 years, developers have submitted plans for this plot. These plans included bars, cafés, and apartments, and all were shot down for one reason or another. Our plan seemed to have merit. The other tidbit I took from this meeting was that, while this project was large for Signature Properties, this was an extremely small project for zoning and planning. They told us that we should anticipate two more approval meetings with the community and the historical preservation society, and following that we should be ready to build. This was certainly a big relief. You see, when it comes to the typical Signature rehab or contract assignment, we buy and profit without giving it a second thought. These deals have become second nature to us. But as you grow into bigger and larger deals, the uncertainty begins to keep you up at night. You wonder why this land has not been built on before. Has the city slammed every proposal before, and is there a chance that we will be sitting on a piece of property that could potentially be worthless to us? Could it be us holding an auction to get rid of it next year because our plans have failed? I'm usually not kept up at night...but unfortunately, Pete sometimes is kept up at night, and with just these types of questions.

I told you that I really have a make-it-happen attitude. I jump into many deals and find a way to work them out. I like to compare my partner and me to Tiger Woods and Fred Couples. Everyone knows Tiger Woods: he's the best golfer in the world. Most of you may have heard of Fred Couples, but many non-golfers probably have not. Freddy is a great golfer. He has been for many years. When I watch golf tournaments on the weekends, I always see Freddy's name somewhere on the leader board. I seldom, if ever, see his name on the first page of the board, but he usually is in the money somewhere. Basically, Fred is a great par golfer. He can go out onto just about any course and shoot pars all the way around. This allows him to make a great living at the game of golf, but never really shoots him to the top of the game. Now, Tiger is a totally different story. Watching Tiger play golf is extremely exciting. I have seen Tiger play out of the woods, out of the traps, over water, out of the weeds, and from just about every other unimaginable place that a professional golfer should not be hitting out of. These are places that only the true hacker like myself gets to see during a round of golf. Do you know why Tiger is always playing out of crazy spots? It's because every time he hits the ball, he is trying to make a birdie or an eagle. He is aggressive and creative with his shot making. Sometimes it works and sometimes it doesn't. If the ball ends up in a not-so-fantastic location, it's not a problem; he provides the solution with a great recovery shot. Tiger may make his share of bogeys, but it's a fact that most of the time he is hitting birdies and eagles, so that everyone remembers his name. You see, he wins tournaments by taking chances. These are chances that Freddy is not willing and may not be able to make. When it comes to investing in real estate, I am willing to take incredible risks in order to shoot the birdies and eagles. We have had some bogeys along the way, but we have certainly had our fair share of winners. This is the looming problem that is starting to become more obvious with Pete and I's partnership at this point in our development.

I do not have the time to do the required due process that Pete needs in order to sleep well at night. Pete requires so much analysis on every decision we get into that we will never have an opportunity to go for the proverbial 'green in two'. We were having lunch the other day, and the discussion was very much directed at risk. Pete asked me if I could delay a decision just another day in order to gather more information about the decision, which would in turn increase my odds for success 100%, so wouldn't I take the extra day? Now, for those of you who don't understand psychology, this is as loaded a question as they come. Of course I have to respond yes, because why would anyone choose *not* to gather more information if they could increase their odds for success 100%. At the time, I didn't have the correct comeback, and wasn't able to truly present a logical argument, but when the subject came up again the following week, I was poised and ready. If you took that extra day to gather the additional information needed to increase your odds of success, would you ever buy the property? You see, if you took yet another day to increase your odds for success another 100%, wouldn't you take just one more day? Continue this on into eternity, and the end result is that you will never buy a property, and completely paralyze the company. For those of you who are not formally educated, this process of careful (and slow) analysis is what you learn in a master's degree program in business administration. The focus of MBA programs is analysis. They want you to think of every possible outcome before it happens. They want you to analyze all potential permutations of a decision, no matter how ridiculous. What they are teaching is meant to be loss prevention techniques to make a complete decision, but in actuality, they are teaching business professionals not to act on their guts. The best business leaders are the ones that have created unforeseen opportunity, acting on their guts. When Bill Gates came up with the operating system for Windows, he was turned down by every major manufacturer of computer equipment, including IBM. Why? The reason is that business professionals were looking for a tool for analysis to compare his platform to. They were looking for research and comparable products, but there were none. Eventually, Bill took his gut and created Microsoft. I'm sure that you have all heard of Microsoft. If Bill had taken years and years trying to find research and analysis to see if his gut theory of an integrated platform would be successful, he never would have pulled the trigger on his idea.

In all fairness, Pete and I do make a wonderful team. He is the analytical yin to my cowboy-shooting risk-taking yang. So don't get the wrong idea about Pete just yet. He certainly has reason to be concerned and lacking in sleep. I recently did the financial accounting for the past few years, and showed you how I have accumulated a net worth approaching a million dollars. One of the key components that is left out of this equation is cash in the bank. At this point, both Pete and I are carrying incredible amounts of debt. The company has lines of credit up to $175,000 that are exhausted, both of us personally have lines of credit that are exhausted, and the overhead at the company continues to grow as we bring on more employees. I am carrying a personal debt of about $40,000, which I would really like to hammer down one of these days. The prospects for the next six months are great, but right now, at this point in time, we are surviving on very little money. Over the past 3 months, I have taken a total of $6,000 out of Signature Properties. And trust me, it's not easy living on $2,000 per month. My wife and I run the bank accounts down to $0 each month, and I hope a deal closes just to carry us through to the next mortgage payment. She grew somewhat concerned when the checking account balance truly was at $17. So, how and why can I continue to buy nice things and go on nice vacations? One thing that I have learned about real estate is that it is, to the extreme, a matter of feast or famine. When we close a deal, I tend to deposit $20,000 in the bank, but when I don't close a deal, the lean times are really lean. One of the biggest problems that we are encountering now, related to cash, is Fells Point.

The Fells property cost us $367,500. We are looking for an

additional $550,000 in construction money from the bank. On a commercial deal this size, the bank is looking for a 20% down payment on the purchase of the land, or $73,500, plus costs we will incur to another $30,000 in fees just to close on the property. We need to come up with $103,500 just to get into this deal. To make a stressfully long story short, we don't have enough money to close, and we go to closing this Friday. We certainly can't tap anymore lines of credit because they are already beat. I've been working feverishly over the past month to try to get lenders to write second mortgages on all of the rental properties in an attempt to try to cash in on all of that equity. On commercial seconds, banks don't like to go higher than 75% loan in relation to value, and that is already where we're at on most of these properties. The fund has about $60,000, we haven't bought anything in over two months due to the cash shortage, and we can't personally take any money out of the company to live on as we have these pestering operating expenses to run the company. So, you may see why this has been a somewhat stressful period for a few months. But a solution is soon to come. I've begun reading a series of real estate wealth-building books about how to buy property for no money down. The key is in the seller financing. Now, I am like most people and I think that these deals just don't exist, but dire circumstances require thinking outside of the box. I contacted the doctor who's selling us the Fells property. I explained to him that this property is going to cost us over $100,000 in out-of-pocket expenses. I told him that we are a growing company and, while we can raise the money to come to the closing table on Friday, it really would strangle the company for about a year, so that if there was any way at all for him to provide $50,000 in seller financing, it would really be a help for a couple of young investors. I was asking him to write a second mortgage on the property so that we can close this week. He would eventually get his $50,000 back and a nice interest rate. He took the easy way out and told me that he had to run it past his wife, as she is his business partner. I then received a quick message on my voicemail telling me that, unfortunately, he wanted to pay off a line of credit with the proceeds, and his line of credit was carrying an interest rate of 12.9%. I was just not ready to give up yet. I thought that if I could cover the payments on *his* line of credit, then it will still solve everyone's problem. Since I was going out of town, I told Pete to call him back and negotiate to pay him 13% or even 15%, just to have him hold that second mortgage.

I got an email back this morning and, wouldn't you know it, the good doctor is going to step in and help us out. He is willing to hold $50,000 in seller financing at 15% interest. Again, it is amazing what can be accomplished by simply asking for things. We would probably not be able to close this deal had we not asked the good doctor to hold seller financing. That frees up $50,000 to grow the company. That was a very exciting email to read this morning, and also gave me a growing sense of excitement in that I may be able to find more of these no-money-down deals. The other bit of fantastic news on that email was that an investor who we have been courting for quite some time is going to buy 10 shares of the Fund for $60,000. Perhaps things are looking up a little bit. I have put myself on a quest to raise money for the Fund. We have been stifled recently by some setbacks and cash flow problems, many of which could be solved with some additional investors into the fund. I sent out a group email to all of my graduating MBA buddies, and as of last week, I have about 10 replies with an interest in becoming investors. We'll see if any of this pans out for us.

April 2004

My last entry was made way back in August of 2003. As the business of real estate gets more and more time consuming, I find that I have less free time to write down my thoughts as they happen. Let me start by running through what is on the plate for this month, and then attempt to fill in with some update reports on the various projects. In regards to the Fells Point project, which is an ongoing challenge, we have finally received the approval of the historic preservation society on the demolition of two of the four parcels. With that, we've commissioned an architect to put together some prospective drawings. Our instructions to the architect were to make them edgy. We would really like to build some super high-end luxury townhouses that could potentially draw the highest dollar per square foot in the area. The drawings that he came back with are fantastic. They have a ton of open space, which is entirely uncommon in the city rowhomes. Within the next week, we should receive what they call bid documents, which include the fixtures and finishes of the whole project. From there, we can get some bids from the various subcontractors and decide exactly how much we want to invest on this project. The numbers keep inflating in my head. I constantly have dreams of how high the area will appreciate, and how much money we will make on a project like this. My current estimate, which changes by the second, is that the homes will sell for $500,000 each. Now, keep in mind that we purchased the properties for $367,000, and we are currently in them for $425,000, which includes all of the architectural fees, carry costs, and closing expenses. So, we are into each lot for about $109,000. We estimate spending about $200,000 construction on each property. That would bring out hard costs up to $309,000, plus another $50,000 in carry expenses to be paid out over the next 12 months. From $359,000, we can add $28,000 in commissions and $7,000 in transfer fees. So, by the time we're ready to sell the properties, we should be in them for $394,000, each. The net profit should be about $106,000 each, times four properties, netting us $424,000 on the deal. We are fairly excited about the deal, obviously, but not nearly as excited as we are about the fact that we picked up 2 more lots over in Federal Hill which have the same financial metrics. When all six of these properties are completed, we should net about $600,000.

Let me tell you a story about another exciting deal which actually started out as a fiasco. About 4 months ago, I sent Jeff (our salaried analyst) to look at an auction in a nice suburb of

Annapolis. He spent well over an hour at the property since it was vacant. He analyzed what he would do to the property if we were the successful bidder. He spoke with me on the phone, and together we decided to pay $230,000 max at the auction. Well, once at the auction, we ended up purchasing the property for $227,000. We went out to lunch, I congratulated Jeff on a job well done, and I proceeded to send out my "get out of the house" letters. Well, the homeowner returned my call and agreed to meet me one night that week. On the phone, he seemed extremely interested in making a deal...so off I went. The numbers on the street were fairly confusing; they seemed to jump around, but I eventually ended up at the vacant house that Jeff had bought. I found it somewhat interesting that this man lived in what appeared to be a vacant house, so I called him from the mobile phone. He answered the phone, and said in a laughing voice, "Hey Scott, you are at the vacant neighbor's house." My heart just about sank. This meant that Jeff had bought the wrong house. At least, he'd thought that he was buying the right house, but had ended up buying a house that no one had looked at, no one had analyzed, and no one had even established a market value for that property. So, here I was proceeding to walk through a house that I just spent $227,000 on, and without having the faintest idea what the house was worth. Could it be worth more? ....I should only be that lucky. The house ended up being slightly smaller, and in slightly better condition, but in the end only worth $275,000 instead of the $325,000 we'd thought we could get out of the other house. Alright, so what kind of trouble did we get ourselves into? After closing costs, we are in the house for $250,000. Once we put the $15,000 in in construction required to make it pretty and resell it, we stand to just about break even. Boy, was that a lucky break.

So, the guy who was losing the house allowed me to try to assign my contract by letting me stick a for sale sign in his yard and putting it into the realtor MLS. The house got a lot of showings, but in its present condition, no one was even willing to give me $270,000 for the house. When the courts finally ratified the sale and we had to step up to close on the property, I pulled it off the market, and at that point I fully intended on doing the work to fix it up. Fast forward to several weeks ago. I'm stopping by the property just to make sure that the family has moved and that we can get started with our cosmetic makeover on the property. I'm perplexed, though, as to why both Jeff and I made the same mistake on the numbering of that street. Well, what had happened was that the house we'd bought has a very large garage, separate from the main house. This garage causes the numbers to skip between the house we thought that we were buying and the house that we had actually bought. The garage sits on its own lot, which would have been the appropriate number. Ahh: that's why Jeff and I made the same mistake. Now is when it gets interesting and, quite frankly, very, very exciting. I raced back to the office to pull up my land survey to see what exactly we own. The property consists of four small skinny lots. The existing house sits on two of the skinny lots, and the garage sits on another two skinny lots. The garage is completely separate from the house. If you haven't figured out where I am going with this, you are not alone. It took my partner a while to figure it out. I faxed the survey to a small builder friend of mine, and said "what do you think?" Well, she informed me that, if you knock down that garage, you have a buildable lot! Bingo. Lots in this neighborhood are selling for $125,000. Subtract out $20,000 to level the lot and remove the garage, and this fiasco just turned into a $100,000 deal. Again, sometimes it takes a little bit of luck to turn lemons into lemonade.

Speaking of big deals, do you remember the wall over at Lombard Street? It seems like years since I talked about that deal...and, well, it has been. We have owned that property for over two years now. That property will go to closing on April 22. The final price on the property will be $341,000. What a roller coaster that property was for Signature. We had trouble building it and then we had trouble selling it. In the end, the project will yield a tidy profit of $125,000, which we shouldn't be unhappy with, however, due to the constant pain over this deal, the money really is bittersweet.

Outside of these projects, we have another 10 foreclosure flips on the board, and we recently put a two parcel piece of land under contract to build a couple of townhomes over in Hamden. Our goal at Signature has been jumping around quite a bit. We want to continue purchasing and selling foreclosure properties. We need the cash flow, as the company burns through about $20,000 in salaries and overhead a month. Rental property income covers much of "our nut" – another term for burn rate – but as we continue to add staff and expenses, our cash needs continue to grow. The company has the tools in place to build itself into a much larger entity; the challenges really lie in the industry. The real estate business is incredibly difficult. You need to be able to negotiate, sell, finance, analyze, and be extremely tolerant of risk. There are only so many hours in the day to build this company, and training employees takes a substantial amount of time and money. I certainly understand that, someday, these employees will be responsible for running this entity and making it successful while I enjoy more leisure, but at present, the sacrifices are great. I find myself working longer hours, which lead to longer days, which lead to weekends, etc. In general, I still find real estate exciting, and I enjoy waking up every day to get into another deal, but in order to build a company and support the overhead, the business is very taxing. But, who ever said that getting rich was going to be easy?

Financing and Fundraising

One thing that I realize about real estate people is that they are asset-rich and cash-poor. I am quickly falling into that category. We currently own 21 rental properties, 10 foreclosure flips, 2 two lot projects, and the four lot project. All in all, there's about $6,000,000 worth of real estate in my portfolio. There are some days that I wake up and feel that this is a huge accomplishment, and there are other days that I stress about the lack of take-home pay Pete and I have. Pete and I have been feuding for several months now. I decided that this was going to be the year that the both of us start taking home a decent wage. My tax return for last year showed a whopping $27,000 from Signature Properties, and I vowed that this was going to be the year to change all of that. At the end of every month, we sit down and go over the financial statements, and each month the result is exactly the same as the month before. We just don't have the cash-flow to take any money out of the company this month. So, you must be asking how we can be having such incredible deals and not taking home any of the money. The reason is twofold. First, as I alluded to earlier, it takes about $20,000 to run the company each month. So while we continue to crank out $20,000 profits from deal, we need to close 12 of them per year just to feed the beast known as Signature Properties. This gobbles down a substantial amount of our profits. Second, we keep investing our money into additional projects, therefore never actually taking out the money. We have decided to solve the second problem by using more OPM, which stands for other people's money. I described the Fund earlier in the book. This money refers to the capital that we've raised in order to buy and sell residential flips and development projects. This is key in our ability to have $3,000,000 in construction projects on the books. But the big problem for us is the rental properties that we own. Over the past 18 months, we have bought and held 21 properties. If each property requires $20,000 to get into, we have reinvested about $400,000 of our money into this rental portfolio. Now, I realize that when I turn 55 and we own these properties free and clear, I will be thankful that I did this, but right now, when I am only pulling out $2,000 per month to live on, it is a tough pill to swallow. So, starting with the last several deals, we've decided to use OPM to purchase the rentals. Allow me to explain. With interest rates extremely low, the average bank account is yielding about 2%. What we offer our investors in the rentals is real estate backed money, personally guaranteed by Pete and me, paying out at an interest rate of 12%. This sounds pretty good to our investor pool, and thus far, we have raised $125,000 for residential rental properties.

The rental portfolio has truly become a focus for Signature, especially the college rental properties. We are learning the incredible cash flow potential in this market, and have tried to capitalize on it as quickly as possible. We started in this townhouse community, purchasing 5 units from the original developer. There are 20 units total in the complex. Over the past 13 months, I have picked up an additional 5 units, bringing my total to 10 units in this complex. Connected to the property are two townhouses on a large piece of land. I have bought both of these, and will probably knock down both houses and build five more college rentals on the lot, with the anticipation of having them online next June. Just last month, the phone started ringing with students looking to sign leases for my 10 units in the complex. The units quickly filled up, but I continued to have phone calls from interested students. Instead of letting this incredible opportunity slide by, I decided to go out with the intent on purchasing houses for these groups of students that were calling. So, imagine this: you are the parent of one of these Loyola students, and you get a call from your son which goes a little something like this: "Dad, you know how we were looking for off campus housing? Well, this guy picked us up at school in his Mercedes, he bought us all lunch, and then he took us out to look at some properties. We found one that we like, so he said that he would buy it for us."

I joked with my wife and thought how absolutely preposterous this must have sounded. In the end, several of the parents did want to meet me at the properties so that I could show them the units. I'm sure that they really wanted to meet me to make sure that nothing funny was going on. At any rate, we purchased two single family houses to turn into college rentals. We bought one for $110,000, which will rent for $1,600 per month, and one for $227,000, which will rent for $2,800 per month. Both will yield a cash flow of about $7,000 per year. So, by the time construction is complete on the 5 new homes, we will have 17 college rentals which are each yielding an average of $8,000 per year, 7 single family homes yielding about $3,000 per year, and an office building kicking out $75,000 per year. When planning for cash flow, we should have about $230,000 a year in positive cash flow from rental properties alone. That means that, if I wanted to stop working next June, I would live off of $115,000 per year for the next 25 years, and more than that after the projects are paid off. This is one of those times I think, wow, I really have accomplished a lot over the past 3 years. However, my goal is to continue to build a vibrant and growing investment development company.

So, where exactly am I on the net worth picture? Using a capitalization rate of 10%, the rental portfolio as it stands is worth $3,200,000, we owe roughly $2,000,000, the equity in my house has escalated to $230,000, and my cash investments stand at $50,000. That works out to be roughly $1.5 million without all of the developer profits that I hope to realize when all of the construction is complete. I will remind you of something that my wife constantly reminds me of, though….it isn't our money until it hits our account. So I am holding back from running out there to spend the profits before they are actually realized

May 2004

As I briefly review the last paragraph or so of text, I see that this is a great time to include my personal financial picture. We have a line of credit at BB&T bank of about $75,000. I have a personal line of credit for $50,000 with BB&T as well. We are in discussions with the bank to refinance our entire loan package, at hopefully a better rate than the 6.75% that we currently pay to Severn Savings Bank. We have about $2 million in loans, and hope to save one percentage point on the refinance. That equates to $20,000 a year, just for completing some paperwork. One of the pieces of paperwork is the personal financial statement. This statement asks you to put down all of your assets and all of your liabilities. In the end, you come up with a number that you are personally worth. They call it your net worth, and this is the crux of this entire book. At any rate, I listed all of my assets…my personal assets, not including my wife's interest in half of our primary residence, and came up with a personal net worth of $1.2 million. In previous net worth analysis, I was using the expected equity that I had in all of my development deals. This $1.2 million does not include any of that. You see, if I look at what projects are up on the development board and try to predict my portion of the profits, the total net worth number would be another $200,000. Basically, I want to be able to say that I could sell everything that I own and have over two million in cash to live off for the rest of my life, and know that that is personally true. Right now, I could indeed sell off everything and have $1,000,000 in my pocket. Again, I go back and forth between if this is a substantial amount of money or not in terms of what I want to accomplish with these same finances, but for now, I am pleased that over the last 18 months, I have managed to set aside $700,000 in equity in my net worth. While I have been relatively cash-starved for the past year, and my tax returns reflect about $50,000 in income, I've actually earned in excess of $500,000 per year, assuming that you include all of the money that I have amassed from savings, appreciation, and all the other great things that come along with owning and investing in real estate. I have absolutely no doubt at all that real estate is the fastest way to accumulate wealth, and I am really just touching the surface of what is out there and available.

If you are reading this book and thinking about real estate as a method of accumulating wealth, take my word for it…it is nice to put together a personal financial statement that says "hey, you are a millionaire by age 35". Let me tell you a scary thing. When I was in my 20's, I said that I would be a millionaire by 35, but I am not sure I knew what that meant. At the time, I was making pizzas for $5.35 an hour, but I had a dream, and it is certainly enjoyable to see that I have fulfilled that dream.

So, what happened this last month or so that was exciting? We finally closed on the wall rehabilitation project on Lombard Street. This project literally beat me to death. It was tough to build, tough to sell, and tough to close. But when we finally closed on the deal, we realized a profit of $110,000. Pete and I paid off some debt from the transaction, and each took a check for $35,000. I tell you what: it felt pretty good to go from a bank account with roughly $700 in it to over $35,000. This year has actually been a pretty rewarding year for me in terms of short-term cash flow. The nuclear seminar has been good to me, and now with Signature beginning to kick in, I have managed to take roughly $90,000 in salary this year, by the end of May. My wife is pleased, my kids have new furniture, my landscaping is complete, and tension is slightly lighter at the Benjamin household this spring. I know that money does not necessarily bring happiness, but it certainly makes the attitude a whole lot happier around the house. The money is coming, albeit slowly, but I am also getting something far more important than the money. I am seeing my boys grow up. I never miss a dinner, I could not imagine missing a baseball game, and I never go an entire day without seeing my family. There is no amount of money, no fast-track to success, that could keep that away from me. I think that I need to email my partner Pete and tell him that I couldn't be happier with our current status. The company rolls along. I should make and save $200,000 this year. I hope to set aside in equity another $500,000 in investment, and all of this with really working less than 40 hours per week. While there are occasions when things seem shaky at Signature Properties, all in all, I have put together something that is extremely desirable to me and my family, and enviable to many young fathers.

As always, I like to provide you with a deal update just so you know what is on the board. The big project is the Fleet Street project. This is the construction of four new luxury townhomes in Fells Point. We are still awaiting the final architectural drawings for this project. Next will come the demolition of the burned down tavern, which will provide for 2 open lots. There have been some grumblings from Pete and Dan recently, considering whether we ought to sell the four lots "as is" and cash out. Since we have already run into roadblocks from the historic preservation people and with the architect, they are seeing the difficulty with actually building these projects. We bought these lots at auction for $367,000. After carry expense, site planning, and architectural fees, we are at $410,000 for the four lots, or about $103,000 per lot. The lots are probably worth $180,000 each with all of the work that we have put in so far. So, after we incur some selling expenses, we would net around $70,000 profit per lot. With four lots, I can certainly see their enthusiasm for a $280,000 profit waiting in the wings. What I am seeing is a new development about 4 blocks down from our lots that has 6 houses being listed for $749,000 - $799,000. Now, they look like super high-end townhomes, but nothing says that we cannot build equally nice homes with the right budget. So, recently I have been pitching Pete and Dan that, if we were to get $650,000 per house and were willing to increase our construction budget from $160,000 to $200,000, we would be into each house for around $350,000 after all of the costs of building out the project. But now each house could potentially yield $300,000, or $1.2 million in total.

No question: these numbers are certainly more exciting to me than $280,000. It's true that I don't expect to get $650,000 for each house, but I can hope and plan on maybe a $800,000 pay-day when all is said and done. Now, the split on that is that 25% goes to the Fund ($200,000), leaving $600,000 to be split between Scott, Pete, and Dan. This would be a $200,000 payday which could be realized somewhere around next spring. That would be an ideal way to start 2005.

The next biggest project on the board is that of 6006 and 6008 York Road. These will end up being rental properties for us if all goes well. We hope to build 5 townhouses to rent to college students by the spring of next year. We should accumulate instant equity of $50,000 per unit, or $250,000 for the project. I originally started looking at this deal about a year ago. The deal was just about as unorthodox as every other big deal that we have had in real estate. Across the street from the main complex of our college rental properties stands this big old house with a sign on it that says "Psychic Inside". The house sits on a huge lot, which should be able to be subdivided into 5 lots. About a year ago, the house had a 'for sale by owner' sign stuck in the front lawn. I called the number on the sign, and the psychic answered and immediate said, "I know why you're calling". That was a joke, if you got it... psychic and knowing why I called…alright, I will stick to writing about real estate. So anyway, I made an appointment to see the house and was met by the owner's nephew. The house was in dire condition, but was certainly a big enough house, sporting over 3,000 square feet of living space. The nephew informed me that the house was going through foreclosure, and that in order to stop the foreclosure, it would take over $130,000. That was close to what I would pay for the house if it was in good condition, but in its current condition, this price appeared to be slightly steep. I let it go and forgot about the house for about a year. Well, just the other day, while culling through the multiple list service database, I came across the house listed as a bank REO property for $52,000. I jumped on it and submitted a cash offer, as is, with a quick close, without even needing to look at the property. If you remember, I had already walked through the property and would probably have paid close to $100,000 for the property. When my contract was accepted, I was jumping for joy. The property offered many options. I could remodel the house into one huge fraternity house and rent it to students, or I could knock down the house and build four or five brand new college rental properties, and really cash in. I was celebrating this purchase at $52,000 and patting myself on the back. Well, two days prior to the closing, I was just reviewing the public records on my upcoming purchase, and realized that according to the city, that house was zoned as a duplex. I didn't remember seeing two separate units – it had looked like one very large house. I went by the house to look at it, and low and behold, someone had put up a wall dividing the house in half. This had not been there when I'd originally looked at the house last year. When I called the REO agent to inquire what exactly I had contracted to purchase for $52,000, it was shockingly explained to me that I had purchased the right half of a duplex.

Are you kidding me? The agent knew that I thought that the purchase was for the entire house; the agent knew that the city had boarded up the entire house, making it appear as if it was one house; and the agent knew that he was sandbagging me into the purchase. Well, you know what, I was a licensed real estate agent and I should have known better. Not only that, but I've bought houses sight unseen before and had dire consequences. Shame on me. So I decided to go through with the purchase. I did buy half of that shack, and I was focused on finding out who owned the other half. After closing, I searched high and low through public records, mortgages, titles… you name it, I searched it. I went through the internet and finally found the name of the person who owned the property (it was the psychic), but I could not find her anywhere. After about 2 weeks of searching, I gave up and decided to fix up one half of the house and make it into a nice 5 bedroom rental unit for next year's students. We put a dumpster in the yard and started gutting the inside. Unbeknownst to me, my property manager Mike had left a stack of my business cards with the crew that was doing the interior demolition of the property. One night, while I was sitting at home with the family, my cell phone rang. The guy on the other end was a private investor who had loaned money to the owner of the other half of the duplex. He was driving by and stopped in to peak around. Mike gave him my business card. "Can you locate the women who owns the other half of the house?" I asked. Not only did he locate her, but he ended up getting her to sign a contract for the purchase of her half of the property for $50,000. We ended up closing about 2 weeks later, with a women who had to be in her early 100's, after the private lender picked her up at her house and delivered her to the closing, and we were now the proud owners of the entire lot. Now we could officially party, and the dance was back on. Since then, we have met with a company that installs prefabricated townhouses, and can have 5 townhouses installed on this site in about 2 months after the completion of all of the engineering work. So, after lot purchase and townhouse installation, we are looking at roughly $150,000 per townhouse, with each one having four bedrooms. We will rent these for $2,000 per month with a debt service of roughly $900. Once you allocate taxes and insurance, and extremely minor repair and maintenance, we should have cash flow of $10,000 per unit, or $50,000 per year.

Rewarding the Crew

Things have been going fairly well this year. We've been accumulating some development deals, some rental deals, some new construction deals, and overall we're making some decent Jack. We decided to reward the crew with dinner last night. We took 10 people to dinner at an extremely fancy restaurant in Ellicott City, Maryland. The place is called Jordan's Steakhouse, and boy do they know how to cook a steak. The total bill for the ten of us was $960, and it was so long that it looked like a grocery bill. Not that we have made it just yet, but it feels pretty good to go out to one of the nicest restaurants around, order the most expensive things on the menu, drink expensive wine, and eat expensive desserts. I think that the crew enjoyed it and I know that both my wife and I enjoyed the food and the company.

There is another part of this business that I have really grown to enjoy. I really enjoy getting people into the business. The intern program has been a great opportunity to introduce young students to the business and watch as they grow through the hands-on experience gained at Signature Properties. I have also helped real estate agents learn a great deal about the business. Not long ago, Laura, an agent in my brokerage office, cornered me and asked me tons of questions about the topic of foreclosure. Apparently, she had been working with an investor in an attempt to find properties, but was not having a whole lot of success in her search. Laura called me about 2 weeks after our talk, and low and behold, she had purchased her first foreclosure. Not only that, but she'd ended up outbidding the guy that I had sent to that auction. I was extremely happy for her, even though I thought that she had overpaid for the property. I subsequently fielded several phone calls from Laura, further describing the process to her and to her investor. To make a long story short, they ended up selling the property and profiting $35,000 off of the deal. I guess I missed out on a good one. She was extremely grateful for the education, and I felt great for being able to help someone get involved in the purchase of foreclosure real estate. On another occasion, I was at an auction in Annapolis one day, and after the auction, a gentleman named Jim walked with me to my car. During the walk, he explained to me that he and his wife were interested in getting involved in buying foreclosures, and that I'd seemed to know what I was doing at the auction; little did he know that I am relatively new myself to the business. I offered to meet him and his wife for breakfast and teach them a little about how I buy discounted real estate. Jim and his wife were bright, and seemed eager to learn the business. Well, after attending about a dozen auctions, they too bought their first piece of foreclosure real estate. Their deal was extra special. It ended up that, attached to the house that they'd purchased, was a buildable lot. The lot alone was valued at $90,000, so they really cleaned up with this purchase. After the purchase, they brought me a bottle of red wine from a vineyard called Caymus.

One evening when my wife and I had just finished cooking up a nice batch of macaroni and cheese, we decided that we wanted to have some wine with this dinner. So upon my wife's request, we opened up the bottle of Caymus and really enjoyed the wine. We have a relatively cheap palette when it comes to wines, but his really did hit the spot as it washed down the mac and cheese. About a week later, we were out and about, and stopped at the liquor store to pick up a bottle of wine. My wife asked me to pick up another bottle of that Caymus which we'd thought was so good the other night. When I came out with our typical bottle of Kendall Jackson (not that there is anything wrong with Kendall

Jackson), she asked if our store didn't carry the Caymus. And oh, they did indeed carry the bottle, but I wasn't interested in spending $65 on a bottle of wine. Call me cheap, but maybe someday I will splurge on my wine to that level. Jim and his wife have since brought me 6 more bottles of wine since they've had further success with their purchases. Thanks, Jim, from both me and my wife!

Since I was getting so much satisfaction from teaching others about the business, Pete and I decided to try our hand at education. I picked two sites to hold some real estate investment lectures at, one in Annapolis and one in Baltimore. I developed a flyer and distributed it to every real estate agent in the three nearest counties. My next target market was investors. I distributed flyers to the local investors club, and attended several auctions and handed out flyers at these as well. I ran ads in the newspapers and in the classifieds. The end result was about 20 people at the Baltimore seminar and about 30 people at the Annapolis seminar. I put together a slide show and handouts, and I was ready to go. I also realized that I needed something to sell at the seminar. I put together a toolkit of forms and documents that I have developed and used over the past several years. I charged $99 to attend the 3 hour lecture and $149 for the foreclosure toolkit. When all of the numbers were added up, we made about $3,000 in profit from the two lectures. Certainly not the boondoggle that I had hoped for, but again, I felt a certain sense of satisfaction in knowing that I had helped 50 people get exposed to my specialty. Where I go from here, I'm just not sure. I am planning on offering several more seminars to other counties in Maryland; I am planning on offering this material on the website, and ultimately I may present this material to different investor clubs around the country. There are a lot of possibilities for the education side, but I just need to find the energy to start to capitalize on them. The downside to the education business is that it is fairly time intensive to organize and market these seminars. If I am spending my time organizing a seminar, it means that I am not out on the street finding my next deal. The money from the seminars is marginal, and the return on the real estate is phenomenal. So, we will see if anything happens with the education side, but I do find it to be a passion for me, helping others get into the business.

The big question: what is on the horizon for Scott and Signature Properties? I am quickly learning that holding onto real estate is the true way to accumulate wealth. On occasion, I will look back to some of the deals that we sold over the past year and see that their value has continued to grow. I try not to have second thoughts about selling them, but I have to remind myself that I needed the cash to live, survive, travel, and have peace of mind. I am hungrier now than ever before to find more and more rental properties. The more that I can find and sock away, the quicker I will reach my ultimate goal. We just picked up a duplex with a 3 bedroom and a 4 bedroom apartment. The contract price is $210,000. We will get a loan from the bank for 90% of the $210,000, which works out to be $190,000. The monthly payment on this, including taxes and insurance, is about $1,500 per month. Our goal over the next 30 days is to raise $30,000 cash for the down payment and closing costs on the deal. We will pay 10% interest on that money, which works out to be $275 per month. When you factor in another $200 per month for repair and maintenance, we'll be out of pocket $1,975 per month. The property is conveniently located between two college campuses. When we fill the units with college kids paying $500 per room, we'll have $3,500 per month coming in revenues. That is a positive cash flow of over $1,500 per month, or $18,000 per year. Kabam, the deals keep getting better and better. Not only that, but let's calculate the market value of the property to an investor using a 10% cap rate. The revenues on the house are $3,500 per month, or $42,000 per year. Subtract out $2,400 per year in repair and maintenance, $2,400 per year in taxes, and another $1,000 per year in insurance, and you have a NOI on the property of $36,200. To an investor, this house may be worth $362,000. We just paid $210,000 for it. We manufactured $152,000 in net worth by locating, financing, and filling the property with its highest and best use. College rentals get contagious, and I hope that you can see why. So Pete and I are truly focusing on purchasing as many of these things as we can find. Our model seems to be working well thus far, and we hope to continue with this growth pattern over the short term.

LESSONS LEARNED

- Don't be afraid to take risks, but make sure that they are educated risks. Requiring 100% certainty will result in the paralysis of analysis.
- Be creative. Sometimes the highest and best use of the property requires you to step back and take a second look.
- Always pay forward your knowledge.

LOCATION, LOCATION, LOCATION

July 2004

I remember reading a book called *Good to Great* by Jim Collins. One of the things that stood out in the book was that great leaders create a list. Most people create a "to do list". This is a list of things that can be checked off one at a time as they are completed. Completing these tasks feels good. It brings a sense of accomplishment as you leave for the day, that you have accomplished a great deal of things during the day. Well, great leaders do not create to do lists. Instead, they create lists of "things not to do". These lists are filled with the daily activities that can be delegated to others in the organization, things that take time and do not provide any advances to the company. Another item that sticks out in my mind about this book was that great leaders work *on* the business and not *in* the business. If you get caught up with the day to day activities of the company, you cannot find the time to look at the company as a whole and investigate what needs to be done to build the business. Now, reading about it and doing it are completely different things. Over the past 6 months, I have been working on Laura, the office manager, and Mike, the property manager wannabe, to take on more of the day-to-day operations of managing the properties. Everything from collecting rents to property maintenance; I had this vision that, as long as I was focusing on acquisition of property, these guys could handle all of the day-to-day management of the portfolios.

Unfortunately, it proved not to be quite so wonderful. As I

find my way back into the office, I am hounding tenants to pay their rent money, and I am telling Mike what to fix and where. Basically, I am getting sucked into the day-to-day operations of the business. As a control freak, I don't feel that I can let go of these responsibilities to others, as I am just not comfortable that they will handle the situations the same way that I would. Furthermore, I get frustrated at the slow learning curve, and simply say that I will do it myself. I understand how detrimental this is to my goals and the company. Delegation is the key to the growth of the company, but it is just so incredibly difficult for me to do! I have fantastic employees. Sometimes I ponder what exactly that means, to have fantastic employees. Well, first of all, they show up at work everyday. To me, this is a very important piece of the puzzle. If your employees enjoy their jobs enough to show up everyday, then you have accomplished 50% of the task. I am also pretty good at getting them to actually produce once they arrive at work. The part that I lack is how to motivate them to take on additional responsibilities without me having to probe and prod them along the way. I fully and completely understand the importance of human resource management…I am just not very good at it. One of the reasons that I enjoy real estate is that it is not a labor intensive business. I can do most of the elements of a transaction by myself, and if I want to find more profit, I simply increase the valuation of the project. I have always struggled with human resource management and I acknowledge this flaw. Well, as you can imagine, my days are running end to end. I look back on my goal of spending time with my children and realize that this goal is quickly slipping out of my grasp. I certainly need to reevaluate the way I am conducting my day-to-day business because I do not have time to even keep this diary, and the business is starting to run my life. For now, I will check out, but hopefully I will return soon, as I see the business taking on more of my time, and frankly, this is not how I envisioned spending my 35th year of life.

January 2005

Wow. Three years have gone by since I started writing this epoch. I don't think that I envisioned the process of becoming a multimillionaire as a three year endeavor…but here I am. I just calculated my estimated tax payment, which is due January 18th to the IRS. In order to do that, I went through all of the deposits that I made into my personal bank account, and estimated 28% of that. I have been making estimated payments along the way, but this year-end thing is really an eye opener. Since January 1st of 2004, I put $225,000 into my bank account. My wife and I still live extremely frugally. We live in the same house with the same $1,500 per month mortgage payment, which I might add is now worth $625,000, with only a $200,000 mortgage left on it. We carry no credit card debt, and I've managed to pay off all of those lines of credit that I ran up over the past 3 years in this business. This is pretty good, and I feel pretty comfortable. Things really clicked for me and the company this last year, and I accumulated a lot of equity and managed to live off of a great salary to boot. This is a far cry from where we were when this whole roller coaster ride began. So, the things that are fresh on my mind, which I hope to scribe on paper this month, include my current financial status, current Signature deals of interest, my recent fascination with the art of negotiation, and a new spiritual journey that I find myself beginning.

First, let me see exactly how much money I am worth. What's funny is that, while this was the goal of this book 3 years ago, now that I have a bank account with over $100,000 in cash, the money side has really taken second place in my brain. My focus is on the enjoyment of how I am spending my life, and the depth and meaning to it. At any rate, in keeping with the financial snapshot, let me pull up the one from the first chapter in order to do some comparisons.

Financial Snapshot

<u>**Written January 19, 2002**</u>	<u>**January 14, 2005**</u>
I own a house. My wife and I bought the house 5 years ago and have done very well with its appreciation. You'll get some details on this in chapters to come,	Still in the same house. New landscaping ($13,000) New baths ($4,000) New paint ($3,500)
Equity in House = $140,000	Equity in House = $425,000
As of January 2002, the stocks and funds markets have not been kind. I have two accounts.	Same two accounts… still suffering. Interesting how the stock market has suffered.
Stocks = $19,000 Funds = $13,000	Stocks = $19,000 Funds = $20,000

WOW… if the above two statistics about the stocks and funds don't hit home, what will? The house made $285,000 in appreciation and the stocks are up $7,000. I bought the house with $25,000 of my own money, and bought the stocks with $50,000 of my own money. Why would people invest in anything but real estate?

No IRA No Savings for College	SEP IRA = $25,000 College Savings = $20,000

Cash in the bank was something that I could not put on the initial snapshot. The reason being that my wife and I were living check to check. We kept a small token of money in the account, but not even enough to write down at that point since it would have been gone by the next sitting.

Now, it is with great pleasure that I can write down:

	Cash in Bank = $100,000
My wife drives a 1995 Jeep Grand Cherokee with 150,000 miles. (My car is a lease)	Wife drives a 2001 Toyota Seqouia with very little equity
Equity in her Car = $3,000 on a good day	I drive a 2000 Mercedes. Equity = $10,000

Now, for the fun stuff…the real estate. Signature Properties owns 21 rental properties. The equity in these properties currently stands at about $2.5 million, of which I own half.

So, the snapshot today is: $425,000 plus $39,000 plus $45,000 plus $100,000 plus $10,000 plus $1.25 million... equals $1.869 million. At the rate that the market has been appreciating and the rate that we are purchasing deals, this book should be done and completed by Christmas of 2005. What a present that would be, to have accomplished my goal in under 4 years!

I'm honestly feeling like the hard work is paying off. My schedule is pretty consistent now. I take my oldest son Noah to school each day. He starts school at 8:10 and it is about 10 minutes from the house. I tell you what – these are 10 of the best minutes of my day. We chat and joke and talk about life. From there, I go to Baltimore, which is about a 25 minute commute. The one thing that I am pretty good at doing is being extremely useful with my time. I am not one to chit-chat with other agents in the office or randomly surf the internet. I am diligent in working the business of real estate, whether it is acquiring properties, managing rentals, or handling the day–to-day operations of our company. I leave the office around 5:30 to 6:00 each day, and I am home for dinner by 6:30 each night. Many times, I'll leave work early for baseball practice, soccer practice, and the like, as these are the things that really keep me going each day. I never, and I mean never, work a Saturday or a Sunday. My only complaint at this point in my life is my relationship with my Blackberry. For those of you who do not understand this phenomenon, the Blackberry is a phone, a PDA, which allows you to receive emails anywhere in the world. This invention has altered the way business is done. I simply cannot remember how business was conducted if you could not be reached by phone or email at any time of the day, and in any location. I constantly check my emails, for what I don't know. If I leave the house without the almighty Blackberry, you'd think that I left the house with the gas running on the stove. I *will* turn around, regardless of how far from the house I have made it, to recover the almighty Blackberry. I can acknowledge this flaw and thank my wife for being extremely patient as I continue to deal with Blackberry Addiction Syndrome. So, you get the idea of my work week. I work roughly a 45 hour per week on an extremely selective schedule. Since last year was hugely successful, and since this year we already have many substantial projects on the books, my goal this coming year will be to work 4 days per week.

Speaking of having many substantial projects on the books for this year, allow me to explain how I have progressed over the past year. We still do the foreclosures. We have hired a 20 year old youngster and taught him how to analyze the properties, take photos of the properties, and bid at the auctions. The auction market is unbelievably competitive lately, but it still remains the bread and butter of our business. We cashed in on about 10 foreclosures last year, netting roughly $300,000. So we continue to peck away at this side of the business, but I am getting tired of evicting homeowners that have lost their house due to hard times. This falls under the category of things I don't want to do in 2005, but for now, we persist. We cleared the books of all but 2 of our foreclosure properties by the end of last year, and it wouldn't bother me one bit if we don't pick another one up ever again. The niche that we have found ourselves in lately is that of properties which can be subdivided into 3-5 lots. If you remember from last year, we were working on a property in Fells Point, which we bought for $367,000 and hoped to build into $750,000 townhomes. Well, Pete and Dave have convinced me to sell out the lots since we did some architectural drawings and historic work with the city. We sold the package for $800,000 and netted $293,000 on the deal, after all expenses had been incurred. This has been the largest return on any of our projects to date. In addition to this project, we are in the process of building 2 super townhouses in another posh Baltimore borough. We purchased the lot for $200,000. The lot was divided into 3 unbuildable lots. Buildable lots in this neighborhood sell for roughly $200,000 apiece. We went to the city, combined the lots into one, and then subdivided the lot into 2 parcels. Basically, we ended up with 2 buildable lots worth $200,000 each, and for only $200,000. We could certainly sell these lots and pocket the quick cash, but we are seeking to build a nice product. After interviewing 4 custom home builders, we have settled on what we think should be a good choice. Their prices are a lot higher than we are used to paying, but their product is good, and if these houses are built well, we could sell them for $650,000 each. This would net an additional $200,000, bringing this project to somewhere around a $400,000 deal. In addition to that, we are still working on the 5 lots on York Road, and have picked up 2 lots in Hampden and 5 lots in Canton. These neighborhoods and streets probably do not mean a whole lot to you, but if you think of each lot netting us about $50,000 per lot, we stand to have a pretty good year, should all things fall into place.

The Big Kahuna

Now, the last deal that I want to share with you is the newest one to come under contract. I am so excited about this deal that I simply can't contain myself. Looking above, I've shared some deals where we were taking lots and subdividing them into smaller lots, and either building on them or selling them off. I shared with you the Fells Point Lots. Remember the psychic's house that we were going to turn into 5 college rental townhouses? We ended up subdividing the land and cashing out up there. We have had some success with smaller subdivision properties, but this particular lot I'm talking about now really propels us into the big leagues. First, let me tell you how we identified this opportunity because sometimes it takes that extra effort to get into the great deals. As a real estate agent with a larger company, you can use the resources at any of their offices. I am an agent with a company called Long and Foster and can use the conference rooms, phones or faxes at any of their many offices. About 6 months ago, I was at the local real estate office near my house to use their fax machine. So, I needed to use their computer system to write up a contract and their fax in order to send it. When I went to the front desk to ask the woman there to fax it, she asked which office I was located out of. I told her that I worked out of the Baltimore office, and we small-talked about a building that she and her husband had owned in Baltimore for about 20 years. It ends up that the building, a 36,000 industrial building on 2.5 acres of land, was used when they had a family machine shop business. They lost the business, but kept the building, and have rented it over the last 10 years. I half-jokingly asked if she had any interest in selling the property, and she provided me with the address and answered, "for the right price, everything is for sale." I sent one of my employees to look at the site, but never really did anything further with it, not for about 2 months anyway. I kept the woman's business card on my dashboard for probably 2 months. One day, while in the city, I decided to go drive by the building. The building was located in a fantastic site on the south side of a rapidly growing neighborhood. It was a really large 2.5 acre lot with an ugly set of disjointed manufacturing buildings on it.

Lot known as 1901 South Charles Street, Baltimore

The catch to the entire deal is that it was zoned for manufacturing. Having never gone through the zoning change process, this presented me with a problem. As I drove around the adjacent streets, I noticed another huge piece of property, with a city council sign on it requesting a change of zoning from manufacturing to residential. Was this possible? Could you convert manufacturing zoning to residential zoning, and then use the piece of land to build houses? It ended up that the purchaser of the big parcel indeed had changed the zoning, and was going to build 180 apartments on the site. Hmmmm, what would 2.5 acres of land be worth if it was zoned for residential, and one could build townhomes on the property? I was becoming good at putting 3-5 townhouses on smaller lots, but how hard would it be to do it on a larger lot? I began discussions with the couple that owned the piece of property. I met with them and we discussed the options for this property. They had already been offered $2,000,000 for the piece of property by another developer. After some haggling and back and forth discussions, we ended up putting the property under contract for $2.150 million, with a 90 day study period. Was I crazy? The largest residential deal we had done to date was the Fells project, and this one was exponentially larger than that one.

During the 90 day study period, which I am currently in, I would have my engineer look at how many lots we could build; I would have the zoning attorney who did the zoning work next door on the big lot see if he thought it would be possible to duplicate his efforts for this piece of land; I would have an environmental engineer perform land surveys to make sure that there isn't any contamination on the site, which might prevent us from building further houses. If I don't like the results that we find, we can always back out of the deal. So, here we sit, a few rookies with a large parcel of property in a desirable neighborhood, with really no idea how to make the deal fly. We have until April 30th to figure out what to do with it, and then we have to close the deal. Oh yeah, and then there is the whole money thing... We estimate that we will need 20% down, plus closing costs. That means that we have to go out there and somehow raise $450,000 in cash. I guess that I should be more concerned about this little snafu, but for some strange reason, I am at ease with this part of the transaction. After our initial meeting with the engineers, the initial yields on the lot are anywhere between 43-60 townhouses, depending on the number of variance we seek. To break it down into numbers, the average lot in this neighborhood sells for $150,000. If we could have only 43 of these lots, the project is still worth $6.45 million. We have a purchase price of $2.15 million, plus maybe another $100,000 in legal and engineering fees. The difference on this is roughly $4 million. Can you imagine splitting this with my partner? Okay Pete, you take $2 million and I'll take $2 million. This would bounce my net worth to over $4 million. That is astounding, mind boggling... What is more astounding is that I just reread the first chapter of this diary to see that, in January of 2002, I had roughly nothing. I started this venture with a goal in mind. The goal was a combination of making a bunch of money and spending time with my family. I am realizing these goals, and the thought of writing this book will hopefully help other people to realize their goals as well. On the dreamer side, let me just imagine for a minute that I could get 60 lots out of the project. That would equate to a resale value of the project at $9 million. The amount of money is really becoming confusing. I am looking forward to seeing where this new and very exciting project takes us. It is all-consuming at the office! I am looking forward to reporting back where we are on this deal located at 1901 Charles Street.

Life is not a Beach

For the past month, I have been looking long and hard at beach rental properties. I think that this would be a good place to store $50,000, and hopefully break even on the investment. Just after Christmas, I took a day off to travel to the beaches of Maryland and Delaware. I started looking at houses on the oceanfront. These houses were listed anywhere from $2 million up. In order to properly calculate the return on these homes, I contacted a property management company that handles rental properties. The rental season for beachfront properties is about 12 weeks. This is the summer months when the kids have off from school. So, in order to make the numbers work on a deal like this, you need to make enough in these 12 weeks in order to cover your expenses for 12 months. Then, if all of the planets align correctly, you could have free use of the property for the remaining 40 weeks per year. I like the sounds of this since my wife and I could take a weekend getaway in the fall to the beach house, or maybe come down for a few days while the kids are on Christmas break. Alright, so back to my vision of the beautiful $2 million house on the beach. The house sits right there on the shoreline. Go out your back door and you are sitting in your beach chair with the surf rolling up to your feet. The house has 4 bedrooms, 3 baths, a game room, a nice kitchen, and is nicely appointed. Now, this house is not the biggest or best on the beach. There are those beach mansions which are about 8,000 square feet with a 24 person movie theatre, 8 bedrooms, etc., but his is not one of them. This is what should be an affordable way to get into the beach rental business, and hopefully break even. The rental property management company tells me that this $2 million house will rent for about $7,000 per week during the best 5 weeks of summer. The other 7 weeks will average about $5,000 per week. So, over the 12 week period, the house will bring in a total of $70,000 in gross revenue. This sounds pretty good, however, now I need to calculate how much the expense side will run. At my interest rates, I can get a mortgage for 90% of the value of the house. With that in mind, if I have $200,000, I could finance the remaining $1.8 million. The debt service on that would run me $12,600 per month, or $151,000 per year. I am having a little trouble reconciling these numbers? If I put down $200,000 of my own hard-earned money (which represents 10% of the $2 million purchase price) and then financed the rest, my yearly payments to the bank on the loan would be $80,000 more than the income coming in from renting the beach house. Wait a second, what about the taxes, insurance, and property management fees, which could run as high as 15% of the $70,000 gross revenue? This deal is getting less and less attractive by the minute. I imagine that the people that buy these huge beach houses don't do it as a cash flowing investment but more as speculation for appreciation, and the joy of using it when they want.

I asked the listing agent: how in the world do people own these properties? Remember now, I come from a world where each rental property that I own kicks back a tidy profit of $6,000-$10,000 a year. She gave me the school lesson on the beach rental market. The people that buy these houses either have a large chunk of cash to invest, which makes the mortgage payment virtually non-existent, or they are fine with losing $100,000 per year in order to keep the lights on in the house, just to have the opportunity for the appreciation. Now, that's a thought that I had not investigated. The average appreciation for the area last year – and keep in mind that we are currently in probably the midst of the best real estate years ever recorded – was 27%. If I owned this house at $2 million, and this next year it appreciated at 27%, I would have a paper net worth on this deal of $540,000. So, even though it will cost me $100,000 for the year, I stand to make $440,000 if I choose to sell the house after one year. Now, in order to get into this deal, I would have to leverage some of the equity in my other projects in order to come up with the $200,000 cash in, plus the $100,000 in carry costs for the next 12 months. This would be a steep nut for me to crack since I just do not have the tolerance for that type of risk. Furthermore, you are gambling (and it's true, I love gambling) on the continued appreciation of this area. So, even though I am fairly comfortable with these numbers, I think that this deal is just a hair too large for me to take on personally. So, put me back in my car driving away from my $2 million beach house, and I'm driving to the bay side of the beach.

Now, you can get into the bay side properties for under $1 million. The rents go down slightly, but the net effect of the bay side rental properties comes to a whopping loss of $55,000 per year. This is better than losing the big bucks on the $2 million property, but of course your appreciation factor is smaller because the property is only worth $800,000. What I really need to decide is this: what are my goals in the beach rental property formula? Well, first and foremost is my desire to capture some of the appreciation on the beach location. If the property can appreciate at an average of 15% per year for the next 10 years, this could yield a great return on any size house. The next piece of information is my cash position. I should have about $50,000-$75,000 to put down on the beach house. This puts me somewhere between $500,000 to $750,000 as a purchase price, using the 10% down theory. Next, I want to have as close to a break-even cash flow as possible. Something about losing money year after year hits me too hard. An investment is supposed to earn money, and having to cough up $5-$10G's per month in order to make money has the potential to keep me up at night. So, now I move on to the next part of the analysis and speak with 3 or 4 agents and property managers in the area. This one guy sends me to a beach community about 2 miles off shore. He says that there are a lot of families that like to be close to the beach, but only want to spend $1,500 per week to rent a unit. They like to be in single family houses that have pools and other amenities, but are willing to take a beach shuttle to get to the water. This community is made up of older 1970's style houses, but I see the attraction for young families to rent in this community. The houses sell for $450,000 and have gross revenues of about $17,000 over that 12 week rental span. Under these numbers, I could put $45,000 down, and have a mortgage of $405,000 and payments of $28,350 per year. So, now I am losing about $11,000 per year, plus management fees of $2,500 per year, plus taxes and insurance, bringing my net loss on this investment to about $16,000 per year. If the property appreciates 5% a year in a down market, it should go up $22,500 per year. Again, as was the case with the larger houses, you still lose money, but you manage to make it up almost proportionally, with some modest appreciation. The only difference is the money that you need to put down and the amount of monthly loss that you can afford. In this example, I would need to come up with about $1,500 per month just to keep the lights on at this house. But, of course I can use the property for the remaining 40 weeks per year, and who knows, as rents increase on the beach, I may at some point actually break even on this investment.

So, follow me if you will to my next stop. There is a community real estate office at the beginning of this development. I stop in to talk with the broker on duty. I tell him exactly what I am looking for, and describe to him my dilemma with the purchase as a losing investment. He turns me on to yet another development, located 3 miles from the beach. These are new construction homes. Basically, his thought is that if you are willing to drive 2 miles to the beach…why not 3? Now you are getting a brand new 2400 square foot house for $350,000. The interesting part about this whole scenario is that this agent tells me that he can get $25,000 per year in gross income from these houses. He showed me his book, which indicates that he is currently managing 5 houses in this community, and that the rents are indeed about $25K per year. Let me quickly run these numbers: at $350,000, I would probably put $35,000 down and take a mortgage for $315,000. The payment on this would roughly be $22,000 per year. The management fees would be about $2,500 per year, plus taxes and insurance of roughly $2,500 per year, and I am looking at expenses of $27,000 per year, on an income of $25,000 per year. This is only a $3,000 loss, and I am buying a brand new house with all new systems. To say the least, I am extremely intrigued. I asked this guy how these houses could possibly rent for $25,000 per year, and he described his average renter as a family or two renting together, and looking for a large house capable of housing 10 or so people. They are willing to drive the 3 miles to the beach for this size house and a reasonable price.

We are in the process of planning our summer vacation with 4 other families that we hang out with on a regular basis. We are looking at the huge mansions on the beach, but several of the couples have commented that $15,000 per week is a bit excessive. If we could rent 2 of these 2400 square foot houses next to each other, we probably would, since it would give us the flexibility to stay next to each other. So the agent's philosophy on why to invest in this community seems to make perfect sense to me. The other part of this investment which really excites me is the new community phenomenon. If you remember from way back in chapter one, I told you that we built our house about 10 years ago. When my wife and I were ready to move, we looked in just about every community in the Washington/Baltimore area. We spent weekend after weekend driving around, looking at both new and resale houses. If you want to talk about a marriage challenging situation…try buying a house with your spouse. Boy, did that take something out of us. So, after spending 8 weekends looking around, we knew just about every house that was for sale in a 100 mile radius. We really liked this little sleepy community called Crofton. We liked the location, as it was 10 minutes to Annapolis, 30 minutes to Baltimore, and 40 minutes to Washington, DC. The community was chock full of young families, with youth baseball and soccer taking over the city on Saturday mornings. We definitely had a good feeling about the community. The next big decision was what to buy in this community. We decided to buy as much as we could possibly afford. We did not want to see ourselves moving into a medium range townhouse with a comfortable payment in the $150,000 range, and then having to move again into the single family house of our dreams in the $250,000 range just a few years later. So, we decided to take the plunge and build a house in a residential community which was in Phase II of a four Phase project. We went with a loan called an 80/10/10. This 80/10/10 loan meant that we could put 10% down on the property, finance 80% of the purchase price of the house (avoiding paying that pesky property mortgage insurance), and then take another 10% mortgage against the 10% we put down. We decided to go with the model that had the best use of space in the community…and the one that was priced in our qualification range. We ended up buying a Rutledge model, which was a 2,400 square foot base priced at $256,900. That meant that we had to come to the closing table with $25,690, plus closing costs. Between the equity in the North Carolina townhouse that we had recently sold, and some savings, we managed to squeak into this house and qualify for the payment. The payment was about $1,500 per month.

We bought this house in December of 1994, and were we excited! We were in a house and in a community well before our years would have projected. Alright, so now we were in this house for $256,900, which was absolutely as much as I could possibly afford. We now sit, 9 ½ years later, in a house worth $650,000, and a mortgage balance of $210,000. We have managed to set aside $440,000 in equity. If I decided to try to save that money instead of invest it in real estate, I would have had to put some

$40,000 per year aside each year for 10 years. This probably would not have ever happened, considering I typically brought home about $50,000 a year in salary. My only complaint is that I did not try to raise the money to buy 2 or 3 of these houses. So, why has my property gone up so very much? Some of the appreciation is due to the phenomenon that I refer to as the new neighborhood effect. When we shopped for houses, we looked at 10-15 year old resales in the area. A resale is a property that has been lived in, and in Crofton, meant the house was typically 20 years old. We compared these houses to the prices of new construction, and low and behold but we found that the prices were almost comparable. Now, I ask you, why would you pay the same price for a 10 year old house with a 10 year old roof and a 10 year old air conditioning system and a 10 year old plumbing system, when you could purchase absolutely brand new construction for the same price? I have not been able to answer that question. So we bought the property in Phase II. Once Phase IV was completed and the entire neighborhood had been completed, there was still demand for houses in this community. With this pent-up demand came an immediate bump in sales price for the first people to resell in the community. This is why I love investing in brand new communities. Then, demand for housing in my county coupled with the lack of new construction to mean that the prices of houses have skyrocketed over the past several years. I certainly don't anticipate it to continue at this break-neck speed, but I like what I have seen thus far.

Back to my beach story. I am looking at a brand new housing community about 3 miles from the beach boardwalk, and right across the street from a 36 hole championship golf course. It has all of the recipes for success. The houses start at $350,000 for the same house that I currently live in at 2,400 square feet. My goal on this purchase is to buy 2 of these houses, with 10% down, thus requiring $70,000 of capital, plus closing costs. My brother is interested in going in on this deal, and I have a substantial amount of cash to invest, so we will probably each put in $40,000 to purchase the houses. My debt service on the houses should be somewhere around $2,400 per month, including taxes and insurance. My choices are to rent it out for the 10 good weeks of summer at $1,800 per week, losing $600 per month plus the extra two months of carry costs, bringing my grand total to a whopping loss of about $12,000 a year, or try to find an annual renter for the place, at $1,200 per month, working out to a loss of $14,400 a year. I am leaning towards the annual rental just because I won't lose sleep on whether or not the place is getting fully leased over the summer, and for the wear and tear factor of a vacation property. Now, my logic…and we'll see if it is flawed in about a year... is that the property should appreciate at more than 4 percent per year. Given the measly 4 percent, it will go up $14,000 a year in appreciation, rendering the investment a break-even investment. While I don't anticipate property values to continue at the break-neck pace of 30% per year that these past several years have seen, I don't think that asking for 10% per year average is asking too much. Say we do the 10% per year average, over a 30 year period, and these two houses which were purchased at $700,000 will be worth $12,214,582. I know what you are thinking, that this cannot possibly be right. Each house will be worth $6,000,000 with this line of thought in place. Let me throw this one at you. My parents bought a nice house in Massachusetts about 35 years ago, for $50,000. If they put the house on the market today, this house would sell for $500,000. This property has increased 10 times over the course of 35 years. Now, if I gave you $500,000 free and clear today, you would be thinking that wow, that is a nice chunk of change. Well, in 30 years, when these two beach properties are paid off, I will be 65 years old, and on just this investment alone, cashing in on my half of $12,214,582. Not bad.

Alright, alright, so maybe I am dramatizing the results just to make my point, but what if the homes are worth $3.5 million each? What if they are worth a measly $2 million each? You get my point. I read a quote the other day about a father who used to drive around with his grown children, pointing out houses in the various neighborhoods. The dad would say, "I could have bought that house for $20,000 back in 1940, and I could have bought that house over there for $22,000 back then." When the grown child asks why he didn't buy them, the dad responds: "they were too expensive." If you learn one thing from my experience and from this book, it is that in real estate, everything is expensive in current dollars. You need to have the foresight to think of 50 years from now, when those same homes will be worth exponentially more. You don't want to be having that conversation that you didn't get into the business because the houses were too expensive.

Unfortunately, I never went back to the beach in Maryland, and never did purchase the houses on the beach. I did mention to Richard, one of my original partners who moved to Virginia, that I was thinking about beach rentals. Well, Richard owns a vacation house on a lake in Roanoke called Smith Mountain Lake. As I told Richard about my goals of buying a beach property up here, he introduced me to the rental market down there at the lake. The rents that people are getting for the 10 to 12 weeks of summer on the lake are fairly comparable to the rents that people owning the beachfront properties here are getting. The difference is, the cost of acquiring the property at the lake is less than the cost of acquiring a beach property up here. So, on Monday of next week, February 28th, we close on our first lake house rental property. The purchase is for a 5 bedroom house on the lake, one with a nice dock, for $460,000. The house was recently appraised at $475,000, so we are getting a discount, but certainly not the discount that I am used to getting when I purchase property.

We have already spoken with a rental management company, and they can rent this property out for $2,400 per week for about 10 weeks over the summer. So, using the metrics described before, I can anticipate losing about $12,000 per year, including mortgage, management, taxes, and insurance. Split that in 2 since Richie is on the hook, as well, and I plan on putting up $6,000 a year to keep this house. Another angle that I hope will fall into place as I get more experience in this resort rental is that I will be able to fill several weeks in the spring, the fall, and around Christmas.

Shangrila down at Smith Mountain Lake

One of my goals will be to make these properties break even every year. As rents increase, this will also help with this goal. As a bonus to owning all of these resort properties, I will get free use of them for about 40 weeks per year. So, I can offer them out to friends and family or take my family down during the off-peak season. With the purchase of the Smith Mountain Lake property, it will not help me increase my net worth immediately, so unfortunately it doesn't help me take this book to press any quicker, but over time, purchases like this will help me retire incredibly rich.

Negotiation and Relationships

I want to tackle something that has been on my mind for a while, but I find it incredibly important to put down on paper… The Power of Negotiation. About 8 years ago, I bought that distressed restaurant in a food court in Annapolis, Maryland, as I mentioned before. The restaurant was having difficulties. It needed a complete face lift, it needed to be entirely restaffed, it needed the menu to be enhanced, and it needed the quality of the produce to be properly managed. The restaurant mainly sold these large salads to wealthy, health-conscious shoppers. My thinking at the time, which sounded logical, but proved to be faulty, was that Annapolis is littered with affluent residents. They shopped at this nice mall and would probably be looking for a healthy alternative to the steak subs, pizza, and fries. The key to me satisfying this type of clientele was to make sure that the produce used in the salads was as fresh as possible. I went into this venture fully knowing that this place would take every ounce of energy and sanity I had to get it all cleaned up. I put the time in during the first two years, doing all of these key elements to make this a new and shiny successful venture. What I remember about my style of management was that things needed to be done my way. I never truly put myself in the position of the opposite party to see what they were experiencing as I continued to fire employees and work my way through upsetting every produce company around. I remember starting a contract with a small produce company, thinking that they could provide me with superior service and hand-pick all of their produce. On several occasions, I would get cases of tomatoes where a number of the tomatoes were rotten. And this didn't happen frequently, but every now and then, the carrots at the bottom of the bag were bad. The way in which I chose to handle the situation was to call the manager of the company and leave him nasty voicemails. Now, at the time, I looked at things as very black and white. If my complete order was delivered on time, freshly, and with no mistakes in the order or the invoicing…they were great. Keep in mind, however, that I never called them up to tell them that they were doing a great job and that I appreciated their attention to my account. Instead, if any one part of the order was incorrect, I called and lashed out with the mantra that the customer is always right. I simply could not understand how a company could survive treating its customers the way that they did.

I treat dealings like this completely differently now. Now I put myself in the shoes of that vendor. They are in business much in the same way that I am. Their goal is to earn a good living by attempting to supply a good product and provide good service. Every once in a while, things do not go properly, and corrections need to be made. The correct way for me to handle a complaint might have been to wait until business hours, contact the manager, and let him know that some of the product was not satisfactory. Give him the opportunity to offer to drop off a fresh case of produce and make up for the deficiency. Applaud the company for providing a good service and make them want to continue to provide good service in order to constantly receive the positive feedback from me…the customer. This mindset of the customer being incredibly nice to the vendor is a foreign concept that is lost on most business people, and was certainly lost on me. The saying 'that's just business' is used far too often to insulate people from being nice. I have found that you tend to get better service and better results just by being nice to the other person. Not only that, but as a person, you tend to be happier if you are not always dealing with conflict in your day-to-day activities.

Now, in real estate, the exact same style holds true. I am extremely good at getting what I want by helping other people get what they want. I want to give you two examples of that. The big deal with the 50 lots that I am working on is a prime example of how performing win-win negotiation will help you achieve exactly what you want. On the purchase side of the project, I have this property under contract with the seller for $2,150,000. After speaking with the seller, I found out that he is interested in retiring to Florida later this year. Cashing in on this property is the main source of his retirement funds. He already knows that 2 other parties have an interest in this property at $2,000,000. What was important to me was the timing of the deal. Since the property needed to be rezoned and subdivided, I would ideally like 6 months before closing to make sure that I can do with this property what I need to do. The price of the property was not as important as the timing because, if I could do with it what I wanted, the resale of the property is close to $6,000,000. My offer came in higher than any other offer that he had on the table. I settled for a 5 month study period to do my work on the rezoning. The seller was pleased that he could get what he wanted, and I am pleased that I could get what I wanted. Next, he had a tenant in the property who was about to exercise a 5 year option to renew. Now, I was not entirely interested in the property if he had a 5 year lease on it. This would mean that I would have to wait 5 years in order to cash in on this deal. I explained to the seller that, if he allowed the tenant to exercise the option, the value of his property would go down substantially for any potential buyer. Now, he could make the 5 year extension price incredibly high, thus forcing the tenant to move out when their lease expired in 3 months. If this were to happen, I would be pained for about a year because I was counting on getting the rental revenue from the tenant for about a year, while I continued to go down the process of rezoning and subdivision. You can see that this is shaping up to be an extremely fun negotiation. To make things even more interesting, the seller is worried that I will mess up the negotiation, and upset the tenant so that they may then want to move out immediately, and if I don't close on the deal, he is stuck holding this property without any tenant, and no buyer on the hook.

So, everyone had a lot at stake during this meeting. All three of us met last week to work out a lease extension. I asked the tenant what would be most important to them, and they just wanted enough time to find a new place to house their truck repair facility. The seller just wants to make sure that the tenant will stay there, just in case I drop out of the deal. I would like to have the tenant in there (ideally for 9 months) and then have the ability to kick them out with 2 months' notice. When speaking with the tenant, I assured him that I would keep him in the loop throughout the entire process so that he understands when I will be asking him to leave. Further, I am attempting to establish a relationship with the tenant by offering him my realtor services in helping him find an acceptable location. To make a long meeting short, in recap, we settled on a 15 month lease with guaranteed 9 months occupancy, and 6 months notice can be issued after that 9 months has elapsed. What this did was satisfy their need for a substantial amount of time to relocate (and 6 months seemed to satisfy them); it gave me 15 months as a far-out date to have full possession of the property (I conceded 7 months on this); and with an extension in place, it satisfied the seller that he can count on this income for enough time to find another buyer if I fall through. This three-way negotiation turned into a win-win-win negotiation, and hopefully I can continue to build these relationships so that we all cash in on this deal in the end.

My next example of a successful negotiation, by being thoughtful, is through the process of foreclosure. Allow me to set the stage: I go to the courthouse and purchase a property at foreclosure. An auctioneer who is hired by the bank's attorney stands at the top of the steps with a folder in his hand. The auctioneer knows what the bank is owed on the delinquent mortgage, and this is where he starts the bidding. The bank opens the bidding at $102,000; do I have $103,000, asks the auctioneer. Now, investors like me know how much that house is worth. On many occasions, the house may be worth a lot more than that bank debt. We bid against the other investors until someone ultimately buys the property. Sometimes, I am the successful bidder, and sometimes the other investors outbid me. It all depends on how we each analyze it, how much risk we are willing to take on, how much repair work we are willing to put into the project, or if we know the market better than the others, as to who will be the successful bidder. So, let's assume that I am the successful bidder at the steps on this property for $145,000, and I believe that the property is worth $225,000 after some paint, carpet, and some freshening up. So far, the process has been extremely analytical. There is no need for negotiation, or even dealing with people and their problems. We simply analyze the deal, look at the exterior of the building, plug in numbers, and show up at the courthouse steps with a deposit check. Imagine, now, what the next step in the process is. People are still living in the house. They are known deadbeats that have not been able to make a mortgage payment in over 90 days. They are probably not the most responsible people, and they are now living in what will soon be my house. The court takes 60 days to approve the foreclosure sale, and at that point, I can go to closing on the property. During that 60 days, I really want to get the people to kindly move out of their lifelong residence and allow me to profit by $70,000 on their misfortune. Does this sound like a difficult task yet?

Now, the legal process for evicting people from their house is somewhat time consuming. Take a property on Walgrove Road that we closed on in December of last year. The people refused to move, and frankly said that they would wait until we carried them out on the lazy boy chair. So, after we closed on the process, I had to file what is called a motion for possession. The judge needs to sign this motion before the court is willing to issue a writ of possession. Once the court clerk issues the writ of possession, I can take this to the sheriff's department. The sheriff will then schedule an eviction, which usually takes about 4-5 weeks, for it to get on their calendar. For the eviction, you need to schedule a crew of 8-10 strapping young men to move every article of clothing, every piece of furniture, and every other piece of personal property of the evicted party out into the street. Now you have legal possession of the property. With the Walgrove property that we bought back in December, we are scheduled to evict on March 3rd. Basically, this women and her son have lived in this property for 3 months before the sale (time for which we paid, through that delinquency at closing), and then another 2 months while the court ratified the sale (again, we paid); then, tack on 2 ½ months while I went through the arduous process of eviction. Not a bad deal for this woman, but keep in mind that she is going to lose about $50,000 in equity once I take possession of the property.

Now, if you are like my partner Pete, and fairly objective, this process works just fine. He can calculate a number which it costs to carry this property, hire the crew, and follow the rules of the law. I see the process entirely differently. If I could get this family to move the day after the sale, I would save a fortune in carry costs, and perhaps be able to assign my contract to another investor, therefore never having to actually close on the property. Many investors, for one reason or another, do not take my route. Similar to Pete, they either fear the interaction with the people, or are just too intimidated by the entire process to try to capitalize on what amounts to be tens of thousands of dollars. I look at this as an opportunity. First, I have to understand what these people are going through. The people losing the house are no different than you and me. They wake up every day, go to work (well perhaps these types of people don't actually go to work), eat their meals, and have families just the way that I do. Unfortunately for them, they have hit hard times, and have been unable to keep up with their financial obligations. This translates into them losing their house, which in some circumstances they have lived in for over 10 years. This is a scary time in these people's lives. They don't understand the process, what it means to be in foreclosure, and most importantly, they are in a state of denial. Imagine what happens if they do not receive a friendly warm letter explaining the process, but instead receive a piece of stale lawyer correspondence or a sheriff's eviction notice. Like a tiger backed into a corner, these people will thrash out. That includes staying in the property until they are carried out on the lazy boy, and that may include stripping the house of every appliance and every fixture, or maybe even feeling so humiliated that they kick holes in the sheetrock and truly destroy the house before the eviction. Unless you can truly understand what these people are going through, it will be very difficult to accomplish your goal of a timely and kind move. So, the negotiation starts with understanding what is important to these people. First, it is information. They simply do not understand that they have lost the house, and what the process is going to be from this point on. Next, they need some options laid out for them. These options include making them understand that they are going to have to move, and at this point, it is just too late to salvage their home. Since so much equity is being lost in the house, this also allows me to offer them some financial assistance to help them get back onto their feet.

Here is how the situation typically plays out... Immediately following the sale of the property at the courthouse steps, I send them out a letter. The letter is sent through regular mail, and is written in an extremely friendly tone. The letter basically tells them that the bank has taken their house due to non-payment (I like using the bank as the bad guy), and has sold the house to my small investment company. I encourage them to contact me in order to discuss the many options available to them. I want them to understand that I am not a bill collector, and that given the chance, I can actually help them in this tough time. Some of these letters are successful, and the people contact me by phone; others do not respond and I need to follow up with a personal visit to the property. My goal is to build a relationship with the people. They have been afraid to seek assistance in the past, and are very guarded about trusting anyone. During the face-to-face meeting, I explain to them that foreclosure happens all of the time. I see people losing their homes for a variety of reasons, including divorce, loss of employment, medical problems, and the like. I will probe them with questions to understand their situation. I can only help them if I fully understand why they lost their house and what their plans are for the future, assuming they have any. From there, I explain the process of foreclosure. I show them the contract I received at the courthouse steps. I explain the 60 day court ratification process. Ultimately, I tell them that the inevitability is that they will have to move, whether on their own accord or by the hand of the sheriff. Now, if I can get them to move within 30 days, I tell them I can offer them $1,000 in cash for their cooperation. This money will certainly come in handy as a security deposit on a rental property. Understand that they have not been able to pay their mortgage for 3 months, and they need cash to move. Understanding their needs is incredibly important in order to accomplish a win-win solution. On properties that are in good condition and are located in neighborhoods with strong markets, the opportunity to assign my foreclosure contract presents itself. For these people, I may be able to give them more than $1,000 if they allow me to put a sign on the lawn, a lock box on their door, and basically list the house as for sale. I will explain to these people that, in this situation, it appears to the neighborhood that they are just moving, as opposed to being foreclosed upon (thus protecting their reputation), and that if I can capture more margin, I am willing to share more money with them. I am under absolutely no obligation to share anything with these people. They have already lost the house, and it is just a matter of time until I take possession, but I find it more satisfying if I am able to at least give something back to these people that are going through extremely difficult times.

Out of about 40 foreclosures, the eviction on March 3rd will be just the second time that I have had to get the sheriff involved in the process. Let me say that again: out of 40 foreclosures I've embarked upon, I've only had to enlist the sheriff's aid on two occasions.

I take pride in being able to meet these people and offer at least a little help in this very difficult situation. I will be honest, though: while there is fantastic money to be made in buying foreclosure property, I am leaning away from continuing to use this as a method of acquisition. You see, the entire process is depressing. People are losing the biggest investment of their lives. People that need the equity in their homes more than I need it are losing it because they simply do not know where to go for help. If I thought that I could be successful in helping people to avoid foreclosure, instead of taking their homes, I would probably spend some time on this. The problem is that these people are losing their ability to manage their finances, and short of adopting these families, I simply do not know what the solution is to this problem. Over my years in the business, I have come to realize that being able to successfully negotiate with people is an incredible skill. I stand in awe of people that are better at it than I am. I try to read as much as I can, attend seminars as often as possible, and really take an interest in understanding how people negotiate in order to become better at this imperative skill myself. I recently took a seminar offered by a famous sports agent. While I was practicing many of the skills that were taught, he really put a name and strategy to these skills. There are very few situations that don't have a possible and successful outcome. They simply require thinking outside of the box for a mutually agreeable outcome.

One aspect of negotiation is understanding your needs and the needs of your opponent. Now that we have the big 50 lot deal looming, the need for cash is becoming greater and greater. You may recall a property that I described as York Road. This was the "psychic house" project where we bought half of a house, and eventually bought the other half through dumb luck. At the time that I wrote that section of the book, our goal was to build 5 townhomes that we would then rent as college rentals and keep in our portfolio. That was our initial plan. As the famous boxer Mike Tyson says, "Everyone has a strategy to fight me until that first punch". The big 50 lot development will present some potential cash flow conflicts on the company, which may cause us to sell the 5 lot deal for cash flow after all, in order to keep funding the 50 lot deal. The 50 lot development currently has the trucking company renting the one usable existing building on the site. Their lease is for $60,000 per year. Now, this is great cash coming in; however, with a purchase price of $2.1 million, the debt service to carry the project will be in excess of $15,000 per month. So, after we receive the rents, we will still have to come up with $10,000 each and every month while we go through the rezoning process and the subdivision process. We estimate that this could last for approximately one full year of carry costs, which brings our immediate cash flow needs to $120,000 per year. So, we are currently looking for something to sell that will help put a cushion of money into the bank in order for us not to feel pinched as this project progresses.

The York Road project may be the immediate answer. We are currently in the deal for $125,000, including engineering expenses and carry costs. The lots alone are worth somewhere between $300,000-$400,000, depending on what the ultimate user will build on them. These lots need to have some final engineering work done, some utility issues worked out, and currently there's an old ugly duplex on the lot, which simply has to be demolished. All-in-all, the ultimate builder may run into $50,000 to $70,000 in lot fees, just to get it ready to build. So, back to my negotiation situation: we have put the properties out on the market for $300,000. We have not had many bites on the property. Frankly, people are slightly weary of that market, and are certainly not flocking to the deal. Finally, we got a builder who is willing to take on the risk of building out this 5 townhouse development project. He submitted an offer for the full $300,000 asking price, and shows some enthusiasm in getting the deal done. At a recent meeting, he showed us his diagram on what he thought could be built on the land. In his drawing, he's looking at a 4 story townhouse, which would be much larger than our proposed 3-story. Now, Pete and I reacted slightly differently to this news. Pete is voting to take the property off of the market and try to resell it as a 4-story project, therefore capitalizing on this guy's ingenuity in adding a 4th story. I don't completely discount this point of view because we certainly want to maximize our return on this deal, and he may have a point. However, we have had this thing out there for quite some time, and regardless of this 4th story vision, people just are not that excited about the location. The most important thing to remember is that our primary objective is *selling the land*...getting a cash cushion in the bank in order to carry the big lot deal. So, through my negotiation training course, I have learned to try to find a win-win solution to the problem. Now, the buyer really wants the project. With his 4th story vision, he thinks that the project could yield closer to $1.5 million, as opposed to our estimates of $1.125 million. Using this theory, he could pay as much as $450,000 for the lots. We walk a very fine line between maximizing our return and blowing the deal by going back to this builder and saying "sorry, your new information shows us that the property is worth more, so now the price has gone up." Now, if I thought for one minute that there was another builder lined up and ready to go on the purchase of this property, with the 4th floor vision, I would not hesitate to re-list it at a higher price. But the market value is defined as what someone is willing to pay for it, and I think that this project has had its fair shake at the market, regardless of any new information. What I would like to see happen in this scenario is to take the $300,000 offer and close on that immediately. This satisfies our primary objective of getting a cash cushion in the bank. Then, what I would like to propose is a back-end kicker on the deal, which would allow us to receive, say, 10% of everything over a $225,000 sales price on each unit. So, if he is lucky enough to sell the properties for $300,000 each (as he predicts), then we would get roughly $7,500 per house, or $37,500 for the project in back-end kickers. This would bring our ultimate resale of this deal to $375,000, or a tidy profit of $250,000. In this situation, the buyer gets the deal, which makes him happy, we get the immediate $175,000 in profit in the bank, which carries the big lot deal for 17 months, and we get a kicker in the end if all goes well, which satisfies Pete's need to try to maximize the profit on the sale of the lot. It will be interesting to see if this actually plays out as I hope that it does. The part of this deal that becomes a non-tangible result is the potential for establishing a relationship with a builder, who could be a great outlet for future land development deals. This type of negotiation is relationship-based, and they preach it in just about every book you buy on the topic.

The last section that I want to tackle on this sit-down is that of the abundance theory. The abundance theory states that whatever you give, you will get back tenfold. I quickly referenced this theory earlier in the book, but how does this theory work in business? Well, ask yourself when was the last time you volunteered to do a community service project. Or, when was the last time you took time away from your bread and butter business dealings, and helped someone who wanted to learn more about your business? Far too often, we find ourselves so tied up with our big "to do" lists that we forget what success is all about. Every day we get into the office, we are flooded with work to complete by the end of the day, deadlines by the end of the week, and just the demand of making more money. This was the way that I lived for many years of my life. The money was the ultimate goal, and I would sacrifice just about everything in order to achieve this "success". Well, somewhere down the line, things have begun to change in the way that I live my life. I truly enjoy helping people get into the field of real estate. I not only find the time, but will truly prioritize my time around helping people learn what I do and how I do it. This brings me a great sense of satisfaction, and in my mind is a better measure of success. I have found that treating my employees more kindly has yielded me better results than the 'my way or the highway theory' that I used to live by when I owned the restaurant. I sit back and look at the success of the past 4 years, and truly believe that I have been blessed by God for my willingness to help others in many different ways. I may dovetail this discussion into a somewhat spiritual one next month, when I find the time to sit down and continue, but before you go on reading, ask yourself when was the last time you sacrificed something important to you to help others. Just last week, my entire staff volunteered to paint a local high school in the "Help the Schools" campaign in Baltimore; simply giving back to a community that has really given to us.

LESSONS LEARNED

- Beach rentals are difficult to make into positive cash flow. This is especially true in the north.
- Bigger deals are inherently more complex. Learn before jumping in.
- Always seek a win-win solution to a negotiation. You might need that adversary to help you in the future

TIME & EFFORT WILL BE REWARDED

April 2005

Back to my abundance theory: these friends of mine that run this investors club were missing a national speaker in March and asked me if I would be willing to talk for 2 hours on foreclosures, and how we make our money as a fill-in. They felt that the local flair would be appreciated. Frankly, I love teaching and sharing the information, so this was a fantastic opportunity for me. That night, 225 people showed up for the talk. It went over great. I told them the full story of the last four years of my life. I told them the true facts on how to analyze a deal and how not to get stuck losing money. I also gave them my cell phone number and told the entire crowd to call me for anything, even just to sniff-check a deal. Well, for 3 weeks after the seminar, I did not have to buy lunch once. At least 20 people came by my office in response to that talk, and I spent an hour to an hour and a half with each of them, explaining to them how real estate works and how they can make money in the business. Some of the folks in my office think that my giving out my time is far too excessive. My response is that the reason that the company is so successful is *because* I am giving with my time. For every hour I give, we reap the rewards of 10 hours of success. Now, I certainly cannot say that any one of these people has helped us with a deal or any certain act that contributed directly to our success, at least not yet, but if you truly believe in my abundance theory, you have to believe that this philosophy of helping people is truly the cause of our success.

And a quick aside to my abundance theory: it works the other way around as well. If you are mean, nasty, difficult, or tough on people, you will ultimately get penalized in life. Last year, we had a mother of one of the college students who was moving in. She worked me continuously about the condition of the property that her son was moving into. I went up to the unit several times, and frankly, while I thought that the unit was in decent condition, I did continue to repaint and fix all of the small minutia that she felt were so imperative to repair. But I also went so far as to tell Laura, the office manager, that if this women is one day late with her rent, she should be sure to slap the late fee on immediately. You see, I try to treat people fairly and honestly. The golden rule of do unto others as you would like them to do unto you should be plastered onto the wall of my office. Well, just last week, this college student's mother called my office. Apparently, her son has had some trouble with the university and is going to have to spend another year in school. Why did this happen? Could it be the reverse of the abundance theory? She also wants to know if her son can stay in his apartment for another year…and also, will the rent go up, and if so, how much? When you burn your bridges, you need to make sure that you have an alternative way back to the other side, or things can get very hairy. Not to worry, though: I will show grace to this women and her son regardless of any lack of courtesy.

So, enough of the Benjamin philosophy class, and back to what is going on in the real estate business... Let me tackle the small stuff first and then hop into the life-changing stuff. In March, we closed on the five Mangold lots in Washington Village. I can't even remember if I ever wrote about this deal in the first place, but I don't think that I did. We bought these as shells for $275,000 in October of 2004. We just closed on them as a resale on March 31, 2005 for $511,000. I saw the houses once and we did absolutely nothing to them. The gross profit on this deal was $236,000 with a net of about $200,000. After we pay the Fund members their 25%, or $50,000, Pete and I get to split $150,000. Pretty good for about

5 hours of work. If you remember, there was an agent in my office that brought me this deal. We've decided to buy her a trip somewhere exotic as a 'thank you'. It was only about an hour ago that we told her about the gift, but I am thinking about a week at the Paradise Island Hotel in the Bahamas with airfare and spending money.

I just paid my quarterly tax payment for January to March of 2005, and I have already taken $115,000 out of the company. Not that I can anticipate this to continue throughout the year, but this business really is fantastic. The next small deal on the plate is 1622 Calvert Street. Last summer, we had an intern from the University of Maryland MBA program who was trying to learn how to get into real estate. He worked one day per week (Wednesdays) for about 4 months. He has since taken a real job in New York City, but when he did work for us, he found two properties on Calvert Street that he liked. One fell through (which we had under contract for $65,000) and the other one we closed on for $32,000. He started by sending out postcards to all of the homeowners in the 2 neighborhoods that he liked in the city. He got several responses to his postcards and followed up with meetings, and ultimately got that $32,000 home under contract. There is no magic to what he did: he just used our template postcards and the rest worked itself out. Now, I have never seen this house, but apparently it is a shell in pretty tough condition in a fringe neighborhood. We thought that the property was worth about $99,000. So we knew that it was a really good buy at $32,000. About 3 weeks ago, we got a letter from the city stating that this neighborhood is being targeted as a rejuvenation neighborhood. The city was sending letters to all of the property owners that had their houses boarded up and had not applied for a permit to repair the homes. Needless to say, we got one of these letters. Then the phone starting to ring and other letters began to fill our mailbox, but this time, the letters were from investors who were in tune with the city's initiatives and they wanted to buy our property from us. The offers came in at $65,000…then $85,000…then $115,000…and our last unsolicited offer came in at $150,000. All the while that these unsolicited offers began to roll in, our next door neighbor property was listed on the market for $79,000. Given the knowledge that we had from these unsolicited offers on our property, we contacted the agent in order to submit an offer – hey, we knew ours was worth $150,000, so $79,000 would be a steal – but he informed us that he currently had had 15 offers on the property, within 3 days of each other. His property finally settled at $210,000. On Friday of last week, we put our property into the MLS system at $99,000. Our goal will obviously be to obtain a similar result to that of our neighbor and end up somewhere around $210,000. Again, you do the math, and we should net about $165,000 off of this one house in about 8 months. We continue to buy property each and every day. Within the last month, we bought 2 lots and 2 houses in developing areas, and we have another 5 lots under contract in a study period.

All of these little deals are fantastic. They are bringing in cash monthly, allowing us to pay the staff to run the company and allowing me and Pete to take vacations; I bought a lake property in Virginia for $460,000 last month, Pete redid his kitchen (Viking, stainless, granite, etc.), I am buying another lakefront house in Virginia this month at $500,000, Pete is paying cash for a 1965 ½ Mustang convertible, I took a week at Doral and Disney…. You get the idea, but something bigger is on the horizon. You see, we are living pretty good right about now. I anticipate that we'll each take about $400,000 home this year in earnings, and probably over $500,000 next year, just from the projects that are on the books right now. Our rental portfolio hovers at about $5,000,000 and I continue to achieve greater net worth based on the fantastic appreciation we have received over the past several years. But, there is something taking shape that is absolutely mind boggling to me…the 50 lot deal on Charles Street. This is the name that we have given to the big 50 lot deal.

Now, just to refresh your memory, know that I am under contract to purchase this piece of land for $2.150 million. Over the course of the past several months, we have met with the engineering company several times. We went out and raised $25,000 from an MBA buddy of ours who we're paying 10% interest to for the use of his funds. With this money, we've paid about $10,000 to the engineers so far, about $2,000 to the zoning attorney, and another $2,200 to the site engineers that completed the Phase I survey for us. Keep in mind that neither my partner nor I have any experience with this type of project. Every step of the way is a learning process, and we hope not to make too many mistakes as we go. April 13th was a big day for us. This was the day that the 120 day study period expired. We could have released ourselves from this deal and received our $20,000 deposit back at any time prior to this date. Essentially, effective as of this date, we are officially in the deal. Our $20,000 deposit money has gone "hard", as they say. It would have been nice to have all of our due diligence done completely by this date. Well, to let you know the reality of all this, we have managed to drop the ball several times so far in this area. By now, we had hoped to have conducted a series of due diligence tests to make sure that the site was indeed capable of being converted to residential use. We did accomplish the first objective, making sure that the soil was acceptable for residential lots. You see, when you convert a site over to residential from manufacturing, there is the potential for the site to be contaminated with metals and lubricants which would have been used on an industrial site. So the first test was called the Phase I study. This test, which ran about $2,200, was a historical review of the site. For this study, the engineers researched the records as far back as 100 years to see what was on the site. What they found was that it was originally a foundry building where they built bells and motors. In knowing they'd been building bells and motors, we could now be sure that surveyors would find some concentration of leads and lubricants in the soil. The next thing that they found was that, over the years, permits have been pulled to implant several 3,000 gallon tanks with oil and gasoline in order to power the foundry building. Also, there was an electrical shed on the property, with transformers which would help to provide electricity to the site. While this seemed a bit daunting at first, the engineer did assure us that, in all likelihood, there would be a method for remediating this site from all of these problems…but it would come at a cost, of course. The ideal goal of this test was hopefully to find that nothing ever existed on the site which could prevent us from building houses that children could live in without any risk of health effects. Unfortunately for us, this Phase I revealed that this was not the case. This meant that we had to take it to the next level, which was a study called a Phase II study. The Phase II study consists of digging holes at different points around the site, collecting samples of soil, sending them to a lab for analysis, and making sure that the land is indeed in a condition acceptable to the state in order that we can build residential houses. The total cost of the Phase II study is $28,000. Well, we got the results of *this* study, and it shows that for approximately $100,000, the tanks can be removed from the land, the lead in the soil can be removed and/or covered with fresh soil, the application for the State of Maryland required to build can be completed, and we can then be awarded the clear sign for construction. Now, we have not gone ahead with spending any of this money. When the time comes, we may decide to sell off the land without doing any construction, and we will probably then transfer this expense over to the ultimate buyer. If we do decide to build on the lots, then we will incur this expense. Okay, so we overcame that hurdle by April 13th. You see, there are a series of hurdles that you need to overcome to accomplish a project of this size, and each and every one is scary, at least for me. So overcoming this one certainly helps me get a little bit more sleep at night.

Now, the engineer and the zoning attorney that we hired are the best in the business. Both of these guys came from the builder who used them to convert his site next door from manufacturing to residential. Our thinking was that they would be most familiar with the project, the area, and with the players at the city level. The way that the process works is that the councilman for the area that the property is located on must submit a bill to the city council, requesting the zoning change. In order to do that, the councilman has to represent the wishes of his constituents. We found the leader of the local community association who had helped the neighboring property get their lot rezoned. I had a meeting with her and she was entirely in favor of the property being converted to residential use. She had some suggestions for me regarding the use of the roads and location of transformers, but in general, she knew the site and was in favor of anything that could be done to it which would beautify this corner of the area. The bad news, however, was that her zone ended at our street, and our lot fell into the next community association's site. This was last week, just prior to April 13th. I had this woman send a nice email on my behalf to the president of the next community association. I have since contacted her and will meet with her on Monday. Over the phone, I gathered that her constituents would like to see a grocery store on the site. Now is when the power of nice negotiation comes into play. Instead of tunnel vision, with her seeing that we have to spend a lot of money on the residential plan and that we are opposed to anything but our vision, I set up an open meeting to discuss the available options with her on Monday. On Monday, I hope to impress her with the fact that we are easy to work with as developers, and will willingly investigate all of the options including both a grocery story site and residential potential. Over the phone, she sounded extremely easy to get along with, and I have high hopes for a very positive relationship with her community association. Eventually, we will need her to contact the local councilman, who will submit a bill to the city council for the rezoning of the property. Without the support of the community, the bill will be dead in the water, so this relationship is incredibly important. The downside, of course, is that I didn't have a chance to meet with her prior to April 13th. Technically, we are into this deal regardless of the support of the community. That is extremely scary. At some point in your career, you have to take some chances and rely on the fact that you understand your craft, and your ability to get things done. This is where I am in my career, and I simply cannot think of any reason why this deal should not go through for us *and* for the community.

Our second missed deadline in this project is our initial meeting with the city planning department. Assuming that we get the support of the local community, we now have to present a plan to the city for approval. The engineers drafted a nice rendition of what they see on that site. Their plan is for 58 residential townhouse units set up in a somewhat of a suburban type community with cul-de-sacs and yards in between townhouse groupings. The catch to their plan is that the community and the planners tend to shy away from this concept in the inner cities and it doesn't maximize the number of units that can be put on the land. There will be four rows of townhouses. Each group of two rows will face each other and have garage access in the rear. Between the two rows will be a sidewalk and a lot of green space (grass). Now, if you are a homeowner, you probably like the community feel of having front doors looking at each other, with a lot of common area for children to play. If you are the local community or the planning department, you probably do not like the suburban style because it creates a separate community within your community. These people tend to be almost like a gated community in an urban setting. This is generally frowned upon by city planners, as their goal is to keep the urban fabric of the city consistent throughout. So, we were originally on the calendar to meet with the planners at the city planning department on April 13th. This would have worked out great as – if we encountered some flak from them on our concept, and left there believing that no matter how we engineered the site, there was absolutely no way that they would approve it for residential – we could turn around and tell the seller that we were out of the deal. Well, two days before the meeting, the engineers contacted the attorney, who was unfortunately unable to attend at that time. We had to make a quick decision as to whether to attend the meeting as planned, without our zoning attorney, or reschedule the meeting after the expiration of the study period and risk getting bad news. Again, you hit a point in life where rewards accompany risks, so we decided to reschedule the meeting after the 13th in order to get the attorney present at the meeting. We only get one shot at making a first impression with the project, so we didn't want to squander that shot by not having our attorney present at the meeting. The meeting is now set up for the 20th of April.

While all of this was going on, we went to the bank for financing. We went to our favorite local bank first and presented the deal to the secondary bank as a back-up. We knew the challenges that the bank would present us with and we were somewhat prepared for them. The bank usually finances our houses with 10% down and 100% of the construction dollars spent. The bank provides us these terms if two very important conditions are met.

First, the completed appraised value of the house is greater than 80% of their loaned money. This may sound confusing, but it really isn't. Allow me to explain in simple terms. If we buy a house at foreclosure that needs paint, carpet, kitchen, and baths, we will probably spend $100,000 on the house and $25,000 in construction. What we want is to put down $10,000, and get everything else financed through the bank. So we want $90,000 in financing on the house, and $25,000 on the construction for a total loan amount of $115,000. With all this in mind, the bank's appraiser does the appraisal as if the house were for sale *after* we completed the renovations. He gives the bank that price. Now, we hope that 80% of that price does not exceed $115,000 (since that is what we are looking for). By taking the $115,000 and dividing it by the 80% that the bank needs, the appraisal has to come in at $143,750 in order for us to have the luxury of only putting 10% of our own money into the deal. We usually know the post-renovation appraisal, and that is how we finance so many deals with cheap money down. Well, now try taking that approach and applying it to our lot deal on Charles Street. If the value of the lots after we complete the zoning and subdivision process is $9 million, according to this first condition, the bank should be willing to loan out $7.2 million if the acquisition costs and costs to subdivide do not exceed $7.2 million. Unfortunately, it is not that easy. There is, of course, a second condition to meet.

Banks are not in the business of taking risks. Their rewards, or returns as they call them, are based on making conservative loans which are guaranteed by the principals (mainly, me and Pete) and backed through the security of the appraised value of the property. So, in my residential example, the bank is pretty well protected. The house is worth $143,750 when complete, and they only loan the construction money after they have inspected the completion of the work, so they know that their loan is 80% of what that property is worth. Sure, the market could adjust and they could own a larger percentage of the house, but they're making only one year loans. That way, if the market begins to adjust, they can collect the loan from us or force us to sell or refinance the project. I think very highly of this local bank. They are entrepreneurial and are willing to take some risks in loaning to smaller players like me, but they do get much higher returns on their money by charging me higher origination fees than larger banks. It all follows the higher risk - higher return model.

Refocusing on our land deal, the lot could be worth $9 million, but many risks accompany this valuation. I previously pointed out just a few of these risks. The community may not give us their buy-in, the city council may not approve the bill for rezoning, and the planning department may not want to see townhouse lots there. In an ideal situation, we would have an option to purchase this property without having to close until we got all of these ducks lined up in a row. This way, the bank would have the assurances that they are seeking before lending us the money. Unfortunately, this is one of the craziest times Baltimore has seen in real estate in recent history. Sellers are simply not giving these conditions before closing. If we don't want to step up to the plate, there are 10 other players behind us that would be willing to take a shot at making this kind of money. So, with the bank, we had an appraisal done on the land as it exists as a manufacturing property. Our goal was to make the deal work for the bank in its current condition. The appraiser pulled down other industrial sites that have recently sold, and came up with an "as is" appraisal on the property with a manufacturing zoned use of $2.6 million. Well, that is good news and bad news. The good news is that it is greater than the $2.150 million that we are buying it for, but the bad news is that the property appraisal would have had to come in well over $3,000,000 in order to satisfy that second finance condition, just to make the bank feel comfortable enough with the deal to loan us up to 90% of the purchase price. And now we have found some additional information. The bank will provide us with $1.6120 million, or a 75% loan toward the purchase price. Now, this is pretty well protected money because this in only 62% of the appraisal value. Unfortunately, this requires us to put down a fair amount of additional capital in cash. With these new factors in mind, Pete and I started to think outside of the box on how to come up with the required capital.

Remember that we owned the office building on Windsor Mill which we purchased at auction? After having a long negotiation with our loan officer, I believe that we've come up with a solid solution. The bank will allow us to pledge the equity in the Windsor Mill building (that we bought at foreclosure for $350,000) for another 10%, or $210,000, as what they call cross collateralization. This leaves us 15% that we have to come to the table with in cash. So at closing, we will need $315,000 in down payment money, plus another $30,000 in closing expenses. As we begin to calculate the massive amounts of capital that this project will consume, my blood pressure rises, my bald spot expands, and years are taken off of my life. We will need $65,000 in additional engineering fees to get it subdivided; we will need about $30,000 in legal fees, and another $120,000 in mortgage payments over the course of the year, while we continue to pound this thing through the process, a process that we are completely unfamiliar with. So, if you add up the capital that we will need to make this project a reality, we need $530,000 in cash. This project could be so incredibly profitable that we have numerous options available to us in order to help finance the deal. Our goal is not to put a whole lot of our own money into this process. I have several developer friends who have offered to put up the lion's share of this cash, but the catch is that they want an equity position in the deal. So, for putting up $530,000 and our personally signing for the remaining portion on our loan documents, the investor/developer is looking for 25% of the profits of the deal. Let us just say, for kicks and giggles, that the project yields $6 million: the investor would like to take out $1.5 million. Sounds like a pretty good one year return if all things go well. Structuring this deal is interesting. We want all of the profit, but we don't have the capital to get the deal done. The project has risk, and investors want equity instead of debt. Perhaps we are greedy because we do not want to give up any equity, but our first stab at this is to try to convince an investor to give us debt financing for the down payment. Here we go again... back on the capital raising roadshow.

We would like to keep as much of the profits off of this deal as possible, which is why we're shooting to raise the half a million via debt. We've been in business for 4 years, and have established a pretty good track record for success on our smaller projects. We want to pay the investors a decent return since we really need their money, and fast – so we decided to try to raise the debt financing with a payout of 12% interest for one year notes with one year extensions. We created a good mailing campaign, and have since sent noticed out to all of our prior investors, along with many potential ones that missed investing in the Signature Property Fund on the first go-round. The end result…so far, $225,000 has been pledged in commitments, with several more inquiries. I have no fear that we will be able to finance this deal. We have made enough contacts over the years that we can raise debt money all day long at 15%. Our challenge is just trying to shrink that outgoing percentage to 12%. That is where we stand on the financial implications of this deal.

Let me digress from real estate for just a few minutes in order to relay a story to you about investing and irrational exuberance. Back when the internet market was going haywire in the late 1990's, people were making millions of dollars in the stock market, investing in these highflying technical stocks. I withheld any investment in internet stocks for quite some time. I heard the pundits commenting on the internet stock bubble and how it could implode at any time. I was committed to staying out of the stock market investing game; I was too good to get involved in the hype....or so I thought. I went back to get my MBA and even took some classes in e-commerce at the time. I could see the writing on the wall, that the internet was going to revolutionize the way commerce is conducted. As I patiently watched from the sidelines as people doubled and tripled their investments in internet stocks, I decided that all of my MBA-style education confirmed that I needed to get "into the game".

So, I am remembering back in January 1998: I had $40,000 sitting in the bank of my old company. This $40K represented money that was paid up front by attendees for the medical seminars that I was holding at the time. This money would need to be equally disbursed for operating costs over the next 4 months of the seminars. Typically, I would make sure that my expenses were covered over the course of the 4 months and take a draw in profits in June; however, the infectious nature and apparent ease of everyone making millions of dollars around me by investing in internet stock finally caught hold of me. I searched the mutual funds and found the fund that had had the highest return over the last 12 months. My plan was to invest the $40,000 into this rocket ship of a fund, which had posted 181% return last year, through until May. This way, if it gained the same rate of return, about 45% per quarter, I could make $10,000 on that money. Besides, it was only earning 1% sitting in the bank, and what could happen over the course of the next 4 months? So I did it, and plunked the money down on a RS Emerging Growth Fund. For the first two months, my hypothesis was true, and the money did increase at a tidy clip through March. My balance was over $50,000. Then, as you almost could have predicted, someone took a pin and popped that bubble that everyone had been warning of. By May of that year, the predetermined time that I was going to cash out, the bubble had imploded. After the dust settled and the carnage had been laid aside, I had lost about $25,000. This may not sound like a big deal now, but at the time, that was a fortune to me. I was so mad at myself for being true to my beliefs for so long, and ultimately could not have timed my investment any worse. As bad as it was for me, the stories for others were even more devastating.

I recall the story of the carpet salesman in Florida. My parents live in Deerfield Beach, Florida. My parents had some friends down there that had children about my age. Well, one of their children married a carpet installer. While I had never met the man, from all of the stories told, he was a genuine guy who made a fantastic couple with the daughter of the family friend. Somehow, he got into the internet game of day trading. While the market was exploding at an incredibly feverish pace, he was cashing in on some super large gains. First, he bought his wife a new Porsche, and then it was a 3000 square foot palace; the stories I heard from my parents on their successes were incredible. He was hitting it so well as a day trader, he even convinced his mother to refinance her house so that he could gamble…I mean invest... her money. Numerous times, my mother would ask why I was not into day trading the internet. She even went so far as to see if she could day trade. This hype has an unbelievable effect on people. Constantly, I would remind my mother and father that what their friend's son was doing was nothing short of gambling. In an up market, he would do well, but I constantly said that I hoped he was setting some of this aside for the time when the bubble burst. I probably don't need to elaborate on the type of damage the bubble did to this family. First, they traded in the cars, and then they were forced to downsize the house; ultimately, his mother was forced to sell her house, as she had lost all of her equity in the stock market. He ended up unemployed and the marriage was on the rocks. The weekly stories from my parents, the parties, the neighbors, the excitement of this guy, the rags to riches and all of the allure that goes with it are so entertaining to hear. So, when I think of my loss on that RS Emerging Growth Fund, which I am still writing off at a tune of $3,000 per year, as per the IRS code, I realize that I was no different than every other person that got caught up in the game. I was gambling money that I could not afford to lose, in a game that I knew to be irrational, all in the quest to make easy money.

There are some learning lessons from this story. The concept of irrational exuberance can be broken down to greed. We all want to get our piece. We buy, sell, and trade assets to drive up the price. The demand increases and we see our gains. As more people become exposed to these gains, they ultimately drive the price of the asset far above its inherent value. Then, the tipping occurs when, all of a sudden, the market realizes this insanity and the demand diminishes. Now, the market has a massive bailout, selling all of the assets at lower and lower prices. As supply floods the market, the prices are driven down, causing losses. While it is obvious to anyone who studies these markets, I can tell you firsthand how difficult it is to keep yourself out of this game. What fascinated me back then, as it does still today, are the few players that cashed out a part of their success smack dab in the middle of the explosion, and only lost their profit. Like a good blackjack player who removes her original principal and only gambles the house's money, these stock market players know these bubble cycles. So, why do I tell you my views on the bubbles? I am beginning to lose sleep at night. Yikes... something inside me is causing me just a little pause. I am beginning to see real estate in the same light. By doing my homework and market research, I see real estate as a method of obtaining great wealth. I could see the renaissance happening right in front of my eyes and decided to hop in with both feet. That is how I ended up currently owning about $5,000,000 in rental properties, and have another $5,000,000 in potential development. I would like to think that this crazy appreciation will continue for another 5 years, but I'm just not sure. I would like to think that it *has* to continue for at least another 2-3 years. Again, that may not be the case. As interest rates begin to creep up, the buying power of the general public, when it comes to long term debt, will begin to diminish: it has to. At some point, the development inventory may begin to be worth less than we anticipated. When this happens, our projects will begin to be liquidated at break-even rates, or even worse, we could actually lose money, as I did in the 1998 internet stock market. What if I'm wrong and this run will continue for another 5 years? I could have $10,000,000 in rentals and $10,000,000 in development deals. This is not an easy business, and banking on predicting the future could have dire consequences.

Enough thinking about the market and bubbles, though. For now, I am focusing on getting Charles Street on the market. Let's take a look at the analysis numbers:

Acquisition $2.15 million
Closing costs $30,000
Engineering $65,000
Site test $30,000
Legal $25,000
Carry costs $120,000

Total acquisition and subdivision cost = $2.42 million

Now, let me assume that we do indeed sell the lots for $130,000 each. I am using that as opposed to $150,000, as I imagine we will have to discount them for the builder to do the necessary site work. Instead of getting 60 lots, say we only get 50 through the planners at the city and the community level. The sales price on the deal would be $6.5 million. That would equate to a net to Pete and me of $4.08 million. Now assume that we get in cahoots with a builder big enough to build all of these houses. Furthermore, assume (in real estate dreaming, we make a lot of assumptions) that, instead of a resale of $500,000, appreciation continues and we can get

$575,000 for each house that we build. With a net building cost of $250,000 and the land cost to me of $40,000, I am into each deal for $290,000. Throw in some additional soft costs for engineering, additional site work, demolition, interest carry, sales and marketing expenses, and we could be into each house for $375,000. At $575,000, we could net out about $200,000 each. Apparently, this is what the big players in the luxury homes market are netting on $600,000 homes, as well. This deal could net out $10,000,000. Of that, the building partner will probably want $3,000,000, leaving Pete and me $7,000,000 to split. Now, I could be getting $3.5 million at the conclusion of the project. You simply have to love real estate.

So, here is the question that I pose to you since I will need to answer this within the next 6 months. Do you sell the project, take the money, and pay off your rental portfolio in cash, then putting another $800,000 of cash into your pocket, and live off of $200,000 a year in free cash flows from the rentals, never having to work another day in your life... or do you take a chance on building the project and capitalizing on an additional $1.5 million at the end of 12 months' worth of risk? Not entirely an easy question to answer right now. Along with the many issues that this project presents, this question is equivalent to the Texas Hold 'em player saying ALL IN. Would you be all in? I could be the internet executive who had the foresight to pull out enough to change his life forever, or I could be the carpet installer who "almost" had everything. For better or for worse, I credit myself with always being the optimist. I imagine that my decision will change and fluctuate on this topic thousands of times over the next 6 months while we develop the project. I am also sure that there is not a correct answer to this question. This is a life changing wager…and this is exactly why I love this business.

Should be interesting and fun to watch this process evolve.

May 2005

Just looking at the last paragraph…things have already changed. We continue to plug along on the Charles Street project. We met with the planning department, which is in the process of tweaking our plan and hopefully agreeing to let us build the 61 townhouses. We've also met with the Baltimore Development Corporation (BDC). This is a quasi-public organization that helps the City of Baltimore with its decisions on how to better develop the properties in the city. In order for us to convert an industrial property over to residential use, we need the BDC's blessing. So, last month we met with the woman who handles the industrial sector of properties in the city. It's her job to preserve industrial properties within Baltimore, so you can imagine how that meeting went, when we went into her office looking to take yet another one of her properties and convert it into a residential development. In order to prepare for a meeting like this, you need to take a totally objective look at the property. When you drive by the lot and look at its current use, you can objectively say that industrial is not its highest and best use. The majority of the neighborhood is residential. The last thing that these people want is large trucks driving in and out of their residential developments. Then take an objective look at what the physical characteristics of the site are. In this case, the site is overgrown with weeds on about 40% of the site. The next 20% of the site is currently used as a parking lot. Another 10% of the site is a burned-out non-functional building, leaving the final 10% of the site to being used as a truck repair center. Certainly, anyone would have to think that this site is not being maximized as an industrial zoned property. The truck repair shop employs about 5-7 people. One of my goals is to relocate the shop to another site within the Baltimore City limits, keeping these jobs within the industrial sector of the city limits. All told, the meeting went well, and while the woman in charge of BDC industrial felt like we were taking yet another one of her industrial properties, and rightly so, she was hard-pressed to make an argument as to why it should be kept industrial. So now we have the blessing of the BDC, we are in the process of getting the final blessing of the planning department at the city, and then we will take the project back to the neighborhood association and see if we can get them to completely buy into our initiative. If all of this happens in the next 2 to 3 weeks, we will meet with the city council person for that area and submit the bill for rezoning. The council takes off over the summer months, which will provide us time to hammer through the items in order to have the subdivision approved by the city. Our goal will be that, once the council reconvenes in September, we can get the property rezoned and subdivided all at the same time. Our subsequent goal will be to relocate the trucking company and find an ultimate buyer for the site.

Speaking of finding the ultimate buyer for the site... it's funny how many people come out of the woodwork when you have a product that's in incredibly high demand. At this point in time – May 2005 – real estate continues to be an incredible investment. We could be at the top of the market, or it could continue to rise, but regardless, large builders are looking for any and all land on which to build houses. People from New York, Washington D.C., and Philadelphia are now looking at Baltimore City for development opportunities. Lots large enough to build 60 houses on are few and far between, not to mention lots located at the outskirts of hot boroughs like Federal Hill. And the bank that is financing the acquisition of the land... well, wouldn't you know it, but the president of the bank has someone interested in purchasing our land. The president of the engineering company... well, wouldn't you know it, but he has someone interested in purchasing the land also. Two of the attorneys that we have used on other projects.... Well, do I need to say more? I am playing golf with one of the largest builders in the country next week. Pete and I remain cautiously optimistic as we continue to meet with buyers, planners, zoning folks, and other stakeholders.

So, what's the property actually worth? This is a question that I contemplate daily, and I hope to get better at honing in on it over the next few months. We use this metric that postulates builders are willing to pay 30% of the final resale of a house to determine the land acquisition for a lot. Don't ask me where we came up with the 30% number, but it works for now. Here we have 61 lots that will ultimately build townhouses worth $500,000. Run these numbers, and each lot should be worth $150,000. Well, 61 of them should produce a land number of somewhere around $9,000,000. Boy, is that a lot of zeros. I'm constantly trying to find comparable properties or developments to use in order to better understand our resale number. Pulte Homes, one of the country's biggest builders, is just beginning to presell a community not 3 miles from my site. They found a manufacturing site that was rezoned to residential, and they are now going to put 121 townhomes on it, with the dimensions of 18 feet by 36 feet. This site provides a fantastically comparable development. So, I check out their website and talk with the sales agent working the trailer as they begin to presell these units. Much to my surprise, they are already 25% presold, months before they are going to break ground on the site. And how much are they preselling them for, you ask? Their base model for the Camden (the smaller unit) is $625,000, and the base model for the McHenry is $675,000. Let's just say that the average unit is $650,000. Using my 30% land acquisition model, our lot price just went up to $195,000, or a total package of $11,895,000. I keep telling myself that we cannot count on this pricing, and that I should tread rather cautiously with this type of dreaming, speculation, and optimism... but it's hard.

Now I am just not sure how much of my life should be changed by the past few pages of this chapter. Again, my wife always says that you haven't earned the money until the cash is in the account. If I were to put my eggs into that basket and put all of my faith in its results, I could probably take this summer off and spend that extra time with my family. It's just very difficult to believe that this type of good fortune could happen, and is going to happen, to me.

So, just to keep things interesting, we are building 6 new construction houses in Canton and Federal Hill. These houses should retail out at around $650,000 and we should be about $400,000 into each. The two in Federal Hill will hit the market come this fall, and the four in Canton sometime next spring. In addition, we are doing the plans for 4 units in Butcher's Hill that should retail out at $500,000, with about $300,000 in each of these. When it rains, it really does pour, and should the market continue at this rate, we should have just an absolutely unbelievable year. For all of this new construction, we have finally found a builder that we can work with. Over the years, we've learned that when doing construction on a budget, you end up with delays, poor workmanship, and complete dissatisfaction with the entire construction process. While, in the first few years, we prided ourselves on being able to complete a rehab project for $60 per square foot, we are now comfortable paying $125 per square foot for a much higher quality of work. This understanding simply evolved over years of learning that it truly is better to sell a luxury product than an entry level product. The builder that we found seems to be a truly professional outfit. The owner is onsite each and every day on our projects, making sure that things go smoothly. We recently took him out for dinner and a baseball game just to show our appreciation for the work that he's done for us, and to better foster the relationship for the future. By becoming affiliated with these guys, we are now able to focus more on what we do best, which is finding land to develop and raising capital, and leaving the construction element, which was incredibly time consuming in the past, to another party. I will comment that paying the $125 per square foot really bothers Pete. He just doesn't seem to understand why the builder should make $20,000 to $30,000 per house. I look at it from a different perspective, in that we are making $200,000 per house, and we are really doing the easier job in the process. While we disagree on things, the partnership between Pet and I is once again going well.

In addition to the new construction element, we are tooling away on the two foreclosures that we bought at the end of last year. We hired a full-time carpenter onto the payroll to do everything from light plumbing to hanging sheetrock. He should be in each house about 3 months in turning them around. The numbers on Howard Avenue come in with a purchase price of $136,000, about $40,000 going into the rehab, with a projected sales price of $260,000. The other house is a buy-in of $185,000, about $25,000 in the rehab, and with a projected out price of $250,000. Also, we have been flipping a few properties here and there. What is funny in all this is that my perspective has changed. I'm not terribly excited or impressed with the Calvert deal, but it will net out about $125,000 without me ever seeing the inside of the house. We plan to use this money to help us carry the debt on the Charles Street Development Project. Other happenings include a two lot deal that we bought from a church in Hampden. This was a parking lot that was actually zoned R-8. We took it to the engineers and had them cut it up into 2 buildable lots. We had plans drawn up, and just before building it, we sold off the lots to another builder. The ultimate sales price of the lots was about $300,000. We made good money, and really shouldn't look back. I have a feeling that I am going to regret this decision in about 9 months, though, when I see the builder making an additional $50,000 profit per each home, but I can't be greedy; we ended up making a few sheckles and not having to deal with the issues of building these two homes.

I can't forget to update you on the lake houses in Virginia. I went to a closing down at Smith Mountain Lake at the end of April in order to purchase the second lake house. Now, I haven't seen either of these houses, and have relied completely on the judgment of my good friend and previous business partner, Richard. The first house seemed to be a great purchase on paper. It rented for $2,400 per week and the purchase price was $460,000. After debt service and management fees, we stood to roughly break even if we were lucky enough to rent this house for 12 weeks. Unfortunately, the management company told me to count on 8 weeks, and thus far, as of May 15, 2005, we only have 3 weeks rented. I am trying not to worry, but this could prove to be a hemorrhage this year, should things not start to pick up. I'm not sure why I keep banging my head against this wall called vacation rental property. I guess I like trouble because Richard has been pitching me to purchase the house next door. But this time, there seems to be a method to his madness. The first house that we bought for $460,000 sits high atop the embankment of the lake. The house is about 150 yards from the actual water. The challenge with the house is the view. On those 150 yards sits a small forest of trees. In order to get to our dock, you need to navigate down a path, through the trees. We could chop down the trees to enhance the view, but what we learned from our land survey is that we don't own the land that has the small forest…the neighbor does. We have an easement through his property, just to get access to our dock. Richard's rationale for this purchase is that controlling the house next door would allow us to cut down some trees and redraw the property lines so that the value of our $460,000 house should go up sharply. Basically, we are trying to create equity by cutting down trees, and giving the property a better view by creating lake front property.

Well, here's the problem with this reasoning: the numbers on the second house are not as compelling as the first. The house was built in the late 70's. It's outdated, musty, only has 3 bedrooms, and needs a complete home makeover. This house was purchased for $500,000, but it only manages to bring in $1,800 per week. I don't think that Richie truly understands the amount of carry expense we are going to incur on the second property, and perhaps we might not have jumped into this investment so quickly if we had sat down together to really run the numbers. At any rate, we are going to make it work. How, you ask? Well, if the real estate market is half as great as both Richard and I believe it is, the outdated 70's style house that we purchase for $500,000 should be worth $600,000 in one year, after $30,000 worth of updates. Over the course of the year, we also plan to cut down the trees, giving property 1 a fantastic view. This should increase the value of this house from $460,000 up to $575,000, probably overnight. We should be able to create $100,000 in equity that easily. This is why I love real estate. There is no better business out there. Unfortunately, we are not going to be able to redraw the property lines. Apparently, there's a law requiring lots to be a minimum of .5 acres. If we redraw the lines, we'd need a variance…not that that is out of the question, but it is another hurdle to the process. If we fail on the variance, we can at least reconstruct an easement that benefits property number 1 forever. We will rent property 2 throughout the season, and then put it back on the market in the fall. If our hopes and dreams are correct, though, we should net out about $50,000 after all of the expenses with this property. We will then take the $50,000 and pay down the note on property 1. With a debt of $375,000 on property 1, our monthly debt service should be about $2,000 per month, or $24,000 per year. If we can get rentals up to 10 weeks per year, we may even have an investment that roughly breaks even…and we get to use it 42 weeks per year for free. Given all of that, this should be a pretty good investment. Theoretically.

Here is another little tool that I've learned about through a good friend and fellow investor, Victor Colucci. Victor has been doing real estate for about 10 years in Baltimore. I first met Victor at the courthouse steps in Baltimore City. It was a hot day in July in Baltimore, the type of day when you would vastly prefer to be at the beach or at the pool instead of looking at houses and pounding the pavement. I was relatively new to the business, and somewhat green. As I was waiting for the auctioneer to show up, this guy and his girlfriend drove up to the courthouse steps in a convertible BMW. They parked illegally in front of the courthouse, got out, and pitched up their beach chairs as they proceeded to sun themselves while waiting for the auctions to begin. I struck up a conversation with the guy because, at that time, I was really thinking that this guy had the life. Mr. Colucci explained to me his story in real estate, and we seemed to really hit it off. Since then, we've become great friends, and I currently manage his entire rental portfolio. Well, Victor introduced me to a way of investing money tax free. There's a small company out in Ohio called Equity Trust. They set up an IRA account for you and purchase real estate in the name of the IRA. So, I started up with just a few thousand dollars in my IRA. The problem with the IRA is that you must purchase the property with all cash. The tax code doesn't allow for recourse loans, which I have to personally guarantee. So after 2 years of squirrelling away money into this IRA, I have around $50,000. I've been looking for a smaller property to purchase with this money, but I've just not been able to find one. Victor is also a big fan of the self-directed IRA, and he has managed to parlay $40,000 into well over $500,000 in just a few years. Well, it is nice to have friends that want to do business with you because Victor and I are scheduled to close our first IRA purchase as partners. We are going into this house as partners 50/50, and each of us put up $37,500 out of our respective IRA accounts. The house is a small 2 bedroom rowhouse in a decent area. We are paying about $75,000 for it, but I conservatively think that it is worth about $110,000. So, through Victor's generosity, he has cut me in on an instant $17,000 in net worth. Pretty nice guy, huh? Now, the unit is in decent condition, and I will put a tenant in there paying $700 per month. That $8,400 per year, minus the taxes of $700, means that Vic and I will split $7,700 per year. My $3,850 will go back into my IRA, yielding about an 11% return on this investment. Again, not bad for a rookie, but this neighborhood has been appreciating like gang busters. Conservatively, I think that this little house should be worth somewhere around $150,000 next year. That means that my and Victor's equity should be at $75,000, or roughly a 100% return on this investment, and don't forget the 11% we got from the rents. If you gave me 40 hours a week for a straight month, I still don't think that I could find an investment vehicle yielding 111% return per year.

In finishing up the entry for May, I have to say that the first five months of this year have been a roller coaster of activity. I have purchased several million dollars' worth of property. I have watched the market continue to push upwards, we are beginning to sign leases for the college rentals at $5,000 more per unit than last year, and the office building just picked up a tenant and its market value is in excess of $1.1 million. But the best part of this year has been the time that I have been able to spend with my family. I have managed to eat breakfast and take them to school frequently. With lacrosse, soccer, and baseball beginning, I am at just about every practice and game. We went to Miami and Disney during the boy's spring break, and hope to be heading to the islands following their last day of school. The plans are in the works for some additional work to be done on my primary residence. Oh yeah, and I have found the time to become a Make-A-Wish volunteer. This was one of my goals for this year, and I am finally making it happen. I attended a full day's training seminar on becoming a wish grantor for the organization. Since then, I have been active in fund raising for them, I have been working with one 18 year old boy with terminal cancer who has a wish to be practicing football with Ray Lewis and the Baltimore Ravens, and I am scheduled to take on my second wish child next week.

May 31, 2005

It is a really big day today. Pete and I settled on Charles Street with a purchase price of $2,150,000. This is by far our biggest acquisition to date. The excitement is palpable. We settled at All-Star title up there on North St. Paul Street. Everything went really smoothly. We were so excited that we decided to stop at a bar for a drink right after closing. Now, we don't have a history for spending money foolishly, but today was different. There was something life changing that happened today…Charles Street. Upon entering the bar, we asked the bartender for a couple of shots of vodka. As we sipped our vodka, we dreamed of what we will do with all of that money that we were going to receive from Charles Street. We then decided that vodka was not celebratory enough, so we ordered two shots of Remy Louis XIII. It comes from a crystal bottle and flows as smoothly down your throat as you can imagine. Now, for the kicker, these shots of Louis ran us $150 each.

PRIME RIB - BALTIMORE

THE PRIME RIB

The Civilized Steakhouse

Date : 5/31/2005 Check#: 79144
Time : 8:19:15 PM Table#: 2755
Covers : 0 Server: 33 Bar
Person#: 1

1	PREMIUM VODKA	9.00
1	PREMIUM	9.00
2	REMY LOUIS XIII	300.00
	Beverage Sub-Total	318.00
	SUB TOTAL	318.00
	Sales Tax	15.90

TOTAL $333.90

THANK YOU!
Bar

Give The Gift Of Good Taste
A Prime Rib Gift Certificate!!

I have many decisions to make about how to proceed to live my life. This is an exciting year for me, and publishing and selling this book may quickly make its way onto my goal sheet for next year. With that thought, I am checking out for this month. Prosper on!

LESSONS LEARNED

- Bigger deals require much larger chunks of capital. Prepare to continue to liquidate cash flowing short term projects in order to fund larger deals.

- Be careful of irrational exuberance. As Warren Buffett once said, *"Be fearful when others are greedy, and greedy when others are fearful."* Stay balanced.

RED TAPE AND TIMING

November 2005

Today is November 17th. This is actually a pretty significant day in the life of Signature Properties. Today is the second reader of the rezoning bill that has been submitted for Charles Street. The process has been fairly smooth thus far. We hired an engineering company in Baltimore to help us design the layout for the 64 lots. They put their team of designers to the test of laying out as many lots as possible, using the current limitations from the city. They designed 64 total lots with houses that would each be 18 feet by 36 feet. In exchange for about $100,000 of my money, they handed me back a drawing that could be submitted to the city planning department for subdivision. Of course, I am joking when I say that the drawing itself cost that much money, but it sure feels like it. They have been a very professional company to work with, though. Over the summer, we met with many various offices within the city. These offices included transportation, environmental, planning public utilities, and every other person at the city who might have a problem with this site getting an additional 64 residences on it. We've had about 3 different meetings with the city, and many iterations of changes to our drawings. The woman who is spearheading the project for us was a previous employee over at the city. She is incredible. She knows all of the city codes and rules, and has been instrumental in us getting as far as we have in the process. We also hired a pretty well-known zoning attorney to help us draft the bill and walk us through the process with the City of Baltimore. Again, paying a premium for top notch people is important: he has proved to be a great asset to the team. He arranged a meeting where we sat down with the local councilman for the area where the site is located. In order to rezone a piece of land, many people have to be in favor of the change. It all started with the support of the neighborhood association. Without their help, we would not have been able to proceed with this at all. Then we set up a meeting with the councilman for that area. When presenting to him, we already had the support of his constituents. Therefore, he was comfortable submitting a bill to the city council on our behalf. So, in August of this year, the zoning attorney put together a bill for the councilman to sign and submit. This step happened without a glitch.

Now, on November 17th, the bill was read at the city council meeting. This is called the first reader. The bill will be read again at a December meeting called the second reader. Finally, on January 2, we will know if the rezoning has been approved. From there, it is sent to the Mayor's office for signature, and viola, the property has been successfully rezoned from manufacturing to residential. While this entire process has been taking place, Pete and I have continued to pay the mortgage, taxes, and insurance on the property. We did a brief cash flow analysis, and realized that in order to carry the property until January, we'd need $116,000. We simply did not have the funds in the Signature account. So, back on the fundraising horse we went again. Within about 3 months, we put together another $100,000, of which I personally convinced my wife to invest $50,000 toward. This project is an absolute bear to carry, and the quicker we can sell it, the better off we will be. There is a saying in real estate that goes like this: 'put together your construction budget and your timeline, and then double it'. Incredibly prophetic for this rather large project. The engineering budget is rolling out of control. One iteration after another costs us tens of thousands of dollars. Wasn't I supposed to be retired by now? I thought that this project would have been complete and I would be finishing up this book from my yacht in the Caribbean... Well, things just take time, and this thing is certainly taking time.

So with the zoning out of our hands and really nothing that we can do to speed up this process, we're brought to our next issue, which is the actual subdividing of the land. You see, the lot is currently known as 1901 South Charles Street. It is one single big lot. After we rezone the property to residential, we need to draw the property lines to make the 64 separate lots. This process is called subdivision. We need to provide numerous documents prepared by the engineering firm in order to get this approved. Once this is approved and recorded, it can then be referred to as "record plat". This is the point at which this lot becomes worth a lot of money. Until then, we have one piece of land. When we change the zoning, this will increase the value somewhat, because we have changed its use. When we divide it up, thought, the sum of the individual lots far outweighs the value of one large lot. This leaves us at a decision making point. At one time, Pete and I discussed building out the houses. Several things have changed. First and foremost is the information that we have gathered about the timeline of development. By February, we should have the almighty record plat. From there, we can have the engineers put together construction drawings for how the sewer pipes will run, how the roads will run, how the electric conduit will run, how the underground storm water management will run, and many, many other items that are required before the city will approve us tearing up the land. These drawings and this interaction with the city is proposed to take until September of 2006. We then can hire a development contracting company to start pushing the dirt around the site. They would be the ones to lay the pipe and the electric and the roads, and all of the other items that go into finishing off the lots to the point that we can build houses. This process takes about 6 months, which would put us at March of 2007. Not only is this project taking a lot of time, but we would then have to go back to the bank and ask them for an additional $3,000,000. We would have to raise more cash to service the additional debt, and the time to carry the loan. We spoke with some big builders, and they predict that we could be able to build and sell 3 or 4 houses per month. If you do the math, it would then take 15 months to sell out the community. On the timeline discussed above, we are now out of the project in June 2008. As amateurs in a project this size, this timeline truly gives me pause. Again, going back to my bubble hypothesis, how long will this market continue to rise? Are we really challenging fate by stretching out the timelines?

Over the past two months, we have seen a significant slow-down in the real estate market. For almost five years, people have been talking about the bubble bursting in the market. Unlike the stock market, real estate is difficult to judge when it comes to the popping of a bubble. In stocks, one day your stock is worth $100, and the next it is worth $25. This has an immediate impact and can be quantified quickly. With real estate, the effects and signs are slower. If you look for quantifiable data, the average time that it takes to sell a house has extended; they call that *days-on-market.* It used to be that if you put a house on the market, it would sell within a week. Not only that, but you would have multiple contracts presented for people anxious to buy that house. As of recently, when you put a house on the market, it can take 30-60 days before someone presents an offer. Furthermore, if you don't get an offer within 30 days, people then tend to reduce the price of the house. These are real time signals that the real estate market is going to experience a period of softening. A good question is, how sudden and how severe will the softening be? Pete and I debate daily on the amount of carnage that will result because of this correction. I am a believer that the market will continue to suffer for about the next six months. This correction will seem more severe as people are just getting used to the fact that their houses are not selling within 30 days. This most definitely gives me pause on our business. So, on Charles Street, we have looked at the timeline necessary to finish off the lots and the risk of an uncertain market. With these two factors in mind, we have decided to sell off the lot once we have achieved record plat, with no development and no construction. One final thought on this bubble issue: I don't believe the bubble will implode, but I do see the writing on the wall as of this November 17, 2005, and it does cause me a lot of concern.

With the realization that we're not going to be the ultimate homebuilders on this project, we now need to identify who will be the ultimate purchaser. At this point in the subdivision process, we are looking at 64 houses to be built, with each one being 18 feet wide. This was the original plan submitted by our engineers. As we talk with various national homebuilders, they all seem to have different ideas of what the actual size of the lots should be. As a result, it's imperative for us to identify and contract with a homebuilder immediately so that we can redraw our final plat submission for the city, according to what the purchasing homebuilder would like. I went ahead and put together a packet containing enough information for homebuilders to analyze this deal and be able to make their best offers possible. In the packet was the Phase I and Phase II survey results, the letter from the community, the notes from our meetings with the city, the proposed bill that is being submitted for the rezoning, some comparable sales prices in the area, and everything else that might sway them to paying us a high number to purchase the lot. We sent out about 10 packets. Are you ready for this? Of the packets that I sent out, I have already received two offers, and I am hoping to receive another 3 LOIs (we call those letters of intent) by the first week of December. I'll reveal the offer prices to you shortly – extremely exciting stuff. In dealing with these homebuilders, they are playing the same games that I play when I buy a single house. First, they sandbag me on what they think the final resale price of these finished houses on Charles Street can be. I believe that they are worth $650,000. Being conservative, there is a chance that they only bring in $600,000. The national homebuilders are trying to convince me that they are looking at $550,000 to $575,000. Now, I don't blame them for trying to reduce their risk by being conservative on the resale value, as I do the same thing. I tend to be a mathematical investor, and expect that from the homebuilder. So the difficulty that I am going to have is accepting an offer that the builder cannot justify mathematically. Don't get me wrong: I want everyone involved in the transaction to make money. With multiple offers, my goal is to work these guys for the highest and best offer. I have given them 3 weeks to finalize their highest and best offers, and I am hoping to get more offers in the door.

Enough about Charles Street. Let's take a closer look at the Signature picture. We do not have so many projects coming and going as we once had in the past. Looking back at earlier chapters, we were constantly buying and selling properties. We had settlements on a basis of what felt like every other week. Things are much more sedate now. I feel like I am working a fair amount less than four years ago. The projects that we are doing are larger deals. They stand to yield higher profits, and involve less and less daily interaction. On the construction side, we are currently building 10 new houses. All of these are in the hands of the general contractors. Unless I am stopping by the houses to check on construction, I don't have that much to do with them on a day-to-day basis. On the rental property side, we have recently hired a management company to begin to take over the day-to-day management of this portfolio. Property management is a time consuming business. I found a large part of my day being spent managing the tenants, showing places, signing leases, collecting rents, calling in maintenance calls, and the list goes on and on. We tried to hire an employee to handle some of these tasks. He was successful on several pieces, but could not seem to put together the whole package. On the college rental side, he only managed to fill 9 of the 15 properties with college students. If you remember from before, the only reason to truly get into the cash flow game is through renting them at above market rents. We now have 6 average producing properties that are not being rented to college students. We ended up letting our property manager go, and are in the transitional phase of moving our portfolio over to this management company. The verdict is out as to how successful this move will be, but it should certainly bring about some consistency in our operation.

The other reason for subcontracting this out is somewhat selfish. I see the Charles Street deal looming around June of next year. This should, and hopefully will, produce a sizeable windfall for both me and Pete. Ideally, I would like to pay off the rental portfolio and live off of the substantial base income I could receive from this investment. Having a management company allows me to separate myself just one more step away from the business. At some point next year, my real estate business may be more of a real estate investment. No different than investing in dividend producing stocks or funds, this investment will kick off solid returns, year after year. If all things are to go as planned, by June of next year, the entire rental portfolio will be paid off. This should produce about $100,000 a year, going to me directly. Think about the gravity of this…for the rest of my life. I can't think of any other career or vehicle which allows you to accomplish this kind of annuity within four years. This number assumes that I will continue to have a property management company, and that my interaction for this money will be nothing more than reviewing a monthly statement. I do realize that I am exaggerating slightly, and all investments require some type of oversight, but I certainly do not expect to have any day–to-day activities for this income. I have to admit, most of the excitement of real estate is dreaming about what the future holds. After four years, I have finally learned enough about real estate to understand how to make money at it.

November 20, 2005

Several things have happened over the course of this weekend. First, if you remember, we had our zoning meeting this past Friday. I exchanged emails with Pete and found out that everything went just as smoothly as it could have been planned. The City Planning Commission had no problems with our layout or the proposed change in the zoning. This was another huge hurdle for us to overcome, and now we plug along until the next meeting. The attorney working on the rezoning did, however, tell Pete that he doesn't expect the final rezoning bill to be signed and in effect until the end of February of 2006. This really shouldn't present a problem on the sale side, as we don't anticipate selling the property until June of 2006, but financially, it will create a minor issue. If you remember, we had to go out and raise about $100,000 in order to carry the project until the end of January of 2006. I ended up putting $50,000 of my own money into the account to offset these expenses. We fully anticipated having the zoning complete and the subdivision recorded by February. The problem remains now, that we need to raise even more capital to carry the project until June of 2006. But, we can always go back to the bank with the new developments, have the property reappraised, and hopefully draw out some of this new found equity to carry our debt for the next few months. Not only this, but we should have a contract in hand from one of the national builders to justify the increase in price on the new appraisal. This is what I envision will make the bankers feel comfortable before they give us more money. So, leaving on that note, I will pick up and follow up in January.

January 2006

Happy New Year to all!!! This is probably going to be a life-changing year, and the year that I actually reach my ultimate goal. I originally set out to accomplish the goal of $2 million. The vision also included having the freedom to spend countless hours of time with my family, which I do enjoy each and every day. Somewhere over the past few years, perhaps through my involvement with Make-a-Wish or my becoming more involved with ministries, I decided I needed more money to free up even more time to donate on and help others. It is completely counterintuitive to the capitalist model, but nevertheless... I have finally found a method of manufacturing money in rental properties. If only I could continue to grow as I have during the past 4 years, I could increase my net worth, my cash flow, and free up more time. This year, though, my goals have drifted. The biggest cause for this is the

Charles Street property, and I will discuss its status shortly. Also, I have been reading more and more books about relationships, and fewer and fewer books about financial success. One of the books quotes: "I don't know anyone that on their death bed only wished that they could have made more money." My thinking really has changed over the past five years. I have watched people without any money have fantastic friendships and relationships in their lives, and I have watched wealthy people exist with complete emptiness. They are one-dimensional and are worshipping the dollar more than any other relationship in their life. I have been guilty of chasing that dollar perhaps to vigorously in the past…even in the past five years in real estate. One can easily claim that there is simply not enough time in the day to have good relationships with kids, spouses, pets, family, and friends. But I will tell you something funny: we find 8-10 hours of our waking days to spend at our jobs. Think about that. If you wake up at 7:00 AM to get dressed to drive to work, work until 5:30 PM, and drive home to arrive at 6 or 6:30 PM, where are you going to find time to invest in your relationships? But, that said... You certainly did not buy this book to hear me pontificate about how to foster relationships; you bought the book to help you understand how to invest in real estate and find the time to enjoy life. So, where am I in my quest?

We decided to sell off the office building that we bought about 20 months ago. If you recall, we purchased it at foreclosure for $350,000. The building was in tough shape both physically and financially. It needed over $125,000 in repairs, including a new roof, new air conditioning condensers (yes, both of them), a new parking lot, new bathrooms, paint, and some minor stuff to give it appeal. We ended up borrowing $100,000 from a friend for the purchase, and borrowed the balance from the bank. We threw about $60,000 of profits from other deals at the building to carry it since it was only about 25% occupied when we bought it. I'm actually not sure why we're selling it. I think that the biggest reason is the $35,000 air conditioning condenser that went in this past summer. Real estate is a passive activity for the most part. Once in a while, something breaks or a tenant does not pay on time. Well, I think that the new AC unit was our breaking point. The building takes about $58,000 per year to run in operating expenses. The majority of this is in utilities since we pay the electric and gas for the entire building. The rest of the money goes to janitorial services, repairs and maintenance, trash removal, grass mowing, marketing, and miscellaneous costs that occasionally pop up. Add these expenses to the mortgage payment to the bank and the 10% return to the private investor (about $48,000 per year), all in, it costs us $106,000 a year to keep the building lights on and the tenants happy. The positive side is that we have gotten 12 of the 13 suites rented. We have run ads in the local papers, put a banner across the top of the building, put it out there on the internet, and one by one we have filled the building with rent-paying tenants. We even had this storage area in the basement (no windows) that we'd used to store office supplies and building supplies. We cleaned that out and now rent it to an exotic reptile distributor for $8 per square foot. The property has gross rents of $136,000 per year. We are netting out some $30,000 per year on the building.

So when I said that I'm not 100% sure why we are liquidating, I meant it. I think we are considering selling the building to cash out. Renting real estate is a great way to have a nice steady cash flow, but the real money is made when you sell. Valuing commercial real estate is unique. If you were investing in a commercial property, you would invest by using a capitalization rate model to evaluate what the building is worth. In order to do this, you would take the net operating income from the project and divide it by the prevailing cap rate. The net operating income (NOI) for my building is the gross revenues of $136,000 minus the operating expense of $58,000. That gives you a NOI of $78,000. If the prevailing cap rate for a commercial property in that area, given current interest rates, is 10%, the building should be worth $780,000. If the market was dictating a 9% cap rate (based on current conditions, and costs of capital and risk), $78,000/.09

would equal a value of $866,666. How does that affect our office property? We are in the building for approximately $500,000 when you count the mortgages and the cash we put in. If we were lucky enough to sell it for $900,000, we could net out $400,000. That would set both me and Pete up for the year with just this one sale. That is the reason that we are looking to sell the building. We would happily take $900,000 from a potential buyer. Too many times in this business, we've run across people trying to sell us something that they don't have: value. They try to sell us the potential to make the project work. This is a big idea. We never try to buy "potential", though, because it is the subsequent actions that bring the "value". That being said, you want to buy value and add potential. For instance, consider a property primed for residential subdivision and development. Well, is the seller selling a piece of land that is already subdivided and ready for me to put houses on? If not, he's selling me a raw piece of land that has the "potential" for subdivided lots, and he should price it accordingly as a piece of raw land. Agents and owners try to sell you the raw land at a price equal to what it is worth *if* it was already subdivided. I think that's ludicrous, and I tell them that all the time. If you want to get the price you want, subdivide the land for me. You see, there is cost and risk in subdividing land, and I am not paying you so that I can take on the risk and spend the money to add that value. Doing that would mean I'd be, essentially, paying for the process of subdividing twice-over, in buying the potential and then adding the value itself.

Interestingly, though, I find myself putting together a marketing packet for the office building and trying to price in all of the potential of the building. Funny how perspective changes when you become the seller. I find myself thinking in phrases such as "once fully occupied" and "once the leases get to their maximum level after several years of escalation", projecting that the building is worth $1,250,000 at a 9% cap rate. The write-up is pretty compelling, and in this time and day when commercial opportunities are few and far between, the right buyer just might step up to the plate in order to buy that potential. Like the famous hockey player Wayne Gretsky once said, "You miss 100% of the shots you don't take." The building has gotten a lot of action on it over the past week. In the end, it produced 3 or 4 buyers with offers from $800,000 up to $900,000. This is exactly what I had expected, until we got the bite that I was looking for. An offer came in for $1,250,000. It is a non-contingent offer with a sizable $65,000 deposit attached. They wanted 14 days to study the financials. Well, the 14 days came and went, and they never contacted me to withdraw from the deal. I've talked with the agent representing the buyer, and as far as she knows, they are in the deal. Regardless, I am entitled to $65,000 if they change their mind. The settlement is supposed to happen in the second week of February. If you run the numbers, it is selling at a cap rate of 6.25%. This is extremely low, given the neighborhood and risk level of the investment. Only time will tell, but if the deal goes through, we should see about $700,000 on the settlement statement. I've already told me wife to expect a $350,000 deposit to be made.

How about a quick follow-up to the Virginia lake properties? Over Christmas week, I went down to check on the properties. To give you the quickie refresher, we bought one newer 5 bedroom house that rents for $2,600 per week now, and this is close to the water, but not on the water. A small forest separates this property from the water and an easement has been granted in order to have dock access. An easement is a path on the neighbor's property that allows our house's property to cross over their property in order to get to the water. In other words, they can't block tenants in the house from that path. When the neighbor's house came up for sale, we pounced on it. Now, as a rental investment, the numbers simply don't make sense. We paid $500,000 for the house and it only rents for $1,500 per week. Even though it is lakefront, it is an older home with only 3 bedrooms. At this point, I feel like we bought it so that it could hemorrhage $3,000 a month from my checking account, but I *think* I remember why we bought it. Over the winter, my partner on that deal had a tree guy come in and remove every single tree separating the 5 bedroom house from the water. He planted grass over the entire area, and wouldn't you know it, but we created a waterfront house where one did not exist before. The 5 bedroom house now has an uninterrupted perfectly elevated view of the lake. It has a rolling lawn right down to the water's edge…simply breathtaking.

View from Deck at Shangrila without forest

Over the Christmas break, I met an engineer down at the house. This week, he's submitting a new drawing of the property lines. We're redrawing the lines so that the 5 bedroom is now officially a waterfront property (of course, at the peril of the 3 bedroom house). We plan on doing some cosmetic repairs to the 3 bedroom, perhaps about $30,000 worth, and reselling that property come the spring of this year. Alright, so how about the numbers, you ask. On the 3 bedroom, we paid $500,000. We had some luck of timing with the market and, after some paint and carpet, that will go on the market for $675,000. As for the 5 bedroom which we plan to own for a long time, we paid $460,000, and it is now worth $750,000. Our little scheme has created $290,000 in instant equity, and in less than a year, as well. With the rents of $2,600 per week, we are shooting to rent it for 12 weeks per year. This should pay the majority of the expenses. We are not planning on selling it until we find a better investment. As for the $175,000 that we should make off of the sale of the 3 bedroom, we are looking into a 1031 tax free exchange, and buying a beach property in North Carolina. Who knows... we could do this whole process again?

For this month, here are a couple of quick updates on some of the projects. We are flipping two properties that have each been in the portfolio for about a year. One, we bought as a package of four about a year ago. The other has already sold, and the debt has been completely paid off. This house (which has been owned free and clear) actually settled last Friday for $75,000. Next week, a small single that we bought for $75,000 will go for $87,000. We may make a few sheckles on this one, but not too much. Lastly is a property on the west side that we picked up for $60,000. The market was smoking when we bought this property, and we thought that we were going to cash out with $20,000 quickly. We had two viable contracts on the property, but one after another, they both fell through. I know that I mentioned before that we're seeing signs of the slowing market. Banks are becoming leery of the speculative investments, and this property on the west side certainly hits that point. However, we have a contract at $84,000, and we're keeping our fingers crossed that it goes through.

Let me take just a quick moment to discuss the market softening. With my being in real estate, people always ask me if I'm concerned about the real estate bubble bursting. Having lived through and been involved in the bursting of the tech stock bubble, I understand the dynamics of a bubble. A bubble is when you own $40,000 of stock one day, and $20,000 of stock 3 weeks later. That, to me, is a bubble. When you can lose 50% of your investment almost overnight…that is *risk*. Housing is not risky. In housing, you may see a softening. Some people call it a 'flattening' and some say a 'soft landing', but they're all saying the same thing. The 2006 projections are for volume to only go up 2.5%. Think about that, when the market for the past 4 years has gone up over 20% per year. That past rate is certainly an unsustainable amount of appreciation, and everyone knows that it has to come to an end. So, when the experts are predicting a 2.5% gain, it may seem like a burst from 20%, but it is still a positive gain, and we have to remember that fact. Furthermore, the 2007 projections do show a reduction, and in Baltimore, they are predicting a loss of 1.7%. Think about that, that if I plan on selling that house for $300,000, I have to be willing to take $295,000 instead. That $5,000 is certainly not going to break the bank. The thing is…we buy conservatively. That is not always the case with real estate investors. In the frenzied market, people were simply paying too much to get into the game. For our property that we bought for $150,000 and from which we should profit about $50,000, rookie investors were paying $200,000 to $250,000 for the same type of shell. By the time they completed the project, they were in it for over $300,000. Well, this works great if your model is based on a continued price escalation of 20% per year, but certainly doesn't work if you are only getting a 2.5% increase, much less a 1.7% decrease in price. The mass carnage is just about to begin. There are so many people that call themselves investors, but should call themselves speculators who are about to get bludgeoned by the market. As this market adjusts, people that were paying too much are slowly realizing that they are in trouble. It's like the childhood game of musical chairs. You dance around the chairs while the music is playing, but when the music stops, you don't want to be the little guy standing without a chair. The music is just starting to stop playing now, and whether you realize it or not, you are standing without a chair if you're in the position of these speculators. These people will feel the pain in the next 12 months, and as a conservative investor, I have to admit that I'm going to enjoy the carnage. Think about it: I missed out on many deals by buying conservatively. For the past few years, we sat idle, buying only deals that made sense at current day prices. We went to auctions and took the time to bid on projects, only to get outbid by speculators in the market. It is now my time to watch it come back in our direction. There was once a day when you had to wait in line to get a lot on a new home community. Now, so-called investors are seeing deals fall through and having to sell these homes as spec homes. Most of these deals we see falling through are coming from investors who put up $10,000 to build a new home, and now that they realize the market is adjusting, they are walking away from their deposit since they just cannot afford to close the deal. And I will go you one better, even. I look at the auction list each week. I am seeing properties that are going to auction that sold at auction 2 months ago. Again, these are investors who put up $20,000 in deposit to buy a property at auction, and now realize that they can't afford to close, so they're simply walking away from their deposits. The auctioneers are being forced to resell the property at the cost and expense of the defaulting purchaser. So, yes, I am looking forward to the correction with open arms. Now, all of the rookie investors and speculators will get out of the market, and I can begin to make more sound investments.

Speaking of sound investments, allow me to update you on the Charles Street project. Let me start by saying that Pete and I were hoping to get a $9,000,000 offer on the project. After all of our expenses, we envisioned being in the deal for somewhere around $3,000,000 – so the potential to make monopoly money on this deal was mind blowing. We felt that $9,000,000 was a reasonable offer, given that properties in that neighborhood were closing at $650,000. We now have a total of 4 letters of intent. We had been dealing with builders of all shapes and sizes. The first LOI came in from a local builder. They'd done some deals in Baltimore City and were very familiar with property values in the area. We thought that this builder was going to come in with a very high offer. We met them for lunch on several occasions to discuss the details of the project, but at the end of the day, they only came in at roughly $4,000,000. This was a big letdown to us. We had anticipated something far larger than the $4,000,000 offer from this group, given their local market knowledge. Next was a regional builder. These guys had built projects in Maryland, Delaware, Virginia, and New Jersey. They were a slick outfit with a pretty refined model for determining value. They came in with a $6,000,000 offer. Again, lower than the $9,000,000 that we were hoping for, but a very respectable company to work with, and one that we will continue to work with in hopes of getting them to raise their offer. Then, we finally made some progress with one of our key national players. They came in with a solid offer of $9.1 million. This was exactly what we were hoping would happen. And then, finally, my guys up in New Jersey, who we had been courting for a long time, came in at $9.3 million. The plan was all coming together. We went back to each of the groups and said that we wanted to be fair with each of the groups. We had no intention of going back and forth, and wanted them all to get a fair shake at the deal. We told them that several offers were very close, and that they should sharpen their pencils and come back to us with a final offer. Well, the $4 million guy stayed put at $4 million, the $6 million upped his offer to $7 million, the New Jersey guy was pretty close to his max, but left the option open for some last minute heroics, and the $9.1 million national is still out there, but they did let us know that they probably did not have a lot of wiggle room. We are thinking about pushing them all once again, trying to illicit one more highest and best offer. Over the years, this has happened to us on multiple residential properties. We seem to always up our offers and get outbid. It's refreshing to be on the selling side of something in such high demand. As we continued to try to get all of the meat off of the bone, I got an offer from another national. Now, we were not actively pursuing this last group I mention. I had dropped a packet off at their office and exchanged a few emails, but I just did not get the feeling that they were that interested in the project. But I was wrong…incredibly wrong. They came in with a first offer at $12 million. You see, we hadn't put a price on it, so none of the parties truly knew where to come in at. This offer was fantastic, including all terms of the letter of intent. This offer came in with the highest deposit amount, the shortest study period, and by far the highest gross number. I literally fell to the floor when I opened up the envelope. WOW!!! I have become somewhat numb to the numbers. At this point, and with these mind-numbing offers on the table, we met with this builder last week. They still seemed interested and we dropped off the Phase I and Phase II studies for them to review. They remain very interested, and should have us a formal contract next week. Upon signing the contract, they will have 60 days to complete their study and analysis of the deal. If they still like it, we will get their $600,000 deposit check, and close once the city has approved the subdividing of the land into the 64 lots.

On the subdivision process, we recently had a city council zoning meeting, at which point the transportation committee voted on our project 4-0 in favor of the redevelopment. Check that box off. The bill will be read at two more meetings, and ultimately voted on on March 6th. If approved, the bill will be signed by the mayor by the end of March, and we will officially have a residentially zoned piece of land. Once the builder signs the contract and agrees on how many lots they want, we will continue our subdivision process. Then, we will continue to finalize the plans in order to get the final recorded plat. This process, in all likelihood, should take until July 1, 2006. On the day that the subdivision is approved and the plat is recorded, we are hoping to close with the builder…immediately. With the softening of the market happening right before my eyes, July 1st cannot get here quickly enough.

March 2006 – My Cause for Concern

In real estate, it is often said that the three most important things are Location, Location, and Location. Well, I'm not sure that you shouldn't throw Timing in there as well. For the past 5 years, and from the beginning stages of writing this book on, all of the entries have been unbelievably positive and favorable. I may not have realized it during the experience of living all this, but this run of the past 5 years could potentially have been one of the best real estate runs in history. Once in a while, I catch myself pondering what exactly has happened in this market. In 5 years, the value of my personal residence more than doubled. Think about that... making $300,000 in equity in just over 5 years, in an investment that I live in. For someone to save that kind of coin, they would need to save something like $60,000 per year. Just this fact alone seems somewhat illogical. So, perhaps the three most important things are Location, Location, and Timing.

I know that I've mentioned it in previous posts, but the pressure is becoming palpable. My sense of certainty in a soft landing for the market is fleeting. I can't help but think back to the internet market again. I held out from this market until the bitter end. Sitting on the sidelines, I simply could not understand how a company with massive debt, and no signs of revenues or profit in the near future, could go from a stock price of $25 per share to $250 per share almost overnight. There were absolutely no fundamentals of any kind going into the analysis of picking stocks. You simply invested in anything that ended in a "dot com" and you were significantly richer the next week. What's funny is that I look back at that phenomenon and wonder how people could be so foolish as to not realize that eventually this market had to come down, and with it, the fortunes of many people, people just like them. Hmmmm. Does this sound vaguely familiar? I have spent years profiting in a market that continues to go up at a breakneck pace, and has now outstripped any logical fundamentals. My primary residence has gone up $300,000, someone offered me $1,250,000 for my office building, and now, I have an offer on Charles Street for over $12,000,000. I've enjoyed my daily entries into this journal as I have ridden this wave for 5 good…I mean, 5 great, years; but am I now stuck in the game of musical chairs when the music is about to stop? My sense of unease continues to grow each and every day.

It's funny when you discuss the real estate market with real estate professionals; they simply refuse to admit that there's any bubble, and certainly no real feeling that a down year could ever occur. Even my partner thinks that, if we continue to discuss this downturn, it will become a self-fulfilling prophecy, and I should stop bringing it up so that I don't jinx our financial progress and success. But let us parallel the craziness that we saw in the internet bubble to the current situation in real estate. Take my neighborhood as a sample point of the overall real estate market. When we moved into our house, the value was $260,000. We were able to purchase the home 10 years ago with a $1,500 per month mortgage, including taxes and insurance. That is a very affordable payment, even for the small salaries that my wife and I were bringing home at the time. There was modest appreciation over the first five years in the house, but over the past five years, the comparable homes have escalated to over $700,000. Now let us try to apply some logic to this analysis. The federal government has kept interest rates relatively low for the past five years. These 5-6% mortgages have allowed buyers to qualify for more house for less money. Even better, mortgage companies have come up with these incredible leveraged products, which allow buyers to get into properties with no money down, interest only payments, and interest rates at 4% for 5 years, payments adjusting to market levels after that. Therefore, if you wanted to buy a house in my neighborhood for $700,000 at a 4% interest only mortgage, your payment would only be about $2,300 per month. Still a pretty affordable payment, but now it may require the borrowers to have income from both the husband and the wife. Not uncommon these days, to have a dual income family, though. So you can see why people have been buying at a frenzy over the past 5 years. This was great, of course, to be able to leverage the bank's money in an up market where, even if the market increased a paltry 10% per year, you would see $70,000 in equity immediately. But....what happens if the market flattens out? What happens if the market, dare I say, actually has a down year, and loses 2-3%? And wait a second, let's say I go one step further, and after 5 years, rates are 9% when your mortgage adjusts, and you now can't afford this payment. So you decide to sell the house. The market is at $675,000 now, you have no equity since it was an interest only loan, and it costs you $55,000 in commissions and transfers to sell the house, assuming you wanted to. You guessed it: you now have to come to the settlement table with $80,000 just to sell your house. Can you say....here comes a huge foreclosure boom? It is coming, too, whether real estate practitioners choose to accept it or not. Deny it all you want, National Association of Realtors....deny it all you want, real estate pundits.... but we are about to see the largest foreclosure market in years.

Pete says: *Scott, the market is not going down; this is real estate and it has inherent value. This isn't like the internet; real estate has sticks and bricks.* And really, isn't this what I've been preaching to you for 5 years now? But seriously: gone are the days of multiple offers on properties. Two homes in my neighborhood have been on the market for 6 months already. Gone are the non-contingent offers. Even the dynamics of financing are changing right before my eyes. But remember, the bubble hasn't burst...right? So, when you go see the banker, he gives you a 30 year fixed mortgage at 7%, since that *is* the going rate these days. And don't forget, since the market is adjusting, you now need 20%, or $140,000, as your down payment. Who has that kind of cash? Think logically and critically about the market....it is overvalued. Housing prices are coming down whether we investors go with it or fight it. If you can't already tell, I really am getting frustrated with the market. What has been the golden calf for the past 5 years is starting to melt away right in front of my eyes. I'm frustrated because I am worried about the future of the real estate market. We are in a lot of real estate deals now and the thought of the market collapsing could have a big impact on my financial condition. I'm frustrated at the agents, bankers and investors that refuse to admit that this ride is coming to a stop. I am just frustrated!!!

So, how is this effecting Signature Properties, you ask? I have concerns about our products. We have 2 super high-end townhomes that will hit the market in about 2 weeks. We are spending a fortune on them, and had hoped to sell them for $800,000 each. I can logically see them going for $600,000 - $650,000 each, at this point. That is a huge swing in price, and I hope that I'm wrong, but this high-end luxury market is drying up like a desert. Next, we have four more super high-end new construction houses on Robinson Street, expecting to come online in the fall of this year. These were slated to be $680,000 homes. We will be in each of these for about $500,000, so we can hope and pray that we come out of these sales with $550,000-$600,000 each. Lastly, and luckily, are the 4 homes on Fairmont. These homes are due to come online in the fall, as well. However, these homes were always slated as $450,000 homes. We bought these lots for $80,000 each and have $225,000 in construction going into each of these. As cautious as I am on the high-end luxury market, I am very optimistic on the middle-range market. This mid-$400,000 market is what I see as the next booming real estate market. People need to be able to afford their payments, as I described above, and $400,000 mortgages are about where they should be. So, these four I have confidence will sell, and we should capture about $100,000 profit per house. Other than that, we have been lucky in that we've not been on a buying spree. Many local developers have really fattened up their portfolios over the past year, and this is where the mass carnage is going to take place. These next couple of years is going to be really interesting as the massive defaulting mortgages all shake out.

So, what you must be saying right about now is, "What about Charles Street?" A day doesn't go by when Charles Street is not on my mind. Just a few short pages ago, I was bragging about these fantastic offers that we had from national builders, all looking to build this fantastic development. The best offer was a $12 million deal. We have been waiting for the $12 million folks to get me the contract. We've been waiting....and waiting....and waiting. Finally, I get a call back from their attorney, who was supposed to have me the contract about 2 weeks ago. First, he explains to me that they're not interested in 64 townhomes, and that their interest lies in 60 larger lots. No problem there, as I fully expected that, and we can redraw the plat map to meet their needs and desires. Next, though, he explains to me that the market is softening, and that the neighboring Pulte Homes development that we've been using as our ideal comparable development has had to slash their prices by $50,000 per unit. After sandbagging me for about 15 minutes during the conversation, he ultimately tells me that their original offer of $12 million has now dropped to $8.4 million for the project. Obviously, this is not good! This is a slight $3.6 million haircut. Man, oh man. Well, $8.4 is still pretty strong.....right? Sometimes I have to tell myself that the craze has ended, and I should just take what I can get for this thing and move on. Other times, I just don't want to roll over and try to scrape together as much of the remaining $3.6 million as possible. This is becoming a very trying time in real estate. Charles Street still has great value. We still have almost $6,000,000 in equity in the deal, but what if I can't get the deal to the table? I am planning on calling all of the prospects that submitted letters of intent. Perhaps I can readjust expectations and get people to submit offers and get something...anything to the table. My concerns begin to rise on this project, but I continue to remain optimistic.

LESSONS LEARNED

- What goes up must come down. The early sign of troubles has been an increase in days on market.
- Form a contingency plan, early and often. Create a series of "what-if" scenarios and make a Plan B, and maybe C.
- Sometimes your gut is telling you something.

WHO IS CHARLES?

May 2006

These days, we talk about Charles so much that people ask who Charles *is*. We really have personified this project to have a life of its own. My friends will ask how things on Charles are going, and my dad always wants an update of the progress through zoning and any interested parties in the deal. The deal fills my head daily with dreams and nightmares, simultaneously. I think about the numbers of the deal constantly. In my head, I go through the iterations: I bought it for $2.1 million, have another $400,000 in engineering, legal, and carry costs, so I am all in at $2.5 million. That number resonates in my head. I have done these numbers so many times and, unbelievably, I continue to come up with the same $2.5 million number in my head. The only variable that is unknown is how much we are going to sell the project for. As I was saying before, we got a haircut from the main player, right on down to $8.4 million. I run this scenario in my head of $8.4 - $2.5 = $5.9. Then I pay taxes on this to the tune of about $1 million, bringing my total down to $4.9 million. We pay off the rental portfolio debt of $2.3 million, and we are left with $2.6 million to split. So, at the end of the day I should have $200,000 in income every year for the rest of my life, and $1.3 million to get the day started. Of course, some days' projections are not as good as others. On these days, I say to myself, what if we just bail on the project and fire sale it for $7 million? $7 - $2.5 = $4.5, minus taxes of $750,000, leaving $3.75 million, minus the portfolio of $2.3, leaving $1.45 million to be split. This math is all-consuming. I do it day in and day out. If I had a nickel for every time I've run this through my head, I'd be a millionaire already and not have to go through with this stressful exercise.

So how close are we to accomplishing all of this? It really is funny to look back on the decisions that we make and evaluate whether or not they were the right ones. They appeared to be the right ones at the time, of course,, but in hindsight, would we have made them? I read this article that describes the Marines' method for decision making. They teach that, once officers have 70% of the available data, their officers should be ready to pull the trigger and/or make the decision. I think that I operate on a similar scale of analysis. Although you do not know what 100% of the available data represents, you do know that, as you continue to gather the data, it gets more and more difficult to ascertain information. At this point, you know that the low hanging informational fruit has been plucked, and you have a pretty good understanding of the situation. At this point, you are probably in the 60%-70% range. If you spend a little more time hunting and pecking for nuggets of information that will help you make a better decision, you will definitively put yourself in that 70% range. At that point, although you know that you do not have perfect information for the decision (perfect representing 100%), you pull the trigger. With this formula, you should achieve success if you make logical decisions. Unfortunately, what seems like a logical decision could possibly be altered by situations beyond your control. Think back to the day when I had a letter of intent from a national builder for $12 million. The market was on fire. Prices continued to go up at a clip of 25% per year. The site down the road had had three price increases for their base model home within the first phase alone. We held a large parcel of land that was unique to the city. Many people wanted the land, and we felt like we certainly were in the power position. We didn't sign the letter of intent because we always thought that we could do a little bit better. As pigs, we were led to the slaughter. Then the air began to be let out of the bubble.

To give you an example, the national builder that was building the 121 luxury townhomes about a mile from our site was at one point selling units for over $700,000. Within 3 months of that benchmark, they are now fire selling these same units for $475,000. Let that sink in for a minute. The homes had a demand that created a buzz that created an artificial sales price of $700,000. The intrinsic value of the homes was equal to about $200,000 in construction costs, plus perhaps $100,000 for the piece of land that each sits upon. The other $400,000 was artificially created by the market. As quickly as the market created it, it came down even quicker.

It's funny how, when things are going up, everyone is bragging about real estate and their real estate riches. Just look at the first part of my book. It was all excitement and optimism. I referred numerous times to buying my house for $256,000 and gaining almost $700,000 in equity. When did my primary residence become my 401(k)? Isn't it just a place to live, and when did society in general turn the place you live into such a hot focus of net worth and equity? How about this... think about the guy that just bought the house up the street for $775,000, and now the neighborhood has 8 homes listed for sale on the market, and the prices are dipping down close to $600,000? He is now in the hole by $175,000. And let's say that he gets another job offer in another state, and wants to move…he can't even think of it, unless he comes to the closing table with $175,000. If this doesn't sink in right away, and I'm guessing it won't (because it's hard for me to believe), reread these last few sentences for just a minute. With all the talk of real estate riches, what about the millions of people that bought at the peak, and now have to wait 5 years just to move? No big deal if you are planning on living there for the long haul, but *I* wouldn't be comfortable in this situation.

Alright, I am done ranting for this month…this market is getting bloody quickly, and I don't like it.

June 2006

The market is really adjusting. Many people in the industry are still holding firm that there's really not a full-blown price adjustment market, and that it's just slowing down, but I would certainly beg to differ on this point. We have two homes on Patapsco that at one point we thought would sell for $800,000 each. I remember spending the money in my head, many times over. I'm just glad that I didn't run out and spend that money for real. After having the homes on the market for 45 days, we are lowering the price from $749,000 to $695,000. That, to me, represents a price adjustment. It's difficult to describe what exactly is happening to the market. When you run the statistics for Baltimore City, there's the same number of homes being sold at this time as there was last year. For example, in May of 2005, there were 1,300 homes under contract and 1,000 settlements. These numbers are roughly the same as they are this year; the difference comes in the number of active homes on the market. During May of last year, there were about 1,200 homes for sale. That means that everyone who put their house on the market had a buyer (and usually within 30 days). This May, there are roughly 4,000 homes that are active, but for just 1,300 buyers. That means that each buyer has 3 to 4 homes to look at before putting a contract in on a house. So, how do these sellers make their house the most desirable? Well, I have the simple solution... lower your price so that, while your house offers the same amenities as everyone else's, you have the lowest price, and therefore should be the first to sell. This dropping of the price is exactly what I am talking about when I refer to a price adjustment. The question is, how far will these prices drop until they finally settle in? This is the scary part of this industry.

We are carrying roughly $6,000,000 worth of construction debt right now. The two homes that I spoke of on Patapsco may have to drop again, to $650,000 in another 60 days. We have four homes on Robinson Street which will be completed in September.

When we purchased the land, the appraiser thought that, upon completion, these homes would be worth $680,000 each. We thought so as well. I am in the process of putting together the marketing piece for these homes, and the prices are starting at $599,000. That is an $80,000 haircut, and multiply it by the four houses, and you get a paper loss from pro-forma of $320,000. Do you remember all of the excitement that I shared throughout most of the book? That excitement has been replaced by cautious skepticism. Just as I explained how I felt bad for my neighbors that paid $725,000 – and simply would not be able to sell their home due to the drop in the housing market…even if they had a job transfer – well, I feel even worse for the people that jumped into the real estate boom as investors at its very end. These people bought homes, property, apartments, and buildings, hoping and dreaming of getting rich like everyone else in the business. Again, there's that thought that it's just plain easy to make money in real estate. This is beginning to resemble my late arrival into the stock market with my investment in the RS Emerging Growth Fund.

But enough of the misery of the market, because there *are* still people making money in real estate. Remember: people need a place to live. There are still 1,300 people putting in contracts in Baltimore City each month. What this should tell you is that, if you buy right and can afford to resell the best house with the best features and the best price, you will still make money. So, even though we have dropped the price on Patapsco to $695,000, we are only in the house for $525,000. There's still a ton of equity to be made in each of these houses. Even though we are lowering our expectations on Robinson to $599,000, we are only in each of these houses for $425,000. If you run the numbers, 2006 should be the best year in the real estate industry for Scott Benjamin and Signature Properties yet. Here's another unique feature about this market, also: it is becoming a great time to be a buyer of property. What I would like you to imagine and critically analyze are the opportunities this type of market presents. People have been used to a market that brings multiple offers within a week. They have seen prices escalate for 5 years at a breakneck pace. Now, they see the signs of a softening in the market. It's on the front page of every newspaper and has been the lead story for about 6 months on the daily news. People that were trying to time the market peak before selling their houses have now thrown them onto the market. The market is flooded with active homes, and a buyer has the power to choose which one he wants. The first 6 months of this shift have seen the sellers refusing to lower their prices. They've been so accustomed to seeing their neighbors getting big bucks, and they believe it's now their turn to cash in. The problem is that there are simply not enough buyers to scoop up the inventory. It's just about now that I am seeing people become slightly more desperate. They are finally coming to the realization that, 'oops, we may have just missed it'. So, homes that were $749,000 (like ours) are now down to $695,000. Imagine if you are a homeowner right now, and your agent just told you to shave $50,000 off of your price. You are now becoming at least slightly edgy and worrisome. Now imagine that the house sits for another 3 to 4 months, and you've hit a deadline where you simply have to move. You will take whatever you can to move the property.

I've been watching a listing that dropped from $395,000 to $350,000. It sat for another 30 days at $350,000, and finally got a contract. When it closed, I noticed that the contract was for $300,000. That is over a 30% discount on retail. People say that real estate is cyclical, and when something is cyclical, the ideal time to buy is when it is at its bottom-most point in the cycle. Warren Buffet always says: "When people are greedy, it is time to be fearful. When people are fearful, it is time to get greedy." The difficult thing is to figure out where exactly the bottom is in the cycle. One thing's for sure... the cycle is on its' way downward now.

So, what am I into these days and how am I trying to use the benefits of a falling market to my advantage? Unfortunately, I'm not actually practicing what I preach. I've explained to you the difficulties with selling off the properties that we currently have under contract. When you're in a market that's behaving poorly, your natural instinct is to pull back and not purchase anything else. This is how I'm reacting to this market. We have 10 new construction projects underway (two of which are not selling and have been completed for several months), we have a full rehab that gobbled up $60,000 in rehab money (plus the $185,000 it cost us to buy), we have a half done house way out in the county that needs fixtures, finishes, paint, a kitchen, and landscaping, and we have a shell of a house that we bought a year ago for $45,000 and would love to dump at $75,000. Then we have four unsubdivided lots that we bought at a foreclosure auction and have owned for over a year, we are knee-deep in 4 tax sale certificates that have been holding $25,000 captive for well over a year, and we have the large lot on Charles Street that we're currently working to complete. In general, I am proceeding with cautious optimism, which I hope will convert into profits over the next six to eight months. As I said before, though, now is the time to start capitalizing on this down market. Now is the time to buy more inventory and have projects filling the pipeline. Now is the time to buy another round of 20 rental properties, as sellers are currently willing to make a deal and banks are at the same time foreclosing on everyone that got in over their head over the past few years. So, why, you ask, am I not going on a buying frenzy? The answer is two-fold: First, we have a ton of money out there on the streets, all tied up in many different projects. We could surely raise more money or refinance to continue to buy, but we're burning money at a breakneck pace since nothing has been selling. Remember: we are carrying debts of somewhere around $25,000 per month, and that money is going out the door quickly. Pete pays the bills in the office on a Quickbooks program. Internet online banking is a wonderful feature, and it makes paying bills as easy as clicking a button. With Quickbooks, every time you make an entry, the computer beeps at you, "blink, blink", just to let you know that the transaction has gone through. I sit next to him and lose clumps of hair every time I hear "blink, blink". Perhaps this is why they say (more and more, it seems) that money can go in the blink of an eye.

I read a stock-picking book recently, from one of those high energy TV-type personalities. The author relays a story about a stock that he got a tip on, one that was a so-called guaranteed winner. He bought a substantial position in the stock as soon as he got the tip. From there, the stock proceeded to go down. He bought more of it. It went down again, and yet again, he bought more of it. At one point, people on the street were in amazement that this crazy hedge fund manager kept buying this dog as it continued to sink deeper and deeper into the toilet. He was so confident in the stock, though, that he got to the bitter end, and was just about to start selling off and taking his losses when the stock finally hit its stride. It went back up to its original position, and then doubled from there. He'd known, down in the gut of his belly, that this stock was a winner.

Even though I have ranted on for the past 3 years about the real estate market, I just don't seem to have that kind of conviction to keep increasing my position in the market. I own a chunk in the market, and certainly I am in no rush to sell off any of the real estate we hadn't already planned to sell, but even though I have been waiting for years for this buyers market, I have not gone after it. This may be, in part, thanks to knowing that the Charles Street property is about to explode, and that I can relax for a while before renewing my energy to work some more deals.

July 2006

Where exactly am I with the Charles Street project? July is here, and I honestly thought that I would be out on a boat in the Caribbean by now. It's funny how pro-forma planning in real estate is truly an exercise in futility. You can try to predict when a project will be through, and how much it will cost, but inevitably, it will take twice as long and cost twice as much. So, here I sit on my back patio, scribbling more notes as I continue to take baby steps toward my ultimate goal of selling off this property. To summarize the progress, first let me review the past six to eight months. We started selling this thing at the end of last year. The market was so hot that we were going to sell the lot raw, just after the zoning was complete. We thought that the sale would be complete by June, and we would be celebrating with the entire summer off. We had two offers over $9 million, and one at $12 million. We had meetings with these national companies and were being selective on which one to choose. We even told the $12 million offer to put together the contract, and we were ready to sign on the dotted line. Then the market softened a bit, the big development down the road had deals fall apart, and their prices of $700,000 quickly sank to a mind blowing $479,000. People began to fear the outcome of the market, and the national builders began to pull back on purchases. Now, we were calling any and all national builders, and begging them to put together a deal on Charles Street. The tables turned just that incredibly quickly. They now held the power, and we were at their mercy. After spending the spring trying to sell this thing ourselves, we turned it over to a land broker with some solid connections with some of these national builders. Within about a week, we had meetings with two companies interested in the lot. He presented us with a letter of intent for 64 subdivided lots with all of the entitlements ready to go. That meant that we would have to complete the entire subdivision development plan with the city, including utilities, transportation, environmental, roads, and a plethora of other time-consuming process of documentation. We countered their letter of intent, explaining that we were willing to hand them back the subdivided plat ready for recording, but we just did not want to invest the additional six months to a year and put together all of the other documentation for the city. They accepted this change, and put together a contract. We just received their contract. They are offering us a purchase price of $9.1 million (which is a full $2 million more than the next two legitimate offers). The 20 pages have everything written to the benefit the builder, and nothing in our favor. We turned the contract over to a recommended attorney to review. Just this past week, we met with him and went over all of the nuances of the document, and low and behold, they are back to asking us to give them permit-ready land. That means that the entire deal is contingent on us going through the whole entitlement process. They are trying to sneak back in the part of the deal that will tie us up for over a year. Now, the subdividing of the land will take us every bit of 6 months, but that is all we are willing to concede. At least, as I sit here feeling powerful about my position, that is all we are willing to concede. At the next writing, I may be willing to give them that and a bunch more. So, this morning, July 3rd, the attorney emailed them the black lined contract with our position on the contract. In the contract were many small items that are certainly not to be characterized as deal-breakers, but are points of negotiation. As a matter of fact, none of the terms are actual deal-breakers in my mind. If you think about it, they want us to invest another year and a half doing another $100,000 worth of engineering so that they can literally pull the permit and start working on the roads. It's funny, though: Pete has a problem with this issue.

They agreed in the letter of intent that they are willing to take the property at record plat without all of the additional engineering complete. Our response is to try to get them back to their original offer of a "record plat ready lot", but if they make this single item a deal-breaker, are we actually going to walk away? They are offering us a purchase price of $9.1 million. Furthermore, we've owned the property for just a year, and we only paid $2 million for the lot. We are still talking about a retirement amount of money, even if we do have to invest another year pushing paper around. Once in a while, Pete and I consider building the townhouses on the property. If we had deeper pockets, or more investors, we might consider trying to make all of the profit on the deal – but then we return to reality and realize that we are not positioned for this.

Sometimes, perspective is a difficult word to understand, and in this case, my perspective is to fight for the record plat decision, but certainly not to walk away from this deal if there ends up being a deal-breaking negotiation point. This is a very confusing time for the company. We are having trouble predicting what will take place in the future market. Pete wonders if I am getting soft in my old years. I think critically about negotiation. When they talk about win-win solutions, whether we have to put in the additional work or not, this is a win-win. They get the 64 lots and a presence in the city that they are longing for, and we get to retire. When I sit down the next time, I will have more information on the contract. It is my goal over the next month to have several of my inventory properties under contract, and to have the Charles lot under contract. I'll let you know how that goes.

Here are a few updates to bring you back to the beginning of the book. Do you remember the wiz kid intern that we had for about a year? This was the kid that bought a flip his first week and netted us out $12,000 between that Monday and Friday. This was the same kid who over-bid on a $300,000 executive house, which brought me our first loss. But also remember that this was a kid who I continued to see amazing potential for, and who had an uncanny ability to make us money. I think he made us $100,000 in his first summer interning with us. He ended up graduating from the University of Maryland. I attended his graduation, as I was extremely proud of him and excited for him as he was starting out in real estate on his own. A few months after graduating, he bought this old local community swimming pool, with its land, for $203,000. I remember asking him what he saw in the land. The pool sat on over 2 acres of land, close to the University campus. He was thinking that, with all of the success that we had in college rentals, that he could potentially build garden style apartments as student rentals. He went on to buy one of the adjacent houses for somewhere around $200,000 in order to rent it out to students. I lost touch with him and this deal for a while. Well, the other day, I was scanning the auction lists to see what was coming up on the auction block in the coming weeks. Then I saw his swimming pool and adjacent house being auctioned off on that coming Wednesday. Luckily, I still had his phone number, so I gave him a call. At this point, the kid is probably 23 or 24 years old. We had a great conversation, catching up on the different projects that he saw us getting started at Signature, most of which are now being sold, and talking about how the college housing market was going. Then I asked him why he was auctioning off his swimming pool. He told me that he didn't have time to work on it since he had three other projects that were monopolizing his time. He was converting a 14 unit building into condominiums in one of the hippest locations in Washington, DC. He also had plans for a 90 unit apartment building on a piece of land that he had in DC. That all just blew me away. I knew that the kid had had potential, but I'd had no idea what kind of a business man this guy had turned out to be. So, back to the swimming pool; I think he had somewhere in the area of $450,000 into the entire deal with the houses. As we closed out our conversation, I wished him good luck on his upcoming auction. So then, I checked the auction results section on Thursday to see how he'd done. The sales price is (I am shaking my head in disbelief even as I write this)... the sales price is $1,475,000. This kid was just minted a millionaire, if he wasn't already. This business remains unbelievable. I will give it 30 days to make sure it closes and he pockets the money, and then call him back so *he* can take *me* out to lunch for a change.

Now an update on the rental property. I just looked back at the pages when I bought the 5 college townhouse rentals. Sometimes, taking a little chance pays off in spades. When we bought them, they were renting for $850 per month. I was excited that I was planning on raising the rents in the second year, up to $1,000 per month. Just a few years later, as I sit here writing this update, these same units are renting for $2,250. That is not a misprint. We were making money, albeit not a whole lot, at $1,000 per month. If you're handy with the quick mathematics, you'll know that our expenses are essentially the same, but our revenues just went up $1,150 per month, or $13,800 per year. In addition to the 5 we purchased back then, we bought another 6 in that community, bringing us to 11 there, plus 4 more college rentals around the corner, plus 5 more homes that we rent to families, plus the office building. To make a long portfolio discussion quick, we are currently seeing $252,000 of positive cash flow per year, after all of our expenses are paid. Part of that money is in Windsor Mill. Sometimes, your initial projections are actually pretty close to what you end up seeing – once in while even a blind squirrel gets a nut. In reading what I wrote when we first bought the Windsor Building, we thought that it would be worth about $1,000,000 once it was 100% occupied. At this time, it is 100% occupied. Actually, it is about 107% occupied. We took some unusable basement space that we were storing stuff in and rented that to an exotic pet distributor. Our gross revenue from the building is about $160,000. This is incredibly close to what we put down on our pro-forma a few years ago. We thought that the expenses would be about $50,000. That too ended up being about spot on. Simply uncanny. We thought that it would be worth $1,000,000 back then. Remember that deal for the purchase price of $1,250,000?…it fell through. The buyer got cold feet on the purchase of the building and pulled out of the deal. Pete and I have decided not to sell the property at all, and are content living on the cash flow for now. Remaining optimistic!

November 2006

I have spent the last 5 years telling you how wonderful the real estate market has been, and it has truly been great. I have bought and sold properties for absolutely crazy profits. I have made some of the easiest money in the world, and had a blast doing it. What made the business fun and relatively safe was the fact that real estate was a stable investment which had inherent value, and should retain its value. All of those chapters of me describing the money coming in like Christmas time were accurate and exciting. For the past 5 years, the real estate market has likewise seen returns in access of 20% per year of appreciation; this, in an industry where the 60 year average of appreciation is slightly over 6%. So, for the past year or so, everyone has been predicting the eminent real estate bubble bursting. Remember my story about investing the money from the seminars into the high flying internet funds and losing most of it during the internet bubble? I swore never to put myself in that position again. OOPS. This time was different on some level, though; at least, that is what I keep telling myself. I did make a bunch of money, and had a great ride as the market went up. Now that it is showing signs of weakness, we are certainly going to hand some of these profits back, but not for an overall loss.

Let me tell you about the two luxury homes that we built on Patapsco. These masterpieces took us over 18 months to build, and stubbornly, we were insistently going to maximize our profitability on these properties. People were telling us to price them at $699,000, and even as low as $649,000. Given that the market had shown signs of weakness, perhaps this was good advice. We did not listen. We originally put the properties on the market at $749,000. After 9 months and about $5,000 spent on marketing, they are both still on the market, and are currently priced at $549,000. Where has all the optimism gone? This month, we had 8 more new construction projects come onto the market. We have four more ultra-high-end luxury townhouses on Robinson Street that were appraised at $680,000 when we went for the original financing, and are now currently on the market for $549,000. Yikes! Then take the last 4 properties on Fairmount that were supposed to sell for $500,000 each, and are now priced at $379,000 each. When you figure out all of the "potential" prices that we thought the houses should sell for, and then look to our current market prices, we are priced at over $1 million less than what we had envisioned just one year ago. That is why they call it paper net worth, and why my wife Jill says she will believe it when the money is in the bank. I have been predicting this market collapse for a while…but it came on us so incredibly quickly. I have also learned that new construction projects take 18 months to develop. This is an awful long time in a deal where you have to try to predict the future. The picture is not quite as rosy as it once looked, just 100 pages ago. The company was flush with cash, as we have stopped buying properties a while back, but as prices continue to drop, we are incredibly close to actually losing money on some of these properties. It is not easy to watch the paper profit evaporate.

Here is the interesting dilemma: we are currently burning through $33,500 a month to carry our vacant non-income producing spec houses. We have enough money to carry us for another 8 months, but with each month that goes by, we increase our basis in the project by that interest amount. For example, we are into the homes on Patapsco for $500,000 each, as of today's date. So, if we sold one of the houses for $549,000, paid out $32,000 in commission, and $8,000 in transfer taxes, we would stand to make about $9,000 on the house. If the homes don't sell by next month, we will have to carry that mortgage for another month, and increase our basis to $503,000. If we don't sell the homes in the next three months, we essentially will break even for the last 18 months' worth of work. At this point, breaking even is looking pretty good to me. We simply can't afford to drop the price, but can't afford not to drop the price. Pretty interesting dilemma, huh? What would you do? Remember, I am the guy with all of the answers, I teach classes on this stuff, and I am still stuck. This market is the worst that people have seen in the last 20 years. There simply are not any buyers out there in the market. Why would there be? The press and the media have taken this thing to the hoop in telling everyone that the bottom is continuing to fall out. The investor market has completely dried up in purchasing homes. The problem has become self-fulfilling. People hold off buying, the press releases poor statistics, the people then continue to hold off buying, and the cycle goes on and on. Now, put yourself in the buyer's position: they have watched us drop from $749,000 to $729,000 to $699,000, all the way down to $549,000 within 9 months. Who wants to be the sucker who bought for $749,000, and then a year later your next door neighbor buys, for $549,000…the exact same house. Perhaps writing a few chapters is therapeutic to me.

Each day, it's difficult to go into work. At one point, you were riding high on the wave of real estate. This book was written through one of the most exciting times in the business. I look back on the deals and the excitement over the past few years, and what a wild ride it was! There's another inevitable problem that continues to keep me up at night. Each time we lower our prices, we expect the people to start coming out of the woodwork and look at our houses. We drop the price, and nothing happens, not one additional showing, and certainly no additional offers. So, then we think, what would happen if we dropped the price below $650,000? Then... yes, then, the buyers will have to see a great product now offered at a great discounted price! We do it, and the same result happens. When I look at the 10 houses that we have now built and are ready to see sold, I am proud of the product that we've built. Each house is professionally designed and decorated. The craftsmanship that went into the construction of the houses is truly impeccable. I am proud to show off the homes to any family or friends that want to see what I have done over the past few years…so then, why doesn't anyone else want to make an offer on the property? Sometimes I think that I am a smart guy and should have the answers, but this is truly a perplexing problem. I continue to compare my product to others on the market, and still come up with the conclusion that it is priced fairly. So what happens if there simply are not any buyers for my houses? I have now dropped the prices down to the absolute rock bottom prices. If they sell, I will be able to pay transfers and commissions, and will happily walk away with absolutely nothing to show for the last 18 months' worth of work.

Like I said, it has indeed been a wild ride in real estate. So, let us just hypothesize a worst case scenario on the properties. Let's say that the properties take an extra six months to sell. As of now, the line of credit that we have currently sits at 10.25% interest. We have $2.5 million on this line, which translates into roughly $26,000 in interest expense per month, and plus we pay separate mortgages on Pataspco for another $6,000 per month, and get a total carry expense of $32,000 per month. If it takes us 6 more months to sell the houses (which is not unheard of in this market), we will now sell the entire inventory and lose $192,000. So where does this $192,000 come from, you may be wondering? If you remember, about 100 pages ago and four years ago in my life, we raised a Fund of money from friends, family, and fools, of $480,000 to start this development company. Well, the losses come from this pool of money. So, instead of returning the $480,000 to our family and friends, I guess that we have to say, "Mom, sorry, but we ended up losing money on the deal, and your retirement money just went down 30%...here's what is left." I guess that's the reason for the third F in that formula (Friends, Family and….that's right, Fools). Hopefully, it is not all doom and gloom. We still have several rehab projects under construction, 4 tax sales certificates in the pipeline, and a very profitable subdivision in process. If these projects survive this market, we should make about $250,000 from these projects. All told, we should be able to return the full capital to the investors, and maybe make a few bucks in the end. If not, Pete and I have decided to pay any deficiency back to the investors out of our own pockets. If I have to liquidate a part of our rental portfolio just to make sure that our investors are made 100% whole, we will do that. Let's hope that this is not the case. There is a moral to this story, and my wife has summed it up many times for me: you haven't made any money until the property sells and the money is in the bank. Paper net worth is exactly that: paper. You can't spend it, you can't trade it, and you can't retire on it. It is all about the cash flow.

The year 2005 was the strongest financial year that I have ever had. My net worth position went up exponentially. 2006 has not treated me as kindly for cash flow. We have had two small properties close this year. All of our capital has been tied up on the 10 new construction projects. We have squeaked a few bucks out here and there on seminars and the like, but the only thing that has truly kept the lights on this year has been the rental portfolio. The college rents are up a ton. Most of the units are renting at rates over $2,300 per month, with $1,000 of that cash flowing. We have a property management company that is doing a mediocre job at collecting money, a poor job at renting to the students for next year, and not handling maintenance at all. The rental portfolio is cashing out around $16,000 per month, which is huge when it comes to carrying all of the office and overhead expenses, not to mention that fact that we are knocking back those mortgages month after month. There is something else happening in 2006 that I wish did not have to happen. We are starting to liquidate our rental portfolio to start paying the bills. We bought a property on Cedar Barn Way at an auction about 3 years ago for $92,000. It's funny, too, because I remember the auction vividly. The property was found by one of our young interns, Josh, from the University of Maryland. This was his first successful purchase, which meant that he was finally going to be paid $10 an hour to work for us. The auction was held at the gallery at the auctioneer's offices. We drove up, outbid several other investors, and then went out for lunch to celebrate. The property was worth $135,000 at the time, so we figured that after some paint and carpet, we could make about $20,000. So we took possession of the property and fixed it up. At that time, I was on my rental property kick. I was trying to keep as many properties as we could and build a rental portfolio. In hindsight, that was one of the best decisions that I could have made. First, since the college rental portfolio is truly the only reason that we are still in the game during this colossal correction, and second, because we have a property like Cedar Barn to sell for some income to live off of. We rented Cedar Barn for the last 2.5 years, to a single tenant. They paid us $1,300 per month, which covered our mortgage, HOA dues, and made us a few bucks at the end of the day. So, 2 weeks ago, I put the property on the market for... are you ready for this? $249,000. I thought it was worth closer to $260,000 but given how miserable the market has been, I thought that I'd underprice it and see how it goes. I'm expecting a contract to be waiting for me when I get back from New York

City. Perhaps underpricing the market is the way to go. Why I'm in NYC, you may ask, but I will come back to that in just a minute. So, let's say that it is a full price contract at $249,000, which is about $10,000 below where I think the property is worth (hey, we need the money, and we are motivated). After we pay 3% to the other agent and 1.5% in transfers, we should see a gross income number of $240,085. My debt to the bank is $82,800. When all of the dust settles on the HUD-1, we should net out about $157,285. When you split that 2 ways, I should get my $78,500. That will carry me for a little while. So, we could have sold the property roughly 2 ½ years ago and made $20K on the deal, and now we are selling it and it is a $157K deal. I really do love this business, even though we are going through a tough time.

While we are going through the largest real estate correction of the past decade, while my interest carry is simply eating me up alive, while I continue to watch my net worth dwindle – I continue to hold my head up high and seem relatively at peace. Cedar Barn will carry me for a few months, the rentals are just chugging along, and Charles is a'coming. Yes, Charles is a'coming. The fantasy days are really gone. I can remember the excitement of the $12 million letter of intent to purchase my piece of land raw. Those days are long gone. But, we have now pushed the property closer and closer to our day of fruition. We had a meeting last week on the 16th with the planning commission of Baltimore City. This meeting is like a court hearing. People who are appointed by the mayor sit on this panel and vote to either approve or disapprove major issues in the city's development. So, a city planner represents us and presents our project to the commission. We showed up with our engineer and our lawyer (now that's an expensive hour) and sat in the audience of the commission hearing. We watched as Irv (our city representative) presented our project on Charles Street to the panel. He explained how the lot was once manufacturing, and is now zoned residential. He explained how the lot should have 64 individual townhouse lots, and showed the architectural renditions of what the houses will look like. He went through the economic impact statement, showing how the tax revenues would go from $20,000 per year to over $1,000,000 per year in additional tax revenue. After his 15 minute power-point presentation, he turned the lights on and said to the chairman of the committee, "do you have any questions?". They asked if any member of the audience had any major objections to the presentation being made for the subdivision of 1901 South Charles Street into 64 residential lots. I did everything in my power not to look backwards at the audience. The next 5 seconds of silence felt like 30 minutes, but when no one spoke up, the chairman put it to a vote. He had a submission, then a second, all in favor….YESSSSSSSS, none were opposed, and the subdivision was approved. From this point, we have another 60 days until the comments are submitted from the various committees, and then we have what is called a recordable plat. This is the 64 lots all cut up and signed, sealed, and delivered to the State. They record that plat, and we are 100% official.

So, what now, you ask. Now I go out and try to sell my piece of land at record plat for whatever I can get for it. Last year, record plat would have been extremely exciting. We certainly would have got $9 or $10 million for the land back then. Unfortunately, it is a little more difficult to sell land these days. The national builders are getting slaughtered in their current subdivisions. They have had huge bailouts, and are simply stuck holding the bag on many spec homes. Their traffic is down significantly, and their new orders are negligible. They have all but laid off their entire land acquisition departments. So why would any of them be interested in buying a new project, especially one that still needs another several years' worth of land construction, engineering, and infrastructure before you can build a single house? Now we are focusing on development companies. We are willing to give up some or all of the profits so that someone can come in, take us out of the deal, put in the infrastructure, and then sell it to the national builders completely finished. We could do that if we chose to, but that would keep us in the deal for another year and a half. I have decided that, at some point, you need to figure out what it is that you do best, and simply stick to these basics. My skills are at buying discounted real estate. We handled the rezoning and subdivision with ease, but I feel like this is where we get off of the bus and let someone else take over. You need to ask yourself how far you want to go. Once we complete the infrastructure and finish the lots, why not just build the houses? Why leave profit on the table then? I feel like I have done enough to this lot. There is still enough profit in this deal for us to make money and for a lot finisher to make money. Why wouldn't you take your chips off the table at the casino and just walk away? Who knows, maybe I will spend the next year or so selling books and giving talks? I remain the optimistic real estate dreamer. Through all the troubled times, I remain faithful to the business.

Speaking of giving talks, I went to New York City for the weekend. It was the annual Learning Annex for Real Estate Wealth Building. I put myself at the convention center for 2 days with 50,000 of my closest friends. These were people of all walks of life, trying to get rich in the business of real estate. I guess the basics of the weekend were speakers trying to get rich selling their disk and CD sets. Everyone had a different angle on how you can get rich with lien certificates, flipping houses, stocks, oil, and just about every other method out there. I went for several reasons. I got the tickets after I made a $200 donation to a PBS television station. I like donating money to public television. My children watch cartoons of public television. Certainly, the government could spend our money on having a local access public television station, but that's unfair to the people that don't take advantage of the station. Instead, once a year, PBS holds a fund raising drive. This fund raising drive is used to support the television station throughout the year. Well, I use the station for my children, and I like the content that they present. So why wouldn't I support the station? For $200, I am supporting a cause that I enjoy. Usually, my donation to PBS brings me a Barney or Sesame Street CD, or a set of stuffed animals that the station sends me as a thank you for supporting them, but this time, it was 2 tickets to the wealth expo in New York City. So, that is one of the reasons that I ended up here this weekend. The other reason is the demand for continuing education. I enjoy going to seminars because, every now and then, you stumble upon a nugget of information that helps you in your business. As soon as you think that you have all of the knowledge, your business will start to plateau. You need to constantly be refilling your brain with new and fresh ideas. Not only that, but these seminars also serve as a means to recharge your battery. That is exactly what I needed for my business development. I have been in a rut lately, watching my net worth dwindle, so this weekend has really been a source of recharging my motivation. Let me give you a few of the highlights from the weekend.

I listened to Jim Cramer talk about the stock market. I've always been fascinated with the stock market, so this was a pretty interesting seminar. He confirmed many of the myths that I'm already familiar with. You may know that 85% of fund managers cannot beat the S & P 500 index. So, why would you put any money into a managed fund? I do have some money tied up in managed funds. After hearing Jim talk, they will all be closed, and the money moved over to the 500 index fund. He also confirmed my theory that stocks really are just another method of gambling. Cramer is a smart, smart guy. He rattled off about 8 stocks that he thinks are going to take off. Wow, can you believe that you risk money and capital in things that we "think" are going to take off? At least in real estate investing, you generally use a set of financial fundamentals to purchase a rental property. Your only risk is that the rental doesn't get a tenant. I don't think I have ever heard an owner complain that they simply could not fill their rental property. My next take-away was that the average return for the stock market over the past 60 years has been 12%. Remember that 85% of the professionals can't seem to meet or beat this number. Then remember that you need to invest 100% of your own money (no leveraging the bank's money) to get this crappy 12% return. Why would you play the market? There are many methods of getting a high return, and I'm not sure that the stock market is the best choice for me.

Just out of curiosity, how does real estate compare with Cramer's stock market? Let me take a quickie analysis of Cedar Barn, that is due to be under contract tomorrow. We put $9,200 as a down payment, we put $5,000 in closing costs, and another $5,000 in paint and carpet. Our all-in cash is $19,200. Then we had a tenant pay the entire monthly mortgage payment, probably reducing the balance of our principal about $3,000. If the deal goes through at our price, and when we sell it 2 ½ years later, we will make $160,000 total return. We got a depreciation advantage which I won't even throw into this equation. So, the return of $160,000 on $19,200 is an 833% return in 2 ½ years. Folks, that is freaky. In the end, the first big item that I picked up on was that I am currently in the right space, and need to continue to bang away at rental real estate. I should be on a buying frenzy of rental properties right now.

Then I went to a commercial seminar. This guy talked about how increasing your rents $1 per square foot on a 15,000 square foot building increases the net worth of the building $150,000 (assuming a 10% cap rate). Wait a second: I have a building at Windsor Mill where I could increase its net worth. Not only that, but we made money on Windsor exactly as this guy taught in his seminar. We bought it for $350,000, put in another $100,000 in repairs, and now it is worth $1.4 million (if we could actually sell it for that). We made about $1 million in net worth in 4 years in the building. Why am I not scouring for another Windsor Mill opportunity? When I get back, I need to be sending out letters to building owners, attending auctions, and talking with commercial brokers to find another commercial deal. I have been singing the praises of residential for a couple of years now, but to make $1 million in residential takes 10 single family properties. Why go through these headaches when I can do it with one address? So, I am really going to get motivated to buy another commercial property by the end of the first quarter of 2007. Deal making is what gets me excited, and I have been out of the game for the past year, messing around with construction. It is time to get back to what I do best. That's it for now. I don't plan on writing again until Charles Street has a contract on it.

LESSONS LEARNED

- Real estate prices are a function of supply and demand. Keep an eye on local statistics because seeing supply increase can only result in a reduction in pricing.

- It is alright to occasionally take a loss. Trying to remain optimistic in a down market can sometimes spiral out of control.

- Never spend paper net worth. Only spend with cash in your personal bank account.

STOP THE BLEEDING

January 2007

Well, here I am again, no contract on Charles Street and the bleeding just keeps continuing. I will get to the depression of Charles Street shortly, but first a quick and very depressing summary of events over the past several months; here we go... I believe that my last entry discussed how we'd performed an analysis of how our burn rate for each property was eventually going to overtake the market price for the homes. In layman's terms, we were upside down on the properties, had more money in them than they were worth, and were losing money, dead in the water, etc.; take your pick of distressing terms, but the properties on Patapsco were just that, distressing. There was a certain irony to the whole Signature Properties Company. For years, we had made money out of buying distressed property from homeowners, and now we were the distressed homeowners with buyers taking advantage of us. So, when we put the two homes on Patapsco Street on the market at $649,000, our basis in the properties was about $475,000. After carrying the properties for a total of 11 months at $3,000 per month, our basis is now around $510,000. Once you add on the commission we are incurring to resell the property, and the transfer taxes that we'll have to pay, you see that we needed to sell these properties for $530,000.

Well, the good news is that both properties are finally under contract. One is going to close on January 31st and the other one on February 15th. We have bent over backwards just to get these offers in the door. The properties would go months without having a showing, so when we finally got interested buyers into the properties, we took their offers. They have us running around like headless chickens fixing this and that, repainting railings, repairing, sanding, installing and rebuilding already beautiful homes. Knowing that our basis is $530,000, the offers we accepted are $519,000 and $510,000, respectively. At the end of the day, we are losing $30,000 on these homes. This is a far cry from how exciting all of the deals were when I began writing this book several years ago. As an analytical guy, I sit around and try to evaluate where I went wrong on these homes. When we bought the land, we pro-forma'd the project at $550,000. I guess that was our first mistake, although I don't know how you could have considered this a mistake at the time. When we got into this project, which was almost 2 and half years ago, the market could support $550,000. As the market kept going up at a breakneck pace, we saw our resale price escalate up to a legitimate $650,000. Over the following 2 years, prices on new construction in the city did indeed escalate about 20%. The problem was, from the beginning of 2006 until now, the market has given back that 20% and more; the 'more' being that it now takes an average of 6 months, and not 30 days, to sell a property. We also made some mistakes in the design of the homes, which has caused them to be less saleable. Parking in the rear of these homes is difficult due to the small alleyway for access. On paper, the plans look great, but after construction, you see that getting an SUV into these rear loading garages is extremely difficult. Uggh... the hindsight of the entire process is disturbing. We are losing money.

The next mistake that we made was blurring our core competency. Core competency is one of the MBA terms that refers to what a company does best. Our core competency was locating discounted real estate and subdividing lots. We've had great success in doing this on many occasions. Somewhere in that process, we decided that we could take the process one step further and become custom homebuilders. Essentially, we became greedy pigs. The problem is this: we are not builders. We went out and hired the builders. So, now we were competing with the finished products of builders that build for literally half the cost that we can build a home. We've found that national builders can build new homes for about $70 per square foot, while our general contractors were charging us close to $135 per square foot. The other issue with taking on this additional step is the time required to build the houses. Since we were living in one of the greatest real estate markets in history, we thought that real estate could only go in one direction, skyward. The construction process took our general contractors over a year, though. In preparing our pro-forma, we hadn't been concerned about timing because we thought that our homes could be worth $750,000 when we were done. Things were great and could only get better…right? We didn't mind holding anything because the appreciation of the assets was outpacing the cost to carry these assets. Similar to the game of musical chairs, when the music stopped, the person holding the most inventory of real estate was going to be left without a chair. I can honestly say that we are chairless right now. So, we took the offers on Patapsco. We wanted to hold out and try to at least break even on this project, but the carry expense was just eating us up. There is something to be said about just taking your losses and moving on. I guess what is difficult to accept is that we worked very hard on Patapsco, and for the past several years, and in the end, we worked for free and have to pony up money in order to cover our losses. I think a valuable take-away from this project is to evaluate how you make money, and stick to your strengths. When we successfully purchased the property and subdivided it, we could have sold off the two lots at a $50,000 profit each. Being so new to the business, I just simply did not have the experience to understand these issues, and subsequently I thought that I had the Midas touch and simply could not lose.

So where do we stand with the other projects? The next big project is Robinson Street. These are 4 townhomes that are priced at $549,000 each and are extremely similar to the Patapsco homes. There is a bit of good news on these homes, though. We have a contract that is due to close next week on the end unit, and at $549,000. After all is said and done, this home should net us out $38,000 in profit. I haven't used the word profit in a long while, and it is music to my ears. This should just about wipe out a little more than half the losses on Patapsco Street. Again, the buyer on this house has been in complete control of the transaction, and has had us reworking the plumbing and finish work for over 2 weeks in order to get this house to the settlement table. When we originally did the pro-forma on this project and had the financing appraisal done, it came in at $680,000. I certainly am glad that I didn't go out and spend the phantom paper money on this project. Unfortunately, we have no other breathing purchasers with any interest in the other three Robinson properties. We are holding open houses, have them listed on the multiple list service, have signs, have banners, and just can't seem to generate any more interest in the project. Inventory levels in the $500,000 plus range are extremely high, and not very many homes are going under contract. We can only hope that, when the first one settles at $549,000, others will see this and soon follow up with some interest. We are also holding our breath for the upcoming spring market. If the media stops running the negative housing reports and starts to show signs of life in the market, I have a feeling that all those buyers in the higher ranges will step up and start buying. These buyers have been sitting on the sidelines, watching homes that have once been priced at $700,000, drop all the way down to $549,000. While they want to buy, they don't have to buy. The interest rates just recently crept over 6% for the first time since November '06.

Just to continue the sobering news on Charles Street, we are having trouble getting any national homebuilder interested in the site. We're expecting to have the plat recorded with the city in two weeks. This was supposed to be a cause for celebration because this would represent the point at which all of the builders wanted the site to be, but that was back when we were getting off-the-wall offers of over $10 million. Instead, we cannot seem to get any party interested in purchasing the site, at any price. I have been out there hawking the site to anyone who'll listen. When they ask what the price is, it's simply the best offer that I can get at record plat. People have now thrown out numbers of $6 million. If you recall, this is half of what we were offered just a year and a half ago. That is part of the game, unfortunately. The builders were once in the subservient position of being price takers. We could demand $12 million and we felt like we were on top of the world with this very precious and unique piece of property. It is incredible how quickly the roles have changed, and now we are taking whatever they are offering. Once they were making offers of taking the deal down at record plat, but now they want us to demolish the building and put in roads, sewers, and connections. Cycles are funny, and I am glad that we did not burn any bridges a year ago. We are meeting with several builders next week to discuss joint venturing with them. With this scenario, we would sell off the land to a third party just to cover what we owe, and take less now and more when the finished lots are liquidated to the ultimate builder for the property. We are open to all possible scenarios that could potentially stop the bleeding. One more update on Charles... the financing. We recently had to refinance the property as the terms for our initial loan have since expired. The new loan is going to be approved when we receive final record plat. The bank reappraised the property and is willing to give us a lot more money. We arranged to recoup some of the cash that we have already spent on engineering and legal. Additionally, they're allowing us to roll the interest expense for the next year into the loan. Basically, we will be paying debt with additional debt. This is a nice play since we were getting worn out of continuing to raise money by selling out our rental portfolio every other month as we burned through it.

My final thought for the month revolves around my future plans. I realize that the last few pages of entries are somewhat depressing and disheartening if you are thinking about getting into real estate as your plan for wealth and riches. I remember the excitement of the earlier chapters, and the deals that were closing and the hundreds of thousands of equity that I was building on a daily basis. As long as you realize that your real estate career is a constantly developing, building, fluid motion, you will see where I am going with this. When I started this whole journey, I had very little money, and essentially the net worth of a homeless person. I was browsing through my hard drive on my computer the other day, and came across a goal sheet that I created when we started the company. Back then, I felt that it was important to establish expectations with my partners, in that my family was my main priority. Certainly, I wanted to have a net worth of $2 million, but I did not want to sacrifice the time with my family to achieve this goal. The sheet includes a time horizon of 5 years. The timing of me finding this document could not have been more apropos. I was beginning to feel the pressures of the market and feeling like the decisions that I'd made over the past several years may not have been the best. When I look back on the past 5 years, though, I realize that I've managed to coach soccer for both of my children every year. I did not miss one baseball game or school event. I have every weekend off, and we took some absolutely top shelf vacations. I didn't miss one holiday, and managed to take 5 weeks a year for personal time. I bought some fantastic material possessions, including new cars, a boat, and jewelry, and managed to afford to get my children started with private school educations. Their college savings have been underway, and I have absolutely zero personal debt. All of this while averaging a 30 hour work week. When you look at this success, the journey has been fantastic. So, right now, I am trying to do some goal planning for the next 5 years. I truly enjoy the industry of real estate, and let me reiterate that I can't think of any other business which allows you to build net worth as quickly as real estate does.

I believe that I mentioned that we put on the market a rental property on Cedar Barn late last year. Well, that property sold and we cashed out $69,000 each. We could have sold that property for $150,000 in 2003 when we finished the project, and walked with a cool $40,000 minus expenses. Instead, we chose to rent it for 3 years. We had one tenant in there the entire time. So, we end up selling it for $240,000 and making $130,000 profit on the deal. The next single house that is hitting the chopping block is one on Fleet Street. Again, we purchased this property at a foreclosure auction for $60,000. We put another $60,000 into the house to rebuild and make it a great property. The tenant who is living in the house wants to buy the property for $230,000. So, on this property, we should net out $55,000 each. When you read my earlier depressing information about miss in timing the market on all of our new construction, let us not forget that we held onto some unbelievable deals over the past couple of years. After Fleet goes, we will be selling off 2 more singles that have very similar numbers. I'm trying to bank some liquid cash so that, when a commercial opportunity arises, I am poised and ready to capitalize on it. My vision is to take the model of these singles where we are making $60,000 and reproducing them with larger commercial investments like Windsor Mill that kick out $500,000 after a few years. Will it work, you ask…you will have to buy the next book to see.

Now, for the most exciting part of the liquidation process. I have told you how smart my wife is, and over a nice bottle of wine one night out at a local seafood establishment, I told her of my plans for 2007. I will say one thing about Jill, that most people cannot say about their spouses: she trusts me 100% with our financial future, and I cannot express my appreciation for this enough. Every several years, I get the bug and jump from job to job, industry to industry, without any knowledge or experience, and reassure her that things will be just fine. Each time I jump ship, she not only trusts me, but encourages me every step of the way. Without this support in your corner, I am not sure that anyone could have achieved the kind of success that I've seen. So, back to the bottle of wine... she asks me why, if the market is the worst market in 10 years, we would be liquidating our inventory. On these single properties, she is exactly right. The house on Fleet Street should have sold for $275,000 in 2005, and now we are going to take $230,000. That is a relatively big hit for missing the market. Unfortunately, holding onto the property in hopes that it returns to $275,000 may take 5 more years, and I need that capital to invest in more profitable investments. We took the lion's share of the profit by holding from 2003 until now, but now it is time to liquidate and put that capital to better use. Secondly, when I talk about liquidating, she wonders what happened to my original plan for the college rentals. Do you remember, years ago, when I was planning on living on $200,000 a year as generated by the college rentals? That was my original plan, but like I said before, your real estate career needs to be fluid. What I have learned over the past several years is that the commercial investments tend to run themselves. You have very little interaction with the tenants and they sign multiple-year leases. There are no residential headaches and payment games. The process is very straightforward, and the returns are also pretty good. So, between sips of the 1997 Cabernet, I tell Jill that the nice thing about the college portfolio is that it will be valued on a cap rate basis, using the income approach versus the market value approach. I've been preaching this theory throughout the book. The townies that we have on Nicoll Avenue are worth $180,000 each to the general public, as homes using the market value approach. If I sold one to a homeowner, he would have to get an appraisal for his financing, and they would realize that the house is worth just $180,000. Now, this isn't all that bad considering I was buying them for $75,000 each. But, as a rental property, the appraisal uses an entirely different process of valuation. The income approach takes the net operating income from the property and assigns it a capitalization rate using other comparable investment properties and the potential for rent increases, vacancies, operating expenses, etc. These houses rent for $2,200 per month, or $26,400 per year. If you deduct the management expense, taxes, and HOA dues, you come up with an NOI of around $22,000 per year. We constantly throw out a capitalization rate of 10% just because it is easy to divide by, which would mean that the value of this home using the income approach would be $220,000, which is great, but I'm not done yet.

In trying to evaluate the best method to sell this portfolio, we are jockeying between two potential liquidation methods. We like the auction route because it is quick and guaranteed. At auction, income producing properties seem to sell between 8 to 10 times gross rents. If that is the case, our portfolio is worth between $3.2 million and $4 million (we gross about $400,000 a year in this scenario, in case the math was difficult to figure out). Now it starts to get a little bit exciting, because we only owe $1.8 million on the package. Therefore, at the end of the day, Pete and I would split anywhere between $1.4 million and $2.2 million. Folks, in six years, this portfolio would have made me around $1 million. This in addition to all of the singles that we are selling, in addition to the building that has $1 million in equity, and did I forget to mention Charles Street, which has an unknown equity at this point, but what should be at least several million in equity.

Let me take a quick breather because I really love talking about net worth, since this is why I am in the business, after all. So, I said that there were two possible methods of liquidating the portfolio, the first being the auction method, and the second method is working with a commercial broker. I came across two young hungry commercial guys from a decent sized national company. They brought a deal to my buddy for a commercial property with a 7-11 in it, and I was impressed with the professionalism. I met with them last week and gave them a shot at preparing a plan for the liquidation of the 15 college rental properties. I told them that the leases for the next calendar year are already signed and in hand, all the way through to 2008. I shared with them the increases in rents over the years, and the fact that this portfolio is just a cash cow. Needless to say, they are extremely excited about getting the listing on this portfolio. They did a very impressive packet for the sale of it, and I decided to give them a shot to see what they can generate. Oh yeah, and I told you that I like using a 10% cap rate because it is easy to divide... well, being in the business, they think that they can get a 7% cap rate on the project. So, with a net operating income of $366,000, they are telling me that they will get me some crazy number like $4.8 million. Yes, that is right, that is a crazy number, but if they can get me more than $4.2 million, they will beat my best day at an auction. I told them that I like the auction route, but I am willing to give them a 60 day shot at selling this thing and making their commission of $288,000. Again, if you are doing the math and they do successfully sell the portfolio at $4.8 million, we pay off the debt of $1.8 million and split $3 million. That would be absolute insanity, if I walk from this with $1.5 million. Again, I am a firm believer that a paper net worth is exactly that, just paper, but still... So, that is all of the dreaming that I can pen for now. I hope that this chapter has brought the real estate market into perspective, but also motivated you to get into the business sooner than later. With the real estate market being as depressed as it is, this is probably the absolute best time to buy. When you think of buying stocks, you buy low and sell high. We are in the trough of the real estate market. The dips that it has taken over the past year have created some of the best residential opportunities in years. Get out there and take advantage of them.

April 26, 2007

Real estate is a business of dreams. Part of the fun of playing in the real estate game is imagining all of the money that you are going to make off of the next big deal. Just look at the past 5 years of my life, and you will see one exciting and promising deal after another. Each entry I've made talks about how much money I "could" make off of the next big deal. Even as I continue to get absolutely killed in what is turning out to be one of the most prolific real estate market corrections in history, I still write about all of the money that I *hope* to earn on the deal. I'm starting to think that I'm bi-polar as I contemplate the absolute highs and lows of playing in this game. Then, reality hits!

Yesterday was absolutely and by far the worst day in my real estate career, or my business career, for that matter. Sit down for this one: I lost $164,000 yesterday. I can't help but laugh at myself as I sit here and write this paragraph. It really isn't funny, because this is the type of stuff that bankrupts people. I can't remember when we first bought the deal on Fairmount, but it had to be around 3 years ago. We had an intern who put together a proposal to buy 4 lots from the city, through the RFP process. Boy, were we excited to get awarded these lots for $320,000. The intern was hailed as brilliant for this purchase. This was going to be the easiest money in the world to make. The process was simple. The intern was an architectural student from the University of Maryland. He would draw the proposed plans for what the facades of these 4 townhomes would look like when they were complete. We would put the plans together, pitch them at the next community meeting, get permits, build nice houses, and have a fantastic payday. The preconstruction appraisals done in order to get the financing showed these houses worth $425,000 each when completed. This was yet another dream deal. While we thought we had all the answers (sort of like my 9 year old son) we saw our total cash in the project coming in at $80,000 per lot, $210,000 construction per house, and $25,000 in soft costs to cover architectural and engineering, for a total of $315,000 per unit. Using the bank's appraisal numbers, not ours, we had created a pro-forma showing that we were going to make $115,000 per house on, or $460,000 on the project, so there was good reason to celebrate…right? What really happened? First, we did have the intern complete the drawings. We went in front of the community and they loved the project that we were proposing. With their support, we went to the zoning hearing and, yet again, got the thumbs up from the city to proceed with the plan. Things were just going swimmingly. We met with our preferred builder and signed a contract for $840,000. So, there you go – we were off and running. Now keep in mind, 3 years ago, the building industry was just booming. It took the builder 6 months to start the project, and a full year and two months to build the project. At that rate, a 9 month project took us 18 months in order to get the final product to the market. This delay was indeed costly. When our builder finally handed us back the keys to the finished products, the market had already started to tank. Pete and I were fairly concerned with the signals of the market adjustment, but we were still relatively optimistic at this point. Instead of going with the bank appraised number of $425,000, we put the properties on the market for $399,000. Thirty days went by without a single showing; we dropped the price again to $379,000. I remember the painful discussions that Pete and I were having on dropping the price. It just seemed like we were chasing the buyers down to their price level. The feeling of a complete lack of control caused my stomach to churn. At this point, we were in each house for approximately $350,000. We decided to drop the price again, to $359,000, thinking that if we could just find a buyer at this price, we would have a shot at breaking even after our commissions and closing costs. I hope that you can see that we are slowly bleeding a painful death. When you have a project that came out just the way you wanted it – with upgraded cabinets, countertops, and top of the line fixtures and finishes – and nobody wants it, this game can get to be very depressing.

So, here we stand, today, in April of 2007. We are in each lot for $80,000, plus the costs of construction of $225,000, plus $40,000 in interest expense per house, plus $8,000 in additional soft costs for a total of $353,000 per house. If we were lucky enough to get the $425,000 that we thought that they were worth, we still would have made about $50,000 per house after commissions. But this is the worst real estate market in decades. To compound the issue of the sales pricing continuing to drop, our bases in each house continues to rise as we have to pay interest expenses to the bank. Each month that we carried these properties, we incurred $10,000 in interest expense, or about $2,500 per unit. Pete and I decided to plot some graphs on the white board that showed a month by month comparison between our price dropping and our basis growing. As stated above, we are at the critical point where the two lines crisscross, and we would break even if they sold TODAY. If you have ever had the dream of becoming an entrepreneur, this is that moment in time that separates the men from the boys and the women from the girls. We decided to literally amputate the hand instead of slowly bleeding to death. We had no other choice; we had to liquidate the properties.

We hired a local auction company to market these homes. They spent $6,000 of our money in marketing fees, plus charged us 4% to sell the homes. They ran ads in all the local newspapers, placed multiple entries on their website, and created extremely colorful postcards highlighting the properties and the upcoming auction. Yesterday was our big day. The auction drew 27 people. I counted, as I wanted to see exactly what our $6,000 bought us. Auctions are a lot different these days. I remember back when we were buying properties 4 years ago. There was auction fever going around. People were raising their hands to up the bids with reckless abandon. Prices were inflating beyond realistic valuations. Yesterday, there was a subdued funeral feel to our auction. There was no hype, no excitement, and frankly, no remotely unrealistic valuations. The good news is that we sold all 4 homes. The nice thing about auctioning off your properties is that the buyer pays all of the transfer taxes and the interest expense, from yesterday forward. That means that, technically, we have stopped the bleeding. When I woke up this morning, I knew that someone else was on the hook to cover my $10,000 a month in interest carry. Some other benefits from yesterday's auction are that the buyer is taking the property "as-is", and they have put down a sizable non-refundable deposit. So, we are grateful to have this peace of mind. Now for the bad news.... We have $353,000 in each property. The first one sold for $330,000, the second for $325,000, the third for $325,000 and the last one for $307,000. So, after backing out from all of the expenses, we will have to come to the settlement table with $164,000. And by the way, I'm not sure that we have $164,000 to come to the table with. So, if you are wondering how I remain sane through all of this, know that I have two strategies. The first is that we have a land deal on 4 lots that we have almost subdivided, which we should net around $150,000 on after all expenses. Here is that bi-polar disorder rearing its ugly head again. I am dreaming about the $150,000 gain from a "potential" property to pay off the $164,000 loss I just incurred yesterday. Perhaps I'm not really that sane. So, we will have worked 2 ½ years on a 4 lot subdivision deal, which hopefully will provide enough profit to offset the loss we incurred on Fairmount, which we invested with 3 years of our hard work and effort. This must sound somewhat depressing…and yes, it is. Do you want to know something even more sobering? What happens if the 4 lot subdivision deal doesn't go through, and instead of having a $150,000 win, I have a $150,000 loss? My therapist says that I shouldn't let myself go there.

So, my next strategy for dealing with this is knowing that, in the end, at the end of the day, at the end of my real estate career, I should have over $2,000,000 in net worth created by real estate. Deal by deal, I may be losing some money, but overall, this crazy market has allowed me to set up retirement at age 38. Of course, I do not have the $2,000,000 in the bank currently, so this could all change as well. I have to pat myself on the back right now, though. I have to be the most optimistic lunatic I know. I continue to lose money on projects, I see the market crumbling before me, who knows when the carnage will stop, who knows when I will stop bleeding to death, and for some strange reason, I keep a positive spin on the entire outcome and my net worth. It is kind of funny. At the end of the day, the rental portfolio may not bring anything near what I am hoping that it will bring, Charles Street lots could completely fail, and I may end up with a flower garden in the middle of Baltimore, but I keep smiling.

Before I cut out for this entry, let me fill you in on what houses we have left on the books. We are settling on a small rehab project on Monday. We should just about break even on this after investing about $100,000 in acquisition and rehab. After marketing it for 4 months, you simply take what you can get and get out. Again, we're viewing breaking even as a victory these days. We have a little lot that we purchased for $80,000 in the Federal Hill neighborhood of Baltimore, and that we are just trying to liquidate. Beyond these couple of deals and Charles Street, we really do not have too much inventory to liquidate. Then we have the 16 rental properties. My strategy has completely changed. I originally had viewed the rental portfolio as my nest egg. Remember that I was constantly writing about how I was going to pay off the entire portfolio and live off of the cash flow? Like the boxer Mike Tyson says, "Everyone has a strategy until I punch him in the mouth." This market has punched us in the mouth and our original strategy is now down for the count. I've got to put some food on the table for my family. We have become accustomed to a fairly expensive lifestyle. As such, I need to continue to fund our account without having the consistent successes from flipping houses. So, Pete and I have decided to start liquidating, dare I say it, our precious portfolio of rental houses. I am in the process of moving out two tenants so I can repair these houses and sell them. We bought these really, really cheap, and our basis is extremely low. Even in this market, we should make about $100,000 each on the sale of these two homes. This money will end up in the bank, and should carry our burn rate for a little while.

May 15, 2007

I don't even know where to start this month. The burn rate of Charles Street to cover the bank, the soft costs of development, and the taxes are eating us up. Not only this, but Pete and I have evaluated the Signature Properties Fund. You may remember the Fund from years ago and my occasional mentions of it in the interim. We raised $480,000 of friends, family, and fools' money to support our buying and flipping habit. The Fund had a couple of stellar years where it was returning fantastic returns to our investors. As we are close to liquidating all of the investment properties in the fund, we realize that, at the end of the day, we will have less than the $480,000 of original capital to return to our family, friends and fools. Now, we haven't nailed down the exact loss, but the thought of telling my mother that I have lost 25% of her original principal from her retirement fund weighs heavily on my mind. Given our cash flow issues and our equity issues, Pete and I have decided that we have no other choice but to liquidate the college rental properties. Yikes... this was certainly not in the cards. I've put a packet of information together for potential investors, and have just started the process of interviewing some potential commercial real estate agents who might be able to sell them for us. At this point, I am gun shy of even speculating how much equity we have in the properties. I promise to keep you posted on how the rental property liquidation event pans out. Needless to say, this continues to be a difficult spring at Signature Properties.

Now, I did successfully sell two rental properties this spring. These were homes that we bought in 2003, right during the heat of the market. We fixed them up and rented them for several years. On both properties, Pete and I each got $65,000, so the beginning of this year has started out well. However, each year brings newer and fresher problems. April 15th was tax day. Here is a little tidbit of wisdom from a guy that has made many mistakes.... When the going is good, remember to set aside a few bucks for old Uncle Sam. Since 2006 was a decent year, I had every reason to believe that 2007 would follow suit. Therefore, I was not too worried about making my tax payment during 2006. Why do today what you can put off until tomorrow? My estimated tax bill for 2006 gobbled up just about all of the $65,000 that I made from liquidating my precious portfolio.

Finally, there's the update on Charles Street. You remember this project. This was the one that we bought for $2.1 million, rezoned, platted, subdivided, yada, yada, yada, and we were going to retire rich. Dreaming is great, and I wouldn't trade the past 5 years for anything. So at one point in time, I was doing a jig because we had these letters of intent for national builders who wanted the lots for anywhere between $9 million and $12 million at record plat. What a wicked world we live in. Oh yeah, and I think

I may have forgotten to mention another offer that we had on Charles Street. We did have these crazy guys who met us for lunch and offered us $6 million, right now, for the raw land. They didn't want it subdivided, entitled, rezoned, nothing. They were willing to take a piece of land that we had just purchased for $2.1 million and allow us to make $3.5 million in 60 days. Remember those guys? These were the guys that we scoffed at and laughed at because we stood to make an additional $3 million just for pushing the paper around for the next 6-9 months to receive that recorded plat. What could possibly happen in the next 6 months that could affect value? Huh. We stood to make $12 million on this deal for taking very "little" risk. Again, it was easy. Once the city had signed off on the subdivision, we could sell the land to the national builders and retire on my boat down in the Caribbean. So, how has the downturn in the market affected this property? First, the nationals are getting clobbered. They can't sell the properties that they currently have. They have had deals falling apart at every turn. They've defaulted on land deals that they bid too much for, and are being foreclosed on for others that they can't afford to develop. When I call their land acquisition guys, they tell me that they've all been laid off. As I sit here angrily writing this post, I know that even if I got the entire thing approved, I'd still have no buyers for it.

Another big day happened a couple of months ago, though. This should have been one of the most exciting days of my life. It's crazy how I've had several entries in my journal, and keep forgetting to write about this one. In March, after the long awaited almost 2 year process of rezoning, meetings with planning, working with the community, satisfying each city government agency, and spending hundreds of thousands of dollars with engineers and architects…we have received the plat back from the city, stamped and recorded. How exciting is that? In ceremonial fashion, I personally picked up the plat map from the planning department and walked it to the recording cashier myself. I handed her the check and recorded this Picasso myself. This day was supposed to be the day when Ryland Homes was "supposed" to hand me a check for $12 million. And now that I finally have something to sell, I don't have any buyers to sell it to. I opened up the rolodex to find all of those national builders who were chomping at the bit to buy my land just 1 short year ago. Some of them were not interested in the property at any price, and some were submitting us embarrassing verbal offers, and ultimately we said that we were not ready to sell it. I will make a prediction right now, that one day, I will be regretting not taking one of these embarrassing offers. I seem to be one step behind every step of the way lately, and the market keeps tanking. I don't know what we were waiting for.... Actually, of course, that is not true. We thought that the spring market was going to turn around and show signs of life, and magically, these guys would change their minds and want my land. Now, we sit on a nice piece of land, rezoned to residential use, subdivided into 64 buildable lots, and we are stuck paying about $20,000 a month to carry it. Pretty good position, huh? To make things worse, we ran out of money carrying the project. The bank account went dry. One of our investors was a buddy of mine who I met in MBA school. He wanted to get involved in real estate, but didn't have the time to get his hands dirty. So he gave us $30,000 to put into Charles Street with a guaranteed 12% interest rate. Sounded pretty good back then. Well, now he is getting married and wanted to get his investment back so that he could pay for his wedding. Ooops. We don't have any more money. How do you go tell your friend that you lost his wedding money, and that you hear the catering at Denny's is supposed to be pretty good? We had just about exhausted most of our business lines of credit, so I went to my personal emergency line of credit and put the $30,000 on my line in order for him to get married. What a position and a predicament that we are in.

You get the picture that we are running out of money, and for the first time in my short real estate career, the concept of bankruptcy has just started to enter the conversation. Pete and I are looking forward, yet again, to all of our liabilities, and we need to make a decision on Charles Street. Sure, we want to hold off until the real estate market comes back, but we are not sure if that is even a reality. With the cost of carrying the mortgage, plus the taxes and insurance, the likelihood of us lasting without declaring bankruptcy is very low. We had pretty good luck using the auction method with the 4 townhomes at Fairmont, and are considering auctioning off Charles Street. I know, I know: this has been my dream property and this was going to be my ticket to get out of here, but it may be time to face the music. I like the finality of an auction. Psychologically, you know that your liability ends at a singular moment in time. You get all of your buyers in one spot at one time, and if you can get two buyers involved, the price gets bid up to an acceptable level. At least we can hope that the bidding gets up to an acceptable level. So, we've decided to do what we do best: cut bait and run.

We've been using two auction houses in Baltimore to sell our properties. Both of them are good groups and both do a pretty good job of bringing in crowds of people to bid on the properties. For this one, we went with the larger auction group. They have an impressive showroom where they can wine and dine larger groups of potential investors. I met with the auctioneer to execute the paperwork and handed him a check that I drew from my line of credit again, for $10,000. This money was to be used for marketing the auction. It's funny how the auctioneers make money regardless if whether the property sells of not. Maybe, all this time, I should have been an auctioneer. At any rate, the auction is going to be held at the auctioneer's showroom next Thursday. I've emailed everyone that has shown any interest in the property at any time over the past 2 years, all of the information about the auction. Every national builder, land developer, independent home builder, and real estate agent that has sniffed at Charles Street has been invited to attend our big event. The auction group has hit all of the major newspapers. It has a nice visual on the website, highlighting the potential that this recorded plat with 64 lots has to offer. The group's mailing list has been hit again and again with this great opportunity. I believe that we have done a pretty good job marketing the property. In the listing agreement, I had to put down a reserve price. The reserve price is the absolute lowest amount that I am willing to accept on the day of the auction. I put a reserve of $6 million on the land, which means that if the auction does not bring in this amount, we don't have to sell it. I came up with that number because most of the builders only want 60 larger lots instead of our 64 smaller lots. That means that they could consolidate and recombine the lots to get their desired number of lots. So, in my feeble mind, $100,000 per lot is a good number, but is it? The national builders like to be in the lots for $150,000, finished. If someone pays us $100,000, puts in the utilities, streets, curbs, etc., and then sell them for $150,000, the developer does not make any money. Again and again, we fall into the same seller trap of thinking that our properties are worth more than they are. It's like a race to the bottom, and I seem to be in the lead. Here I am again, coming up with the same crazy high analysis. I just simply cannot learn my lesson.

Before the auction, we are trying to think this through a little more critically. We really don't know who the final buyer will be for the lots. It could be a developer and it could be a national home builder. We do know that we want to be done with this deal next Thursday. If the land developer wants to make $1.5 million for their risk and effort over the next 3 years of putting in the utilities, that works out to be $25,000 per lot. Therefore, our sales price would have to be $75,000 per lot, or $4.5 million. This is quite possibly the outcome that we get on the day of the auction. So, the question becomes: do we take this or not? What if the auctioneer says to us, 'this is it, we got up to $4.5 million, boys'? If we don't take it, we're then committed to finishing the lots and selling them on a takedown schedule to a national builder over the next 3 years. How much money could we make if we go through that ritual and invest the time over the next couple of years? Or, we just take the $4.5 million. We have about $3 million in the deal, and we walk with $1.5 million, or $750,000 each. Again, I sit here and find myself laughing. Business is funny. At one point, I thought that we were selling this thing for $9 million and I was going to have $3 million. Oh, the dreams... how funny is that? That guy who offered us $6 million when we had just a measly $2.2 million in the deal and not a whole lot of work done on the property.... Then we would have made $1.9 million each. I am excited about the prospects of next Thursday, but at the same time, I am scared…really scared.

I know that I keep kicking myself about the internet bubble, but I have to bring it up one more time. The one thing that I recall reading about was all of these executives who had made millions and millions of net worth, but ultimately lost it all due to the crash of the market. The smart ones cashed out, but the majority of them lost everything. How foolish and greedy were these guys? They always thought that the market would continue to go up. It reminds me of the casinos in Vegas. You may go up, but you never leave up. People are wired to continue to gamble because they believe in streaks and luck. They say to themselves, 'if I made this much already, just wait, I am going to make even more'. Are these people are fools... but, wait a second: I fall into the category of "these people". I mean, I could have made $1.9 million just for walking away from Charles Street about 1 ½ years ago. I could have banked that money, paid for college tuition, retired, and who knows, bought whatever I wanted to, but instead, I was ready to sit at the table and gamble just a few more hands. I could have doubled down and walked away with $3 million. Hindsight is 20/20, and sure, I can look back and think, 'why didn't I cash out and walk when I had the chance?' We were in a bubble, just like the stock market, only we convinced ourselves that real estate had intrinsic value and that value could never be taken away. We convinced ourselves that people will always need a place to live, and there will always be a demand for housing. We convinced ourselves of a lot of things that were simply not true. So, in the end, I hope that I can publish the book. I have been waiting on Charles Street to settle in order to publish, and I am pretty sure that I will have accomplished my original goal of $2 million. They say that we learn more from our mistakes than we do from our successes. Without the bottom falling out of the market, without me losing millions of dollars in speculative purchases, I may not have developed as broad a mind for business as I now have. There will be other businesses and other ventures, and these past 7 years in real estate will definitely help me in executing them better. So, the next entry will be short, just a summary of the Charles Street auction next week. Wish me luck. For the record…and don't tell anyone this... I will take $4.5 million if I can get it.

June 19, 2007

This is like a nightmare, and I just can't seem to wake up. It is like a train wreck, and I can't stop watching. Only in this train wreck, I am the one with the train. What in the world is going on with this real estate market? It is making me absolutely nuts. At this point, I am not sure if I am making bad decisions, or if there is just not a whole lot that I can do in these circumstances. I'll cut to the chase…I still own Charles Street!!!!! Before the auction, we met with the auctioneers to discuss our strategy for the auction. We did a great job marketing the property. When it came time for the big dance, we had about 12 people there. Not a very good draw for $10,000 in marketing expenses. There were some smaller builders, and smaller investors, but also a few big players in the city that could easily have pulled off taking down the property and making something happen on that site. Needless to say, we were somewhat bullish as the time got closer to the actual auction. I dressed up in my Hawaiian shirt and straw hat, anticipating my trip to the Caribbean that I was going to buy when we sold this property.

So here we are, sitting with the big wigs of this auction company, discussing what our minimum acceptable bid would be. Pete and I were trying not to tip our hand on what our lowest acceptable offer would be, as we just wanted them to work hard to get the highest possible price. They decided (and I guess we acquiesced) to start the bidding at $4 million. Their logic sounded, well, logical... at the time. They claimed that if it didn't sell at auction (why wouldn't it sell at auction?), then the market would see the property at a value of less than $4 million. They explained that it would be difficult to ever sell the property for greater than $4 million at that point. Dumbfounded and stupid, Pete and I looked at each other and agreed that it sounded like a good plan. If this doesn't make sense to you, don't worry, because it still doesn't make sense to me. I still don't see the issue with starting the bidding at a point that covers our debt and gets people into the game. Once the adrenaline is rushing, we hoped that people continued to bid up on emotion, and eventually get to the point that we wanted them to be at. So, the auctioneer stands up there on the podium, reads the ad describing the 64 lots, and describes the other possibilities for the site. Then the auctioneer says, "will someone give me $4 million?" Before you know it, he says, 'we have $4 million, how about $4.1 million'…and again, within a split second, he says, 'we have $4.1 million'. At this point, everyone is looking around to see who the bidders are, and frankly, so were Pete and I. We didn't care, we had the bidding started, and we were already up to $4.1 million. Now, keep in mind, we needed about $3.2 million just to get out of the deal and break even. Needless to say, the tight feeling that I had had in my chest just hours prior had now loosened up a bit. This auction should continue to take off from here, I thought. All of our worries were washing away like the tide I'd be hearing at the beach in St. John. But pay attention, because the plot thickens. Then he throws out there, 'who will give us $4.2 million?' Again, 'who will give us $4.2? I said looking for $4.2'.... Bueller, Bueller. Can you say 'absolute silence'? You know, crickets–chirping-outside silence. There was not a peep in that room. But hey, that's alright, I thought: I've achieved my goal.

At this point, the auctioneers take us to the back room to re-discuss our strategy. What is there to discuss, though? – We've got

$4.1 million. The auctioneer tells us that we really don't have $4.1 million. As a matter of fact, we don't have any bids on the property. I was confused, as I'd heard someone yell out $4.1 million. Surprise, though: the $4 million and the $4.1 million bids were thrown out there by auctioneer plants in the audience. This usually gets the bidding going, but in our case, it didn't. So, here we stand, Pete and I in the auctioneer's office with no bid, no bidders, and a 64 lot subdivision with $240,000 a year in carry costs still sitting in my portfolio. I ask the auctioneer, why not just start it again at $3 million and try it all over again? They deter us from doing that, saying that since we had these 2 bids at $4 and $4.1 million, that we just cannot go back and do it. In hindsight, that doesn't really sound like my problem, but ultimately, it is. The employees of the auction company are now going person to person out there, asking if anyone is interested, and at any price. People are all trying to keep it under $4 million. It appears that, when people go to an auction in a buyer's market, they want a discount. Go figure. So, after working the crowd relentlessly for about 15 minutes, we let everyone go home, and the auction is officially over. As quickly as we'd signed the listing agreement and put up the $10,000 in advertising money, this method of liquidation was over. I just can't seem to buy a break.

Since the auction, we have been working some of the attendees, calling them, negotiating with them, but nothing has solidified. People in this market are cautious. They don't want to overspend in a market that continues to sink like the Titanic. So that leaves them buying land for such a deep discount that they are protected even if the market continues to tank. Let me chalk this one away for lessons learned for the next real estate market.

Dream with me for a minute, and put yourself in my shoes: your dream piece of land, your retirement house, your kid's education, the cause of all of your dreams over the past 2 years, and it's now a liability. We are paying about $20,000 in payments on the land, we have no income coming in off of the land, and now, we have no prospect of selling it. We've tried everything, including auction. I am worn out both physically and psychologically. I try not to think about it too often because it could be somewhat depressing. So, what do you do?

My friend Vic recommended this book called *Who Moved My Cheese.* I read it about 3 years ago, and maybe even wrote about it back then, but the book says that when you are used to doing something over and over again, you get caught in this rut. Then, when someone moves your cheese, you have to be alert enough to know that the cheese will no longer be where it used to be. One of the mice in the book realizes this and finds a creative way of locating the cheese. Hmmmm. How can I apply these simple lessons to my situation? I've tried all types of different sales strategies, but none have seemed to work. Perhaps the situation isn't in how I am selling the property, but in what I am selling. I remember when the original intern looked at Charles Street, and only saw an old beat-up warehouse and truck repair shop. I was a townhouse guy, and that was what I was comfortable building. Now, think way back to when we bought this thing. We bought a 2.5 acre site that was zoned industrial, and was one single piece of land. It took us hundreds of thousands of dollars, and almost 2 years of my life, and I now own a piece of land zoned residential, and I have successfully divided it up into 64 lots. These 64 lots are worthless at this point, as nobody in this era wants to build new houses since the market is absolutely flooded with residential properties for sale, and yet I continue to go to the same place, thinking that a buyer will emerge. Perhaps it's time for me to step back and apply the same logic that was taught in *Who Moved My Cheese.*

So, today, I try to envision anything else on that lot. I am now investigating the possibilities for alternative uses for the site. The fear that I get stuck spending almost $20,000 a month forever, and I go into bankruptcy, is unbelievably salient, and I will do everything in my power to avoid this happening. I've got a family that relies on me. As I sit in my car on the side of Charles Street, staring at an overgrown lot with a large burned-out brick two story warehouse, I begin to run various scenarios through my head. First, I consider that I could turn the land back into industrial use, and try to build self-storage units there. Pete and I run this scenario and figure that we would have to wait another 12 months, and have to rezone it back to its original use, and this could potentially bankrupt us. Next, we look at its current zoning. Under the current zoning of R-8, we can build up to 64 townhomes on the site, but we can also do multi-family housing. This presents us with an interesting alternative. With everyone losing their houses to foreclosure, people will still need a place to live. I may have been wrong about houses always having some real sustained value no matter what the market did, but I wasn't wrong in saying that people will always need a place to live. Apartment living may be the answer to our prayers. The R-8 zoning allows for a density of 140 apartment units. I have now had 3 meetings with a multifamily architect, and I'm beginning to put together a pitch packet to sell, or joint venture the land with a larger company who specializes in apartments. The vision is this: I contribute the land, and the builder arranges the financing and handles the construction of the apartment complex. At contract execution, I get a small stipend to pay back my architectural and engineering fees, and get some investors back their money, and then I hand off the piece of land to the larger well-capitalized company. From there, I am partners in a 140 unit apartment building forever, with this larger company. Once rents have stabilized and it's producing income (which may take upwards of 3 years), I will begin to receive investment return checks. That's right... I will actually have a 50% stake in a large apartment building with a huge company, and they will take care of the entire process, and I will get a return. Who knows: maybe my kids will inherit it. After 40 years, the loan will be paid off, and I will own 50% of the building, which may have a residual value of $30 million. That is a pretty swanky deal for having had my cheese moved. Now, there are no guarantees for any of this, but I am certainly starting to figure out all of my options. I will keep you in the loop as to the progress of these meetings, and how things fall out.

Let me think about what else is happening in the world of real estate. We settled on the Fairmount debacle properties. The bitter sweetness is that we are not paying another nickel on these properties. That, I will say, is nice. It helps me sleep a little better at night. Actually, I never have trouble sleeping at night, but it does feel better to have $1 million less debt on the books. Remember, though, there's the bitter side…when the dust settled and we paid out all of the debt, auction fees, commissions, and expenses, we ended up losing almost $200,000 on this deal. We haven't truly realized this loss until the fund is 100% liquidated because we are still losing our investor's money. We acknowledge that we are losing our families' and friends' money, but Pete and I continue to kick this can down the road until the Fund is completely liquidated. Given the stress recently, we keep ignoring this issue.

The Fund cashed out of 3 tax certificates that we bought almost 2 years ago. Tax certificates are owned by the city and sold at an annual auction to the highest bidder. Subsequently, the bidder can foreclose upon the properties in order to gain ownership of the properties. So, if you remember, we bought 3 of them for about $30,000 total - $10,000 each. The learning process on how to foreclose on tax certificates is quite steep. Over the two year period, we had 3 separate attorneys prepare the documents to file the foreclosures. We had to serve papers of foreclosure to the defaulting homeowners, the mortgage companies and anyone else that had a financial interest in the property in order to properly follow the procedure to foreclosure on these properties. In the end, we successfully received the deeds on all of the properties. The condition of these homes varied, but there is a pretty good market for really cheap fixer-up type properties. We put them on the MLS and had contracts on all 3 within about a month. When the dust had settled and we had paid out all of our expenses, we made just over $22,000 on the 3 tax certificates. Now, that is not a ton of cash, but we really did not have to do too much on these deals. As I look at the various ways of making money in real estate, the best methods are those that do not require the swinging of the hammer. Anytime we have to fix up properties, we end up working very hard for our money. The tax certificates are a perfect example of making money without having to swing the hammer. We pushed the paper around for 2 years, and eventually the Fund received a $20,000 payday. This could be a fairly good opportunity to ramp up and reproduce on a larger scale, and many law firms do engage in this as their primary activity. I may come back to this method eventually, but right now, I am just trying to evaluate what we do and how best to make money in what is left of the real estate industry.

The next activity which has been occupying my time is the sale of the college rental portfolio. I think that I mentioned interviewing candidates to be the commercial listing broker for the portfolio. This portfolio is now listed with the two young commercial guys from Washington, DC. Over the past 2 weeks, I have given tours to 5 different parties, and we are confident that someone will step up in the next week or so to make an offer on the homes. The eleven townhomes that are bundled in the same community have the greatest appeal. People like the fact that they are all close together and easier to manage. They like that they were built in 1989 and are in relatively good condition. They like the fact that all 11 are identical residencies, and repairs and maintenance is pretty homogenous. So, that leaves me with the 3 single family homes. Also, we have gained access to two other rentals. Both of these were being rented to difficult tenants. One of the tenants was a Section 8 government subsidized tenant, and the other was questionable when we first put them in there. Both of the properties were bought at foreclosure auctions, and we fixed them up about 3-4 years ago. So, after filing the failure to pay rent paperwork and finally getting both of them evicted (they each owe me about $2,000 in back rent), I gained access to the units. It is absolutely sinful that they would take these newly remodeled units and destroy them within 4 years. The necessary repairs include new carpet, paint throughout, broken cabinets, destroyed appliances, a ton of time and energy spent in hauling garbage from both units, repairing broken windows, etc. So, at this point, you need to ask yourself if you want to be in the residential landlording game. This is pretty common, though I hate to say it, and if you let it bother you, you will end up being burned out of the industry very quickly.

I walked through the first one, which took us about 3 weeks and $10,000 to put back together. We bought this at the auction for $26,000 back then. The first time around, we put $15,000 in fixing it up, so we are all in for about $45,000. We had a tenant pay the rent for the past 4 years, and then we put in another $10,000, so at this point we have $55,000 in the house. The comparable property right across the street just settled at $175,000. Remember that this will be the 4th property of this type that we have liquidated this year.

Just a few paragraphs ago, I was writing about the 5 tours that I had through the college rental portfolio. Well, today, the listing company emailed me 4 letters of intent. The first was for the 11 townies, with an offering price of $2,000,000. The next one is for the 11 townies, and it is for $2,365,000. The next one is for the entire package of 14 (including the 3 single family units), and that offer is for $2,500,000. The last letter of intent is for the 14 units, and that one is for $3,500,000, with the catch on this one being that we hold $500,000 of financing for 5 years, and at an interest rate of 5.5%. So put yourself in my position, and let's see which way to go with this. First of all, these are all just letters of intent. If I have learned something from the Charles street LOI's (us big timers use this acronym), it's that you can use them to wallpaper your bathroom because that is about all that they are worth. It is a one-sided document that brings the major terms to the forefront, it forces you (the seller) to stop negotiating with any other party, and it allows the buyer to reconsider for the next 14 days. I may sound somewhat cynical about this, but these letters are really worthless. I completely understand the process, as the buyers don't want to tie up time and money having their attorneys draft a purchase and sales agreement if we can't agree on the basic terms; however, why is the seller required to give up any rights in negotiating with other parties? So, I have now decided to refuse to sign any letters of intent. We can verbally discuss the major issues of the transaction, and once we seem to have a consensus, we'll let them put together the final purchase and sale document. So, where were we... oh yeah, looking at the 4 letters of intent that we have. Obviously, the 11 townies for $2.365 out-matches the one for $2 million, so that one is out. First, I am trying to put a value on the other 3 homes. They have a gross income of $36,000, minus taxes and insurance of $4,000, and minus management and the cost of repairs at another $4,000, this all leaves us with an NOI of around $28,000 per house. At a cap rate of around 9%, these homes are worth roughly $310,000 each. The 3 together are probably worth somewhere in the range of $1 million. If the best I can get for the townies is $2.35 million, the entire package should have a value of $3.35 million. Therefore, the 3rd LOI, which is a $2.5 million offer for the package, is certainly out, and this puts the 4th LOI for $3.5 million into the mix. This offers me a premium of $165,000 over the 11 townies alone offer...which is great. The fact that I can sell all of them at one time is also great. But, this offer is asking me to take back $500,000 in financing at a cheap rate. So, take the $165,000 premium and subtract it from $500,000, and I could come out worse off if he defaults by about $335,000. If he stays true to his word, I get 5.5% interest on the $500,000, which equates to about $27,500 per year for 5 years, which is $137,500, plus the premium of $165,000, and I will come out almost $200,000 ahead of the game. That would be a $200,000 return on the $335,000 investment, by going with that deal over 5 years. That is fairly compelling. Right now, we are waiting on 2 other investment groups to come in and present offers at some point in the near future. Just for kicks and giggles, I looked up our debt position on the townies, and it is $880,000, and on the whole package it's $1.4 million. Hopefully, the sale of this package will kick off a net to me of around $800,000 after-tax dollars. This is where I have to analyze the last 6 years in the business. This is actual cash in hand. The pretax value of this payday is about a million dollars. If I had tried to save this kind of money over the past 6 years, I would have had to put $166,666 per year aside. Sure, if I was making a salary of $300,000 per year, that might indeed have been possible, but most people don't have that kind of base salary, and real estate has allowed me to compete with the big corporate executive boys while achieving the work/life balance that's been so important to me over the years. And I have been able to play with the real big boys for the past 6 years, except my big boys are 9 and 6 years old now. Just saying that I have been able to spend the better part of every day with my boys has put a smile on my face.

The other meetings that I have this week include meetings with 3 apartment companies. On Charles Street, we are trying to make some final decisions on what to do with this piece of land. We do have a new letter of intent that came in a few days ago. This LOI is for $5 million "as is". They want to build townhouses on the land, and are willing to give us reasonable terms. The catch to this one is that they want us to hold $1 million of financing with some creative terms. This business is not just funny... it is downright maddening. It creates mental warfare. It puts rose-colored glasses on you everyday, erases your short-term memory, and causes you to make extremely illogical decisions. Let me explain: I just described an offer for $4 million, with a $1 million kicker over the next 5 years. Just one month ago, we would have taken $3.8 million at auction just to be done with this project and stop the bleeding. But now, we've talked to some of the big apartment guys. These guys are telling us that the land could be worth $6 million or $7 million. I'm now discounting the offer for $4 million, with the potential of collecting on a $1 million note, because now I have the potential for earning another $1 million. What the heck is wrong with me? The only catch to it is that we are taking a look at all of our options right now, and trying to make the best decision possible. I have a feeling that the apartment offers are going to be a much longer-term play, but incredibly lucrative if we can hang in there for 5 years. I will keep you informed as to what happens at these meetings in the next few chapters.

LESSONS LEARNED

- Evaluate your motivation. Charles Street has taught me that I should be motivated to stop the bleeding as opposed to maximizing the return on the deal.

- Bulls make money, bears make money, and pigs get slaughtered. Liquidating Charles at the beginning of the deal would have allowed me to walk away with a great return. Don't be greedy.

- One in the hand is better than two in the bush. Sometimes, it is alright to leave some profit in the deal and take the early offer. Especially when the returns are so great.

LET ME OFF OF THIS RIDE

August 7, 2007

So we just sold the 3rd rental off in the first seven months of this year, and each one will have kicked out about $60,000 to me and to my partner. We have another one to go which will be done in about 3 more weeks. One thing that I've learned about the market is that buying right can heal many mistakes. We bought these houses at the right time. The problem properties that we have are the ones that we bought at the highest levels in real estate history. We have liquidated many of them, but still have a few in the Fund. We have 3 more brand new construction homes to get rid of on Robinson Street, all in the Fund. At this point, the debt amount on them is $485,000 each, and wouldn't you know it, but we have them listed on the market for $485,000. If we were to get a list price offer, we would lose the transfers and commission fees, which would equate to about $20,000 each. But as you know, this is a buyer's market, and we will probably be offered something like $450,000, which equates to $55,000 loss times the 3 units, and we are buckling in for another $165,000 hit. You just gotta love this business... one day I am celebrating the thought of making a half a million dollars on this project, and now I am envisioning coming to the table with $165,000 just to get out of it.

I am trying to liquidate my entire inventory. I am selling off the losers as quickly as I can in order to try to stop the bleeding, and selling off my winners to cover the losses from the losers, and trying to bank some of that money in other investments. I am trying to think about 2008…even though we are only half way through 2007. I need to start investing this money on some new projects that will come to fruition next year. Like I said before, the industry works if you buy right. Now is exactly the time to be buying. I have been kicking around the idea of building out medical condominiums with a buddy of mine, and recently I have begun talking to another buddy about buying groups of underperforming mortgages that we can foreclose on. I've found that you need to be nimble and able to capture the next best hot segment in order to thrive in this market. My goal for the rest of the summer is to try to take my time, conduct a little research on the possibilities, analyze the data, and come up with the next best opportunity in real estate to continue to grow to the next level.

October 1, 2007

The summer is over, and as I review the previous few pages, I see that not a lot has changed. I will say that I enjoyed a ton of time off with the family this summer. We spent two weeks traveling England, Scotland, and Whales, and made many other trips around the U.S. I slept in every day, had the luxury of having lunch with my family most days, and enjoyed the pleasure of relaxing with the family in the evenings. All in all, this summer was exactly the reason that I got into the business in the first place. All of this lounging does come at an expense. Over the past 6 months, I have watched my net worth diminish. The market continues to drop 5-10% a year, and this has caused me great anxiety about getting deeper into the game. The big events of the summer, which turned out to be non-events, were the college rental properties and the office building. We did indeed take the $3.5 million offer on the package. The offer had a study period in it which would expire in 30 days. After 30 days, the buyer requested an extension for an additional 15 days. During this period, we provided their bank with tax returns, tax bills, insurance declaration pages, leases, contracts, and just about every other piece of paper associated with the ownership of these properties. Now, keep in mind, the offer price reflected an 8% capitalization rate which we thought was extremely fair to all parties in this transaction. The final piece of information for the bank was their appraisal. I spent a full 4 hours as the appraiser went through each and every rental property. He measured rooms and exteriors, and wrote down finishes and fixtures. What he did not ask for was information on rental rates, vacancies, or expenses. I found this rather strange since we are selling a commercial property which generates a substantial amount of cash. Following the appraisal marathon, I explained to the 2 young brokers my concern about this process, and that the bank had clearly hired the wrong appraiser for this transaction. He appeared to be a residential comparable method appraiser trying to conduct a commercial income method appraisal. As suspected, on the final day before the contract would go hard (the day the study period expired) we received a letter of withdrawal from the buyer. Apparently, the appraisal had come back at $2.875 million, based on a residential approach. Pleading our case that this was a commercial transaction did us no good. With the current state of chaos in the financial markets, banks are tightening up their credit substantially. This particular bank wanted a back-up plan if their borrower defaulted, and this plan was to liquidate the houses, one by one, at market rates to homeowners.

When they talk about real estate being a cyclical business, here is a perfect example of a knee-jerk reaction to a terrible mistake. About 5 years ago, mortgage brokers and banks were writing these loans on a promise. A buyer could go in and purchase a home with no money down, no income, no assets, and no real right to being loaned money. Better yet, they could actually get 105% financing and walk away from the settlement table with cash. This, in and of itself, seems incredibly foolish, because what makes a homeowner pay the mortgage is the fear that they can actually lose the house. With no "skin in the game", homeowners have very little incentive to pay the note, right? True, they do have a reason if the market continues to go up, but what about a down market? And alright, now let's go one step further... how about an interest only loan where you are not even paying down any of the principal? Better yet, how about a negative amortization loan where you don't even pay all of the interest, and the principal continues to grow? How about that... the fact that you can actually owe more money than you borrowed? Is this beginning to sound crazy? Through these adjustable loans which require you to pay very little money down, people's payments could potentially skyrocket when rates go up. I think about this, and think to myself, what in the world were these financial institutions thinking? How about this for the cherry on top... how about a stated income, no asset verification loan, using one of the products that I described above? On this loan application, you write down how much money you make and what assets you own, and the bank doesn't even check on it. They completely trust you to be honest. All of this was fantastic while the markets were climbing up at the breakneck speed of 25% appreciation, but what happens in a down market?

I am just as guilty as the next guy because I didn't think that there was any chance of there being a down market. I was living the dream and making millions of dollars in the process. So, to make a long story short, the buyer of our college rental properties had trouble getting his financing in line, and subsequently dropped out of the deal. The 2 young brokers have gathered some additional interest in the properties, but we are taking a step back to think about our plan. Just today, we deposited a $16,500 check from the rental portfolio, and that comes in handy when you have to pay the bills to keep the lights on. I spoke with the property manager today, and he is already getting interest for students who want to sign leases for 2008 and 2009. Not only that, but I told him to increase the rents across the board. This rent increase will kick out an additional $47,000 directly to the bottom line. Once my mind gets going on this track, I realize that I should actually keep the units. If I am able to increase the bottom line every other year by $50,000, I will be sitting pretty in about 10 years. Every day is an adventure in this business, and every day I manage to change and alter my business plan. While extremely frustrating, I do enjoy each and every aspect of the business.

Finally, let me bring you up to date on the apartment building that we used to call Charles Street. You may remember me mentioning these two hot-shot young commercial real estate brokers who we interviewed for the college rental properties sale. I really like these guys, Peyton and Dan. They're a couple of hustlers who are really good at networking and wining and dining. I mentioned to them the problems that we were having with the Charles Street deal, and we agreed to let them list the property in search of a buyer. They were convinced that they could get... are you ready for this? $6 million for the apartment deal. I have to laugh because this thing has become such a liability to the company that I'd be happy just to walk away from it and hand the keys to someone. So, we signed a trial listing agreement with them about 3 weeks ago, and they have been peddling the potential for a 140 unit apartment deal in Federal Hill for us. Recently, they had an inquiry from a large apartment company out of Texas. We had a lunch with their local division president, who seemed legitimately interested in our project. These buyers are way out of our league. They have over 10,000 apartment units under management, and are currently building almost 1000 units. I'm trying to remain optimistic about the entire process, but I just feel like we've been beaten down so much that nothing good will come out of this process. When I dream about the ideal offer on Charles Street, I dream of someone taking over my debt. I don't even need to make any money off of the project at this point, but I can't keep pulling off of lines of credit and liquidating rental properties in order to keep this thing afloat. It is psychologically damaging to continue down this road. On a positive note, we are advertising a project for $6 million, and there still remains interest in the project. It is not all doom and gloom, and once in a while, I catch myself thinking that I'm going to sell this project for $6 million, and then trying to figure out how I'll spend all the profit.

I recently renewed my line of credit and prepared the personal financial statement. If you remember from the beginning, this statement is how you measure your net worth on a piece of paper. In modern-day society, this is how you gauge yourself against others. If you remember back in high school, you would compare your grade point average (GPA). Once you enter the professional ranks, it's done by how much money you are worth. That alone is a crazy concept, to say that a person has a net worth of "x" number of dollars. How many times have you heard that such and such a celebrity or business person is worth $10 million? This, to me, is just a fascinating concept, and one that actually disturbs me. I would rather someone start to classify how much time you dedicate a week to your family. So if each day offers 16 hours of waking time, you could refer to me as a 65 hour guy. Between work and commute, the typical business person spends 12 hours a day focusing on their career and trying to increase their net worth. This leaves 4 hours a day for family, and 16 hours on each of the weekend days. So they may be a 52 hour woman. You see, both of these concepts work in absolute polarity to each other in the working world. Each hour that you commit to increasing your net worth actually takes an hour away from your family time. That is why the passivity of real estate has lured me, and hopefully you, into this business. Alright, I have managed to stand on my soapbox for just one paragraph, and thank you for indulging me. Back to my net worth, as I need to fill it in for the bank's personal financial statement...

Financial Snapshot

Written January 19, 2002	**October 1, 2007**
I own a house. My wife and I bought the house 5 years ago and have done very well with its appreciation.	Still in the same house. New landscaping ($13,000) New baths ($4,000) New paint ($3,500)
Equity in House = $140,000	Equity in House = $425,000
As of January 2002, the stocks and funds markets have not been kind.	Same two accounts… still suffering.
Stocks = $19,000 Funds = $13,000	Stocks = $19,000 Funds = $20,000
Retirement Account	$110,000
College Savings Plan	$50,000
College Rental Portfolio	$550,000
Additional Rental Properties	$110,000
Office Building	$250,000
Charles Street	$750,000

Total Net Worth, but is it really? Remember it's only on paper!

2002 = $175,000	**2007 = $2,295,000**

Now, I hope that you've learned a few nuggets from my experience. First, when you read the financial statement above, you should question the accuracy of the validity of using this technique in a falling market. My wife has always said that she'll believe it when it's in her bank account in cash. I can't emphasize the accuracy of this enough. We have about $10 million of projects that we just can't realize until a buyer shows up at the table with a check in their pocket. The past year has been difficult. We have had a number of deals fall apart for various reasons. In my head, I have found the primary residence of my dreams, but I simply won't allow myself to go out and buy it until I have enough cash in the bank to afford it.

The dreaming is what I love about this industry. You can take the trips around the world in your head, and dream about the huge homes and fancy cars with the money that you should make, but until it is in your bank account, you simply cannot afford to over-extend yourself financially. The second lesson that I have been learning, and just cannot seem to get my hands around, is the concept of a falling market. For years, I have been preaching the power of leverage, but when you are losing money, you need to understand when to get off this crazy ride. Let me use my example of the 4 homes on Robinson Street to illustrate my point. When we bought this land for $125,000 per lot, we were excited about the prospects of building this great project. When we were successful subdividing the land 6 months later and our architectural drawings were complete, our excitement rose to another level. As we watched the next year unfold and the builder take our plans, ideas, fixtures, and finishes, and actually build them into something beautiful, we proudly showed it off to everyone that would look. While this entire process of the past year and a half has been extremely satisfying in this respect, we are still in business to make money. So, after buying the land for $125,000 per lot, we spent another $310,000 building the homes of our dreams. After you add in the soft costs, including the engineering and architectural work, we were in them for around $470,000 each. When we started this whole process, we envisioned these homes selling for $600,000. The initial appraisal had them pegged at $680,000. At any rate, this was going to be a hugely successful project, and if I read back a few chapters, I'll probably find that I was touting how much money I was worth because of it, at least in part. Fast forward a few years. The market has begun to show signs of weakness. We have just come off of the largest appreciating real estate market in the history of real estate. As smart MBA folks, we see the market starting to turn. As not-so-smart MBA folks, we don't adjust our strategy to reflect the shift. We had the homes priced at $550,000, which is what the general market was selling for. Luckily enough for us, we had someone buy the first one at $550,000. Even back then, we knew that we were lucky because this buyer really took advantage of us, and we let them get away with it in order not to lose them as a buyer. The problem with selling the first one in a decreasing market at $550,000 is that now we thought that they were all worth $550,000, so we left our prices there. All around us, inventory swelled, and all around us, prices started to drop. Eventually, we were at the high end of the pricing scale, and had to lower our price. Again, there was the same cycle of prices dropping around us, and we ended up at the high end of our scale again. In hindsight, we should have dropped the price all the way down to break even and simply gotten the heck out of the project. But after working 2 years on the project, we just didn't want to give up that easily. I remember people offering us $450,000 when the price was $525,000, and we would not make that kind of concession. We watched buyers come and go, and did not want to give up our phantom profit. So here we sit, another year later. We have the one that sold for $550,000. We have rented one out for $2,900 per month…even though it costs us $4,500 per month to carry it. I have a contract on one for $450,000, even though it is contingent on them being able to sell their house. I am ready to take a contract on the other one for $415,000. And the kicker is that we are now into each one for $510,000. So, you can do the math to figure out that we are in the hole about $300,000. Guess what? The bank has figured this out as well, and they called me yesterday to ask for some sort of additional collateral in order to protect their money. I would not wish this situation on my worst enemy. I told the bank that I'd be happy to default on the loan and give them the keys back to the three houses. That was not a popular answer. Unfortunately for them, there is nothing that they can do. They certainly don't want underwater houses, so they can ask for additional collateral all they want – but, I'm not giving it.

These past few months have provided several reasons to celebrate, though. First, I am about to sign a contract for the 11 college townhouse rentals for $2.3 million. I know, we had offers for $3.5 million, and I know that I provided a lot of quantitative analysis on why our portfolio should sell for that number, but desperate times call for desperate measures. Well... not exactly desperate. We have about $900,000 in these homes, so this could yield a tidy profit. We will need some of that to offset the losses on the Robinson Street deal. If this deal doesn't solidify, we will liquidate any and all remaining capital from the family and friends Signature Fund, and may have to start accessing my personal equity. I don't even want to go down that road for now. Let me focus on the positive and believe that the college stuff will provide the much needed infusion of capital. The contract calls for a 30 day study period and a 30 day settlement, so we will see if that materializes around February.

Second, unbelievable news! Do you remember the large apartment guys from Texas that expressed some interest in Charles Street? Well, they are so interested that they submitted an offer for the land. They first offered $5 million for the land. I did everything in my power not to jump on that offer. The two young agents, Peyton and Dan, told us to slow-play the offer and come back with a counter offer at $5.75 million. While I thought that they were absolutely nuts, the worst thing that they could say was no. So we countered. After several rounds of negotiation with the apartment group out of Texas, we have a signed contract for $5.64 million. Unbelievable. This contract is chock full of contingencies, though, with the biggest one being final subdivision approval for the construction of 188 units of apartments. The land is entitled for 140 units, so we need to go in front of the zoning board to get a variance for the additional 48 units.

Architectural Rendering of 188 Apartment Units on 1901 South Charles

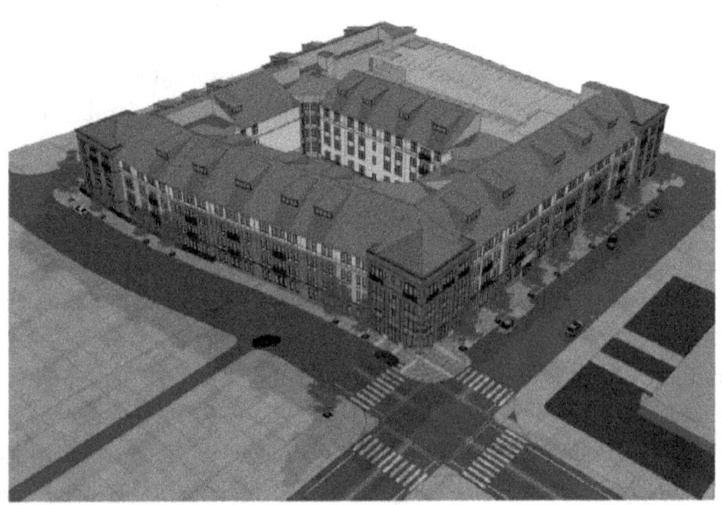

Second View of 188 Apartment Units on 1901 South Charles

Here are some of the terms of the deal that we worked out in the contract. They will deposit $480,000 into an escrow account. They will settle when we have the building permits in hand. Now, getting building permits is no easy task. This requires a full set of construction drawings, including electric, plumbing, HVAC, framing, foundation, and everything else that goes into the construction of a 200,000 square foot building. So I am tempering my excitement because there are a lot of issues to work out in the building permitting area, and they could easily cause this deal to fall apart. The nice thing is, though – they will pay for everything up until the building permits are issued. They will pay the architect and engineer. They will pay for soil remediation issues and legal issues. The best part of the entire contract is that they will pay us a non-refundable $20,000 per month for us to pay our interest payment to the bank and the taxes on the property. So, this prayer may have been answered. Now, if this sounds all too good to be true, it is. They have a 90 day study period during which they can cancel the contract for any reason that they want. You should be able to see why I am excited about having the contract in hand, but somewhat unexcited since we've seen so many of our deals fall apart for any number of reasons.

Oh yeah, and another reason why the timing of this offer is perfect... we are running out of money. I mean *really* running out of money at Signature Properties. The Fund which has been so successful over the years is down to $30,000 in cash in the bank. We have been servicing the debt on the 4 Robinsons and a few other smaller deals with the cash, and we now have about 2 months' worth of carry until we are completely out of money. This would weigh heavily on the minds of many responsible investors, but there is just nothing that the banks can do to us. So, we have lost all of our money, all of the lines of credit money, and all of our friends' and families' money. As bad as the market is to us, it is equally as bad to the banks. We have been smart enough to bank a fair amount of capital over the years so that we have been hanging on for years now in a miserable market. Many of my colleagues in the industry were not so lucky. My good friend Bob had a 10 unit townhouse deal that he was building. He worked so hard on the land deal, construction element, and ultimately almost completely getting them built. He just didn't have enough capital to continue to make the interest payment, though, and just last week, he handed the keys to all of the units over to the bank, and told them that he was flat broke. We met for a beer the other night, and he thinks that his only option at this point will be to declare bankruptcy and hopefully live to fight another day. So, what happens to me in two months when we run out of money? Hmmm, I don't know. Hopefully, the 90 day study period on Charles goes without incident, and they start giving us $20K per month to service some of our debt. This is pretty close to coinciding with the time that we will run out of money. Otherwise, I may be in the same situation as Bob.

March 2, 2008

You remember how I was coining money for the first couple of years in business. It was truly an amazing ride as the roller coaster climbed up the hill. One thing that I've learned on this journey is that the market cures many mistakes. I made many mistakes that were masked by the fact that the real estate market was appreciating at an alarming 25% per year. During that time period, these mistakes were, very simply, masked by success. I could overpay for a project and, by virtue of appreciation, I'd make money by the time it hit the market. The losses became singles and the singles became home runs. What has changed in the market has had the exact opposite effect, and now these mistakes are fatal. The glory days are truly gone.

The homes on Robinson Street are complete, and they are truly magnificent. They came out exactly how I envisioned them. The fixtures were unique and flashy, the layouts are open and inviting, and the view from the decks is breathtaking. Everyone that previewed these homes has been extremely complementary about our incredible attention to perfection. Regardless of the financial outcome of the project, I do have to pat Pete and myself on the back. We make a really nice product, and I am very proud of it. When we first bought that piece of land, the bank had its appraisers guestimate what the value of the finished product would be worth on the open market. At that time, with the market rising faster than the hot summer DC sun, the appraiser thought that these homes would bring a tidy $680,000 each. I am not looking back at our analysis, but on paper, we were supposed to have $450,000 invested in each of these homes, and turn a profit of $230,000 per house, or almost $1 million on the project. What a bunch of amateurs we were. We needed 8 months to subdivide the land, and then another 12 months to build the houses. We were gambling on profits that were 20 months away. At the time, we thought that the market could only go up. Life is full of cruel lessons. The only good thing about the project is that we did indeed hit the construction costs somewhere close to our budget. By the time all was said and done, we had roughly $480,000 in the deal. We did get lucky on one of them. I can't remember if I mentioned that we did sell the first Robinson right out of the gate at $550,000. So we cashed out about $60,000 after costs. You say great, Scott is making some money, but not so fast. Before I run out and drop $1,000 on a dinner at Ruth's Chris, I have to remind you that the profit on this house made just enough to cover our losses on the 2 dogs that we sold on Patapsco Street. Again the optimist, we are still hanging in there at break even. I've got 3 more Robinsons to go, and we are out of the weeds on the 2 Patapscos and the 1 Robinson. One last thing, too: keep in mind that I haven't drawn a salary or taken money home to Jill in a long, long time. So my definition of breakeven really needs to be taken with a grain of salt.

The remaining 3 Robinson homes have sat on the market for about a year now. Our basis in them is now an astounding $508,000 each. Sometime about 6 months ago, we decided to rent one of them out for $2,900 per month. Not bad, considering we were burning $4,500 per month in carry, taxes, and interest. Like a train wreck continuing to pile up, we will bleed on this house for a while longer, but we are managing to slow down the bleeding. Now for the other two, we tried selling for $499,000 for a long time. We weren't going to be the guys that undersold the market just to liquidate. We were better than that, and we had 2 long years of sweat equity built into this project. Did I forget to mention that these Robinson homes are beautiful? It's funny how, when I wear my real estate agent hat, I'm quick to tell sellers to drop their prices if they want to sell their homes, but when it comes to my project, my personal property, I am always the last one to face the music. So, at the end of 2007, we decided we could no longer deal with the painful torture of carrying these properties month after month after month. We had just about burned all of our investors' money by trying to hang in there, and now it was time to pay the piper. We dropped the prices to $479,000. Finally, I got a hit at $479,000…but they wanted $29,000 in closing assistance. Our net would be $450,000, minus the back taxes that we had no chance of paying at $10,000, minus the commission to the other agent of 3%, or $14,000, minus some miscellaneous garbage, which left us a tidy proceed at a closing of $422,000 to pay off the $508,000 in bank debt owed. I hope that you see that there is a problem here. Our choices were to come to the settlement table with $86,000 or tell the buyer that we were sorry and we just couldn't afford to sell them the house. Let me reread that line because it sounds somewhat ludicrous, "I can't afford to sell you my house". Imagine that... 2 years of hard work and we can't afford to sell the house.

I tried to solve the problem by meeting with the bank. I asked them if they would reduce the payoff on their loan to match the proceeds of the deal. Apparently, this is called a short sale. They refused to budge, and I'm not sure why. To make a long story short, we did indeed come to the settlement table with $86,000 in cash. I'll tell you how in just a minute. I also had another agent interested in one of the other properties at Robinson Street.

Remember that we are in a buyers' market, so this particular buyer told us that he was going to "take us to the hoop." At the end of round after round of negotiation, we ended up with a sales price of $420,000. The net proceeds to pay off the debt after taxes and commissions on this one…just $394,000. Not only that, but this buyer had us installing a $1,500 washer and dryer, and $2,500 in hardwood floors in the bedrooms. Pete and I spent days and days running this through the wringer. We had no choice. The properties had sat for months without a showing. The agents that showed them told me that $420,000 was good in this market, we were flat out of money, and all that we could do was punt.

I mentioned that the bank which financed the Robinson Street deal refused to short sell the properties. Our $1 million line of credit with them was up for renewal on February 1, 2008. The bank wants to know what we are going to do. I tell them that I have 2 of the 3 remaining properties under contract. They're excited for us until I tell them that one will net $422,000 and the other will net $394,000. Now, put yourself in the bank's shoes. We owe them about $1.5 million. These homes are done, and we have been pushing them as agents and paying their interest payments regularly for over a year. If they insist on us coming to the table with $86,000 on one and $112,000 on the other, the homes simply won't settle. So, the Vice President of the bank calls us in for a meeting. We are so worn out by the whole process that we tell them to go ahead and have the keys. Cancel the closing and foreclose on the properties because there is just nothing else that we can do. This is a classic case of lose-lose negotiating, and in this scenario, no one will benefit. We intend on making good for every last penny that we borrowed from the bank. Pete and I are good to our word, and we will beg, borrow, and steal (maybe not steal) to make good on all of our debts. Their concern is that we're uncollateralized for the money that we have out on the street. Basically, the properties on Robinson Street are worth less than what we had borrowed from them. Sounds like a problem. The VP is a good friend of mine, and knows that we are good to our word. He's willing to work with us to come up with a win-win solution to the entire debacle.

We gave them a blanket second mortgage on another property in Glen Burnie (the 4 lots) as additional collateral against the balance on the $1 million. The bank agreed to release the 2 Robinsons to settle by accepting the net proceeds from the sale (which, as I stated, was almost $200,000 in deficient payments). So, as of January 16th and January 28th, we are now officially two properties lighter in our portfolio. We gave the bank the proceeds from both of the sales (we end up with absolutely nothing) and our line of credit is down to somewhere around $700,000. The bank now has only one Robinson Street as collateral (on the market at $419,000) for this $700,000. I'm beginning to see a problem here with the whole banking/collateral model; therefore, we are currently signing the paperwork to give them the second mortgage on the other property in Glen Burnie. Let me get something out in the open that is really bothering me about this whole scenario. We don't want to give the bank a second mortgage on a piece of land that they have nothing to do with. We did our best to make the Robinson deal work…it just didn't. We worked years for free on this, and a part of me thinks that the bank should bear some of the risk. Now, I am not talking about writing down the note and giving us a free handout, but when we tell them that we will make good on the money when the Glen Burnie deal settles, I want them to cut me some slack. Times are tough for everyone. They are foreclosing on developers left and right. They are working the little guy for a second mortgage where we will incur filing fees, processing fees, legal fees, and a bunch of other bank fees. Sorry to rant, but this one has been getting under my skin for a while. Part of me wants to mail them the keys to the last Robinson Street and say 'here you go, sleep in it. You made great coin off of us for the last several years and when the music stopped, you want nothing to do with any risk or loss.'

All this leaves us with one more Robinson (that has a tenant in it), the four lots in Glen Burnie (that have a contract on them), and the other stuff that I will get to shortly. The tenant in the other Robinson Street is an attorney at a large law firm. Since this is a buyers' market, he knows a good deal when he sees it. I called the attorney and told him that our loan was maturing, and we simply needed to get out of the property, so would he be interested in buying the property for his daughter who's renting it from us? He pondered the idea for a day or two, and called me back with instructions to fax over a contract. I gave him a great price at $440,000. We have the contract signed with a settlement coming by the end of March. Assuming that goes through, we have no commission on that sale, so our net proceeds there should be around $428,000. That will knock the balance of the line down to $272,000. This will be approximately what we lost on the Robinson Street deal. We worked almost three full years on this project for free, and the benefit of having to cough up $272,000, and oh yeah, I don't have $272,000…do you? This is not exactly the excitement that I was writing about 4 years ago. So, the bank's collateral is now backed by all of the profits we expected to see from the past 3 years work on the 4 lot subdivision in Glen Burnie. We have a contract on that lot and the subdivision should be recorded within the next 3 weeks. Once that is recorded, the buyer will have 30 days to settle on it. The problem is, the buyer is a home builder who has been trying to pre-sell the homes there for the past 6 months. Just last week, we received a request for an extension of their study period since it has not yet been recorded. We've analyzed this request 1000 ways, and we're really unsure if they are asking for the extension because they are getting ready to bail on the deal, or if they legitimately need a few more weeks to work with our engineer to complete the subdivision. This market is leaving carnage everywhere you look, and this builder is being extra cautious about taking down our lot. If this deal falls apart, it will be back to square one in trying to find another buyer willing to take down lots in a market that just has no homebuyers, and the bank will be breathing down my neck for their balance.

Let me dream or nightmare, depending on how you look at it, for just minute. If the last Robinson does indeed sell this month, and the 4 lots do sell, what do we have left? We have a rental property that we have fixed up and have on the market at $199,000, and the price has now dropped 3 times. We have about $130,000 in it, so we should cash a small check off of this one. We have a miserable property in a bad area that we fixed up and just can't seem to sell. This is one that Pete bought at an auction to keep our handyman busy. We overpaid at the auction and I knew it right away. We tried to flip out of it, but our basis was just too high. We decided that we could fix it up and break even. That would have been better than taking a loss... at that time. So after 6 months of roofs, HVAC, kitchens, baths, paint, carpet, siding…we ended up with a sloppy rehab. Now it is on the market for $169,000 and we haven't even had a nibble. And by the way, we have over $169,000 in it already. We just can't get a break in this market, and it is eating us for lunch. The goal on this dog will be to put a Section 8 government subsidized tenant in it. You know, the ones that destroy all of the work that we did to it and leave us with another $20,000 rehab bill? I'm frustrated that we bought it, I'm frustrated that we decided to fix it and not just take our lumps, and finally, I am going to be frustrated by managing the garbage tenant that we are probably putting into this ghetto property.

You must be wondering if things could get any worse. Stop wondering, though, because you are really going to enjoy this story.... We went back to trying to fix our problem by selling off the office building at Windsor Mill. We decided to put the office building up for auction a few months back in order to generate some cash. The building was 95% occupied, had rental revenues of $165,000 and a net income of around $110,000. We figured that, at a 9%-10% cap rate, we would be looking at around $1.2 million for the building. We hired one of the well-known auction companies, paid them $5,000 for advertising, and were off to the races. The day of the auction came and the parking lot filled up with potential buyers. The first buyer of the day was a middle-aged man who pulled up in a large white pickup truck. He found me and asked if I could provide a tour of the building. I was more than happy to show off this prime piece of real estate. As we waited at the elevator, he told me that he was nervous that day, as this was a big deal for him. He had never bought a commercial property, and really didn't know how the auction process worked. I kindly explained the entire process to him, and went off to get the keys to show him around. He waited at the elevator while I snuck off to grab the keys from the storage closet. When I returned, he was nowhere to be found. After looking around the stairwell and hallway, I watched him dash out of the men's room to the parking lot. He then stopped by the auctioneer, who was setting up his table to get ready for the auction, got into his truck, and sped off. I asked the auctioneer what had happened, and he informed me that he'd had a little accident while waiting for me at the elevator, and had needed to run to the men's room. We had a good laugh and waited for the excitement of the auction to begin. As I looked back on the Charles Street auction failure, I was sure that this was going to be a better outcome. The auctioneer then addressed the 25 or so people waiting in our parking lot to begin bidding. The auctioneer asked the audience for an opening bid, and it was opened at $500,000. This was reasonable. I thought that the building was worth about $1 million, but let's get the crowd warmed up to the thought of buying it and then see how high we could get this puppy to go. The bidding went up by $100,000 increments. He asked for $600,000, and sure enough, someone raised their hand. Then $700,000, and again a hand went up. $800,000, $900,000 – at this point, Pete and I were feeling that euphoria of auctions once again.

'Do I have $1 million?', shouted the auctioneer…and yes, a hand went up. As a seller, you do everything in your power not to smile as buyers bid frantically on your property. I was doing the numbers in my head; we owed $450,000 on the property, so at that point, Pete and I would split over a half million dollars. Just as it hit $1,000,000, my good friend in the white pickup truck that had soiled his underwear sped into the parking lot, jumped out (with a fresh pair of pants on), and quickly raised the bid to $1.15 million. The other bidder, a seasoned well-dressed gentlemen wearing a sports coat, raised it to $1.17 million. Mr. Pickup Truck went to $1.175 million and then Mr. Sports coat bowed out. Going once, going twice, sold to Mr. new pants pickup truck. Pete and I exchanged a grin like that cat that ate the canary, and walked over to the table that the auctioneers had set up in order to finalize the contract. Mr. Pickup walks over to the table and says, "What did I just get myself into?" The auctioneer, the consummate professional, explained that he now had to give over the $50,000 non-refundable deposit, and that he had 45 days to settle on the property. The gentlemen handed over the deposit and now we were in business. The auctioneer assured me that even if this guy had trouble closing, the number two guy with the sports coat was a reliable buyer, and he would close at $1.15 million. Well, as could almost be predicted, we get the call 44 days later that Mr. Pickup Truck just can't seem to get the deal done. He went to the bank and they're refusing to finance a class C building in this market to a rookie investor. This is so unbelievable that I couldn't make this stuff up. The auctioneer takes the $50,000, subtracts out some fees, and mails us ½ of the deposit or $22,000. Now, a part of me was excited that we'd just found free money, but the other half was extremely disappointed that we were still stuck with the building. So, I remind the auctioneer that the number 2 guy was a solid bidder, and that he'd said he would "close" if Mr. Pickup Truck didn't. Of course, the auctioneer calls the number 2 guy, and as I might have predicted, he has no interest now. So, had Mr. Pickup Truck not changed his pants so quickly at home, I might have sold the property for $1 million. I usually write "this business is funny" to make me smile and feel better inside, but I'm beginning to think that this business is not so funny anymore, not one bit. Now don't get me wrong, I don't hate the building. We generate about $40,000 a year off of it, and it is fairly low maintenance, but we're selling it (or trying to) because the commercial market is showing signs of the same fate that the residential market has suffered. Credit is tightening up in the wake of the residential debacle, and people are having a more difficult time getting financing done. We vowed not to hang onto this until the market changes, and we want to sell something we own while it is high, for once in this stage of our career. The building is rescheduled for auction on March 11th. I can only hope that we have a better result.

Things just go from bad to worse. Deals are tough to get financing for, all around. We just saw Mr. Pickup Truck lose $50,000 due to a lack of financing, and now we're seeing other deals find the same fate. If you remember, we had the college rental portfolio under contract a while back. The deal fell apart because the buyer could not get financing. This is why I simply don't get excited when I get a contract anymore. Even the Charles Street contract doesn't excite me. You witnessed how the residential real estate market collapsed several years ago, and now the capital markets are falling apart right in front of my eyes. I put the college rental properties right back on the market, and got another contract on it in late December. Unfortunately, this one was only for the 11 townhomes, and instead of the valuation of $2.5 million, we accepted $2.3 million. The difficulty in getting financing is causing our equity to erode. The buyer this time is a group out of New York that finds these deals and then syndicates a group of investors to take them down. This means nothing to me, as they are just as likely to default as every other contract purchaser that we've gotten involved in this deal. So we negotiate hard with these guys for days as they continue to press us for a longer study period and delayed settlement. To this point, I just don't understand the need for these 60 day study periods. Typically, the buyers do no due diligence for 55 days, and then ask for an extension because they're simply lazy. How long does it take to review some financial documents and some leases? It drives me nuts. So, after the dust settles on our negotiation, these guys get 45 days to evaluate this rental portfolio. During that period, they met with our property manager, and we got them copies of leases, financial statements, expenses, maintenance and repair items, and everything else that would help them evaluate the net operating income right down to the penny. February 26th is coming up, and that's the day when their study period ends and their $35,000 deposit goes hard. 'Deposit going hard' is a real estate term meaning the day that their deposit actually means something. You see, for the first 45 days, they can change their mind for whatever reason they want and get 100% of their deposit back. We have to take the property off of the market and wait while we sit on our hands until they officially decide that they like the project. And what happens in this deal? On day 44, the New York guys call me to tell me that they are cancelling the deal. Their syndicated equity partner has decided that they don't like it. This means that we send them back their 35 G's and we're back to square one. Lesson number 1 for you: real estate is perhaps the most liquid asset that I can think of right now. There is a slight silver lining to this most recent fall out. I do have a sniff of life in the college portfolio deal. I managed to find a group of buyers that seems to understand college rentals. I've asked them for the same price and terms as the deal that just fell apart. I figured that would save me the legal fees of recreating the wheel after we just went through this exercise. They agreed. The bad news is that they need 60 days for financing, so here we go with beginning the process all over again. The good news is that I negotiated a nice deposit of $35,000 now, and another $15,000 on day 31. This way, we get some non-refundable money, and perhaps they won't walk away like everyone else. As you can see, this market is very tentative, and I continue to proceed by wearing kid gloves with every buyer we get on the hook.

As if the bad news were not raining in like cats and dogs, we then have Charles Street. On Charles, the buyer's study period was due to expire on February 26th as well. That was a big day for us. At that point, their $60,000 deposit would go hard and we would be more convinced that they were in the deal. Now, with these guys, I feel fairly confident that they want to buy the property.

They've spent in excess of $50,000 in due diligence tests to make sure that they can build what they want. They have ordered soil tests, sound tests, traffic tests and every other test that a big company with deep pockets can order. They have pushed the zoning through the department of planning and have the zoning hearing for the variance for those additional 48 units on March 18th. They spent money, their hard-earned money, on getting the hearing for the variance for more units. At that point, we will have a site that is ready to build 188 units, and the value of the land will officially be higher. So, what happened on February 26th? Pete and I met with the 3 heads of the Mid-Atlantic office of this apartment builder. These guys are hard core apartment guys. Watching them operate is a learning experience. Where Pete and I are small-time shop keepers, these guys are the real deal. The company was recently bought out by a huge Japanese Corporation, and the owner, now infused with a bunch of capital, has begun reinvesting in more apartment deals. We are extremely different, in every aspect, from a well-funded company. When Pete and I go to the community with a plan, our drawings are nothing more that scraps of tracing paper with a rendition of what we want to build. Our instructions to the architect are always to not spend too much money. It's tough being a little shop because we have to watch every penny. These guys are the exact opposite. The presentation to the community last week was a 3-D computer model full of fly-overs and walk-throughs. Their presentation was extremely impressive, and outlandishly expensive. Regardless of what happens with this buyer, I am seeing what real property development looks like. So again, what happened on February 26th? We had a meeting scheduled with the head honchos from their regional office. We decided to meet in neutral territory at a Starbucks. Their lead guy comes in with a stack of papers and binders about 2 feet tall. This guy is in his late 50's. He's a seasoned veteran of the apartment industry, and probably has built more complexes than we have rehabbed single homes. He's polished, well-spoken, and a snappy dresser. He starts by telling us that he likes our site and really wants to buy it. This is when I get that smirk on my face because, as you can imagine, a "but" is coming. 'But'…he says, 'the due diligence has turned up some issues that would need to be resolved'.

First is the environmental. In addition to the typical boring holes that they drill to check what contaminates may be in the soil, they decided to have a magnetic resonance imaging specialist do a thermal diagram of the site, whatever that is. But what it produced was a glossy picture of the site with colorful areas representing what could be underground issues. Who knew that technology existed? "What issues could there be?" I asked, like a student to the professor. He believes there could be additional underground tanks on the site. Alright, issue one is out there. Then he hands us a copy of a report from our engineers, showing a conservative estimate to clean up the site at $500,000. Cleaning up the site from chromium and other contaminates in the soil. Next he breaks out a marketing report from a consulting company out of Texas. Now, perhaps you can tell me what a company in Texas knows about the potential rents in Baltimore. We all had the rents pegged at $1.75 per square foot, or $1,750 for a 1000 square foot 2 bedroom apartment. All along, I thought that this was a low number and that they should be able to command closer to $2.00 per square. At any rate, this report has them at $1.40 per square foot. Now I'm beginning to see the case that they are trying to build. Next, he follows it up with a tax estimate. They had thought that the taxes on the site would be around $360,000 per year, and this estimate has them coming in at $700,000 per year. So here I am trying to choke down my latte as they break out one bit of bad news after another to build a case for price reduction. At the end of the meeting, I sit there in disbelief, waiting for them to drop the hammer. The hammer could be dropped in one of two ways. First, they could simply say that they want out of the deal and ask that we give them back their deposit. After investing the kind of cash that they have already, I didn't think that it was going to be an option. If that was the case, we would have all saved a trip to

Starbucks and done it by fax and email. So next, I am waiting for them to renegotiate the price. Our current price is set at $5.45 million. Pete and I have about $2.2 million in equity, so we do potentially have some room. But to my surprise, they don't ask to renegotiate the price. What they do want is an extension of the study period for 7 days to reevaluate this information. Wow, now that really took me by surprise. So if you were me and your goal was to try to figure out what the other side had in mind, were would you think we're going with this?

Pete and I discussed it briefly before I had to catch a plane later that afternoon, but our gut feeling is that they do this regularly. This is a scripted routine, they give us 7 days to contemplate our fate, and then the renegotiation goes smoothly. At any rate, we can't see the problem with granting them this request, so we give them the 7 days. That will allow me to validate some of their information anyway. So, I began the next day by calling the environmental company that originally gave me the $200,000 quote for cleaning up the soil. Their estimate was $500,000. The environmental engineer assured me that the site indeed was pretty clean, and that the $200,000 number is good. She hates putting out these worst case scenarios for anyone because of this reason. She also told me that the magnetic test tends to yield a ton of false positives. Sometimes when dirt has been disturbed underground, it shows up as what looks like a tank, but in actuality is nothing. The only way to verify this is to dig a hole in the ground. We have the market study to tackle, and the taxes to tackle, on Monday and Tuesday of next week. The market study should be easy, as they already have the rates of several other comparative properties. This outfit from San Antonio is using the worst comparisons available. Last is the taxes, and for this we don't have a solution. In the end, it will come down to who has better information. I would love to play hardball with them when the time comes. One of my goals next week will be to find another buyer. I need some bigger muscles to challenge them when they inevitably try to renegotiate the price. Nothing would make me happier than to say 'thanks for trying, guys, but if you can't make the numbers work, then we need to find a more cost effective buyer who can'. Of course, part of me thinks that we are over-analyzing this and that they just need another week to become comfortable with the numbers.

April 25, 2008

I just reread the last line of the paragraph above, and I must have been intoxicated when I thought that perhaps they just needed another week to become comfortable with the numbers. Alright, brace yourself, because here is what actually happened.... The study period ended on March 6th. So at 3:15 PM on March 6th, I get an email from the principal of the Texas Company stating that they've confirmed all of the terrible news that they presented to us just a week earlier. With the increase in the taxes and the increase in the environmental and the decrease in the market prices, they simply cannot make the numbers work. Their answer that they simply cannot get the numbers to work did not mean that they wanted out of the deal. What that translated into was that they wanted to renegotiate some numbers in the original contract. So the email finishes by stating that, since the total damage was going to be about $1 million, they wanted us to eat $500,000 of that damage. At first, we were extremely angry. These guys were going back on their original word and renegotiating the deal. We were sure that this is the strategy that they employ with every small farmer who sells them land, and they successfully, suddenly, take a half a million dollars off the table. They know how much we paid for the property, and have a good idea of how much we stand to make at the settlement table. Together with all of their high-priced lawyers, they came up with the guess that we would be willing to eat $500,000 and still stand to make $1.7 million. That was probably not a terrible strategy to employ since we have been and continue to be in some serious pain about the entire project. However, I'm not ready to roll over yet. This dog still has a little fight in him.

This was probably the most difficult week that I have experienced since I started in the business 7 years ago. If we tell them that we will give them the $500,000 off, we lose profit and we lose leverage. Is this the end of the renegotiations or are we going to have them come back at us in a few months with some other deal-breaking issue, and then ask us to waive another $500,000? During the 7 day extension period, I was feverishly trying to come up with ideas that might provide me with the leverage for me to play hardball with these guys. Unfortunately, I could not find an alternative buyer. The folks that I spoke with were not looking for more acquisitions in Baltimore City. It is a terrible feeling to be a price taker. So, I decided to think outside of the box and tackle some of their issues. Now, before you go and feel all bad for me, let me tell you about a eureka moment that I found by aggressively researching the tax issue. Baltimore City is looking to take these underdeveloped manufacturing sites and turn them into tax producing functional properties. They have an environmental tax initiative which will give developers a phased-in tax credit on the redevelopment of deficient sites. I won't go through the calculations with you, but after they take this $2 million site and turn it into a $43 million apartment complex, they stand to save $412,000 in tax dollars each year for 10 years. That is a huge coup for that piece of land. If it saves $412,000 per year at a cap rate of 10%, that money is worth $4 million to the developer. So, needless to say, I was doing a dance when I stumbled upon this program.

Back to 3:30 PM on that dark day in Signature history after I received their renegotiation email. I've finished throwing chairs and notebooks across the room. I've picked up the broken pieces of my desk that I kicked numerous times and which nearly broke my toe. Finally, I gathered myself together and tried to evaluate what exactly we were up against. I knew that they liked the site. They've spent upwards of $100,000 in due diligence, with surveys and studies and zoning and the like. That gives me some pretty large bear muscles if we're going into a fight because they can't possibly want to lose that money. On the downside, they can start waving the big company flag at me and saying that $100,000 is a drop in the bucket for these guys, and if we don't concede that, they will simply move on and find another site to develop. Again, this is indeed a buyers' market. So this is where the rubber hits the road. We have 3 alternatives to evaluate and respond to in the next 2 hours. First, we could concede and simply agree to give them $500,000 off the purchase price. It's funny how large dollars tend to blur your vision. Since the purchase price is $5.6 million and we stand to make $2.2 million, we started to look at giving up $500,000 as no big deal. Did I just write that? No big deal? I've been stressing about saving for college education for my two kids for about a decade, and will continue to stress about it until it is all paid off. The combined total of my kids' education will be around $500,000, and now I am ready to write off $500,000 with the stroke of a pen while giving it the grand total of thought of an hour and half? The second alternative is to tell them 'no'. To flat-out say that we are not willing to renegotiate the original terms of our contract, and if the deal doesn't work for you, then thanks for playing and we'll put it back on the market. This option would be great if I thought that I had another buyer keyed up and ready to go. Not such a good plan if we put it back on the market and start spending $20,000 a month to carry the property while nobody wants the thing. My memory shouldn't be so short as to forget that we held an auction on this property not so long ago, and had not one bidder raise their hand. The third option would seem to be the most reasonable, and which would involve going through their expenses one by one with them, and trying to figure out a fair and reasonable solution to each one, then placing out a dollar amount for the sum total of the problems. Then we could go on to signing an addendum with a number somewhere in the middle which would make both of us happy.

Are you curious what we did? Well….we did nothing. Absolutely nothing. We played an old fashioned game of chicken. This was perhaps the most daunting thing that I've ever done.

They perceived a position of power. The contract was due to end at the close of business. They had submitted their $500,000 reduction and were waiting for us to sign this addendum. I simply decided not to respond…and I let the contract expire. I can't believe that, after the history of deals that have fallen apart for us, and given the fact that we don't have any money to service the debt (they've been supporting us for the past couple of months), and the current state of the real estate market – I still played hardball. Either I'm crazy, or they really want the deal and this will work out.

About 6 PM that night, I get a call on my cell phone. It's a conference call with the principal of the company, his attorney, and his operations guy here in Maryland. The principal opens up the conversation by saying…and I quote, "Scott, I am sorry we pissed in your cornflakes." They were interested in hearing my thoughts about the deal, the environmental, and the taxes. At the end of the conversation, they wanted me to simply bring back the original deal, and we could get this thing going again. I couldn't resist getting one shot in at these bastards. Remember, they showed me all of these issues with the land, and why each issue should result in a price reduction. So, I told them that I'd found a $400,000 tax incentive that the property would qualify for. Since I'd found this $400,000 tax incentive, I now wanted to raise my price to $6 million if they wanted to stay in the deal. Holding back the quiver in my voice... I actually told them that I would consider a new price of $6.5 million. After about 10 seconds of silence (the small things in life give me pleasure), I agreed to consider just keeping the old contract. Now, we were feeling pretty proud of ourselves by calling their bluff and staying in the game. Unfortunately, these guys have been doing this a lot longer than we have, and they weren't done taking shots at us. The addendum prepared by their attorney comes back and it's for the same financial terms, but now they want to extend the settlement date another 9 months. They continue to extract a pound of flesh from us at each turn. Pete and I really just want to settle on this deal now. We hold off on getting back to them again. Here we go again, trying to figure out how to deal with these bullies. They know all about leverage. The zoning hearing to boost the number of units that we have been waiting for is coming up at 3 PM on that same day. They are refusing to go to the meeting until we sign the addendum. Without their attorney, this meeting will be cancelled. They have, again, pinned us up against the wall, and are ready to flatten us with renegotiation. I think I lost most of the hair on my head in those two days. Well, we were successful the first time we played chicken, so here we went again. With the zoning hearing, which had been 90 days in the making, coming up at 3 PM, we agreed to meet their local guy here at 2 PM to sign the addendum. Think about this scenario for a minute: we worked out the deal on the phone, they've waited 90 days to get this zoning approval for the variance for the 188 units (which makes this whole thing work for everyone), and we end up at the attorney's office 1 hour before the hearing in order to sign the extension addendum just so that they keep this meeting on schedule. If we don't sign the addendum, they could threaten to not go to the hearing, and we then have to get back on the court docket and risk the whole deal falling apart. This is crazy pandemonium. We show up at the attorney's office at 2PM to meet with the local principal for the apartment builders. We want to take control of this process, so we spend the money with the attorney to have a counter offer ready for them. Our counter offer wants them to close the deal under the original price terms in 30 days, or we walk. How about them apples? They're not the only ones that can walk away from this deal.

We meet around a small circular table at the attorney's office and gently slide our counter offer across the table for him to evaluate and sign. Now, I like their operations guy at the meeting. He seems like a straight shooter and wants this thing to work for everyone. I can tell that he feels terrible that his bosses have tried this bullying style of negotiation. He can't stop staring at the ground when he speaks to us, avoiding all eye contact. We are two honest hardworking guys trying to make this deal work for everyone. We feel that we have offered them a good price, and when they have an issue, we are quick to solve it; we are helping them out like partners in the deal and not adversaries, and still we got treated like yesterdays' trash. We show him our addendum, he calls Dallas, he comes back to us with changes, we contemplate and hold strong to our footings, and he calls Dallas again. They claim that they simply cannot and will not close in 30 days. I turn it around on him and say that the 9 months is fine, but I have a price. Again, everything in this world revolves around a number. If they want to play this game, it will cost them $100,000 per month (non-refundable). That means that they can take their sweet time getting comfortable with the entire process over the next 9 months, but now I am going to get justly rewarded.

I have a feeling that this is around the point when things really began to break apart and get ugly. We were upset at their sliminess and they were upset at our emotional responses. But wait, what about the zoning meeting? We left the meeting without any resolution. The addendum was not signed, and at this point in time, we had no contract on the property. Rather stressful…I might add. So, we left the attorney's office believing that they would show up at the zoning hearing; even though we hadn't gotten the signature, I was sure that they were bluffing and would show up at the meeting, as I thought they had to. These guys had spent 90 days, and probably about $30,000, to get the plans to this point, and it would seem silly for them not to show up. Pete and I walked the 3 blocks to City Hall and patiently waited in the hearing for these guys to strut in and get their approval. We're sure that they will come, they have to come... won't they come? Well, at 5 minutes to 3 PM….their zoning attorney shows up. They have instructed him to cancel the zoning hearing. I looked back at Pete in utter disbelief. Does this mean that they're no longer interested? Have we pushed them back just a little too far and now they don't want to deal with us? Or is it that they're digging their heels deep in the ground and preparing for an all-out battle? We left the meeting with an uneasy feeling about the entire deal.

When you go out on a date with a person for the first time,

people seem to follow this ritual of questioning, when do you follow up with a phone call? If you call too soon, you may give them the impression that you're interested in them (and don't ask me what would be wrong with that). If you don't call them, but you did have a good time, you may be losing out on something special. Well, I was about to embark on a follow-up dating phone call with my buyer. After we'd had our first fight, I had to wonder, how soon should I give them a call? If I called the very next day, they might get the impression that I'm extremely motivated to stay in this deal. This may give them a sense of leverage over me, and that kind of leverage may end up costing me hundreds of thousands of dollars. Is my date going through the same issues as me, and will they call me up to invite me back to the dance? I wait a full day and the phone doesn't ring. Each hour goes by and I reevaluate my strategy. Perhaps I should be the one to hold out the olive branch and try to make peace with these guys. I certainly do not trust them, and I can't see myself playing the win-win scenario anymore. You see, win-win only works when both sides are employing this strategy. If you're trying to work on a win-win approach with an opponent who's looking to take down the whole kitty, then it will end up being win-lose, and needless to say, I would be on the losing end of it in this case. So, finally, day two comes around and I decide that I will get off my horse and make the call. I believe that their principal is actually breathing a sigh of relief that I have extended him this olive branch. We end up coming up with a solution. With the new information about the tax situation and the credit being offered by Baltimore City, he's fairly comfortable with these additional expenses. His biggest concern is the environmental. When we wrote up the original contract, their two conditions were the zoning approval and entry into the voluntary clean-up program. Well, we just blew the zoning appeal by not showing up, and now we have to wait an additional 2 weeks to get on the calendar.

Let me take a second to describe what the legal term "entry" into the environmental cleanup program actually means. The way the process works, once you submit your application, you are technically entered into the program. This works great for us, as we can close the transaction within the next 60 days. It does not work out as beneficially for them, as they really wanted to know what their maximum out-of-pocket cash expense was going to be in cleaning up the site. So, what they actually wanted, but misstated in the contract, was approval of a remediation plan. This plan is a step-by-step set of directions for cleaning up the site so that it can be put into the program. In the end, we decided to allow them to get the remediation plan from the state, with a maximum out of pocket expense of $500,000 before we settle the transaction. For us, that means that we'll have to wait another 6 months before we close the transaction. I'm expecting this to come to fruition around September of this year, but with the track record that I've shown over the past year, like my wife says, I will believe it when the check is sitting comfortably in my back account.

I can fast forward to 2 weeks later at the zoning hearing. We show up, and this time their entire party from Texas is there for the hearing. The attorney presented the case for increasing the density to 188 units, and kabam, right in front of us, the board granted approval. We should have been jumping for joy, but this deal has simply taken the life out of us. I congratulated Pete, and the attorneys congratulated us all, but it felt relatively anticlimactic with all of the issues that we'd faced over the past 2 weeks. Now they are working on the submission of the voluntary cleanup application with the state. The environmental engineers have just finished the application, and it went in just last week, around April 18th. From this point on, the process should take around 45 days for an initial response, with another 30 days for a secondary response. There will be a public hearing at which the neighbors can come and comment, and then the voluntary cleanup plan is put together with engineers and the state. After several more revisions, this plan should be finalized, and we will be clearing for settlement. While this sounds dandy as I sit here at my kitchen table, I can foresee many bumps in the road.

This is another point where I want you to put yourself in my shoes and imagine everything that can go wrong with this transaction. The hearing may have community members there who put up a stink about disturbing the site. This could cause delays and additional expenses. The most glaring issue that I predict is that they fluff the environmental numbers to show expenses far exceeding the $500,000. They could insist that the entire site be capped with new soil, just to protect them and try to push this expense onto us. So, if you were sitting next to me at the kitchen table, I would ask you how we can be better prepared for round 2 of this negotiation, and before we get to that point. The last thing that I want to happen is that I am as ill-prepared for the next round as I was just a few weeks ago during the zoning hearing fiasco. My first order of business will be to find a buyer or joint venture partner who might be willing to spend some time reviewing the site. It's always good to have a backup offer in place. The challenge here is that most people don't want to spend any time or money on a site that is currently under contract. While I'm not sure how to cross that bridge, that is how I will spend a large portion of my time over the next few months. Next would be to get some general estimates for the environmental cleanup, those coming from several engineers. I would rather not have their engineers come to me with a large number that's unconfirmed, and then they again ask us to eat some cash from the deal. This process has been a fantastic learning experience of how large companies do business. As the little guys, we tend to take risks without thinking twice. We don't seek out enough information during our due diligence, and we are afraid to spend the money upfront without having some sort of guarantees. This is the big difference between us and them. They have been doing these projects for decades. They have already seen every issue in residential apartment developments. They are calm and cool and they take their time putting together the information to make the best informed decision. We tend to shoot first and ask questions later. While this strategy has certainly served us well during the most prolific real estate rise in the past 100 years, this buyers market is an entirely new ballgame. So, while this past month has frustrated and angered me to the point of actually losing sleep on a few nights, it has been a great learning opportunity on how to do business. I can only wish that this thing progresses smoothly and that I am depositing my million at the end of the summer.

The last and final entry for the month deals with the college rental properties. We have settlement scheduled for April 30th. This is a local buyer who's been looking over and reviewing this portfolio for well over 3 months. At this point in the process, they appear to have all of their ducks in a row. The financing appears to be secured, the title work appears to be complete, and the legal formation of their LLC (which, incidentally, is buying our LLC to save on transfers) has moved slowly, but seems to be ready to go.

There was once a time when I was the eternal optimist. I was confident that settlement would happen and would daydream about how I was going to spend the money. While I have earmarked this half a million for a down payment on a new personal residence, I am yet to actually start looking for that new house. Even though I may have a personal bank account swelled with $500,000 next week, I am forcing myself to not even look on the MLS computer for a new personal residence to buy until the check is cashed and deposited in my account, and my wife would be proud. It's funny how one's attitude can change after a series of successes or failures. I will find the time to write a new entry come May 4th. Even though it is just 2 weeks away, this could prove to be two of the weeks that I have been waiting for for 7 years. Remember, the college rental properties were all part of Signature Properties and not the Fund. If things go well, Signature Properties will still own Windsor Mill, 3 college rental houses and 2 other rentals – a portfolio that we want to keep long term, the Fund will be a few projects away from being completely liquidated and Scott and Pete will be happy campers. This book may indeed end up getting published. Thanks for hanging in there with me – it continues to be a difficult journey.

LESSONS LEARNED

- You make your money on the buy. Always buy at the right price. Construction and resale numbers are market driven. Buying at a discount is within your control.

- The market cures many mistakes. It's difficult to learn how to do things correctly if the market hides your mistakes. You do indeed learn from failure.

- Development is a long term gamble. We started flipping houses with short turnaround times. This had less risk. Our projects now take over 18 months – it's just hard to predict the future that far out.

A WIN… MAYBE

May 15, 2008

I waited a full 2 weeks before sitting down to write about this euphoric feeling. On several occasions, I've come close to dragging the laptop outside to the back deck to write this chapter, but my emotions have been changing so incredibly quickly that I have resisted each time. These past two weeks have been everything that I've imagined. It started on April 30th. We had the settlement scheduled for the 11 college rental properties at the attorney's office in Baltimore at 1:00 PM. The previous week had been spent in sending and resending documents to the title company, the lender, the buyer, his attorney, and everyone else even mildly associated with the transaction. I'd been convinced that something was going to fall apart at the last minute. In order to mentally protect myself from any kind of letdown, I continued to work diligently every day, not counting on a big payday. Even up to the point that I showed up at the settlement table and saw the HUD-1 financial statement sitting on the long oak table, I still was in denial, or D'Nile…and that is not just a river in Egypt. I seriously thought that the buyer was going to back out of the deal completely when he didn't show up on time. The buyer showed up about 15 minutes late. This guy is sort of like a syndicator. He sets up these groups of investors and locates deals like ours which he thinks have 10 year growth prospects. He's not much older than I am, and has been doing this for about the same time that I have been in the business. Here, he reviews the HUD-1 statement and, as just so easy as "It looks good to me", the attorney has initiated a wire from his account to ours for the total of his down payment,

$645,000. Then the settlement attorney calls the bank to check on the wire, and of course, there are no funds available from the bank. Are you kidding me? The guy comes to the settlement without the down payment portion of the settlement. I'm assured by both the buyer and the settlement attorney that the money is indeed available. They convince Pete and me that we should continue to execute the documents of the transaction. I continue to sign all of the documents and execute what is called a dry settlement. This means we sign over the right to the property without actually receiving the funds. Actually, though, all of the documents sit with the escrow agent – so we really are pretty protected. The process had been fairly smooth up until then, and I was confident that, in the end, the wire would come through if they said it would.

A half an hour later, I shake hands with the buyer and walk out the door. Seven years of work had culminated in this quick half hour – but still I had no money in my bank account. What I find funny is that I didn't have a big celebration with Pete, and I didn't have a big fancy dinner with my wife. I simply went home, not quite understanding the magnitude of what had happened that day. The next day, around 10AM, Pete accesses our bank account online, and low and behold, we have $1,437,000 in our bank account. I was on a field trip with my first grader when I got the email that said "The Eagle Has Landed". That is our code for 'the wire has hit'. Again, I continue to go about my day without it really hitting me that I have almost a million and a half dollars in my bank account. That field trip was on Thursday, and I made it to the office on Friday. I typically do not go into the city on Friday, but this was a ceremonial day. This was the day that I paid back all of my friends, family, and fools that had lent me money. This is when I paid down all of my lines of credit. This is when I finally got some cash back for all of the out-of-pocket money that I had spent for the past 2 and a half years, and never had the money in the business account to pay me back. So, Pete and I sat down at the computer and started to spend the money.

First, we paid off all of our debt money that we had raised at

10-12% from friends who were investors. We paid off everyone that had invested in Signature Properties. We paid off old MBA buddies, we paid off my brother, and we paid off our old instructor and mentor. These were people who had trusted us with their money, and it felt incredibly liberating to get them their money back. Boy, did that feel good to clear that hard money debt off the books. Next, we paid off all of our accounts payable that had showed up in quick books for the past 6 months: nice to have a few bucks to do that.... We had been stringing along all of the contractors and vendors as long as possible. Again, these people had to trust that we were going to be able to pull out this debt. Actually, they had very little choice *but* to wait and pray that they would get their money back. After everything possible was paid off, then we looked to see what was left in the account. When all was done, we had spent $400,000 in just about 25 minutes. The debt and the loans had weighed me down for years. The lines of credit being constantly pinned at their limits had begun to wear on me, and the thought of being debt free was incredibly rewarding. Debt free for Signature Properties. Wow, that has sounded so unrealistic for so, so long that I still can't believe that we've done it. It's difficult to describe the feeling. Before, when we were cashing out huge numbers, we felt like rock stars. We went out for 3 martini lunches and ordered expensive meals and bragged about our winnings to everyone who would listen. This was a completely different feeling. I didn't feel like a rock star. I felt more like a gambler who had just been able to make good on a bad situation. It's really hard to explain, almost like you've had this promise hanging over your head that you never thought you would be able to keep, though you wanted to desperately, and then all of a sudden, you have been lifted. After the checks had gone out, that left us with $1,050,000 in the bank to split. We had made plenty of money over our years in business, but had never had a singular pay day this large. I also have to say that the timing of making a $1,000,000 in this real estate market also seems somewhat unbelievable.

Amid all of the celebration, though, one fact has not gotten lost: the college rental portfolio was always intended to be my retirement nest egg. I was always planning on paying them off and living off the incredible cash flow that they produced. I also realized that this has been the cash flow that's kept Signature Properties alive for these past two years. The symbolism of selling this portfolio is actually one of shutting down the business. This portfolio kept me from going bankrupt, kept me from losing friends and families' money, and kept Signature and the Benjamin family alive on financial life support. I am witnessing the end of a great ride unfolding in front of my very eyes. It is a touch depressing. Given the current state of the real estate market – this marks the beginning of the end of Signature Properties. While we still plan on holding the remaining portfolio, Pete and I don't see any further growth or development.

We decided to leave about $20,000 in the bank to handle expenses that would crop up while we continued to liquidate the portfolio, leaving us $1,030,000 to split. I took great pride in cutting myself a check for $515,151.51. Don't ask me why I went with the crazy 5's and 1's, but I thought that it would be a unique number. I copied the check and have it in my file. Incredible that we generated over a million dollars in 5 years, with passive investments... but who am I fooling? These were not passive in the least. Chalk this up to a lesson learned from this book, that real estate is far from being completely passive. I hope that the gentleman who sold me the original 5 units is still alive in Florida, and raises a toast to me for the success that this project brought me. I deposited the money into my local BB&T account, and it cleared the next day. I have been banking with this bank for the past 15 years. The bank offers competitive products and has a convenient location, so I have always been happy there. Well, wouldn't you know it, but within hours of the check clearing, the customer service representative at my bank calls me and acknowledges seeing a large deposit made, and offers her wealth advisory and investment services. I was quick to inform her that I had already put the transfer in for that money to go over to ING, where it would earn a paltry 3%, which was still higher than BB&T's 2%. So, today, I scanned the internet to find another banking institution that could offer me a higher interest rate, and found that Capital One had a no fee account paying 3.75%. I've arranged to move $639,000 (I had a few bucks in the bank already) out of ING and into Capital One. That .75% difference will translate into about $4,800 per year for a few clicks of the mouse. I'm excited about potentially looking for a new primary residence in the near future. Houses on the water have always attracted my attention, but the closing down of the Signature Properties Fund looms in the back of my mind. Recount that the sale of Robinson Street and Fairmount Avenue resulted in massive losses to our friends and family who invested in this portfolio (these folks were different than our 12% hard money investors). Pete and I are still kicking the can down the road as to how to handle the final liquidation of this Fund which has lost a substantial amount of the invested principal.

Life has changed a little bit since the big deposit. While I have never been a heavy spender, I have noticed my loosening of the wallet strings. The lunches are now running $15 instead of $10. The day at the ballgame costs $100 with food and drinks. The wines we order are $15 a glass. These small perks will not have a significant impact on the nest egg, but the pleasures are truly being enjoyed. This week, I spent a significant amount of time on the computer planning our summer trips, including a week in Florida, a week in New Orleans, and finally a week in the British Virgin Islands. I've decided that the culmination of the book will be the HUD-1 settlement statement for Charles Street. This project has been such a large part of my life, and for so very long, that it would simply not be fair to publish the book without some closure on this.

I realize that my original stated goal was to accumulate $2 million of net worth, and real estate was going to be my vehicle to achieve it. Here is a snapshot of my personal financial statement to date:

2002	**2008**
Equity in House = $140,000	Equity in House = $325,000 (Lower than earlier)
Stocks = $19,000	Stocks = $19,000
Funds = $13,000	Funds = $20,000
Retirement Account	$200,000
College Savings Plan	$100,000
College Rental Portfolio	$150,000
Additional Rental Properties	$110,000
Office Building	$350,000
Charles Street	$750,000
Cash in Bank	$639,000
2002 = $175,000	**2007 = $2,704,000**

My wife always says that I have a short attention span. In the 20 years that she has known me, we have moved 7 times and I have had 3 completely different careers. After graduation, I wanted to be a restaurateur. Having managed a couple of different restaurants and through finally buying my own, the challenge of turning around a food service establishment lost my interest. Then I wanted to be involved with medical consulting. After working 3 years in the business, I went out on my own and started teaching seminars, and selling products and services to hospitals around the country. Again, that nagging feeling – that I was working for the almighty dollar and not for my passion – pulled me away from that industry and into the next big thing…real estate. So now, after I've continued to get the seven year itch, my desire for the next big real estate deal has slipped away. Perhaps setting my goal at $2 million was my downfall. If my goal were $4 million, would I be writing more chapters and trading more deals? My partner Pete has bought 8 more rentals over the past six months. My good friend Craig has flipped and wholesaled a dozen properties in the past year, and made pretty good coin at it. My mentor and colleague Victor now sits on several commercial office and retail properties, and has a net worth that's twice mine.

Why have I decided to get off the bus now, after 7 years, after finally finding my groove? There's no doubt that I could duplicate my success again in 7 more years. I've lived and survived the most difficult real estate market in history – so why stop now? My wife can tell you why – I get bored. This entire journey has been one to prove that I can identify a challenge, climb a mountain, do anything that I set my mind to and ultimately stop once it is achieved. This is the way that I am wired. I am doing it just to prove to myself that I can. At this point, I am not sure that the goal was *retirement* as much as taking on a big hairy audacious goal (BHAG) and reaching it. I also really enjoy teaching people. I enjoy inspiring people to take on big challenges. If my experience can help anyone – this entire journey was worthwhile. If you're trying to retire and have learned anything from my successes and failures, I hope that you can enjoy the freedom that real estate has provided me. With all of that being said, I have another big announcement.

On August 11, I begin a four year PhD program in Strategic Management at the University of Maryland. Realizing that the thrill of making money just to make money was gone, I did some soul searching to try to figure out exactly what it is that wakes me up in the morning. You know, what lights the fire in your belly. What drives me, or you? Remember way back at the beginning of this book when I spoke of the different kinds of wealth – well, I am seeking a wealth of societal contribution. I want to give back some more. Of all of the activities that I have been a part of over the course of my career, the one that I've truly enjoyed the most is teaching. Whether it's real estate, nuclear cardiology, mentoring or helping out at a local school, or working with the interns over the years at Signature Properties, the adrenaline rush from speaking and helping people learn business skills far outweighs my thirst for money.

Did I just write that?...Maybe I need to go to therapy again. I have always been one to chase the dream, though, and I am ready to chase this one. I also realized that I have a love for learning. The PhD program will allow me to understand business from a theoretical prospective. I know how business works and the functions of business from a practical application, but have never really studied the academic theory side of business. I believe that if I can accomplish this goal at age 43, I will have an entire second half to my life in which to experience this dream. On occasion, I feel like I have some sort of business deficit disorder. I can't seem to find peace in any one industry. You know something, though: that is who I am, and only time will tell if the PhD program and academics can scratch this most recent itch.

June 4, 2008

Let me start with a quick recap on where we are in the liquidation of Signature Properties. The 4 lots sold on Lincoln, and now we have the single house on Lincoln under contract at $290,000. At the end of the day, we are in the project for $325,000, including fixing up the house and paying the engineer to subdivide the lots. So, take the net of the $290,000 deal (which should be about $275,000 after commissions and closing), and add the $290,000 that we netted out on the sale of the three lots, and we have gross revenues of $565,000. Subtract out the $325,000 that we have in the deal, and we still cashed out a cool $240,000 on the Lincoln deal. That is good coin considering that we didn't do any heavy lifting. This will be the last property in Signature Properties Fund I, LLC. So, once this settles, which is scheduled for 3 weeks from today, we can cash out the Fund members. I've already started to prepare for this day of reckoning. Each time we've sold a project for a loss, we dipped into the principal of the fund to come to the settlement table. While we knew that we were doing this, we truly never calculated the gravity of how much money we were stripping in principal each time. In case this is lost in translation, every time I wrote about losing money, I was losing my mother's and my brother's money. When the dust settles on the Fund, we will have $170,000 in cash left. Now, I am sure that you can't remember way back to 2003, but we originally raised $480,000 in investor money. Over the 5 years, we returned $60,000 in capital to the investors, meaning that we currently should have $420,000 of their money in principal. When I say that we returned $60,000, though, it's actually an accounting trick. We were sending them back dividend checks every time we made a profit on a deal. With some of those dividend checks, we labeled them as return of capital. We did this to minimize their tax exposure. If these checks were returned as dividends, the investors would have to pay gains taxes on the income. By our labeling them return of capital, they don't have to pay the taxes, however, they will get less money back when the fund liquidates, at just $420,000. So, we now have a few options in returning the capital. If we were true Wall Street sharks and we set up an investment fund that we'd marketed to the general public, we would tell everyone, "Sorry, we make no guarantees that you will get your original capital back, and thanks for playing." Now, keep in mind, our investors have received a lot of money on this investment in dividend checks. Over the years of making money off of profitable deals, we sent back many profit-sharing checks which actually accumulated to around $250,000. So, in essence, they have already received $250,000 of their $420,000 back. Take into account the $170,000 that we should have left in our account after Lincoln settles, and they will have received just about all of their original $480,000 in equity back. The catch to this scenario is that labeling dividends as return of capital means that they will not have received any return on their investment over the past 5 years. Basically, they took a shot at the real estate game, and ended up with a 0% return. That is not a bad option. And who knows, the way the financial markets have been getting crushed, this could happen in stocks, or worse, you could have simply lost most of your investment without any return by investing in the stock market. There is another option that Pete and I have been kicking around.

Much of the money invested in this Fund is from friends and family. We used their money over the years, and it afforded us an opportunity to make solid salaries for the past six years. The other extreme would be for Pete and I to try to make them whole by returning all of their equity ($420,000), which would mean we would have to come up with $250,000 of cash to make it happen. If that were the scenario, the investors would be able to enjoy all of the ups of making money, and this while the market was going haywire via all of the tidy dividend checks that we sent out over the years, but see none of the downs and the risk of investing. That certainly doesn't sound fair to us. The real estate market got flushed down the toilet over the past 2 years, and the investors need to have seen some risk for their money. Pete and I have now gone through this mental exercise for days. I have money from my mother, my brother, and my friends in this Fund. Let's be honest: in real life, the result would be to return all of the $170,000 left in the account and call it a day. I mean, that's what investing is all about. You stand to make great dividends and returns, but you also stand to lose money. Why would I liquidate other investments that I personally own to make the fund investors whole? Do I have to make the phone call to my mother telling her that I lost her principal? Boy, what a dilemma.

So, we decided to meet somewhere in the middle. Pete and I had to agree on what a fair return on their investment should have been if they had not invested in us. What if they had put their money into Fidelity or Vanguard, or one of the equity investment companies? The investor would have taken on the risk of the market, and the investment houses would have let them deal with the consequences. A loss would be a loss...but given the relationship with these investors, I'm just not comfortable with that answer. I have polled friends on what they think a fair return would be in this situation, and most of them tell me a return of zero. Risk is risk. How can you have risk if you don't have loss? Over the years, the Fund has paid us handsomely, to both the investors and Signature. It has allowed us to keep the college rentals and Charles Street on our own while investing their money into development deals. Without the constant cash flow from the successful development deals, we may not have been able to be as successful with these other divisions. So, we are both in agreement that we need to give them some sort of return on their money. We came up with using the S&P 500 return as our baseline. We looked at the beginning value of the S&P 500 on the day that we took in our first Fund investor's money. Then we looked at the day when we expect the final sale to happen, and liquidation to occur on Lincoln. Whatever the return will be for this period of time (had you invested in the stock market), that will be our final payout. If the S&P remains at its level today, we owe $160,000 out of our personal money, which represents a total return (not annualized) on investors' money of roughly 6%. This means that the investors will receive their total principal back, plus a nice return of 6% on their money. The end result will be the same as if they had invested their money into an S&P 500 index fund and left it there for the past 6 years.

Here is how it will all play out. When the dust settles from Lincoln in a few weeks and the checks from settlement clear, we will split up the $170,000 left in the Fund's bank account, as proportionate to each investor's interest. Then we will stroke checks to each investor out of our personal bank accounts for $80,000 each, or $160,000 total. Imagine this: if you invested in a Fidelity Mutual Fund that lost money, it would be pretty cool if the fund manager sent you a personal check out of his personal bank account for money that he lost you. Next week, I am bringing in my personal checkbook and doing exactly that for each Fund member. While it is an expensive lesson to me, I am comfortable with this course of action that we have chosen. The learning lesson from this entire process: I will never take money from friends and family ever again. I repeat again: I will never take money from friends and family again. I find it bothersome that I need to give investors money back that they technically don't deserve. I don't mind being penalized for mistakes and poor investments, but in order for me to be able to look these people in the eyes, I need to treat them differently than I would treat another investor. So heed my advice: don't do it, don't take the money.

August 7, 2008

On the summer front, things down at the lake have been going gangbusters. We still own both of the lake houses, but this year, rents have been fantastic. On the larger of the two homes, I pushed rents up to $2,900 a week, and we have 13 weeks booked. At that rate, we are within $10,000 a year of breaking even. We pay off about $15,000 a year in principal, plus we get a swanky depreciation write off. Don't forget that now that the market has bottomed out, we should start to see the 6-7% appreciation again on this $650,000 house, and kabam....this is why I love real estate. The other house is limping along as well. We have that home on the market for $499,000. At this point, we would happily take a loss just to get rid of the property. On the positive side, it has 11 weeks rented, and should also be within about a $10,000 loss per year. At the end of the day, I will still shovel $15,000 into the upkeep and payments of these houses, but I love the long term prospects of both of them.

On the rental side, we are left with 5 houses. One is the ghetto property that we are in with way, way, way over our heads. We have about $170,000 in the house and it is only worth $150,000. So, we decided to stick a section 8 tenant in the property for $1,295, and at this point, it pretty much breaks even. Pete and I will end up owning this thing forever, but as long as the government is knocking back my mortgage month after month, I don't have any issue with that. Do you remember the property that I call the blue-collar property, the one that was on the market? We thought it would bring $219,000, dropped the price 3 times over the course of 9 months, and guess what... it is now a rental property again. This is a classic case of missing the market. We bought it for $92,000, put in $15,000 to fix it the first time, and stuck a tenant in it, but misjudged the market by about a year. By the time the tenant had had sufficient time to break the windows and destroy the house, we needed another $30,000 to put it back together. By this time, the great recession had set in and no one was going to buy the house. So, in true cyclical fashion, it is back into the rental pool. We have a new tenant in there for $1,200, which just about covers the mortgage, taxes, and insurance. When the next real estate cycle comes, I'll definitely see the signs and not let this little prize stay in our portfolio. Then we have kept the 3 single family college rentals. At the end of the day, these houses will help pay a few small bills with the positive cash flow that they create. They are all in decent neighborhoods and will continue to generate cash flow, depreciation expenses, appreciation, and of course keep knocking back that mortgage. So I will keep those as long as I can continue to get college students to pay me high rents for them. I walked through them all this week, and 2 of them are in pretty good shape, while the third one most definitely looks like a college fraternity house. We still own the office building also. Not for lack of trying, but this just seems to be very difficult to get to the closing table. After 2 auctions and 2 other contracts, I have accepted the fact that it will continue to be ours while I get my PhD. I think I forgot to update you on the second auction on this property. They drew a nice crowd, but the highest bid that they could generate was $750,000. It's about 95% occupied and generates a small positive cash flow, though, so the demand for selling it is relatively small at this time. So I continue to manage the property, which only takes a few hours per month, we have a management company continuing to manage the three college rentals, and Pete is doing a great job at taking care of the ghetto property and the blue collar property.

Last on the update list is Charles. I spoke with the environmental engineer today. They have commenced with soil remediation and contamination removal. They have been working diligently on the remedial action plan, which will entitle the property to qualify for a $400,000 tax credit. This is the final condition to the contract. Within the next 2 weeks, we could hear that the site is ready to go, which would mean a settlement within the next 30 days, or it could need additional environmental remediation. If this is the case, then the next step will be another 30 days for a community hearing. The buyers down in Texas continue to fork out $20,000 a month for the continued development of this project. I can tell you that, right now, they are in control of the entire process. I am cc'd on each email, and it is a thing of beauty to watch them operate. They are bidding out the construction of the project, from foundation to finishing fixtures. They are a truly competent group, and at this point, I am very confident that they will get this thing across the finish line. I'm keeping both my fingers and my toes crossed that we get the green light in the next 2 weeks. I will keep you posted. Cheers for now.

LESSONS LEARNED

- Never, never, never take money from family and friends.
- Real estate is really not a passive investment. It requires active monitoring.

THE FINAL DEAL

January 21, 2009

As I scan the past entry, my optimism makes me smile. Investing in real estate has been like a roller coaster of emotions. The highs that I experienced during the hay day were like walking on air. We were making money, cutting deals, celebrating with expensive dinners, and enjoying the ride. As I enter 2009, things have certainly been brought into perspective. First, I want to acknowledge the economy as it stands. We inaugurated a new President yesterday, Barack Obama. I am certainly hoping that he can bring some stability to the economy. I have been trading in the stock market over the past 4 months, and watching the Dow as it has plummeted from its high around 15,000 to settling in around 8,000 this week. I don't like to make predictions, but I think we are far from done with the Dow. I imagine that we'll see 5,500 before this thing is over. I am still day trading stocks and doing fairly well. As the market goes down, there is incredibly volatility. I tend to trade 2 stocks every day. I like Pulte Homes (go figure) and CCJ, a uranium mining company. These stocks swing 2-4% per day, and if I am lucky, I manage to make $500 per trade. In the past 30 days, I have cashed out $3,300 worth of dividend checks. I set up a little portfolio with Scottrade to execute my day trades. After a successful trade, I call Scottrade and have them issue me a check for $1,000. This gives me the impression that I am taking cash off the Vegas table. I like to buy something with the cash so that I feel like my earnings have accomplished something tangible. At any rate, I have cashed 3 checks totaling $3,300, and I am feeling pretty good at this point. The overall economy is really tanking, though. People have watched their 401k accounts turn into 201k's. Retirees are being forced to work longer and put off retirement. I have watched my kids 529 college saving accounts lose over 30% of their value in the past 2 years. Friends and family are losing their jobs, and their houses are facing foreclosure. Overall, things are very tough.

One shining light in my investment portfolio is my real estate holdings. I currently own 3 college rentals with Pete that could together be worth around $1 million. We have tenants in there at $3,000 each until June, with the new leases through 2010 already signed at $3,300 each. We are gaining positive cash flow and watching the mortgages get chipped away month after month. We own one ghetto property and one blue collar property, with tenants in both. On these, we barely get cash flow on either one, but again, that mortgage is being chipped away at. These homes are worth $350,000. The office building remains at approximately breakeven with its 90% occupancy (we just lost a tenant there). The building scares me a little, as the economy has claimed several of our tenants, there may come a time when we don't have enough rental income coming in to pay our monthly expenses. At this point, we have not had to infuse money into the building from our personal accounts, and we have a few prospects for new leases this month. At one point in time, the building was worth $1 million (or so we thought), and now we would be lucky to get $750,000 for it. Perhaps we should've sold it at auction when we had the chance, but oh, that's right, we tried. We are electing to keep the building until the next real estate cycle.

Down at the lake, Richard and I have become comfortable with owning both properties forever. We have tried to sell one of the houses for going on one year now, only to have the only contract (received in November of 2008) blow up due to a dock issue. We were willing to accept this contract at $419,000. Not exactly what one would expect for a house purchased at $500,000 just a few years ago. At any rate, I continue to pump $20,000 of my personal money into the carry costs of both of these houses, per year. Jill and I take one week a year down at the lake to go fishing and tubing. At $20,000, this could potentially be the most expensive vacation we ever take. I have a feeling that liquidating this final project down at the lake will be our swan song of losing money. We are almost $100,000 in the hole on this one house.

Finally, there is Charles Street. Charles Street is the jewel that I am waiting to cash in on before I send this book out to the publisher. As of the last chapter, we were waiting on some approvals before we were ready to force the buyers to settle. Last June seems so far away that I'm not even sure what the original closing date was. I believe that it was an August settlement date. As you can imagine, with this market, the settlement did not happen. The buyers called us to negotiate an extension of the settlement date. I am not that concerned because they have been carrying this project to the tune of $20,000 per month for a long time. They have $480,000 in non-refundable deposits into it, and they have got to have $300,000 in architectural and engineering expenses already paid out for the work that they've done on the project. Their reason for the extension request was the tightening up of the financial markets, and that they simply were not able to come to the table with the money on the given date. The markets are crumbling like financial dominoes. It started with the housing crisis. We watched as our portfolio of homes was liquidated at auction, at massive losses. Then, the new construction market completely dried up as we couldn't liquidate the Charles property as subdivided lots. We then turned to apartments, and the larger commercial buyers were so gun shy to spend money that we had a tough time getting even this well-qualified buyer into the project. And now, are you kidding me... the financial markets have tightened up their lending criteria as financial institutions are beginning to bite the dust. As a point of reference, this was about the time that AIG, Lehman Brothers, Wachovia, and Merrill were falling apart, and Indy Mac and other banks were closing their doors. Just when I think that I'm sitting comfortably, something in the external markets, beyond my control, crushes my dreams. So, long story short, we had another famous "we've got a problem Houston" meeting with these big time bullies from the Mid-Atlantic office from the Texas company.

We set up a meeting at the Starbucks near my college campus. The principal of the company and his attorney showed up at the table, asking for the extension. Pete and I were upset that they were asking for an extension at all, but we were mentally prepared for their request. We had decided that, in exchange for giving them more time to settle, we wanted a few things of our own. First, we wanted them to continue to pay the $20,000 a month in carry costs. Then, we wanted them to reimburse us for the $40,000 in taxes that we'd just spent. Then, we wanted them to pay us an additional $50,000 just for the right to give them an extension – we've got to extract some pain money. Finally, we wanted them to pay us an additional $250,000 on top of the purchase price, as the new President of the United States had threatened increasing capital gains taxes during his campaign. After this, we threw the kitchen sink in there just for good measure. I figured, they've got almost a million dollars at risk in this deal if they choose to walk away. Why not go for broke? You know the saying, go big or go home. Hopefully, I won't be heading home on this one.

The end result was that they agreed to all of these terms. We were extremely excited. Finally, after they had spent over $1 million in fees on this project, we had them just where we wanted them. They were pregnant…in the deal, *all in*, and we could finally demand some concessions out of them. It was a very liberating meeting for both Pete and me, and we celebrated with a beer, (not the Louis the thirteenth scotch, but a Budweiser). My how things have changed.

I would say that, about the time the buzz wore off two days later, the buyers called us to set up another meeting. Apparently, their partners down in Dallas were thinking about bagging our deal all together. They had 28 deals in the works, and ours was not high on their list. They sent us a letter listing a series of 14 title objections that they had, and that we should prepare to return the $250,000 in deposit money. Wait a minute, and hold the phone. We went from a screaming high to having our intestines pulled out through our navels. Pete and I were flabbergasted. What title issues? This period had expired months ago. Was it possible that we would have to return the $250,000 in deposit money which had long been spent in carrying this project? This was another painful period (of about a week) that we had while we decided what to do. We went from doing a jig just a week before to wracking our brains on "what if's" if this buyer were to walk away. We'd just gone from 'go big or go home' to 'when you mess with the bull, you get the horns'. There is so much volatility in the market that I just can't get comfortable with the thought that I'd be able to find another buyer if this group were to walk away. During the course of the week, I tried finding any other breathing buyer. I spoke with the local developers, agents, guys in New York, and regional builders. Everyone had the same response – work with the buyers you have because nobody is buying these days. How could this happen? I was supposed to be retired and sipping a margarita on the beaches of St. John by now.

I need to stop dreaming and smell the coffee. This has been one tough market to survive. In the end, we decided to forego everything that we had talked about at that Starbucks meeting. All of a sudden, we would be happy with the $20,000 a month carry and the $40,000 in taxes. We didn't need any more money. Things were great the way they were, so why would we want to rock the boat now? It is really funny how we went from guns a'blazing to completely laying down our arms in the course of about a week. We seem to be a day late and a dollar short at every single turn. We first wanted to develop this piece of property to become a 64 lot subdivision. We envisioned beautiful townhouses with flower pots and kids playing soccer in the streets. We just couldn't get the rascal subdivided in time. The entire process just took too long, and in the end, the townhouse market dried up. Back to the drawing board we went. Next, we had the brilliant idea to change its use to apartments. By the time we had received the variances and approvals to build multi-family apartments, the number of qualified buyers had dried up. After searching the entire country for a qualified buyer, we finally find this group out of Texas who my banker over at Wells Fargo tells me is one of the top 10 apartment developers in the country. One year later, the financial markets crumble, and no one can get financing. At first, these guys were going to put 15% down on the deal. This worked out to be about $4 million. The financial markets crumbling, though, means that banks are no longer financing deals. Many would say that they are still lending money, but as of this writing, I can emphatically say that banks are no longer lending. Their method of mitigating their risks is to require a larger down payment on any project. Essentially, they want the builders to have more skin in the game. While we haven't yet seen how this will affect our deal yet, I simply can't imagine what happens when the next shoe falls. I continue to be the eternal optimist, and things could be worse. These guys continue to spend $20,000 a month to carry this thing, so I need to just hang in there. If they were to drop out of the deal, they would lose their deposit, all of those $20,000 a month payments, and all of the work that they have done on this project. I think that they will try to do whatever it takes to remain in this deal. If they walk, well, I'd be stuck again trying to beg, borrow and steal $20,000 a month.

After our final discussions on accepting whatever the Texas guys wanted, we decided to just give them the extension, as long as they remained willing to pay the $20,000 per month. I am not completely nuts. This extension would give them until March 30, 2009 to settle. This was a six month delay, and we were happy just to stay in contract. There is simply no way to describe the completely uncomfortable feeling of not having any control over the situation. I did get them to give us a copy of their construction and architectural documents before we signed the addendum. This was actually very important. If they walked from the deal, I still have access to their entire work product. Not that there are any active buyers out in the market, but they have invested $1 million in the preparation of these documents, so having them at my disposal may give me a little leverage. So, in preparation of the settlement date in 60 days, I am now mounting my horse to take those plans around town to see if there are any other breathing buyers out there, buyers who may want this fully developed deal. I always want to have a backup offer in my pocket. I am predicting that they will come back at us yet again before March 30th. The weakness that we have shown up to this point can only result in them banging us on the price before March. I need a little leverage, and having even a phantom buyer in the background may help me establish the leverage I need to force them to close on March 30, 2009.

February 27, 2009

It's funny how I have less and less to write about as this recession continues to chip away at the economic fabric of the country. We were once rolling with excitement as we were literally growing dollar bills on a tree in the back yard. The party is over, though, and the hangover is very difficult to get used to. I own the 5 residential properties with Pete, and hope to hold them for a long time. They are positive cash flowing and the mortgages are being paid off month after month. I own the office building which – thank you, God – is once again 100% occupied. We have one tenant who is behind several months on his rent, but the rest of the building is operating smoothly. At the end of the day, we are making a few bucks off of the building, and perhaps one day I will start to take a small stipend from these investments. Down at the lake, Richard and I have dropped the price on the one house to $425,000 (hey, we were ready to accept $419,000 a few months ago), and we have agreed to drop it to $399,000 in a month. Remember this house? The one that we bought for $500,000 just a few years ago? The economy is also causing me stress on the rents for these 2 lake houses. At this time in 2008, we had 8 weeks already rented out, and we ended up with over 10 weeks of income for each of the houses on the year. As of this posting, I have 2 weeks booked for next summer, and I dropped the rental price $200 on each house in order to be ahead of my competition. So this is definitely a cause of concern as we go into the spring. I'd feel a whole lot better if I could just shed off this one house. I've got to cut off the arm just to stop the bleeding.

Of major concern is Charles Street. We have our next drop dead date on March 20th. This is the date we extended the contract to, way back when we were negotiating in the Starbucks and they beat us to a bloody pulp. As the date approaches, I'm seeking to gather all of my information before we are forced to meet again. I have this queasy feeling in my stomach that they are going to try to re-trade with us yet again…and this time it will be on price. The positives that I have going for me are that they continue to pay my $20,000 per month in carry expenses, with the most recent wire showing up a few days ago. They continue to meet contractors at the site for demolition quotes, construction quotes, and development quotes. I have a friend who's renting them space across the street from the site as a construction office, and he tells me that they're buzzing around there with full intentions of closing. So, why should I be concerned, you ask. I called their Mid-Atlantic office a few days ago to chat with the architect, and found that they'd had to lay off the chief architect/developer from the company. Yikes! At one point in time, they had 3 different development deals under contact in Maryland and Virginia, totaling the construction of almost 750 new apartments. They've bailed out of every deal that they had in the Washington metro market, and just last week they bailed out of their only other Baltimore City project. At one point, they were gaining some massive economies of scale by accumulating more and more projects out of their Mid-Atlantic office. As they continue to get out of projects, it feels like I'm waiting for the last shoe to drop. You are watching in real time as a train wrecks. At this point, they have got to have over $1 million of their capital in our deal. They've got to have countless hours of work putting all of the pieces into place. Can they possibly walk away from all of that? The settlement is tentatively going to happen in 3 weeks. At this point, I have not heard anything from the buyers as to their financing, projected settlement date, or even a sniff of good news about the project. Tell me that this isn't happening.

In preparation for the ultimate renegotiation, I continue to contact commercial appraisers, other developers, and multi-family agents in order to start banging on some doors to see who might be interested in this project. I'm thinking that the value has to have gone up since the buyers have brought this project all the way to permit-ready status. Pete met with a local architectural firm, and they're calling on potential buyers. We've contacted several large scale builders to see if they have any interested potential buyers who might have a sniff of interest in this project. In preparing for the inevitable, we are trying to gather as much information about the market value and the current market conditions as possible before the dreaded phone call. I keep reminding myself that living through this is truly the best education I could ever have, and if I can get through this, it will make me a better businessman on the other side.

I would like this book to be somewhat of a teaching tool for those who are reading it. So, take a moment and put yourself into my shoes right now. My basis (what I owe) in the project is right around $3.4 million. At the current sales price of $5.645 million, Pete and I stand to take home almost exactly $2 million at closing. Imagine, if you will, that I get that re-trading phone call when they say, "Scott, we like the project, and we have spent a bunch of money on it so far, but with the economic situation as it is, our financing is going to be more expensive than originally anticipated, and the cap rates have shot up, making our ultimate sell-out less lucrative, and the only way that we will close on this thing is if we pay $4.645 million. Now, instead of me taking home $2 million, we are only taking home $1 million. My response could be, 'no way…go pound sand, it is $5.645 million or no deal'. But, the real possibility exists that they are telling the truth, and then the entire deal falls apart, they sue me for the $280,000 in deposit that is actually rightfully mine, I end up carrying the property at $20,000 a month, which burns my available line of credit in 10 months, and then I have to start eating away at money in the bank and other personal equity... just to service this debt. The possibility exists that they are bluffing me, and at the end of the day, they will come to the settlement table and settle at the price which we originally agreed upon. Another alternative would be to basically hand out a freebie to make them feel like they have achieved victory. I could take about $200,000 off the price so that they could offset some of the financing issues related to the change in the market. I can tell you for sure that, right now, I have no idea what my best course of action would be. We are in a recession, and the possibility exists that the current external financial issues continue for another year. In this case, if I get too demanding on the buyers in Texas, I could bankrupt my family in order to gamble on this one deal. Of course, there may be a rebound sooner than later, and the possibility exists that the value of a permit-ready project which can have ground broken immediately may be worth well over $6 million. I certainly wish that there was a manual which I could read that would help me evaluate the many permutations of a probability of success and all those financial outcomes. I can't help but liken this situation to the hit television show *Deal or No Deal.* On this show, contestants are given 36 cases to pick out at random, one at a time. Their goal is to find the million dollar case. Most of the people are working class people earning under $40,000 a year. As they continue to knock out the lower valued cases, they are presented with an offer which they can take with them, and hence give up the chance at becoming a millionaire. The banker on the show offers them $100,000 at one point, and the decision is tough. That is a fair amount of money to make for spending 10 minutes on a game show. As they continue to knock out the lower values (the cases that are on the game show), the offer that the banker offers is raised to, say, $250,000. I find myself yelling at the television set, trying to tell them that $250,000 represents 6 working years of their life. At no time will they ever receive a lump sum of money that high. Inevitably, they all gamble the $250,000. It's funny that people will gamble 6 full years of their life. They have to know the concept of statistics and probability. If they are lucky enough to hit $500,000….they all take it. Very few contestants ever have the fortitude to hold out until the million dollar level.

Over the next few weeks, I need to reflect and understand that $500,000 is truly a lot of money. Sure, during the heyday of the market, we stood to make $10 million on Charles Street, but those days have passed. I need to recalibrate what I consider to be a good return - $500,000 is a good return. It was the first $500,000 that we made on the college rental deal that allowed me the luxury of going back to school for my PhD. This decision weighs very heavily on my mind. While I am trying to prepare for the inevitable renegotiation that I am about to face, I need to gain a better perspective on the value of money at this point of time in my life. At any rate, my next posting should be relatively interesting.

April 24, 2009

Well, the good news is that I have yet another contract on the house down at the lake in Virginia. I think that it is good news because it has been on the market for something like 2 years. Allow me to refresh your memory on this prize. We bought a nice 5 bedroom house on the lake at 105 Shangri La Court for $460,000. That was a pretty good buy since it rents for $2,600 a week during the summer. Then the neighboring property came up for sale for $500,000. The reason for buying the house at 103 Shangri La Court was to redraw the property line in order to make the house at 105 become waterfront, and then we could cut down the forest of trees so that the view from the deck would be a direct water view. So, things were going great back then. The bank gave us $1,000,000 worth of money (crazy???), and we put up another $125,000 in cash to close on the houses (crazy again), and we broke out the chain saws and created waterfront property where it once did not exist. Then, being smart enough to see the market crashing right in front of our eyes, we put the $500,000 house up for auction. Success, as we had a bidder at $556,000. Two months later, they defaulted, losing $35,000 in deposit, and we're now stuck with trying to resell the property. Last fall, after 2 years, we almost had a contract on the house for $419,000. They ultimately decided that they didn't want to ratify the contract. We took the house off of the market, updated the kitchen, bath, paint, and carpet, bought new furniture to stage it, plus new blinds, and $10,000 of construction later, the house is back on the market again. Within one week of relisting the property with its new swanky kitchen, we had an offer. We had it listed for $425,000, and the offer was for $385,000. We go a few rounds of back and forth, and end up with a signed contract for $405,000, and we agree to build them a 12 x 17 shed. I'm not sure that we are celebrating, but it could actually stop the bleeding on this house. If we close as scheduled…in two weeks... we have the wonderful opportunity to come to the table with $40,000 cash just to get rid of the house. I now really see why people that simply can't afford to sell their properties just pack up, move, and let the banks take them back. If I think about it for too long, it really becomes depressing, so I try not to let myself think about it.

Speaking of trying not to let myself think about things, I got a huge surprise 3 weeks ago. Remember that the Texas Company had laid off the chief architect from the Mid-Atlantic office: well, I got a call from Gary, the project manager who has been killing us on behalf of the big Charles Street buyer in Texas. Apparently, the folks in Dallas asked Gary to gather all of his employees from the Mid-Atlantic office together for a conference call at the office. About the time that they were waiting for the phone to ring, the partner from Dallas actually entered their office. That had to be weird. You're waiting for the folks from Dallas to call, and in walks one of the partners into your conference room, in person. Everyone in the office was quite surprised. The partner went on to explain that times are tough in the real estate market, and proceeded to fire each and every employee in the office. They've decided to close down their Mid-Atlantic office, and with it, any hopes of us closing on our Charles Street property. I am still in shock when I think about 2 years of work with these guys, 2 years of variances, permits, financing, issues, and all of the garbage that went along with a long relationship with these guys, and they are now officially abandoning the project. I think that they have like $1.2 million in cash in the deal, what with architectural and engineering costs, and they are just going to walk away from the deal. Now, they haven't formally defaulted on the contract, and nor have they told me that they intend on walking from my deal. Being in complete disbelief, I idly sat on the sidelines, waiting for the April 1st payment of $20,000 to arrive. April 1st, 2nd, 3rd, 4th , and 5th came and went, and no wire fee.

Wow... for the first time in who knows how long, we needed to hit a line of credit for $20K to pay that mortgage. I'm no Einstein, but without a Mid-Atlantic office and without a wire payment, I guess that they are out of the deal. Who do I call now to discuss this deal? All of the Mid-Atlantic folks have now officially been fired, and that's pretty much everybody who I've been speaking with over the past couple of years in relation to this project. So I stepped out of my comfort zone and cold-called the main number down in Dallas, and spoke with the big wig partner. He explained that the numbers simply did not work for them, and that they are going to stay on the sidelines for this deal. As a matter of fact, he explained that in his 30 years in this business, he has never walked away from as much money as he's had invested in my deal. He proceeded to try to offer me a cash number to close immediately. The number was well south of $5 million. I'm a little pig-headed, though, and I haven't waited this long to make less than $1 million on this deal. Ask me again in 12 months, after I've run up another $240,000 in mortgage payments, and I am sure that I'll have wished that I would have taken up his low ball offer. But for now... Now what?

Where do we go from here? Not ready to give up completely on these Texas folks, I asked them what exactly their problem was with the deal. Well, right now, the capital markets (the banking industry, in other words) are completely messed up. The banks went from loaning money without giving it any thought to increasing the underwriting standards that, in the end, make it very difficult to get a loan. These buyers are probably one of the most qualified buyers out there in the market. The principal has a net worth of over $100 million, and they are seasoned in the multi-family business. Don't just believe me on this, either: I called my bank, who was trying to underwrite the loan, and heard from my loan officer that I'd be hard-pressed to find a buyer as qualified as these guys. So, why can't they get the deal done, you ask. The bank is willing to loan them 70% loan to value on a $35 million deal. That works out to their putting up $11.5 million in cash. Then the bank wants them to put up $2.5 million in additional deposits, interest free, to provide them with additional protection. At the end of the day, the buyer simply refuses to tie up $13 million for this deal. The numbers just don't work well if they need to tie up that much cash, and frankly, I understand why they don't want to do it. So, my solutions to their problems are to either find them an equity partner who may be willing to participate in the deal, or find them another bank that's willing to participate in the deal to make the whole thing come together. This is turning out to be a bloody mess. So, this past week, I've been talking to equity partners, banks, and anyone that may know someone who knows someone that might want to invest with this Texas group on this deal. One glimmer of hope came through this week when a local developer called with some interest in the project. They've promised us a letter of intent, forthcoming next week. As if this thing is not stressful enough already, I really can't speak about the project with anyone else until I officially call the Texas folks in default. If I don't, I risk being sued (which, in all honesty, I expect from these sleezebags anyway), and they've already sued another Baltimore guy in an effort to try to get back a non-refundable deposit on his project. So, I need to tactfully send them a default letter, even though I know that they are my best shot at actually selling this thing.

June 3, 2009

We settled a few weeks ago on the lake house in Virginia. After I charged $3,000 to my credit card for the purchase of the new shed that the buyer required for settlement, I went to my bank and wired the required $20,000 (plus $20,000 that my partner had to wire) in order to sell the property. Something tells me that, when you have to wire money in order to sell your house, something is wrong with the picture. It's just not bad enough that I have to come up with $40,000 just to sell the house, but the bank has pointed out that we have a prepayment penalty on the house if we sell it within 5 years. Ooops... we must have overlooked this small detail when we originated this loan. The bank has asked us for a $9,000 prepayment penalty on the loan, which apparently I agreed to do when we first originated the loan. At some point, you just get fed up with the, pardon my French, bullshit, that the banks are lobbing at you. This is one of those points. I decided to email them the HUD-1 statement that showed us coming to the table with $40,000 in cash so that they could get their entire mortgage paid back in full. Shouldn't being paid in full, when I am taking over a $100,000 loss on the property, be enough for them? I told the mortgage company that they have two choices: they can accept the payment in full at the settlement table, or we can let this deal fall apart and I will put the keys into the mail to them, and they can initiate foreclosure. Enough!!!

At the end of the day, the property has settled, it is no longer on my balance sheet, and I no longer have to cut a check for $3,000 each and every month to carry the property. I know, deep down inside, that this is probably the worst market to have to sell a property in, and I should not have sold it at the absolute bottom, but I simply cannot continue to maintain my mental health while writing these checks out every month. The part that gets lost in the analysis of this deal is that I also lost the $25,000 that I put down on the deal when we first bought the property. So, at the end of the day, chalk this property up as costing me $25,000 to get it, about $20,000 to carry it over the 3 years, another $10,000 for new windows, basement, gutters and repairs, another $3,000 for the shed, and yet another $20,000 to sell the property. A total of $78,000 lost, vaporized into thin air in order to play the real estate game. I knew upfront that the rents on this property could not cover the mortgage for this property, and that buying it would be total speculation. We wanted to redraw the property line for the other property, though, and that objective blurred our vision in buying the neighboring property. I look introspectively into this deal again and again, and try to decide what I would change. At the end of the day, I think I bought into this deal because I wanted to share in the excitement with my buddy down at the lake. This was not a prudent purchase, and a risky endeavor, and I have no one to blame but myself for making a foolish purchase. I also think that I was caught up in the moment of having a lot of money and doing no wrong – call it the Midas Touch Phenomenon. So, now, I lick my wounds and get back into the ring to fight for my remaining projects.

The college rental properties (just 3 single family houses) are going through their turnover process this month. We moved out 18 kids, and are making the required repairs to the units to prepare them for the incoming crop of students. Another thing that has changed over the years is my perspective on the damages. Early on, the fact that these kids were destroying my properties really upset me. Now, it is just a number, just a cost to repair, just a deduction from their security deposits to cover these expenses. I seem to be treating them as an investment and not a career now, and it is somewhat comforting. As a matter of fact, I just signed the loan modification agreement for one of the rentals. We had a loan 5 years ago for $212,000 on the unit. The loan renewal is for another 5 years, but this time the balance of the loan is $193,000. So, over 5 years, we paid off $19,000. This is what real estate is supposed to do. The crazy appreciation that I was lucky enough to participate in was just a Christmas bonus. This was not typical for real estate investing. Take the $19,000 we paid off on this unit, and multiply it by 3 more college rentals of the same value. We have paid off close to $60,000 in 5 years on these units, and plus we paid off some money on the 2 other rental houses that we have. It is not a kill-it-quickly, retire-quickly strategy, but little by little, we continue to chip away at the principal on these loans. If we can own them for another 20-25 years, the principal balance will be 0, and my net worth will reflect this equity. So, I'll continue to plug away at repairing the rentals and getting the new tenants into these properties. On the cash flow side, my partner and I continue to take draws of $1,500-$2,000 each per month. All told, the units are doing everything that they're supposed to do. Once in a great while, I regret selling off the 11 townhouse units. Early on, these were my cash flow cows that would allow me to retire with that steady income. I needed the cash to live. I have kept these funds in cash in the bank, and it has allowed me to continue to live my lifestyle for the past year as I pursue my further education degree.

Let me update you on Charles Street... not that there is a whole lot to update. I continue to stay in contact with the guys in Texas that were our original buyers. When they first decided to bail on the deal, they came in with a number under $5 million to take the property down. We wanted to test the waters for ourselves with the general public before we went back to them. After testing the waters over the past few months, with several brokers and several buyers, we have learned that there are absolutely no conventional buyers out there, not at any price. Who would ever have imagined that we could be sitting on a fantastic property, in a fantastic location, with first class architectural drawings, all of the entitlements ready to go and done by one of the country's most prominent builders, and we just cannot seem to liquidate the property. I have tried everything to try to liquidate this property over the past 5 years, and I just don't think that I have anything else to give. For the past 2 months, we've continued to shell out $20,000 per month, off of the line of credit, and we simply can't seem to find anyone interested in taking this liability off of my books. I just swapped calls with the Texas buyer, and now we have completely lost our leverage position, and are going to be price takers. They know that the $20,000 burn rate each month is killing us. I know that he is going to come back around $4 million this time, and at some point, we are going to just have to sell it.

I can't put into writing the pain and suffering that we are experiencing by carrying this thing without any signs of recovery in sight. First we saw colleagues in the real estate industry lose their jobs. I felt sorry for them, but felt somewhat insulated, as I was not on anyone's payroll and that could never happen to me. Next, I've seen several friends who own their own real estate businesses file for bankruptcy. Again, I felt for these buddies because no one wants to see your friends going through the pain and suffering of having to admit that you failed and need legal help just to stay afloat. The effect that it has had on their pride and ego is unbelievable. But, again, I felt for them, but thought, there is no way that this can happen to me. Well, it has recently hit me that I am about 6 months away from being in this position, with Charles Street still on my books. When we run out of lines of credit on this property, we will start to work through personal expenses to carry it. I can foresee carrying the property for 12 more months, and blowing $250,000 in carry costs, and then having to tap the equity that I have in all of my real estate. At some point in time, this one project could bring me to the brink of bankruptcy. My self-confidence has been challenged, officially, and while I pride myself on not giving up and I continue to plug away at Charles and the business, I am slowly coming to the realization that I am one blink away from losing it all. I hope my wife forgives me.

I pride myself on always having a plan B. So, assuming that I continue to try to find a buyer for this property and continue to fail to identify anyone capable of purchasing it, we are now considering the option of building it ourselves. If this sounds absolutely ridiculous to you, think of how ridiculous it sounds to me. Building a 193 unit urban apartment complex is a far cry from the $200,000 rehabilitation project that we did on Andre Street 7 years ago. But, given that we are out of bullets in the gun, this may be our only solution. Our first problem that needed addressing is the capital. In a nutshell, we don't have any. To build a $25 million construction project, you need several million dollars of cash. Now, I can go out and raise some capital on the project. This is one area that I have always been solid in – I'm just not sure that I can raise the $11 million that would be required to pursue this with a conventional loan. So, back to the internet I went to try to identify any and all loans available that would require less than 30% capital in the deal. I stumbled across a special HUD loan that is specifically meant for urban redevelopment of multi-family rental properties. I can't remember if I discussed the benefits of the HUD 221 d4 loan guaranteed by the government in the book prior to this, but I'll refresh. With this loan program, we can get $25 million of financing if we can raise $2 million in equity financing, assemble an experienced team of developers, hire HUD approved builders, satisfy the market study and appraiser, carry the project for 9 months, and meet a litany of other conditions. Sounds daunting, but not impossible, and I like a challenge. We have many boxes to check off before we begin the process, and who knows how much it will cost just to apply for the loan. Think of how many things can and will go wrong with this process. We have environmental issues, development issues, builder issues, financing issues, and then we have to lease it up....yikes, the process is indeed daunting. If we get an equity partner, our capital contributions go away, so check that box off. We don't have to fork over any more money, and the threat of bankruptcy dissolves. If we are successful, we could own 50% (25% mine) of a project that is worth $40 million. What a great project it would be for a developer and me, so perhaps it will go smoothly and I will thirst to build more units. You've got to give me credit – I remain an optimist.

So, this is my first cut at looking into trying to solve the capital markets problem by locating some government backed financing. We will see where it goes from here. We have two strategies. I will continue to hawk the project to brokers, builders, and developers. Pete and I have now dropped the price to $4.5 million. We still make some money at this price point. While I pursue that strategy, Pete is pursuing the HUD loan by ordering the appraisal and market research data in order to see if we can get financing. At the same time, we are both trying to find the equity partner ready to pony up $2 million in financing. Optimistically yours, Scott.

July 19, 2009

The only deal that I am currently working on these days is trying to get Charles Street off the books. This project, which was once filled with equity and excitement, now drains my emotions and drains my checking account, month after month. The carry cost on it is $20,000 per month, the tax bill of $40,000 is coming due again, we just got vacant building violations from the city, and the outlook is not looking much better. So, if you want to get into my head to understand my financial situation on Charles, listen to this.... We originally took out a loan on the project from the bank for $1.7 million. We raised $700,000 from friends and family to cover the down payment, closing fees, and engineering fees when we began this as a townhouse project. Then, we set up a $600,000 line of credit against the project, and then we set up a $215,000 line against the Windsor Mill office building, and then we had the $75,000 unsecured line of credit from our original days in the business. Right now, today, we are left with about $50,000 in available credit…which, as you can see, will get burned out in about 2 ½ months. The bank with the original $1.7 million is calling us, as the original debt is coming due in the next couple of months. Our loan officer, the VP of lending, and the president of this small bank are all extremely worried that we won't be able to pay off the loan. They should be worried, too, because our deal has fallen through. We have no buyer lined up. We plan on asking them for an extension, but that will put them into a precarious situation. Nobody has any idea what the property is worth. Without any buyers in the market, it is very difficult to figure out a market value for the property. This should be an interesting course of events. We've asked some of our friends and family to not take interest payments on their loans until the property sells. We've thought about trying to raise more money, but frankly, I'm not sure how to raise more money when the prospects of an investor getting it back at this point in time are slim to none. Once the money runs out, I could take some of my personal money to continue to feed the bleed, I could refinance my house to feed the bleed, or I could just lie down and accept my fate on this project. I have tried again and again to remain upbeat and positive about this project, and my future financial situation, but each day, the inevitable grinds on me that this project may indeed cause me to go bankrupt. I take some solace in knowing that we took profits off of the table when we sold the college rentals. That has afforded me a significant amount of breathing room during this extremely dire period of time in the market; however, I have a sneaking suspicion that I'm about to pile all of those winnings back into the casino called Charles Street, and will end up losing all of my winnings.

I think great entrepreneurs have a resolve that keeps them coming back to the fight, month after month, to fight and battle to make things work. On this project, we have come up against challenge after challenge, and continue to slug it out. It does no good to wonder why things haven't worked out or what I could have done differently, but I am honestly getting weary of not having a victory on this project. At this point, this project is mentally sucking my enthusiasm for any entrepreneurial venture, but I know that nothing good will happen unless I step up and make something happen. I mentioned, last month, about my seeking the possibility of getting the HUD financing on this project. To summarize, every developer and investor that I hawk this deal to says that the project is great. The Baltimore market is great, the fundamentals of the deal are sound, and the design plans for a high-end luxury rental project are top-notch. The only thing between someone scooping this thing up and me getting out of it are the capital markets. The banks are simply requiring too much capital to be put into the deal, which makes the return on capital too small to make the deal worth the investment. So now, again straddled with a problem, I need to come up with the solution in order to make the project more saleable. That is why the HUD financing route seems so attractive. This is the point in the game of Texas Hold 'em where I push all of my chips to the middle of the table and declare that I am ALL IN. Remember, I am running out of money quickly, and in order to get the HUD application submitted, I have to dig deep into my pockets to put out cash. Just last month, I put up $18,000 for a HUD appraisal and market study in order to shoot for the moon and try to get a HUD loan in place. I will get the results of these two surveys in the next 3 weeks, which will essentially tell me my fate. Bankruptcy may be a result, at which time I'd default on loans made by my family and friends, and risk losing everything I own. Doesn't real estate sound like fun?

I've got to spend money even when it hurts. I hired a consultant last month to help me with the HUD application and market the property. I am paying him a sizeable retainer, monthly, to have him submit all of the information to the appraiser and market research firm, and this guy knows how to work the system. He is very good at talking the talk and walking the walk. In addition, he is sending out packets of information to potential joint venture partners or purchasers. I realized that I needed help with this aspect of the transaction because, after meeting with two very well qualified parties, they both seemed extremely tentative about investing anything in this real estate market. Firms are extremely fearful these days, and while deals like mine are fantastic opportunities, gun shy developers just can't seem to generate the positive vibes enough to be willing to commit to anything. I eventually realized that even finding a JV partner at this point in time was going to be extremely difficult with my limited rolodex. The consultant has now brought me a few well-qualified leads. We had a conference call last week with one of the potential groups, and they seemed to be viewing this market as an opportunity to aggressively pick up deals and get developments into the pipeline. The initial call was extremely positive, and we threw around some deal structures and terms that would be perfectly acceptable to us. At these early stages, our primary goal is to retire all of the debt that we have on the project. We are in the neighborhood of $3.5 million. We threw out the number of $4 million so we could pay the consultant a success fee and make a few hundred thousand at the end of the day. Ahh, remember when I scoffed at the sub $5 million number from the Texas guy? Life is ironic. I've put down the lessons learned at the end of each chapter and still have trouble taking my own advice. This entire transaction is confusing. Pete and I are at the point where we want out of the deal and to just eliminate our debt and get ourselves out of trouble.

One last thing before I sign off.... Like an alcoholic falling off the wagon, I went out last week and looked at 2 houses for acquisitions. An investor/agent buddy of mine called me. As a casualty of the business of being an investor, and having lost his shirt at the end of the wave, he is now focusing on being an agent and helping sellers sell their houses while shorting the bank. There are a ton of homeowners out there these days who have to sell their homes for one reason or another. Take into consideration that the markets have adjusted about 30% in the past few years, and that people have stripped every penny of equity out of their homes, and homeowners simply can't afford to sell their homes. So, the banks are in quite a quandary. Their inventories are growing as they continue to foreclose at record paces, and they can't sell what they have on the books, so now they are willing to accept 70 cents on the dollar of the loan, and let the homeowners sell their homes just to save them the trouble of foreclosing on them and having to take possession. So, the two houses that I looked at were cosmetic rehabs that are worth in the neighborhood of $200,000 when complete. The agent is going to list them for their debt amount…which is about $200,000. So, knowing that the homes have no chance of selling, I will submit an offer for roughly $100,000 (50 cents on the dollar) to the bank. If the bank bites, I can put $20,000 into fixing them up and turn a quick $70,000 in profit. At least, that's the theory. The purpose of me throwing this tidbit into this chapter is that fear has officially set into everybody. The banks are finally willing to accept their fate and are beginning to try to write off the bad debt so that they can move on and recover. So, now is an opportunity to pick up some absolutely killer deals, and I would regret not taking advantage of this market. To quote Warren Buffet yet again: when people are greedy, it's time to be fearful, when people are fearful, it's time to be greedy. Fear has indeed set in. I'll keep you posted.

August 6, 2009

Before I get into the property update, I want to pat myself on the back for accomplishing a goal. I have always thought that if I had $2 million of cash in the bank, I could live off of $200,000 a year. This was based on receiving dividends of 10% per year. I had the opportunity to go through my self-directed IRA statements for the past couple of years. From 2008-2009 I made 15%, from 2007-2008 I made 12.75%, and from 2006-2007 (a year in which I flipped a house in my IRA) I made 38.25%. If nothing else, I think that I have validated my hypothesis that I can get good returns writing hard money loans, and indeed make 10% per year on my money. After completing that exercise, I went through my Scottrade account to see how my day trading performed. I managed to pull out $3,200 on an account where I maintain $25,000. So, that money has made about 12.8%. Now, if I only had $2 million of cash to invest.

HUD application update!!!! The first 2 steps in the HUD application were ordering a market study and having an appraisal done. Remember, I wrote about stroking the $18,000 check last month, and as we see it, this is our last hurrah, the only chance of surviving bankruptcy…all-in at the poker table. So, a few days ago, I received back the market study report. This report is ordered by the bank that we are using to try to secure the funding. The purpose of the market study report is to validate that there is indeed a demand for our apartment product and that the rental rates which we are using in our analysis are validated by comparable properties. The bank calls in an objective third party appraisal company to evaluate everything about the market. They look at the demographic information, household income levels, other apartment units in the area, vacancy rates, amenities, shopping, commuter status, and just about every other possible variable that might go into evaluating what a single apartment unit at my location would rent for if the building was built. Originally, we thought that our site would bring in about $1.75 per square foot. Basically, this means that a 1000 square foot apartment would bring in a total of $17,500 in rent for the year. You can use this number to calculate your gross revenues on a 170,000 apartment building with 193 units, and it is quite important to maximize what you think the market can bear. So, right off the bat, you can see how important it is to convince these market research folks that your place will be the most desirable, mack-daddy location. The number $1.75 came from the original purchaser down in Texas. We never verified it either way, but they tended to be a conservative group, so we were fairly optimistic that the market research should kick out a number close to $1.75.

I just received the emailed version of the market study yesterday, all 130 pages of it. Like the good student that I am, I read each and every page, waiting patiently to get to the part in the document that would tell me how much per square foot I could rent my property for. On page 83, first paragraph, I slowly read the page titled "Subject Property". Are you ready for this? After comparing every aspect of our site against the entire city of Baltimore, these guys think that our site will bring $1.97 per square foot. This is huge for us. We needed a high number to come back with in order to be able to substantiate our pro-forma numbers and push up the limits of the appraisal. Finally, after a long period of bad news, we get our first break. I am expecting the appraisal to come back today in the mid $6 million range for the land. This takes into consideration the gross revenues (which are now substantiated by the market study), the proposed expenses per unit (which we put in at 6K per unit), and the comparable land sales (and we sent them 4 pages of legitimate comps to see). Now, we do have a loop hole with the expenses. We estimated 6K per unit, but had trouble finding a comparable property to use to validate this number. The only numbers that we could gather on this were older properties which had much higher per unit maintenance expenses. It will be interesting to see how this turns out. Even if this whole thing falls apart and I lose everything, it has been a crazy education.

Now that you know where we are with the HUD process, my next goal is to step out and find a buyer or joint venture partner for this thing. Follow my logic for just a minute – I thought that the land was worth $5.5 million before. Now I have an objective third party appraisal done that shows the value to be $6 million, based on the net income approach. The reason I can't sell it is that the banks are not giving money at reasonable rates. Assuming that I can get some favorable rates for a potential buyer, perhaps the deal will indeed be worth $6 million. That is why we are jumping through these hoops to get the HUD financing in-line. This loan is a fantastic product. It requires buyers to put down around 10%. This is huge, considering it was the 30% down payment that killed the Texas deal. The loan is non-recourse. While most conventional loans require the developer to pledge their personal assets to qualify, this is a government-backed loan that doesn't require any personal guarantee. Again, a huge selling feature. Finally, the loan is amortized over 40 years. That means that the monthly bank payment is lower each and every month. The final owner of the project will make more profit on a monthly basis. I hope that you can see why we are so aggressively pursuing this loan. It could be exactly what we need to ultimately sell the project. The smart developers know that this is definitely the time to pick up some deals, so 2 years down the road when institutional buyers are looking to purchase completed income producing assets, they can have a prime new project ready to be sold. With the total loan package on this being close to $30,000,000, the buyer would have to put up around $3 million for the HUD loan to happen. I am trying to figure out a way for a developer to jump in for even less than $3 million. Apparently, in this market, buyers want even less exposure that that, so I'm looking to sweeten up the pot even more. Here is the deal that I came up with.... Assuming our appraisal comes in-line with the market study at $6 million, Signature would pay off with $4.5 million of debt at the closing of the HUD loan, and I would contribute my $1.5 million in equity (the difference between $4.5 million debt and appraisal amount) to a joint venture which would essentially drop the cash to close from a JV partner down to about $1 million. What do you think? Have I made this one an incredibly attractive deal to a builder? Someone could be into a 193 unit apartment building, with a great loan in place, for around $1 million. If I can identify a builder who might be willing to participate in this type of structure, we can come up with a favorable profit and ownership split going forward. I put up my $1.5 million in equity and they put up $1 million in equity and we are both off to the races with some huge upside potential. Hopefully, you agree that this seems like a logical way to approach the sale of the property.

I try not to talk to my wife anymore about the possibility of selling this project because she is so tired of me saying, "When Charles settles". So, how can I possibly still dream about this project working? Well, since I submitted the project to the HUD office for financing, and I might add that I'm the first on the queue for Baltimore HUD financing, the project has been given new life.

Everyone that had looked at the project before, but could not make the conventional financing route work, is now giving it a second look with the HUD financing in place. NOW IT MAKES SENSE. We had a dinner last night with a group of apartment developers who have a keen interest in the joint venture partnership that I proposed above. They know the site and love the project. The recent market study validates our bullishness on Baltimore as a viable submarket for multi-family housing, so now we are just waiting for the appraisal. I'm meeting with another group this week to go through the same song and dance to see if they are interested in either a JV or a purchase. My excitement has been extremely tempered since I have been left at the altar several times, but I can't help but get a few butterflies in my stomach when I think about this thing ultimately succeeding. The process has been grueling for 5 years, and certainly not how I thought things would shake out. In the end, I think that I will have a good story to tell, and hopefully an informative book for you, my envisioned reader, to read. I will leave room for one more paragraph that I can fill in at the end of today…..the results of the appraisal.

By the way, I also need the appraisal to come in high for another reason. My loan with the Annapolis bank is due. I need to ask them for an extension. If the appraisal comes in well, I can refinance the entire loan. I could include carry costs for another year, which will keep me alive until the recession eases. It basically translates into borrowing money to pay back money that was already borrowed. If the appraisal comes in poorly, well, the bank doesn't renew the loan, they foreclose on the property, they take the Windsor office building (because we pledged all its equity to keep this thing afloat), they take the 5 rental properties (because we will be equity deficient), and I lose all of my family's hard money loans... sorry brother Larry... and basically end up with nothing.

Yep, today should be a fun day!!!

August 12, 2009

Today was a big day for us. We received back the appraisal for Charles Street. Hold onto your seat for this, because it came back at $5,989,973. That is just shy of $6 million and exactly what we were hoping for. This helps us in so many ways. First, it is a great base number for submitting our formal HUD 221 (d)(4) application, and it may buy us more time with the bank in order to get this deal to the finish line. The next step in this is to submit the entire HUD application. Since we're using a consultant on this, we have a pretty good handle on what's going on. We've developed a pro-forma statement for the rents and expenses of a 193 unit apartment complex. If all units are occupied, it will show a gross income of $3.9 million with approximately $1.5 million in expenses. The estimated net income from this building should be in the neighborhood of $2.4 million. Working our way through the sheet, it should qualify for a mortgage of $29 million.

We now have a pretty good idea of how much money it will qualify for with bank financing, we have a pretty good idea of what it will cost to build (since our Dallas buddies did all of the bidding and due diligence), we know how much our debt is, and we know how much it appraises for – which only leaves how much we can sell it for, or how much we need to raise if we want to joint venture in this project. I am feeling pretty good right about now. We have our fingers on something special that could be salable, now that we've solved the capital issues.

I've now been beating the streets for potential buyers and partners. In the past two weeks, I've met with two groups that are very interested in a potential joint venture, pending the ultimate HUD financing. The deal structures are very similar, where we would defer our $2 million of equity into the deal and the developer would pay the difference in funding in order to get the deal closed. The rest of the construction will be 100% financed. We will end up splitting the annual net income, and have a 48% ownership in what could be a $35 million apartment complex. One group is sending us over a full blown operating agreement for the structuring of the deal and the new LLC. I remain optimistic about the outcome, and hopefully, there is a deal to be struck there. Incidentally, this group is also out of Texas.

January 28, 2010

Here we sit, 5 months later, and still no deal. Now, when the Texas guys defaulted, they lost the $250,000 deposit that was sitting in an escrow account. That money found its way into our bank account because that's what happens when you default on a contract. It is liquidated damages. Over the past 5 months, we've burned through $100,000 of that money. We are not stressing out yet, but things just can't seem to happen fast enough. We are getting closer to a deal with the JV folks. The terms of the deal are now a 50/50 equal equity position for both parties. These guys will be allowed to earn a developer's fee for building the project, of $1,466,064. Once the building is up and running, we will split the operating income 50/50. Upon disposition of the building, we split the profit 50/50. In early December, they submitted the initial letter of intent on what the structure of the deal will look like. We recently signed these initial terms of the agreement and we are awaiting the formal contract to execute. I am trying not to be overly excited about this, but it does look and smell like a killer deal.

Here is an update on the HUD financing, as well. We submitted our formal application this week. This isn't your run of the mill standard application. It included detailed descriptions of the property, maps, photos, narratives, existing buildings, flood plain information, market studies, pro-forma financial statements, drawings of the finished projects, architectural renderings, and many more documents. Overall, the packet was almost 150 pages long. We received our notice that the application had been received by the US Department of Housing and Urban Development just today, and that they are beginning the process of evaluating our application. Our consultant tells us that there is about 90 days until we even get the initial approval for our application. So, now we sit tight, continue to work these JV guys, and look for backups in case they drop off of the face of the earth. I'll focus on the academic studies this quarter, and check back in when I have something good to report. Hopefully, it won't take too long.

Oh yeah, and one more entry before I check out.... As you can imagine, the entire process is dependent on receiving this approval from HUD. I have tried networking with anybody who'll listen to me in order to make a compelling story as to why this project is exactly what Baltimore City needs. I have spoken with the neighborhood folks, environmental folks, city councilmen, and many folks at the Department of Planning. Over cocktails the other day with my wife and some of her friends, I learned that one of their childhood friends is now the Deputy Secretary for the Department of Planning. So last week, I hooked up in his office downtown to pitch him the project. This is one of those things where you just don't know if it will have any effect on the final outcome of the project. He tells me that he doesn't have any influence or connection with the people at HUD, but I've got to imagine that this project landing in Baltimore City would be a huge boondoggle for this guy. We had a wonderful meeting, and I hope that he may pass on support for our project with the powers that be. You never know – you've got to work every angle possible.

March 19, 2010

I told you that I'd report back good news, and sure enough, here it is. I just received a copy of this letter from HUD. I'll copy you on the first couple of sentences from the letter:

"The purpose of this letter is to inform you that our staff has completed the review of the pre-application exhibits for the subject proposal. Based upon our review of the proposal and the market study, we have determined that there is a potential market for the proposal. Thus the application is found to be worthy of further consideration should you decide to submit an application for Firm Commitment for FHA Mortgage Insurance."

Of course I'm going to submit my application – this is my only hope in saving myself from bankruptcy! They gave me a three page list of things in the application that would need to be addressed in order for there to be firm commitment. Each of the items is easily remedied. Guys, this is the best news that I have heard in years! Pete and I went out for a two martini lunch today to celebrate. Perhaps there really is hope for us down the road.

One of the issues in the pre-application letter regards the railroad that runs behind our property. Apparently, the title shows that CSX, probably the largest railroad company in the U.S., has the right to run a railroad track right up against the West wall of our proposed project. I've walked the site, and this simply isn't going to happen. The railway has been completed for decades, and they did not ever build on the elevated portion of Charles Street. This objection is fallacious. It is just never going to happen. And I can see this, of course, but some HUD reviewer isn't looking at the building, and is only going from their review of the documentation in the title search. The next issue that I will need to resolve will be figuring out if I can get CSX to deed over to me an extremely small piece of land in order to satisfy this objection. Does this sound crazy? I mean, how can I figure out how to get in touch with the right person at the railway, and what are the chances that they will deed over to me a piece of land…for free? Ugh. This business just gets harder and harder at each turn.

When it rains, it pours. The JV partner group has withdrawn their offer to participate in the deal with us. We asked them to pick up the $20,000 a month in carry costs for the next 6-9 months until the HUD financing is in line, and they simply refused. Sure, if Pete and I agreed to pay the carry costs until the HUD financing was in line, these guys would certainly agree to stay in the deal. But honestly, if we had the money to pay the carry costs, we really wouldn't need a JV partner. Pete and I can only speculate that they liked the deal if and only if the financing was in place. They didn't have the tolerance to actually put up their hard earned money to have the chance of making a mint on this deal. You know what I find incredibly frustrating? Pete and I are little guys in the realm of real estate development, and at any point in time, we have millions of our dollars invested and risked in these deals. When it comes to the big players in the industry, they are so gun shy of risking any of their own money. I guess that as long as they can get into deals without having to risk their capital and they still finds deals to invest in, why should they? Just a thought. I've got some work to do over the next couple of months. First, I need to resolve this CSX issue in order to satisfy this HUD issue, and second, I need to find me a buyer or JV partner. I leave this entry with mixed emotions. I am stressed that I keep striking out on finding a suitable buyer, but I am at peace knowing that we continue to line up the HUD financing. I also think that having the PhD program is a great diversion from me having to stress out. On occasion, Pete calls me, all worked up. I spend time on the phone talking him out of a tree, and getting him to feel confident that we have made it this far, and are so very close to closing this thing out.

July 25, 2010

I don't have long to check in right now, but wanted to fill you in on a couple of updates. I cold-called CSX and spoke with the people in their real estate department. After my giving them the sob story of the poor little developer who needs this deal to go, they've put me in touch with local counsel here in Baltimore who can hopefully help me out with this issue. I met with a really nice woman up in Towson, Maryland the other day, someone from a local firm up there. She was an alumnus of the University of Maryland and we made some connections right away. While she did not want to make me any promises, I think that she's going to help me with the deed issue. Also, our consultant has identified a local company up in Baltimore that *is* interested in the property. I was down at the beach with my family this week, and had several in depth conversations with this group. They seem like the real deal. I went onto their website and they have developed a fair amount of multi-family units around the country. To think: these guys are right in our backyard, and we've been messing with these companies from around the world. I have asked myself why they have never been identified as a potential buyer, and I have come to realize that hiring real estate brokers does not guarantee that they are going to turn over every rock and find every available buyer. Now I don't want to exclusively blame the brokers, because I also failed to find these guys. I've scheduled a meeting with this group to meet in person and deliver them some of the work product on the site. Keep your fingers crossed.

September 3, 2010

So, imagine this... while you've been watching the train wreck for the past 3 years, I've been living the wreck. The depression and anxiety of the industry have been wreaking havoc on my personal finances. While I consider myself a pretty optimistic person, the series of events that's rolled out of the history of Charles Street has challenged my optimism. Well, things are really starting to look up. I know that the pre-application approval was a big step in the right direction. Today, we executed a deal with that group out of Baltimore which I mentioned. The consultant brought us these guys way back in July. I met with them and almost immediately took a liking to their lead guy. He seemed honest and straightforward. I got a radically different feeling than when I met the guys from Texas. With those guys, I always prepared for battle, and felt like I had to take a shower to wash off their stench when I left a meeting with them. These new buyers from Baltimore could not have been more opposite. I told them that we were having trouble paying the $20,000 in carry costs. With almost no negotiation, they agreed to pick up this payment, and right away. They didn't hem and haw about a promissory note or being repaid for it: they simply said that if they want the deal, they are willing to invest some of their hard earned cash in order to get it across the finish line. Wow, this has been refreshing. In my meeting with them in July, I shared the entire application packet for the HUD financing. They have access to the market study, appraisal, full sets of construction documents, and everything else that went into that 150 page application. They really loved the design and the work that we did to get the project up to this point.

So, I'm sure that you are curious to hear the terms of the deal; here we go. They know that it appraised for $6 million in the HUD application, so they agreed to give us $5.9 million. Outstanding. I knew it! I just knew that someone would see the value that we were creating with this thing. I'm so glad that I didn't take the $4 million offer from those scoundrels from Texas. Yes, $6 million. They agreed to put up a $200,000 deposit of which I can draw $20,000 a month to pay the bank my carry costs. The only catch, and it's really not a catch, is that they want to hold back $600,000 for one complete year. One of the items in our HUD application was the approval of a remedial action plan (RAP) in order to qualify for the $400,000 tax credit associated with cleaning up the manufacturing site, and turning it into revenue producing residential real estate. The structure of the promissory note for the $600,000 would be that they would release $300,000 once the RAP is approved, or 6 months after settling. The remaining $300,000 will be released one year after closing. In all honesty, we really don't care about the $600,000. I mean even if they default on the $600,000, we still manage to pay off all of our debts and walk away with almost $2 million in profit. So, here I sit on September 3rd with a fully executed contract and a check for $200,000. I feel on top of the world right now. Again, I find myself daydreaming about what I'd do with my $1 million payday. There is one contingency to this whole deal happening – we need to get the HUD financing. If we don't get the financing, the whole deal falls apart.

December 28, 2010

Things have been moving along great. The Baltimore group has been aggressively working with HUD to get the financing in line. HUD had an issue with the noise level of the train tracks and the highway, and the Baltimore group had a decibel test done and shut down this hurdle before it even became an issue. They've tackled architectural issues, engineering issues, traffic issues – you name it, these guys are on it. I am really impressed with their ability to take problems and solve them with great ease. They also have a stockpile of capital to throw at these problems. I've realized that being able to hire the best professionals to deal with these issues is far easier than the bootstrapping method that Signature Properties has used for the past 8 years.

Maybe things are not entirely great.... The taxes are due. We have been drawing down their $200,000 to pay the bank, and now we owe Baltimore City $40,000. I called Baltimore City to see if I could cut the tax bill into 4 installments. No dice. They are not in the business of lending money. Pete tells me that we may have drawn down their entire $200,000 by the middle of January, and be out of money to pay the February mortgage payment. I told you that I like these guys in Baltimore, so I made my problem their problem. I sent an email to the principle of their company, explaining my dilemma. I didn't ask him for money, just for some suggestions. God must be smiling down upon me with these guys, though, because they have offered to give us $150,000 for additional deposit in the deal. They have so much invested in this deal that the last thing that they want is to lose the property due to some tax complication. Not only that, but they are more pregnant in the deal as a side effect of this last development. Instead of $200,000, they now stand to lose $350,000 if the deal goes south or the HUD financing doesn't solidify. They have promised to wire us the $150,000 next week to pay the tax bill. I'm telling you, these guys are the real deal and they are a pleasure to work with.

While I was on the phone talking with Pete about how we keep stringing along this deal, begging and borrowing money from anyone and everyone, I asked him to run me a quick report on who we owe money to if this deal ever closes. Picture this: when we first bought the property, we borrowed $200,000 from our mentor. We borrowed $1,720,000 from the bank for the mortgage, and we put $200,000 down from cash in our account. Then we burned through a line of credit of $215,000. Then we started tapping friends, family, and fools. I owe my relatives $100,000 and Pete's relatives $110,000. As this deal took years and years, we hit the bank for $636,000 as we collateralized the office building. We also burned through $118,000 that we had in the office building's bank account. Pete invested $60,000 of his personal money, I have $50,000 of my personal money invested, and some friends have another $40,000 of their money tied up in this property. We owe all of these people money. Not only that, but we burned through all of the money that the Texas buyer gave us, plus the $200,000 that the Baltimore crew gave us. That was a lot of money to go through on this one deal. Can you imagine if this deal doesn't go through and we end up losing the property? This would affect a lot of people. So, let's hang in there and keep our fingers crossed.

February 14, 2011

Yesssssss. Things are coming together. I spoke with our HUD consultant today and he has reported that HUD is going to approve our loan by the end of the month. I'm trying not to get too excited about the prospect of settling this thing in March, but at this point, it is a distinct possibility. Imagine that... after waiting years, developing and redeveloping the project, after deals falling apart from townhouses to apartments, having the financial markets collapse, and finally, we just may see this thing actually get brought to the settlement table. I am trying to contain my excitement.

On another note, the lady from CSX came through for me. I owe her a box of chocolates or a dozen roses. She knew that I was working on a tight time schedule. As she knew that the potential for a real estate close could happen as early as March, she worked miracles. Last week, we met and executed a deed which signs over to Charles Development, LLC a small piece of land that was owned by CSX. This is no small feat to accomplish. I once thought that this was going to kill the whole deal. I didn't think it was going to be possible for a little guy like me to be able to work out a deal like this, not with a massive behemoth like CSX. I've got to say that my attitude has been changing over the past 6 months. Dealing with the Baltimore group and the attorney for CSX has really changed my perspective. I am beginning to have faith that people can indeed do the right thing. Things have been looking good, and I look forward to reporting a sale in the next entry.

March 9, 2011

LIFE CHANGES TODAY. What an incredible journey it has been. Today, we settled on the property known as 1901 Charles Street. This has been one long roller coaster of a ride. I've scanned in the HUD 1 settlement sheet for you to review. We did indeed end up at a sales price of $5.9 million. We paid off the bank's $1.7 million, the $640,067 we owed them for collateralizing the building, and the $217,448 line of credit, leaving us with $1,984,267.97. We need to pay out $450,000 to completely get out of debt with all of our friends and family. That will leave Pete and I about $1.5 million to split right now, with a $600,000 kicker coming to us over the next year. When all the dust settles, we will have made over $1 million each on this deal. This is a far cry from the dreams of retirement that I had back in 2006, but it is enough to prime the pump for my kids' educations and a tidy little nest egg. Better yet – I achieved a goal and survived a gauntlet.

I figure that it is appropriate to end the book with a net worth comparison. It's funny how my original drive towards a net worth of $2 million has completely changed over the course of this journey, coming to one of simple survival. I am pretty confident that my net worth has indeed achieved my financial goal, but my perspective of money has really changed over the years. What a great journey it has been.

2002	**2011**
Equity in House = $140,000	Equity in House = $300,000
Stocks = $19,000	Stocks = $50,000
Funds = $13,000	Funds = $75,000
Retirement Account	$273,000
College Savings Plan	$205,000
College Rental Portfolio	$100,000
Additional Rental Properties	$50,000
Office Building	$30,000
Cash From Charles Street	$1,067,000
2002 = $175,000	**2011 = $2,420,000**

3/8/11 3:03 PM — OMB No. 2502-0265

A. U.S. Department of Housing and Urban Development

Settlement Statement

B. Type of Loan

1. [ ] FHA 2. [ ] FMHA 3. [ ] Conv. Unins.
4. [ ] VA 5. [ ] Conv. Ins.

6. File Number: 58844
7. Loan Number:
8. Mortgage Ins. Case No.

C. Note: This form is furnished to give you a statement of actual settlement costs. Amounts paid to and by the settlement agent are shown. Items marked ("POC") were paid outside the closing; they are shown here for information purposes and are not included in the totals.

D. Name of Borrower: (

E. Name of Seller: Charles Development, LLC, P. O. Box 6596, Annapolis, MD 21401

F. Name of Lender:

G. Property Location: Lot 024, Block 1037, N/A, Section 10
1901 S Charles Street, Baltimore, MD 21230-4527

H. Settlement Agent: Residential Title & Escrow Company (410) 653-3400
Place of Settlement: 1829 Reisterstown Road, Ste. 330, Baltimore, MD 21208

I. Settlement Date: 3/9/2011 Proration Date: 3/9/2011

J. Summary of Borrower's Transaction			K. Summary of Seller's Transaction		
100.	Gross amount due from borrower:		400.	Gross amount due to seller:	
101.	Contract sales price	5,900,000.00	401.	Contract sales price	5,900,000.00
102.	Personal property		402.	Personal property	
103.	Settlement charges to borrower (line 1400)	452,657.50	403.		
104.	Reimburse seller for permits ($110,000.00 POC)		404.		
105.	Reimb seller 3d party costs ($30,000.00 POC)		405.		
	Adjustments for items paid by seller in advance			Adjustments for items paid by seller in advance	
106.	City/town taxes 3/9/2011 to 7/1/2011	12,284.48	406.	City/town taxes 3/9/2011 to 7/1/2011	12,284.48
107.	County taxes		407.	County taxes	
108.	Assessments		408.	Assessments	
109.			409.		
110.			410.		
111.			411.		
112.			412.		
120.	Gross amount due from borrower:	6,365,141.98	420.	Gross amount due to seller:	5,912,284.48
200.	Amounts paid by or in behalf of the borrower		500.	Reductions in amount due to seller	
201.	Deposit or earnest money	200,000.00	501.	Excess deposit (see instructions)	
202.	Principal amount of new loan(s)		502.	Settlement charges to seller (line 1400)	89,085.00
203.	Existing loan(s) taken subject to		503.	Existing loan(s) taken subject to	
204.	Additional Deposit	450,000.00	504.	Payoff of first mortgage loan Severn Savings Bank	1,730,799.33
205.			505.	Payoff of second mortgage loan S.A. Lynd **	
206.			506.	Deposit or earnest money	200,000.00
207.			507.	Payoff Severn Savings Bank	640,057.96
208.	Seller Take Back Note	600,000.00	508.	Seller Take Back Note	600,000.00
209.			509.	Additional Deposit	450,000.00
	Adjustments for items unpaid by seller			Adjustments for items unpaid by seller	
210.	City/town taxes		510.	City/town taxes	
211.	County taxes		511.	County taxes	
212.	Assessments		512.	Assessments	
213.			513.	, 1/1/2011 to 3/9/2011	
214.	Water 1/10/2011 to 3/9/2011	404.87	514.	Water 1/10/2011 to 3/9/2011	404.87
215.	Ground Rent		515.	Ground Rent	
216.			516.	**payoff Lynd 151,136.22 POC	
217.			517.	Open City of Baltimore Citation	210.98
218.			518.	Water - $3,589.03 POC	
219.			519.	Payoff Severn Savings Bank	217,448.37
220.	Total paid by/for borrower:	1,250,404.87	520.	Total reduction in amount due seller:	3,928,016.51
300.	Cash at settlement from/to borrower		600.	Cash at settlement to/from seller	
301.	Gross amount due from borrower (line 120)	6,365,141.98	601.	Gross amount due to seller (line 420)	5,912,284.48
302.	Less amount paid by/for borrower (line 220)	1,250,404.87	602.	Less total reduction in amount due seller (line 520)	3,928,016.51
303.	CASH (X)FROM ()TO BORROWER	5,114,737.11	603.	CASH ()FROM (X)TO SELLER	1,984,267.97

SUBSTITUTE FORM 1099 SELLER STATEMENT - The information contained in Blocks E, G, H and I and on line 401 (or, if line 401 is asterisked, lines 403 and 404), 406, 407 and 408-412 (applicable part of buyer's real estate tax reportable to the IRS) is important tax information and is being furnished to the Internal Revenue Service. If you are required to file a return, a negligence penalty or other sanction will be imposed on you if this item is required to be reported and the IRS determines that it has not been reported.

SELLER INSTRUCTION - If this real estate was your principle residence, file form 2119, Sale or Exchange of Principal Residence, for any gain, with your income tax return; for other transactions, complete the applicable parts of form 4797, Form 6252 and/or Schedule D (Form 1040).

You are required by law to provide Residential Title & Escrow Company (410) 653-3400 with your correct taxpayer identification number.
If you do not provide Residential Title & Escrow Company (410) 653-3400 with your correct taxpayer identification number, you may be subject to civil or criminal penalties.

Charles Development, LLC

Final HUD-1 Statement from Charles Street

Demolition of the vacant warehouse at 1901 S. Charles Street

Arial of 1901 South Charles Street After Demolition

Construction Beginning on Apartments

Finished Product at 1901 South Charles Street

EPILOGUE

On July 5, 2011, the balance of $600,000 was paid in full by the Baltimore Group. The property was indeed developed into 193 high-end luxury apartments. You can check out their website at http://1901southcharles.prospectportal.com/. I finished my PhD in May of 2011 and am now teaching entrepreneurship at a small beachside school in Melbourne, Florida, a place called Florida Tech. I use many of the lessons that I learned in these business dealings to teach my students about all elements of real estate development. On October 30, 2013, I bought a single family house with one of my students in order to teach him how to rehab and resell real estate to make a profit. We sold it on December 31, 2013 for a $13,000 profit. Over the following 6 months, I have been working with 6 interns, and have purchased 6 additional properties, and a piece of land for development. The next journey begins.

ABOUT THE AUTHOR

Scott Benjamin is a serial entrepreneur with a recurring passion for real estate. In 1991, he received his real estate salespersons license in Florida but only earned $230 in commissions. Following a stint in the restaurant business working for Domino's Pizza and Rudy's Hamburgers, Scott went back to school to get a graduate degree. With the help of some young partners, Scott created Signature Properties.

Over a ten year period, Scott learned the real estate business from the ground up. Seeing the eminent crash of 2008 approaching, Scott pivoted careers and earned a PhD in Strategy at the age of 42 from the University of Maryland. Dr. Benjamin now teaches at a small private University in Florida.

In 2014, Scott began investing in real estate once again with an eye on capitalizing on the rising real estate market. He enjoys sharing his passion and knowledge for real estate with others through teaching and public speaking.

To correspond with Scott, send requests to Scott Benjamin, 7777 N. Wickham Road, Suite 12-714, Melbourne, FL 32940 or electronically to scott@ridingthebubble.com.

www.ingramcontent.com/pod-product-compliance
Lightning Source LLC
Chambersburg PA
CBHW060004210326
41520CB00009B/813

* 9 7 8 0 6 9 2 4 0 5 3 2 1 *